Old-Fashioned Labor-Saving Devices

Old-Fashioned Labor-Saving Devices

*Homemade Contrivances and
How to Make Them*

Skyhorse Publishing

Copyright © 2015 by Skyhorse Publishing

All rights reserved. No part of this book may be reproduced in any manner without the express written consent of the publisher, except in the case of brief excerpts in critical reviews or articles. All inquiries should be addressed to Skyhorse Publishing, 307 West 36th Street, 11th Floor, New York, NY 10018.

Skyhorse Publishing books may be purchased in bulk at special discounts for sales promotion, corporate gifts, fund-raising, or educational purposes. Special editions can also be created to specifications. For details, contact the Special Sales Department, Skyhorse Publishing, 307 West 36th Street, 11th Floor, New York, NY 10018 or info@skyhorsepublishing.com.

Skyhorse® and Skyhorse Publishing® are registered trademarks of Skyhorse Publishing, Inc.®, a Delaware corporation.

Visit our website at www.skyhorsepublishing.com.

10 9 8 7 6 5 4 3 2 1

Library of Congress Cataloging-in-Publication Data is available on file.

Cover design by Jane Sheppard
Cover photos courtesy of Thinkstock

Print ISBN: [978-1-62914-520-4]
Ebook ISBN: [978-1-63220-075-4]

Printed in the United States of America

Contents.

I. Farm Conveniences

Bin for Oats	3
Fastenings for Cows	4
Movable Nests for Hens	5
How to Get Rid of Straw	7
The Management of Young Bulls	9
A Convenient Ice-Hook	11
Hints for the Workshop	11
A Non-Patented Barrel Header	13
Building Ribless Boats	15
To Mend a Broken Tug	18
Business Habits	19
Hay Racks	21
How to Extricate a Mired Animal	23
How to Save and Keep Manure	24
Grinding Tools	27
A Method of Hanging Hogs	28
Relief for Bog Spavin and Thorough-Pin	29
Tool Boxes for Wagons, Etc	30
Making a Hinge	32
Shelter for the Head	34
How to Level with Square and Plumb Line	35
How to Keep Cattle under Cover	36
Watering Places for Stock on Level Land	37
A Shaving-Horse	38
A Milking-Stool	39
How to Treat Thrush	40
A Western Locust Trap	41
Manure Spreading	43
Putting Away Tools	45
Self-Closing Doors	46
Ventilators for Fodder Stacks	47
Corn Marker for Uneven Ground	49
A Home-Made Harrow	50
Clearing Land by Blasting	51
Preventable Losses on the Farm	56
A Cradle for Drawing a Boat	58

Contents.

Feed-Rack for Sheep	59
How to Manage Night-Soil	60
The Use of Lime in Blasting	62
A Water and Feed Trough	63
The Construction of Stalls	64
Hog-Killing Implements—Ringing	66
How to Mix Cement	68
Ringing and Handling Bulls	72
Sled for Removing Corn Shocks	75
A Tagging Trough	76
Lime and Lime Kilns	76
Fall Fallowing	80
Unloading Corn	81
Stone Boats	82
A Dump Cart	83
To Prevent Washing of Hill-Sides	84
A Log Mink-Trap	86
Plowing From the Inside of the Field	87
A Wire-Fence Tightener	89
Planting Corn—A Marker	90
Feed Trough and Halter	93
The Horse-Show and Its Application	93
How to Make a Fishing Scow	95
Crows and Scarecrows	98
Flood Fence	101
Clearing Slough Land	101
How to Dress a Beef	103
A Farm Cart	105
Braces for a Gate Post	107
Whipple-Trees for Plowing Corn Safely	108
What Trees to Plant for Fuel and Timber	109
To Steady Portable Mills	110
Splitting Rails and Posts	110
A Mixture of Grasses	112
Hitching a Crib-Biter	113
How to Increase Vegetable Matter in the Soil	114
Open Links	115
Care of the Root Crops	116
Trap for Sheep-Killing Dogs	117
How to Use a File Properly	120

CONTENTS.

A Mitre-Box	123
The Manure Harvest	124
Fastening Cattle with Bows	125
The Preservation of Wood	128
A Nest for Egg-Eating Hens	129
Plowing Gear for a Kicking Mule	130
A Leaf Fork	130
Preservation of the Wheat Ground	131
How to Drive a Horse-Shoe Nail	133
Screw-Drivers	134
To Prevent Cows Sucking Themselves	136
Abuse of Barn Cellars	136
Hay-Rack and Manger	139
A Barn Basket	139
The Treatment of Kicking Cows	140
How to Build a Boat-House	141
Waste Lands—Make Them Useful	143
A Rat-Guard	145
A Crupper-Pad for Horses	145
A Dam for a Fish Pond	146
A Wagon Jack	148
Will You Feed Hay or Wood?	149
A Brace for a Kicking Horse	150
How to Save Liquid Manure	151
An Open Shed for Feeding	153
Shade for Horses' Eyes	154
Test All Seeds—Important	155
A Field Roller	157
A Portable Slop Barrel	157
Where and How to Apply Fertilizers	158
A Mill for Crushing Bones	159
Lime and Limestone	160
A Farm Wheelbarrow	162
To Prevent the Balling of Horses	163
To Prevent Cattle Throwing Fences	164
Feed Boxes	165
A Cattle Tie	167
A Beef Raiser	168
A Cedar Stem Soil-Stirrer	169
A Hint for Pig-Killing	170
Mending Broken Tools	170
A Large Feed-Rack	172

Contents.

Barn Door Fastening..173
A Fork Stable Scraper..174
A Method of Curing Hay...175
Granary Conveniences...176
A Non-Slipping Chain for Boulders..178
A Pitchfork Holder...179
A Convenient Hog Loader..180
A Home-Made Roller...181
A Land Scraper...181
A Home-Made Rag Holder...183
A Safety Egg-Carrier...184
A Bush-Roller..186
Brood Sow Pens..187
A Rabbit Trap...188
Wooden Stable Floor...189
A Rail Holder or "Grip"...191
A Cheap and Durable Grindstone-Box and Hangers..................192
A "Ladder" for Loading Corn...194
Protecting Outlet of Drains...195
A Log Boat..196
Cheap and Durable Wagon Seats..197
A Bag-Holder on Platform Scales..198
Making Board Drains..200
Put Things in Their Places..201
Water-Spout and Stock-Trough...203
A Desirable Milking Shed...204
Wear Plate for Harness Tugs and Collars..................................205
Potable Water Fence...206
Ditch Cleaner and Deepener...206
How to Build a Dam..208
Driving Hop and Other Poles..209
A Convenient Grain Box..210
A Road-Scraper...211
Aids in Digging Root Crops...212
The Wood-Lot in Winter..213
Swinging-Stall Fronts..215
Save All Corn Fodder Everywhere...216
Improved Brush Rake..217
Digging Muck and Peat...219
Cleaner for Horses' Hoofs...220
Cold Weather Shelter for Stock Profitable................................220
Good Stone Troughs or Tanks...221

CONTENTS.

Artificial Feeding of Lambs..223
A Convenient Bailed Box...224
Sawdust for Bedding..225
A Cheap Ensilage Cart..226
Milking and Milking Time...227
A Revolving Sheep Hurdle..228
Lights in the Barn..230
A Nest for Sitting Hens..230
Barn-Yard Economy...231
A Cheap Manure Shed...232
A Sheep Rack..233
A Good Picket Pointer...235
Sterilizing Oven and Bottle Truck.......................................236
Inexpensive Building Construction.....................................239
Cover for Sap Buckets...240
A Handy Trough...240
Substitute for Flood Gate..241
Hooks for Shop or Store House..242
Improving a Pasture Spring..242
A General Farm Barn...243
Handy Clod Crusher and Leveler..244
Giving Seeds an Early Start in the Garden........................245
A Post Anchor..245
Stoneboat from Two Boards..246
A Handy Garden Barrow...247
Homemade Trucks and Wheels...248
A Roller from Mowing Machine Wheels.............................248
Making a Picket Fence Hen-Tight.......................................249
Barrel Strawberry Culture..250

II. Farm Appliances

CHAPTER I. RACKS, MANGERS, STANCHIONS AND TROUGHS

Racks and Feed Boxes for Horses..253
Covered Horse Manger..254
Feeding Trough and Hay Shute..255
Device for Box Stall...256
Various Cattle Stanchions..258
Feeding Crib for Pork-Producing Sections.........................263

CONTENTS.

Sheep Rack and Feed Box..................264
A Barrel Rack..................265
Improvements in Pig Troughs..................266
A Plank Trough..................269
A Protected Trough..................270
Troughs for the Pasture..................271
Improved Grain Bin..................273
Straw Baler..................273
Watering Troughs for Stock..................274
A Guarded Horse Trough..................278
Box for Watering Pails..................279
Home-Made Heating Vat..................279

CHAPTER II. VEHICLES, ROLLERS, HARROWS AND MARKERS.

A Cart for Breaking Colts..................281
A Home-Made Cart..................283
Apparatus for Lifting a Wagon-Body..................284
Jack for Wagon Box..................285
Serviceable Wagon-Jacks..................286
Adjustable Wagon Seat..................287
Lubricating Axles..................287
A Light Sleigh or "Jumper."..................288
A Substantial Sled..................289
A Dump Sled..................291
A Triple Land Roller..................291
A Cheaper Triple Roller..................293
A Double Land Roller..................293
Stalk Leveler..................294
Useful Clod Crusher..................295
A Brush Harrow..................296
An Improved Harrow Frame..................297
Land-Markers..................298
Combined Marker and Clod-Crusher..................301
A Land Leveler..................302

CHAPTER III. SMALL TOOLS AND APPLIANCES.

Bag Holders..................303
Handling Potatoes..................306

CONTENTS.

Grindstones and Frames..................308
Tool Holder..................310
How to Repair a Grindstone..................310
A Wooden Manger Fork..................311
Home-Made and Useful Chaff Forks..................312
Stable Scraper and Broom..................313
A Straw or Hay Hook..................314
Fork for Handling Stones..................314
Salt Box for Stock..................315
Safety Single-Tree..................315
Root Pulpers and Cutters..................316
Root Washers..................318
Clamps and Stools for Repairing Harness..................320
A Box Saw-Horse..................322
Long Saw-Bucks..................323
How to Tie a Bag..................324
A Home-Made Rake Head..................325
Working Building Stone..................325
Block for Sand-Paper..................327

CHAPTER IV. APPLIANCES FOR THE BARN, PASTURE AND DAIRY.

Convenient Stable Ventilator..................328
Light Needed in Barns..................329
Lanterns in the Barn..................330
Safety Stick for Mare's Halter..................330
To Keep a Horse from Jumping..................331
Coupling Horses in the Pasture..................332
A Simple Tether..................333
Chain Cattle Tie..................334
An Unpatented Calf Feeder..................335
Two Kinds of Milking Stools..................336
Vat for Deep Setting Milk..................337
Home-Made Butter-Worker..................338
Reins for Driving Oxen..................339
Vat for Dipping Sheep..................340
Sheep-Shearing Bench..................341
Ear Tag Punch for Marking Animals..................341
Sewing Up Wounds in Animals..................342

Contents.

Chapter V. Wells, Pumps, Cisterns and Filters.

Windlass and Tilting Bucket	343
Well-Curb of Staves	344
Hemlock for Well-Curbs	345
Securing the Well-Bucket	346
Curb with a Bucket Shelf	346
Covered Well-Curbs	347
Impure Water in Wells	349
Hook for Cleaning Wells	350
A Non-Freezing Pump	351
Agitation of Air in Wells	351
Deepening Wells	353
Digging a Well	355
How to Build a Cistern	355
Water in the Barn Yard	357
Wooden Water Pipes	358
Filters for Family Use	359
Connecting Cisterns	362
Build and Dimension of Cisterns	363
Cisterns with Filters	364

Chapter VI. Appliances for Handling Hay and Corn Fodder.

Revolving Horse Rake	367
Care of Mowing Machines	370
Sweep for Gathering Hay	371
Hauling Hay or Stalks	372
Derrick for Stacking	373
Hay Carrier for Horse Fork	374
Hay Barracks	375
Supports for Stacks	378
Home-Made Hay Press	379
Twisting Hay and Straw	381
Standard for Corn Shocks	385
Ventilator for Stacks	386
Bench for Husking	387
Corn-Stalk Band	388
Convenient Fodder Carrier	389

CONTENTS.

CHAPTER VII. STUMP-PULLERS, DERRICKS AND SLINGS.

Stump-Pullers 390
Derricks for Farm Use 393
Slings for Hoisting Heavy Objects 394
Derrick for a Cellar 396
Lever Apparatus for Lifting 397
A Home-Made Horse-Power 398

CHAPTER VIII. PREPARING AND HANDLING FERTILIZERS.

Hauling Barnyard Manure 400
Implement for Fining Manure 402
Muck and Peat 403
How to Burn Lime 404
Value of Gas Lime 406
Burning Clay and Sods 407
Converting Straw into Manure 408
Manure from Marl and Shells 409
Making Fertilizer from Bones 409

CHAPTER IX. APPLIANCES FOR THE GARDEN AND ORCHARD.

Paper Plant Protector 411
Muslin-Covered Plant Screen 412
Protected Plant Label 413
Poles for Beans and Other Climbers 414
Potting Strawberry Plants 414
Stand for Berry Baskets 415
Tube for Watering Plants 416
Movable Trellis for Grapes 417
Tool for Cutting Edgings 417
Substitute for Pea Brush 418
Trellis for Tomatoes 418
Tools for Killing Weeds 420
Various Fruit Pickers 421
Fruit Ladders 424
Japanese Pruning Saw 426
Rabbits and Mice in the Orchard 426
Implements Used in Cranberry Culture 428

CONTENTS.

CHAPTER X. APPLIANCES FOR SLAUGHTERING HOGS AND CURING THE MEAT.

Sticking Hogs 430
A Better Way 430
Heating the Water for Scalding 431
Scalding Tubs and Vats 432
Hanging and Cleaning the Hogs 436
Packing Pork 438

III. Fences, Gates and Bridges

CHAPTER I. RAIL AND OTHER PRIMITIVE WOOD FENCES.

Virginia Rail Fence 441
Laying a Rail Fence 443
Staking and Wiring 444
A Fence of "Stakes and Riders" 445
A Pole Fence 446
Fences for Soil Liable to Heave 447
Other Primitive Fences 449

CHAPTER II. STONE AND SOD FENCES.

How a Stone Wall Should Be Built 452
Building a Stone Fence 452
Truck for Moving Stones 454
Reinforcing a Stone Wall 454
A Composite Fence 455
A Prairie Sod Fence 456

CHAPTER III. BOARD FENCES.

Building Board Fences 458
Fences for Land Subject to Overflow 460
A Fence Board Holder 463
Reinforcing a Board Fence 464

CONTENTS.

CHAPTER IV. PICKET FENCES.

A Good Garden Fence 465
A Southern Picket Fence 465
Fences of Split Pickets 467
Ornamental Picket Fences 468
Rustic Picket Fences 470
Light Picket Fences 471
Hand-Made Wire and Picket Fences 473
Fence of Wire and Pickets 475

CHAPTER V. BARB-WIRE FENCE.

Barb-Wire Fence 477
Steel Fence Staples 483
How to Get Barb Wire Fence 484
Unreeling and Stretching Barb Wire 485
Wire Stretchers 489
Splicing Barb Wires 492
Building Wire Fences on Uneven Ground 494

CHAPTER VI. FENCES OF BARB WIRE AND BOARDS.

Combined Wire and Board Fence 495
A Bracketed Fence 497
Dog-Proof Fences 500

CHAPTER VII. HEDGES.

The Best Hedge Plants 501
Planting and Care of Osage Hedges 502
Hedges for the South 507
Ornamental Hedges and Screens 508

CHAPTER VIII. PORTABLE FENCES AND HEDGES.

Portable Board Fences 509

CONTENTS.

Portable Fences of Poles or Wire..511
Portable Fences for Windbreaks..513
Portable Poultry Fences..514
Portable Folding Fence..517
Temporary Wire and Iron Fences..518

CHAPTER IX. FENCES FOR STREAMS AND GULLIES.

Flood Fences..519
Portable Tide Fence...527
Watering Place in a Creek..528

CHAPTER X. MAKING AND SETTING POSTS.

Making Fence Posts...529
A Post Holder..530
Driving Fence Posts By Hand..531
To Drive Fence Posts Without Splitting......................................532
A Powerful Post Driver..534
Setting a Gate Post..537
Live Posts..539
Mending a Split Post...541
Hook for Wiring Posts...542
Drawing Fence Posts...543
Lifting Posts By Hand..544
Splicing Fence Posts..545
Application of Wood Preservatives...546
Iron Fence Posts..548

CHAPTER XI. GATES AND FASTENINGS.

Wooden Gates...551
A Very Substantial Farm Gate..555
A Strong and Neat Gate..556
Light Iron Gates..557
Self-Closing Gates...559
Gate for Village Lot...562
A Chinese Door or Gate Spring..562

CONTENTS.

Lifting Gates 563
Rustic Gates 569
Balance Gates 571
Gate for Snowy Weather 572
West India Farm Gates 573
Double Gates 577
Double-Latched Gates 580
Improved Slide Gate 581
A Combined Hinge and Sliding Gate 582
Gates of Wood and Wire 584
A Good and Cheap Farm Gate 585
An Improved Wire Gate 586
Taking up the Sag in Gates 588
Good Gate Latches 591
Top Hinge of Farm Gate 595
Gateways in Wire Fence 596

CHAPTER XII. WICKETS AND STILES.

Iron Wickets 598
Wooden Wickets 599
Stiles for Wire-Fences 602

CHAPTER XIII. FENCE LAW.

Fencing Out or Fencing In 604
Division Fences 605
Highway Fences 607
What is a Legal Fence? 608
Railroad Fences 609

CHAPTER XIV. COUNTRY BRIDGES AND CULVERTS.

Strength of Bridges 610
Braces and Trusses 611
Abutments, Piers and Railings 614
Bridges for Gullies 616
Ornamental Bridges 618
Road Culverts 619

I.
Farm
Conveniences

FARM CONVENIENCES.

A CONVENIENT BIN FOR OATS.

The usual receptacle for oats, corn, or mill **feed, or other** grain for domestic animals, is a common bin **or box** about four feet in hight. It is difficult to get the **grain** out of such a place when the quantity is half **or more** exhausted. To obviate this inconvenience, there **may** be affixed, about one foot from the bottom on one **side** of the bin, a board, (*B*) figure 1. This is nailed so **as to** project into the bin at an angle sufficient to allow **the** filling of a measure between the lower edge of board *B* and top edge of the opening at *M*. The opposite **lower** side of the bin is covered with boards, as indicated

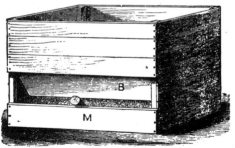

Fig. 1.—A BIN FOR OATS OR OTHER FEED.

by the dotted line at *R*, for the purpose of placing the **contents** within easy reach. The top can be completed **with** hinged cover as well as the delivery space. By using a bin of this form, the last bushel is as easily removed as the first one.

FASTENINGS FOR COWS.

Although stanchions are really the safest fastening for cows, yet some persons object to them because the animals are held in a too confined position, and one which is supposed to be painful, or otherwise objectionable to the cows. Most owners of valuable cows consider safety to be the first requisite in their management, and the question as to what the cow would like as of minor importance. Stanchions have the valuable recommendation that one always finds his cows in the morning just where they were left at night, if they have been properly secured. Nevertheless, for those who dislike stanchions, there are other safe ways of fastening cows. For some years we used the method shown in figures 2 and 3. In

Fig. 2.—FASTENING BY SLIDING RING ON A POLE

the first a strong smooth pole was inserted through the floor and "stepped" into the beam beneath and into the floor above. It was also fastened by an iron strap bolted through the front of the trough. A steel ring to which a steel chain was attached was made to slide up and down upon the post, and a leather neck strap, or, in some cases, a leather head stall, was attached to the chain by a suitable ring or loop. The ring could not fall so low as the floor, being held by the edge of the feed-trough, and the cow's feet could not, therefore, be entangled in the chain by getting over it. This is the chief danger in the use of neck straps and chains, but it may be avoided in this way. Another plan is to have an iron rod bolted to the feed-trough, upon which the ring may slide. This is equally secure, and gives more room for movement to the cow. With these ring-ties it is best to have

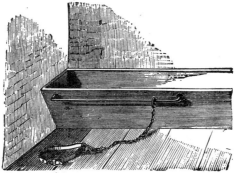

Fig. 3.—FASTENING ATTACHED TO FEED-TROUGH.

short stalls to prevent the cows interfering with each other, else one of them may step on to another as it is lying down. The teats are sometimes injured even when stanchions are used, but the danger of this is greater with chain ties.

MOVABLE NESTS FOR HENS.

Hens, as a general thing, are remarkably self-willed and obstinate. Perhaps an exception may be made as regards the Brahmas, which are very docile and easily managed. On account of this general peculiarity of fowls, many people who possess a somewhat similar disposition, find no success in keeping them. Their hens will not lay in the nests provided for them, or after sitting a few days upon a nest of eggs, leave them and never return. The consequences are, either no eggs at all, or nests hidden where they cannot be reached; no chickens, and time and labor lost. This may all be avoided if the owners will only study the habits and instincts of their poultry reasonably. One of the most inveterate habits of hens is that of hiding their nests, or seeking them in retired, shaded places. Those who would have plenty of eggs must make their arrangements accordingly. A very cheap and convenient nest is shown in figure 4. It is made of pieces of board eighteen

Fig. 4.—A MOVABLE HEN'S NEST.

inches long, nailed endwise to three-sided cleats at the top and bottom. The box need not be more than eighteen or twenty inches in length. Some corner pieces are nailed at the front to make it firm, and the back should be closed. These nests may be placed in secluded corners, behind sheds, or beneath bushes in the back yard, or behind a barrel or a bundle of straw. The nest egg should be of glass or porcelain, and every evening the eggs that have been laid during the day should be removed. A little cut straw mixed with clean earth or sand, will make the best material for the nest. This should be renewed occasionally, for the sake of cleanliness. When a hen has taken possession of one of these nests, it may be removed at night to the hatching-house, without disturbing her. Before the nests are used, they should be thoroughly well lime-washed around the joints, to keep away lice.

HOW TO GET RID OF STRAW.

Many farmers in "the West," and some in what we call "the East," are troubled as to what they shall do with the piles of straw which lie about their fields. Upon the same farms with these nearly useless straw piles, many head of stock are kept, and many more might be kept, which could be made useful in reducing the straw to a condition in which it would serve as manure. If the already urgent necessity for manure upon the western and southern fields were realized, there would be little hesitation in taking measures to remove the difficulty. The chief obstacle is, that these involve either personal or hired labor; the first is objectionable to many, and the second cannot be had for want of the money necessary to pay for it. The least laborious method of using this straw and making it serve the double purpose of a shelter for stock and a fertilizer for the field upon which it has been grown, is as follows: Some poles are set in the ground, and rails or other poles are laid upon them so as to form a sloping **roof.** This is made near or around the place chosen for thrashing the grain. The straw from the thrashing-machine is heaped upon the rails, making a long stack, which forms three sides of a square, with the open side towards the south, and leaving a space beneath it in which cattle may be sheltered from storms. In this enclosure some rough troughs or racks may be placed, from which to feed corn. Here the cattle will feed and lie, or will lie at nights under shelter, while feeding during the day upon corn in the field. As the straw that is given them becomes trampled and mixed with the droppings, a further supply is thrown down from the stack. The accumulation may be removed and spread upon the field to be plowed in when it is so required, and the stakes pulled up and carried to another place, where they may be needed for the same purpose. Such a shelter as this would be very serviceable for the purpose of making manure, even where straw is scarce, as in parts of the Southern States. There pine boughs may be made to serve as a covering, and leaves, pine straw, dry pond muck, swamp muck, "trash" from cotton fields, corn stalks, or pea vines, and any other such materials may be gathered and thrown from time to time beneath the cattle. Cotton-seed meal, straw, and coarse hay would keep stock in excellent order, and although there may be little snow or ice during the winter months in those States, yet the animals will be very much better for even this rude but comfortable shelter. In many other places such a temporary arrangement will be found useful in saving the hauling of straw, stalks, or hay from distant fields, and the carting of manure back again to them. It will be found vastly easier to keep a few young cattle in such a field, and go thither daily to attend to them during the winter when work is not pressing, than to haul many loads of hay or straw to the barn at harvest time, or many loads of manure in the busy weeks of spring.

THE MANAGEMENT OF YOUNG BULLS.

Many farmers want a method of disciplining bulls so that they may be made more docile and manageable. To do this it would be advisable to work them occasionally in a one-horse tread power. They should be used to this when young, and thus being made amenable to restraint, there will be no " breaking " needed afterwards and consequently no trouble. We have used a Jersey bull in a tread-power in which he worked with more steadiness than a horse, and twice a week he served a very useful purpose in cutting the fodder for the stock. Nothing more was needed than to lead him by a rope from the nose-ring into the tread-power, and tie him short so that he could not get too far forward. He was very quiet, not at all mischievous, and was a very sure stock bull ; and besides this, the value of his work was at least equal to the cost of his keep. Where there is no tread-power, a substitute may be found in the arrangement shown in figure 5. Set a post in the barn-yard, bore a hole in the top, and drive a two-inch iron pin into the hole. Take the wheel of a wagon that has an iron axle, and set it upon the top of the post so that it will turn on the pin as on an axle. Fasten a strong pole (such as a binding pole for a hay wagon) by one end to the wheel, and bore two holes in the other end, large enough to take the arms of an ox-bow in them. Fix a light-elastic rod to the wheel, so that the end will be in advance of the end of the larger pole. Yoke the bull to the pole, and tie the nose-ring to the end of the elastic rod, in such a way that a slight pull is exerted upon the ring. Then

Fig. 5.—MANNER OF EXERCISING A BULL

lead the bull around a few times until he gets used to it; he will then travel in the ring alone until he is tired, when he will stop. Two hours of this exercise a day will keep a bull in good temper, good condition and excellent health.

A CONVENIENT ICE-HOOK.

A very handy ice-hook may be made as shown in figure 6. The handle is firmly fastened and keyed into a socket; at the end are two sharply-pointed spikes, one of which serves to push pieces of ice, and the other to draw them to the shore, or out of the water, to be loaded and removed. It may be made of light iron, horse-shoe bar will be heavy enough, and there is no need to have the points steeled; it will be sufficient if they are chilled, after they are sharpened, in salt and ice pounded together.

Fig. 6.—ICE-HOOK.

HINTS FOR THE WORKSHOP.

A grindstone is very seldom kept in good working order; generally it is "out of true," as it is called, or worn out of a perfectly circular shape. A new stone is frequently hung so that it does not run "true," and the longer it is used, the worse it becomes. When this is the case, it may be brought into a circular shape by turning it down with a worn-out mill-file. It is very difficult to do this perfectly by hand, but it is easily done by the use of the contrivance shown in figure 7. A post, slotted in the upper part, is bolted to the frame. A piece of hard **wood**, long enough to reach over the frame, is pivoted in the slot. This should be made two inches wider than the stone, and be pivoted, so that an opening can be made in the middle of it, of the same width as the stone. This opening is made with sloping ends, so that a broad mill-file may be wedged into it in the same manner as a plane-iron is set in a plane. At the opposite end of the frame a second post is bolted to

Fig. 7.—TRUEING A GRINDSTONE.

it. A long slot, or a series of holes, is made in the lower part of this post, so that it may be raised or lowered at pleasure by sliding it up or down upon the bolt. If a slot is made, a washer is used with the bolt; this will make it easy to set the post at any desired height. It should be placed so that the upper piece of wood may rest upon it, exactly in the same position in which the file will be brought into contact with the stone. A weight is laid upon the upper piece to keep it down, and hold the cutter upon the stone. When the stone is turned around slowly, the uneven parts are cut away, while those which do not project beyond the proper line of the circumference are not touched.

A Grinding Frame to hold tools is shown in figure 8.

Fig. 8.—HOLDER FOR TOOLS.

It is made of light pieces of pine, or hard wood. The tool to be ground is fastened to the cross-piece. A sharp point, a nail, or a screw, is fastened to the narrow end of the frame, and, when in use, the point is stuck into the wall of the shed, which forms a rest.

A NON-PATENTED BARREL-HEADER.

Not long since we saw in operation a useful contrivance for pressing the heads of apple or egg barrels into place. Both apples and eggs require to be packed very firmly to enable them to be transported in barrels with safety. Apples loosely packed in a barrel will come to market in a very badly bruised condition, and if the packing around eggs is not very firmly compressed, the eggs and packing change places or get mixed up, and it is the eggs, and not the packing, which then suffers. A barrel of eggs properly packed, with layers of chaff or oats an inch thick between the layers of eggs, and three inches at each end of the barrel, will bear to be compressed as much as three inches with safety; without this compression, eggs are almost sure to be greatly damaged. A barrel of apples may fill the barrel to about two inches **above** the chime, and will bear to have the head brought down to its place. When barrels containing these perishable articles are thus packed they may receive very rough usage without injury to the contents. The header referred to consists of a bar of half-inch square iron rod, with a large eye or loop at one end, and at the other end two diverging hooks which grasp the bottom of the barrel. The bar is bent to fit the curve of the barrel. When in use, the hooks are placed beneath the lower chime of the barrel, one end of a short lever is placed in the eye, and the lever rests upon a block, which is set upon the head of a barrel properly placed in position. A strap or cord, with a loop or stirrup at one end, is fastened to the other end of the lever. The foot is placed in the loop or stirrup, and the weight of the body thrown upon it brings the head of the barrel into its place; the hands being free, the hoops can be driven down tightly without the help of an assistant. Without the

Fig. 9.—BARREL-HEADER.

use of the cord and stirrup, two persons are required to head barrels, but with the aid of these the services of one can be dispensed with.

BUILDING RIBLESS BOATS.

A method of building boats, by which ribs are dispensed with, has recently been brought into use for coast, lake, and river crafts. These boats are light, swift, strong, and cheap. They have been found to be remarkably good sea boats, and to stand rough weather without shipping water. By this method of building, fishermen and others who use boats can construct their own at their leisure, and in many cases become independent of the skill of the professional boat builder. The materials needed are clear pine boards, one inch thick, a keel of oak or elm, a stem and stern-post of the same timber, and some galvanized iron nails. For small boats the boards and keel should be the whole length of the boat intended to be built ; for boats over sixteen feet in length, splices may be made without injuring the strength, if they are properly put together. The materials having been procured, a frame or a set of tressels are made, and the keel is fitted to them in the usual manner, by means of cleats on each side, and wedges. The stem and stern-post are then fitted to the keel in the usual manner, the joints being made water-tight by means of layers of freshly-tarred brown paper laid between the pieces, or by the use of a coating of thick white lead and oil. Previously to being fitted together, the sides of the keel, stem, and stern-post are deeply grooved to receive the first strip of planking. The boards are then ripped into strips one inch, or an inch and a half wide, according to the desired strength of the boat. For rough work,

Old-Fashioned Labor-Saving Devices

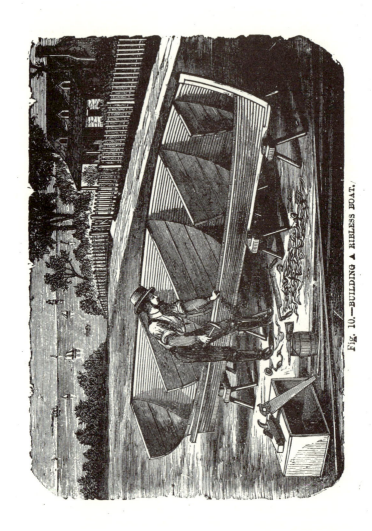

Fig. 10.—BUILDING A RIBLESS BOAT.

such as fishing with nets, or dredging, an inch and a half would be a proper width for the strips. The ripping may be done with one of the hand circular sawing machines, or at a saw-mill, with great rapidity. The first strip is then nailed to the keel, a coating of tar or white lead having first been given to the groove in the keel already prepared for it. The broad side of the strip is laid next to the keel. A set of molds, corresponding to the lines or form of the boat, are cut out of inch boards, and tacked to the keel in the manner shown in figure 10, with the help of cleats upon each side. Then one strip after another is nailed to each preceding one, and the shell of the boat is built up of these strips. Each strip is trimmed down at the ends in a proper manner, with a drawn knife, or a plane, and as each one is nailed to the preceding one, some of the tar or white lead is brushed over it, to make the joint tight and close. A sufficient number of nails is used to hold the strips firmly together, and the heads are driven down level with the surface of each strip. The work proceeds in this manner, forming the strips as each is fitted, bending them to the shape of the molds, and nailing one alternately upon each side, so that the molds are not displaced by the spring of the timber. When the sides of the boat are completed, the fender and gunwales are fitted, and bolted to them to strengthen them, and cleats are bolted inside for the seats to rest upon. The molds are now removed, and the boat consists of a solid shell an inch and a half thick, with not a nail visible excepting on the top strip, and conforming exactly in shape to the model. To give extra strength, short pieces of the strips are nailed diagonally across the inside, from side to side, and across the keel. In this manner a great deal of additional stiffness and strength is given to the boat. A boat of this kind is easily repaired when injured, by cutting out the broken part and inserting pieces of the strips. For a larger boat, which requires a deck, the strips are wider and thicker, or a diagonal lining may be put into it; knees are bolted to the sides, and the beams to the knees, the deck being laid upon the beams. The method is applicable to boats of all sizes and for all purposes, and its cheapness and convenience are rapidly bringing it into favor. If the material is ready for use, two men can finish a large boat in two weeks, and a small one in one week. These boats being very light and buoyant, considerable ballast will be necessary to make them steady enough in case sails are used.

TO MEND A BROKEN TUG.

No one should go from home with a buggy or a wagon without a small coil of copper wire and a "*multum in parvo*" pocket-knife. This knife, as its name implies, has many parts in a little space, and, among other useful things, has a contrivance for boring holes in leather straps. In case a strap or a leather trace breaks, while one is on a journey, and at a distance from any house, one would be in an awkward "fix" if without any means of repairing damages. With the copper wire and an implement for boring some holes, repairs can be made in a very few minutes. The ends of the broken strap or tug may be laid over each other or spliced; a few holes bored in the manner shown in figure 11, and some stitches of wire passed through in the way known among the ladies as "back stitching." The ends of the wire are twisted together, and the job will be finished almost as quickly as this may be read. If it is a chain that breaks, the next links may be brought together and wire wound around them in place of the broken link, which will make the chain serviceable until home is reached. In fact, the uses of a piece of wire are almost endless. Nothing holds a button upon one's working clothes so securely as a piece of wire, and once put on in this manner, there is never any call upon the women of the house at inconvenient times for thread

Fig. 11.—REPAIRING TUG.

and needle to replace it. The wire will pierce the cloth without any help, and nothing more is needed than to pass it through each hole of the button and twist the ends to secure them, cutting them off close with a knife. There is scarcely any little thing that will be found of so great use about a farm, or a workshop, or in a mill, or even in a house, as a small stock of soft copper wire.

BUSINESS HABITS.

There is probably not one farmer in ten thousand who keeps a set of accounts from which he can at any moment learn the cost of anything he may have produced, or even the cost of his real property. A very few farmers who have been brought up to business habits keep such accounts, and are able to tell how their affairs progress, what each crop, each kind of stock, or each animal has cost, and what each produces. Knowing these points, a farmer can, to a very great extent, properly decide what crops he will grow, and what kind of stock he will keep. He will thus be able to apply his labor and money where it will do the most good. He can weed out his stock and retain only such animals as may be kept with profit. For the want of such knowledge, farmers continue, year after year, to feed cows that are unprofitable, and frequently sell for less than her value one that is the best of the herd, because she is not known to be any better than the rest. Feed is also wasted upon ill-bred stock, the keep of which costs three or four times that of well-bred animals, which, as has been proved by figures that cannot be mistaken, pay a large profit on their keeping. For want of knowing what they cost, poor crops are raised year by year at an actual loss, provided the farmer's labor, at the rates current for common labor, were charged against them. To learn that he has been working for fifty cents a day, during a number of years, while he has been paying his help twice as much, would open the eyes of many a farmer who has actually been doing this, and it would convince him that there is some value in figures and book accounts. It is not generally understood that a man who raises twenty bushels of corn per acre, pays twice as much for his plowing and harrowing, twice as much for labor, and twice as great interest upon the cost of his farm, as a neighbor who raises forty bushels per acre. Nor is it understood that when he raises a pig that makes one hundred and fifty pounds of pork in a year, that his pork costs him twice as much, or the corn he feeds brings him but half as much as that of his neighbor, whose pig weighs three hundred pounds at a year old. If all these things were clearly set down in figures upon a page in an account book, and were studied, there would be not only a sudden awakening to the unprofitableness of such farming, but an immediate remedy would be sought. For no person could resist evidence of this kind if it were once brought plainly home to him. If storekeepers, merchants, or manufacturers kept no accounts, they could not possibly carry on their business, and it is only because the farmer's business is one of the most safe that he can still go on working in the dark, and throwing away opportunities of bettering his condition and increasing his profits.

HAY-RACKS.

We here illustrate two kinds of hay-racks, which have

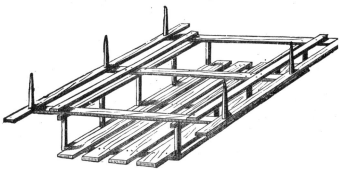

Fig. 12.—HAY-RACK.

been found more convenient in use than some of the old

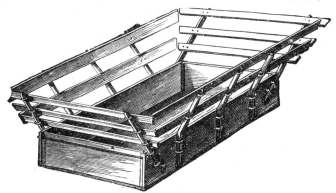

Fig. 13.—RACK FOR GRAIN.

kinds. That shown in figure 12 consists of a frame made

Fig. 15.—Extricating a Mired Cow.

of scantlings, mortised together, and fitting upon the wagon after the box has been removed. Cross-pieces, which project over the wheels, are bolted to the frame, and to these one or two side-boards are bolted. A few short, sharpened stakes are fixed into the sides of the frame, which help to hold the load, and prevent it from slipping off from the rack during the loading. A strong rack of this kind may be made to carry a very large load of hay. We have seen over thirty hundred-weight loaded upon one of them, and more might have been easily added to the load. The plan of building this rack is readily seen by studying the engraving. At figure 13 is shown a rack made to fit upon a wagon body. When grain is hauled, much is sometimes lost through the rack, by shelling. This is almost always the case in hauling ripe oats, and always in drawing buckwheat. To avoid this loss, we have used a strong wagon-box of rough planks, fitted with iron sockets, bolted securely to the sides. Into these sockets were fitted head and tail racks, as shown in the engraving. For the sides we procured natural crooks, shown in figure 14.

Fig. 14.—SUPPORT FOR RACK.

HOW TO EXTRICATE A MIRED ANIMAL.

An animal mired in a swamp gets into a worse predicament the longer it struggles. The effort to extricate it should be made in an effective manner, so that the animal may not be encouraged to exhaust itself in repeated exertions, which are useless, and only sink it deeper in the mire. The usual method is to fasten a rope around the animal's horns or neck, and while this is pulled by some of the assistants, others place rails beneath the body of the animal for the purpose of lifting it out of the hole. This plan is sometimes effective, but it often is not, and at best it is a slow, clumsy, and laborious method. The materials needed for the method here referred to are all that are required for a much better one, which is illustrated in Figure 15. This is very simple, and two men can operate it, and, at a pinch, even one man alone may succeed with it. A strong stake or an iron bar is driven into the solid ground at a distance of twenty-five feet or more from the mired animal. Two short rails, about nine feet long, are tied together near the ends, so that they can be spread apart in the form of a pair of shears, for hoisting. A long rope is fastened around the horns or neck of the animal, with such a knot that the loop cannot be drawn tight enough to do any injury. The rope is cast over the ends of the rails as they are set up upon the edge of the solid ground, and carried to the stake or crow-bar beyond. The end of the rope is fastened to a stout hand-spike, leaving about a foot of the end of it free. This end is laid against the bar or stake, and the other end is moved around it so that the rope is wound upon it, drawing it up and with it drawing the animal out of the mire. The rope being held up by the tied rails, tends to lift the animal and make its extrication very easy.

HOW TO SAVE AND KEEP MANURE.

There is no question more frequently or seriously considered by the farmer, than how he shall get, keep, and spend an adequate supply of manure; nor is there anything about the farm which is of greater importance to its successful management than the manure heap

There are few farmers now left who pretend to ignore this feed for the land; and few localities, even in the newer Western States, where manure now is thought to be a nuisance. We have gradually come to the inevitable final end of our "virgin farms," and have now either to save what is left of their wonderful natural fertility, or to restore them slowly and laboriously to a profitable condition. We have reached the end of our tether, and are obliged to confess that we have trespassed over the line which bounds the territory of the locust, or have improved the face of the country so much that, the protecting timber being removed, the water supply is becoming precarious, and springs, brooks, and rivers no longer flow as they did heretofore. To some extent the tide of emigration, which has flowed westward so many years, is now eddying or even ebbing, and the cheap, worn lands of the East are finding purchasers, who undertake to bring them back to their former condition. At the same time Eastern farmers are discovering more and more certainly that they must increase their crops, and make one acre produce as much as two have heretofore done. The only way in which either of these classes can succeed, is by keeping sufficient stock to manure their farms liberally; to feed these animals so skillfully and well that they shall pay for their feed with a profit, and in addition leave a supply of rich manure, with which the soil can be kept in a productive state, and to save and use the manure with such care that no particle of it be lost. It is not every farmer who can procure all the manure he needs; but very many can save what they have, with far greater economy than they now do; and this, although it may seem a question secondary to that of getting manure, is really of primary importance; for by using what one has to better purpose, he opens a way to increase his supply. We have found this to be the case in our own experience, and by strict attention to saving and preserving every particle of manure in its best condition, we have succeeded in so enlarging our supply of fodder that the number of stock that could be fed was largely increased each year, and very soon it was necessary to go out and buy animals to consume the surplus. To bring a farm into improved condition, there is no cheaper or more effective method than this.

The ordinary management of manure, in open barnyards, where it is washed by rains, dried by the sun's scorching heat, and wasted by every wind that blows, is the worst that is possible. In this way half or more of the value of the manure is lost. By figuring up what it would cost to purchase a quantity of manure equal to what is thus lost, the costliness of this common method would be discovered, and the question how much could be afforded to take care of the manure would be settled. When properly littered, one cow or ox will make a ton of manure every month, if the liquid as well as the solid portion is saved. Ten head would thus make one hundred and twenty tons, or sixty two-horse wagon loads in a year. A pair of horses will make as much manure as one cow, or twelve tons in the year. A hundred sheep, if yarded every night and well littered, will make one hundred tons of manure in the year, and ten pigs will work up a wagon load in a month, if supplied with sufficient coarse material. The stock of a one hundred acre farm, which should consist of at least ten cows, ten head of steers, heifers, and calves, a pair of horses, one hundred sheep, and ten pigs, would then make, in the aggregate, three hundred and sixteen tons of manure every year, or sufficient to give twelve tons per acre every fourth year. If this were well cared for, it would be, in effect, equal to double the quantity of ordinary yard manure ; and if a plenty of swamp muck could be procured, at least six hundred tons of the best manure could be made upon a one hundred acre farm. If this were the rule instead of a rare exception, or only a possibility, what a change would appear upon the face of the country, and what an addition would be made to the wealth of the nation!

GRINDING TOOLS.

The useful effect of many tools depends greatly upon the exact grinding of their edges to a proper bevel. A cold chisel, for instance, requires an edge of a certain

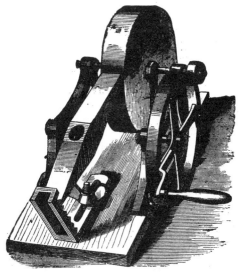

Fig. 16.—DEVICE FOR GRINDING MILL-PICKS.

bevel to cut hard metal, and one of a different angle for softer metal; the harder the work to be cut, the greater should be the angle formed by the edge, and the softer the material, the more acute the edge. The same rule is to be observed in wood-cutting tools. But there are no tools which require more exact and careful grinding than mill-picks, and the first business of a miller is to know how to grind his picks. Upon this depends the dress of the stones, and the quality of work turned out by them. Figure 16 represents a small grindstone for sharpening picks, which is run by means of friction wheels covered with leather, and provided with a gauge for setting the pick at a variable angle to the stone. This gauge, shown in the engraving, is so serviceable as to be well worth a place in any farm workshop. It consists of a series of steps raised upon a slotted plank, which is screwed upon the frame of the grindstone. By means of the slot and a set screw, seen below the pick, the gauge can be set for tools of different lengths, and each step causes the tool set in it to be ground at a different angle.

A METHOD OF HANGING HOGS.

An easy method of hanging a hog or a beef, is by the use of the tripod shown in figure 17. It is made of three by three oak scantling, six feet long, connected at one end, in the manner shown, by means of an iron bar one inch thick, passed through a hole bored in each piece. The two outside pieces are fastened together by two cross-pieces, bolted to them, so that they are spread at the bottom sufficiently, which would be about three feet. A hook is fastened to the lower cross-piece, upon which the hog is suspended.

Fig. 17.—TRIPOD SET UP. To hang the hog the frame is laid upon the ground with the hog between the outside

legs, the third leg being drawn backwards. The hog is hooked by the gambrel stick to the cross-piece, the frame is lifted up, and the hinder leg is spread out so as to support it, as shown in figure 17. The frame may be lowered easily when the hog has to be taken down, and as the frames are cheaply made, and occupy little room, it will be well to have several of them. They may be made to serve other useful purposes.

RELIEF FOR BOG-SPAVIN AND THOROUGH-PIN.

Bog-spavin, and thorough-pin, which are in reality the same disease, differing in position only, and that very slightly, may be considered as incurable. But like many chronic disorders, they may be very much relieved by proper methods. They are caused by an inflammatory condition of the synovial membrane of the hock joint, and are chiefly located in the vicinity of the junction of the bones of the leg, or the capsule between the tibia and the astragalus. This inflammation may be primarily caused by sudden shocks, or by continued strains from hard work, and the troubles are common among those horses which are of a lymphatic constitution, soft boned, or hereditarily subject to scrofulous or inflammatory conditions. They are also found lower down the leg, in which case they are the result of inflammation of the sheath of the tendons. They do not always cause lameness, except when the horse is first brought from the stable, and after a short time the stiffness may pass away. At other times there is great heat and tenderness in the parts, and the animal is decidedly lame. The best treatment is by cold applications and pressure upon the part. Blistering, which is sometimes resorted to, generally increases the trouble, and may cause a permanent thickening of the tissues, and a stiff joint. Pressure is best applied by a sort of truss, or strap, provided with a single pad in case of spavin or wind-gall, or double pads in case of thorough-pin, which is simply a spavin or wind-gall, so placed that the liquid which is gathered in the sac or puff may be pressed between the tendons or joint, and made to appear on the opposite side of the leg. In this case it is obviously necessary to apply the pressure upon both sides of the leg, and a double pad strap will be needed, of the form shown in figure 18. A common broad leather strap, lined with flannel, or chamois leather, to prevent chafing, is used; pads of soft leather, stuffed with wool, are sewn to the strap, and the exact spots where the pressure is to bear, disks of several thicknesses of soft leather or rubber are affixed. The pads must necessarily be made to fit each individual case, as success will depend upon their properly fitting the limb. The pads should be worn continually until the swelling disappears, and meanwhile, at least twice daily, the parts should be bathed for some time with cold water, and cloths wetted with cold water, with which a small quantity of ether has been mixed, should be bound around the parts, and the pads buckled over them so tightly as to exert a considerable pressure. Absolute rest is necessary while the animal is under this treatment.

Fig. 18.—SPAVIN PAD.

TOOL-BOXES FOR WAGONS, ETC.

To go from home with a wagon without taking a few tools, is to risk a break-down from some unforeseen accident, without the means of repairing it, and perhaps a consequent serious or costly delay. Those who do business regularly upon the roads, as those who haul lumber, wood, coal, or ores of different kinds, should especially be provided with a set of tools, as a regular appurtenance to the wagon, and the careful farmer in going to market or the mill, or even to and fro upon the farm, should be equally well provided. We have found by experience that a break-down generally happens in the worst possible place, and where it is most difficult to help one's self. The loss of so simple a thing as a nut or a bolt may wreck a loaded wagon, or render it impossible to continue the journey, or some breakage by a sudden jerk upon a rough road may do the same. It is safe to be provided for any event, and the comfort of knowing that he is thus provided greatly lightens a man's labor. At one time, when we had several wagons and teams at work upon the road, we provided the foreman's wagon with a box such as is here described, and it was in frequent use, saving a considerable outlay that would otherwise have been necessary for repairs, besides much loss of valuable time. It was a box about eighteen inches long, sixteen inches wide, and six inches deep, divided into several compartments. It was supplied with a spare king-bolt, a hammer-strap, wrench, some staples, bolts, nuts, screws, a screw-driver, a hammer, cold-chisel, wood-chisel, punch, pincers, a hoof-pick, copper rivets, a roll of copper wire, a knife heavy and strong enough to cut down a small sapling, a roll of narrow hoop-iron, some cut and wrought nails, and such other things as experience proved to be convenient to have. The shape of the box is shown in figure 19. The middle of the top is fixed, and on each side of it is a lid

Fig. 19.—WAGON BOX.

hinged to it, and which is fastened by a hasp and staple, and a padlock or a spring key. The box is suspended to the wagon reach, beneath the box or load, by two strong leather straps with common buckles. Being only six inches deep, it is not in the way of anything, and is readily accessible when wanted.

MAKING A HINGE.

A gate with a broken hinge is a very forlorn object, and one that declares to every passer-by, "here lives a poor farmer." If there is one thing more than another worthy of note and a cause of congratulation in this one hundredth year of the existence of the United States, it is the infinite number of small conveniences with which we are supplied, every one of which adds to the sum of our daily comfort. More than this, the majority of these little things, which are in use all over the world, are the inventions and productions of Americans. So plentifully are we supplied with these small conveniences, that we cannot turn our eyes in any direction without coming across some of them. It is these small matters which enable us to have so many neat and pleasant things about our homes, at so little cost of money, time, or labor. One of the greatest of the small conveniences around the farm, or the mechanic's rural home, is the small forge. To make a gate-hinge with the help of this portable forge is a very easy thing. We take a piece of half-inch square bar-iron, as long as may be needed, and heating one end, round it for an inch or two; then, heating the other end, flatten it out gradually to a point for the same length, and bend it over a mandrel, or the nose of an anvil, into the shape shown

in figure 20. We then cut off a piece of round half-inch
bar, about two inches long, and
drive it into the loop, tightening
the loop around it as much as pos-

Fig. 20.

sible. The loop-end is then brought to a welding heat,
and the joint closed around the pin, and neatly worked
smooth with the hammer. Another piece of square iron
is then taken, and worked at each end the same as the
first one, the loop, however, is worked open upon a piece
of cold ⅜-inch round bar, so that it will be large enough
to work easily upon the pin of the first piece. A thread
may now be cut upon the round ends, or they may be
riveted over a piece of iron plate, or a large washer,
when they are driven through the gate-post and the
heel-post of the gate. It is best, however, to have a
screw-thread and a nut, using a washer under each nut,
to prevent the wood from being crushed. The whole
then appears as at figure 21, and is a hinge that cannot

Fig. 21.

easily be broken or worn out. In
boring the holes for a hinge of this
kind, a bit or an auger of only
half-an-inch diameter should be
used, so that the edges of the iron
should cut their own way into the wood, and when the
hinges are driven, a piece of hard wood should be laid
upon the ends that are struck, so that they will not be
battered by the hammer. Care must be exercised to
have them driven in squarely, so that the gate may
swing without binding on the hinges. For lighter
hinges, the same sized iron may be used, but the ends
should be hammered out to a point, and the edges
should be notched or bearded with a
cold-chisel, as shown at figure 22.
These may be driven into a post
Fig. 22.
very readily, if a hole smaller than the iron be bored to

lead the way, and when driven in, will not be easily drawn out. When it is necessary to draw a hinge out of a post or gate, that has become rusted in, or that has been very tightly driven, it may easily be done by boring a hole above it, or on one side of it, or beneath it, a little larger than the iron, and then forcing it into the hole by means of a wooden wedge driven close to it. It will then be loose, and may easily be taken out without difficulty.

SHELTER FOR THE HEAD.

Many a severe headache, and a restless night after an exhausting day's work in the harvest field, might be prevented by the use of some simple precautions. The sun beats down upon the head and neck with great force, when the thermometer marks ninety degrees and over in the shade, and the scorching effect of a heat of one hundred and twenty degrees in the direct sunshine is both uncomfortable and dangerous to the health. The head should be protected in such cases by wearing a straw hat, or one of some open material, with a broad brim, and by placing a leaf of cabbage or lettuce, or a wetted cambric handkerchief in the crown of it. The very sensitive back of the head and neck is best protected by means of a white handkerchief fastened by one border to the hat-band, figure 23, and the rest made to hang down loosely over the neck and shoulders. The neck is thus shaded from the sun's rays, and the loosely flapping handkerchief causes a constant current of air to

Fig. 23.—NECK-PROTECTOR.

pass around and cool the neck and head. We have found this to be a most comfortable thing to wear, and its value as a protector to the base of the brain and the spinal marrow is so well known in hot countries, that the use of a similar protection is made imperative in armies when on the march.

HOW TO LEVEL WITH SQUARE AND PLUMB-LINE.

The common carpenter's square and a plumb-line may be made to serve as a substitute for the spirit level for many purposes on the farm or elsewhere, when a level is not at hand. The manner of getting the square in position to level a wall, for instance, is shown in figure

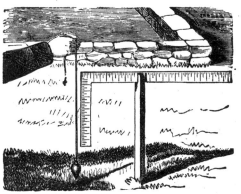

Fig. 24.—MANNER OF LEVELLING A WALL.

24. A piece of board, three feet in length, having one end sharpened, is driven into the ground for a rest: a notch is made in the top of the stick large enough to hold the square firmly in position, as shown in the engraving. A line and weight, held near the short arm, and parallel to it, will leave the long arm of the square level. By sighting over the top of the square, any irregularities in the object to be levelled are readily discovered. A method to find the number of feet in a descent in the ground is illustrated by figure 25. The square is placed as before directed; then a sight is taken over and along the upper edge of the square to a pole or rod placed at a

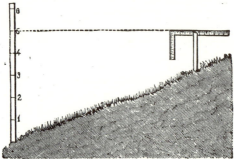

Fig. 25.—MEASURING A SLOPE WITH A SQUARE.

desired point. The point on the pole which is struck by the line of sight shows the difference between the levels of the two places. This method will be found applicable in laying out drains, where a certain desired fall is to be given to the ditch.

KEEP THE CATTLE UNDER COVER.

Even now, in some of the newer regions of the West, the easiest way to get rid of the manure is considered the best. The English farmers have long been obliged to feed farm animals largely for the fertilizers they yield, and this has proved that covered yards are the most economical. These covers are not so expensive as might be supposed at first thought. Substantial sheds, large enough to accommodate a hundred head of cattle, may be built at a cost all the way from $1,000 to $1,500, according to the locality and price of labor and lumber. The roof may be made with three ridge poles resting upon outside walls, and two rows of pillars. There should be ample provision for ventilation and the escape of the water falling upon the roof. The original cost will not be many dollars per head, and the interest on this will represent the yearly cost. If this should be placed at two dollars for each animal, it will be seen that this outlay is more than repaid by the increased value of the housed manure over that made in the open yard, and exposed to the sun and drenching rains. The saving in food consequent upon the warm protection of the animals has been carefully estimated to be at least one-tenth the whole amount consumed. In the saving alone, the covered yard gives a handsome return upon the investment.

WATERING PLACES FOR STOCK ON LEVEL LAND.

It is frequently the case that there are underdrains of living water passing through level fields, in which there is no water available for stock. In such a case, a simple

Fig. 26.—TAKING WATER FROM UNDERDRAIN.

plan for bringing the water to the surface is shown in figures 26 and 27, in which is indicated an underdrain of stone or tile; a pipe of two-inch bore of wood or tile, and about 15 feet in length, is laid level with the bottom of the drain, and connecting with a box one foot or more square sunk into the ground. If the soil be soft, the box is surrounded with stones as shown. **A low place or small hollow** at some point along the **drain is selected** for the watering box, or, should the **land be**

Fig. 27.—THE WATERING PLACE.

nearly level, then with plow and scraper an artificial hollow is soon made at any point desired. Two fields may be thus easily watered by making the box two feet in length, and placing it so that the fence will divide it.

A SHAVING-HORSE.

The shingle-horse, shown in figure 28, is made of a plank ten feet long, six inches wide, and an inch and

Fig. 28.—SHAVING-HORSE FOR SHINGLES.

a half thick. A slot is cut through this plank, and a lever, made of a natural crook, is hinged into it. A wooden spring is fixed behind the lever, and is fastened to it by a cord. This pulls back the lever when the foot is removed from the step beneath. The horse may have four legs, but two will be sufficient, if the rear end is made to rest upon the ground. Figure 29 is made of a plank, six feet long, ten inches wide, and two inches thick. Four legs, two feet long, are fixed in inch and a half holes, as shown below. A bench, eighteen inches

Fig. 29.—HORSE FOR GENERAL USE.

long, eight and a half inches wide, and an inch and a half thick, is fixed upon the horse. A slot, eight by one and a half inches, is cut through the bench and the plank, and the lever, two feet eight inches long, is fixed in this by means of a pin passing through the bench. Some extra holes are made in the lever, by which the height of the head above the bench may be changed to suit different sizes of work. A head is put upon the lever, six inches square each way, but bevelled off at the front. The foot-board, five by ten inches, is fastened to the bottom of the lever by a strong pin.

A MILKING-STOOL.

The front of the stool (figure 30) is hollowed to receive the pail, which is kept in its place by a wire, fixed as shown in the engraving. The front leg has a projecting rest upon which the bottom of the pail is **placed to** keep it from the ground, and also from **breaking**

Fig. 30.—A MILKING-STOOL.

away the wire by its weight. The milker may either **sit astride** of this stool, or sideways upon it.

HOW TO TREAT THRUSH.

Thrush is a disease of the horse's hoof, quite **common in** this country. It results oftener from neglect in **the stables** than from any other cause. The symptoms **are** fetid odor and morbid exudation from the frog, accompanied with softening of the same. A case recently came under our observation. A young carriage horse, used mostly on the road, and kept in the stable through the year, showed lameness in the left fore foot one morning after standing idle in the stable all the previous day. On removing the shoe, and examining the hoof, a fetid odor was observed. The stable was examined, when the sawdust used for bedding was found to be saturated with urine. The stable was cleaned immediately. Dry sawdust was placed in the stall, and a few sods packed in the space where the horse usually rested his fore feet. The lameness diminished without medical treatment, and in ten days disappeared altogether. A bedding of sawdust or earth, covered with straw or leaves, promotes the comfort of the horse, but it needs watching and systematic renewing. The limit of the absorbing power of the driest soil, or sawdust, is soon reached. If a horse is kept most of the time in the stable, his bedding soon becomes wet, and unfit for his use. It is all the better for the compost heap, and for the horse, to have frequent renewals of absorbments of some kind, that fermentation may not be in progress under his hoofs. The proper place for this fermentation is in the compost heap. Too often the care of the horse is left to a servant without experience in the stable, and the result is permanent disease in the hoofs and legs of the horse. This is most certainly one of the cases in which "an ounce of prevention is worth a pound of cure."

A WESTERN LOCUST TRAP.

A great many devices have been used for the destruction of the locusts in those Western States where they have done so much mischief for a few years past. Whether the locusts are to remain as a permanent pest to the Western farmers, or not, remains to be proved. It is certain, however, that through some effects of the climate, the attacks of parasitic enemies, their consumption by birds and other animals, and by the efforts of the farmers themselves, the locusts have of late been greatly reduced in numbers, and their depredations have become almost inconsiderable. Many methods have been adopted for their destruction. Rolling the ground; plowing furrows, and making pits in them in which the insects are caught; burning them in long piles of dry grass; catching them in large sacks, and upon frames smeared with gas tar, and upon large sheet-iron pans containing burning fuel; all these have been tried with more or less success, as well as the negative means of diverting them from their course by means of thick smoke from smothered fires of prairie hay. A most effective method is one invented by a woman in Minnesota. This consists of a large strip of sheet-iron, figure 31, from ten to thirty feet long, turned up a few inches at the ends and one side; a wire is fixed to each end, or at proper places in the front, by which it can be drawn over the ground by a pair of horses or oxen. A light chain or rope is fixed so as to drag upon the ground a foot in advance of

Fig. 31.—TRAP FOR CATCHING LOCUSTS.

the front of the sheet-iron, by which the locusts are disturbed and made to jump, and as the machine is moving on at the same time, they drop upon it. A thick coat of gas-tar is smeared over the surface of the iron, in which the locusts are imbedded and stick fast. The vigorous kicking of the trapped insects helps to keep the mass stirred up, and present a sticky surface. When the trap is full, the locusts are raked off into a pile, and set on fire and consumed. This machine can be drawn over young wheat without injury, as it is not heavy enough to break it down, and being flexible, conforms to the surface of the ground it is passing over. The engraving shows the manner of preparing the sheet-iron for this purpose. The season when the locusts have formerly damaged the newly sprouted wheat is in the spring, and it will be useful for many Western farmers to know of this cheap and effective method, which is not patented, and for which they may thank a farmer's wife of more than usual ingenuity and habits of observation.

SPREADING MANURE.

The winter is a good season for spreading manure. It is immaterial whether the ground is covered with snow or not, or whether it is frozen or soft, provided it is not too soft to draw loads over, and that the ground is not upon a steep hill-side, from which the manure may be washed by heavy rains or by sudden thaws. We have spread manure upon our fields several winters, and always with advantage, not only in saving labor and time, but also to the crops grown after it, more especially to oats and potatoes. In spreading the manure, it

Fig. 32.—WAGON WITH RAISED BOX.

is the best to drop it in heaps, leaving it to be spread by a man as soon as possible afterwards. This may be done most readily by using a manure hook, with which the manure is drawn out of the sled or wagon-box. Sloping wagon-beds are used for hauling various heavy materials, and why should they not be used for this, the heaviest and most bulky load a farmer has to handle? A wagon, having the box raised (figure 32), so that the forward wheels could pass beneath it, would be very convenient on a farm. It could be turned in its own length, and handled with vastly greater facility than the ordinary farm wagon, which needs a large yard to be turned in. Such a wagon could be unloaded with great ease and

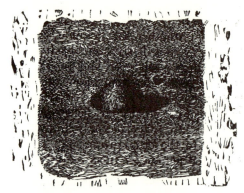

Fig. 33.—MANNER OF SPREADING.

very rapidly by the use of the hook, and in case it was desired to spread the load broadcast from the wagon, that could be done perfectly well. But to do this keeps the horses idle the greater part of the time, and is an unprofitable practice. Two teams hauling will keep one man busy in the yard helping to load, and another in the field spreading; the work will then go on without loss of time. In dropping the heaps, they may be left in rows, one rod apart, and one rod apart in the row; each load being divided into eight heaps. This will give twenty loads per acre. If ten loads only are to be spread, the rows should be one rod apart, and the heaps two rods apart in the rows. In spreading the manure, it should be done evenly, and the heaps should not be made to overlap. If there is one heap to the square rod, it should be thrown eight feet each way from the centre, covering a square of sixteen and one half feet, as shown in figure 33. One heap then is made to join up to another, and the whole ground is equally manured. There is more in this point than is generally supposed by farmers, many of whom are careless and wasteful in this respect, giving too much in some places, and too little in others. The consequence is uneven growth over the field, rusted grain, or perhaps laid straw in some places, and in others a half-starved crop. Another important point in spreading is, to break up the lumps, and scatter the fine manure. Unless this is done, the field cannot be evenly fertilized. There is work about this, which would tempt some hired men to neglect it, but it should not only be insisted upon, but looked to, and its performance insured.

PUTTING AWAY TOOLS.

The wearing out of farm implements is, as a rule, due more to neglect than to use. If tools can be well taken care of, it will pay to buy those made of the best steel, and finished in the best manner; but in common hands, and with common care, such are of little advantage. Iron and steel parts should be cleaned with dry sand and a cob, or scraped with a piece of soft iron, washed and oiled if necessary, and in a day or two cleaned off with the corn-cob and dry sand. Finally, paint the iron part with rosin and beeswax, in the proportion of four of rosin to one of wax, melted together and applied hot. This is good for the iron or steel parts of every sort of tool.

Wood-work should be painted with good, boiled, linseed oil, white lead and turpentine, colored of any desired tint; red is probably the best color. Keep the cattle away until the paint is dry and hard, or they will lick, with death as the result. If it is not desired to use paint on hand tools, the boiled oil, with turpentine and "liquid drier," does just as well. Many prefer to saturate the wood-work of farm implements with crude petroleum. This cannot be used with color, but is applied by itself, so long as any is absorbed by the pores of the wood.

SELF-CLOSING DOORS.

A self-opening, rolling door is shown in figure 34. A half-inch rope, attached to a staple driven into the upper edge of the door, passes parallel with the track, and be-

Fig. 34.—SELF-CLOSING SLIDING DOOR.

yond the boundary of the door when open, over a small grooved pulley and thence downward; a weight is attached to its end. The door is shown closed, and the weight drawn up. As the door is a self-fastening one, when the fastening is disengaged the weight will draw the door open. By a string or wire connected to the fastening, the door may be opened while standing at any part of the building, or if one end be attached to a post outside, near the carriage way, the door may be opened without leaving the vehicle, a desirable plan, especially during inclement weather. The weight and pulleys should be located inside the building, but are shown outside to make the plan more readily understood. By attaching the rope to the opposite side of the door, it may be made self-closing instead of self-opening, as thought most convenient.

Fig. 35.—SWING-DOOR.

The manner of closing a swing-door, as in figure 35, is so clearly shown as to need no description.

VENTILATORS FOR FODDER STACKS.

The perfect curing of fodder corn is difficult, even with the best appliances; as usually done, the curing is very imperfect. The fodder corn crop is one that merits

Fig. 36.—FRAME.

not only the best preparation of the ground and the best culture, but it is worthy of special care in harvesting and curing. The French farmers are giving much attention to this crop, and by good culture are raising most extraordinary and very profitable yields. Seventy tons per acre is not unfrequently grown by the best farmers. We do not average more than eight tons per acre, yet with us the corn crop may be grown under the most favorable circumstances. In a few instances, a yield of thirty tons per acre has been reached by one farmer, but this is the highest within our knowledge. One of the most prominent defects in ordinary American agriculture is, the neglect with which this easily grown and very valuable crop is treated; and one of the most promising improvements in our advancing system of culture is, the attention now being given to fodder corn. A drawback under which we labor is the difficulty of curing such heavy and succulent herbage; this, however, will by and by be removed, both by the adoption of the French system of ensilage, and by better methods of drying the fodder. On the whole, the system of ensilage offers by far the greatest advantages; the fodder being preserved in a fresh and succulent condition, and the labor of preparing the silos, cutting the stalks, and properly protecting them from the atmosphere, being actually no more than that of drying the crop in the usual manner, storing it in stacks, and cutting it afterwards for use when it is needed. It is impossible, however, that even the best improvements can be introduced otherwise than slowly and with caution; the old system, although it may be less effective and profitable than the new, will be long retained by many; and even in the old methods improvements are being made from season to season by the ingenuity of farmers. We recently saw a very simple but useful arrangement for the ventilation of stacks, and mows in

Fig. 37.—VENTILATOR.

barns, which is applicable to the curing of corn fodder. It consists of a frame, figure 36, made of strips of wood, put together with small carriage bolts. The strips may be made of chestnut, pine, or hemlock, the first being the most durable and best, two inches wide and one inch thick. The illustration shows how these strips are put together. The length of the section shown may be three or four feet. In figure 37 is seen the manner in which the sections are put together. A small stack may have a column of these ventilators in the centre; a large one may have three or four of them; in a mow in the barn, there may be as many as are needful, two or three, or more, as the case may be. When made in this shape, they are so portable, and easy to use, that the greatest objections against ventilators are removed. In stacking fodder corn, it is safest to make the stacks small. Three of these sections, placed together in one column, are sufficient for a stack containing three tons, and which would be about fourteen feet high. The sheaves should be small, and the stack somewhat open at the bottom, so as to freely admit currents of air. The top of the stack should be well protected to keep out the rain; a hay cap fastened over the top would be very effective for this. If a quantity of dry straw could be thrown in between the bundles, and on the top of each layer of them, the perfect curing of the fodder would be then secured.

CORN-MARKER FOR UNEVEN GROUND.

The corn-marker, shown in figure 38, is so constructed that it will readily accommodate itself to uneven ground. It consists of two pieces of plank, these form the middle set of runners. Upon these pin two straight pieces of two by four scantling, with each end projecting over the runner six inches; through these ends are bored holes for a four-inch rod. Two other pieces of plank, like the former, are procured, and one end of two other pieces of scantling are pinned to each runner; then these beams are connected to the middle pair by the

Fig. 38.—FLEXIBLE CORN-MARKER.

bolts, as seen in the engraving, so that, while one runner is on high ground, the other may be in the land furrow. In turning around, the two outside runners may be turned up against the seat.

A HOME-MADE HARROW.

The harrow, figure 39, is a square one. The teeth are set twelve inches from centre to centre, each way. There are four beams in each half, and five teeth in each beam. These beams are four feet eight inches long, mortised into the front piece, which is three feet seven inches in length. The rear ends of the beam are secured by a piece of timber, two by one and a half inches, halved on to the beams and then bolted. The harrow is made of two and a half by two and a half-inch scantling, using locust wood, because of its great durability and firmness. There is nothing particularly new about this harrow, except that it is larger than common, and the novel way of hitching to it by which it is kept steady.

The teeth can be made to cut six inches or one inch apart. The manner of hitching is shown in the engraving. The draw-bar is made of three-eighths by one and three-quarter iron, three feet four inches in length.

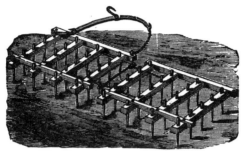

Fig. 39.—AN EXCELLENT HARROW.

The chain is attached to this by a hook at one end, the other being fastened to the harrow by a staple. The chain is about two feet long. The entire cost is about twelve dollars.

CLEARING LAND BY BLASTING.

The explosive used is dynamite or giant powder. It is a mixture of nitro-glycerine with some absorbents, by which this dangerously explosive liquid is made into a perfectly safe solid substance, of a consistence and appearance not unlike light-brown sugar. It is not possible to explode dynamite by ordinary accident, nor even by the application of a lighted match. A quantity of it placed upon a stump and fired with a lighted match, burns away very much as a piece of camphor or resin would do, with little flame but much smoke, and boils and bubbles until only a crust is left. There is not the least danger, therefore, of igniting the powder dangerously, until properly placed for the blast. In this respect it has a very great advantage over ordinary blasting powder, which may be exploded by a spark. The powder, as it is manufactured, is made into cartridges about eight inches in length, and of any required diameter. The cartridges are wrapped in strong parchment paper, covered with paraffine, and the true form is shown at figure 40. They are fired by a cap (also in figure 40), which is inserted into the end of the cartridge. The fuse, which is of the common kind, is inserted into the open end of the cap, which is pinched close upon it with a small pair of pliers, so as to hold it firmly. The cartridge

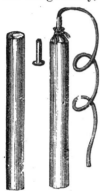

Fig. 40. Fig. 41.

Fig. 42.—THE STUMP BEFORE THE EXPLOSION.

is then opened at one end, the cap with the fuse attached inserted, and the paper tied tightly around the fuse, with a piece of twine. The cartridge ready for firing is shown at figure 41.

Our first operation was upon a green white-oak stump, thirty inches in diameter, with roots deeply bedded in the ground. To have cut and dug out this stump with axe and spades would have been a hard day's work for two or more good men. The shape of the stump is shown at figure 42. A hole was punched beneath the stump, as shown in the figure, with an iron bar (figure 43), so as to reach the centre of it. Two of the cartridges were placed beneath the stump, and were tamped with some earth; a pail of water was then poured into the hole, which had the effect of consolidating the earth around the charge. The fuse was then fired. The result was to split the stump into numerous fragments, and to throw it entirely out of the ground, leaving only a few shreds of roots loose in the soil. The result is shown in figure 44, on the next page; the fragments of the stump in the engraving were thrown to a distance of thirty to fifty feet, and many smaller ones were carried over one hundred feet. The quantity of powder used was less than two pounds. A portion of the useful effect produced by the explosion, consisted in the tearing of the stump into such pieces as could easily be sawed up into fire-wood; by which much after-labor in breaking it up, when taking it out in the usual manner, was saved. This test was perfectly successful, and proved not only the thorough effectiveness of this method, but its economy in cost and in time. Several other stumps were taken out in the same manner; the time occupied with each being from five to ten minutes. Smaller stumps were thrown out with single cartridges, and in not one case was anything left in the ground that might not be turned out with the plow, or

Fig. 43.

that would interfere with the plowing of the ground. The explosive was then tried upon a fast rock, of about

Fig. 44.—THE EFFECT OF BLASTING THE STUMP.

one hundred and fifty cubic feet, weighing about ten tons. The shape of the rock before the explosion is

Fig. 45.—THE ROCK AS IT WAS.

shown in figure 45. A hole was made, with the bar, in the ground beneath the rock, and three cartridges were inserted and exploded. To have produced this result (shown in figure 46), by the ordinary method, that was here done in a few minutes by one man, would have occupied, at least, two men, with drills, sledge, etc., two or three days. The application of this method is seen to be of great value where the saving of time is an object. An acre of stumps or rocks may be cleared in one day by one or two men, and the material left ready

Fig. 46.—THE ROCK AFTER BLASTING.

for use as fire-wood, or as stones for fences or buildings. The cost in money is also reduced in some cases very considerably, and almost absolute safety to the careful operator is insured. It would be generally advisable to secure the services of an expert, and that the parties who have work of this character to be performed, should jointly engage such a man, who could either do the whole work, or do it in part, and instruct a foreman or skilful workman sufficiently in a day to perform the remainder. The most favorable seasons for operating upon stumps and rocks are fall and spring, when the ground is saturated with water. It should be explained that this explosive is not injured by water, although a long-continued exposure to it would affect some qualities of it.

PREVENTABLE LOSSES ON THE FARM.

It is a "penny wise and pound foolish" system, to breed from scrub stock. There is not a farmer in this region who has not access to a pedigreed Shorthorn bull, by a payment of a small fee of two to five dollars, and yet we find only one animal in ten with Shorthorn blood. It is a common practice to breed to a yearling, and as he is almost sure to become breechy, to sell him for what he will bring the second summer. Many farmers neglect castrating their calves until they are a year old. We think ten per cent. are thus permanently injured, must be classed as stags, and sold at a reduced price. Fully half the calves so stunted never recover.

With many, the starving process continues through the entire year. They are first fed an insufficient quantity of skim milk; then in July or August, just at the season when flies are at their worst, and pastures driest, they are weaned, and turned out to shift for themselves, and left on the pastures until snows fall, long after the fields yield them a good support. They are wintered without grain, spring finds them poor and hide-bound, and the best grazing season is over before they are fairly thrifty.

The keeping of old cows long past their prime is another thing which largely reduces the profits of the farmer. We have found quite a large per cent. of cows, whose wrinkled horns and generally run-down condition show that they have long since passed the point of profit. A few years ago, these cows would have sold at full prices for beef, now they will sell only for Bologna at two cents per pound. Thus cows have, in a majority of cases, been kept, not because they were favorites, or even because they were profitable, but from sheer carelessness and want of forethought. Another fruitful cause of loss to the farmer is, attempting to winter more stock than he has feed for. Instead of estimating his resources in the fall, and knowing that he has enough feed even for a hard winter, he gives the matter no thought, and March finds him with the choice of two evils, either to sell stock, or buy feed. If he chooses the former, he will often sell for much less than the animals would have brought four months earlier, and if the latter, will usually pay a much higher price for feed than if it had been bought in autumn. Too often he scrimps the feed, hoping for an early spring, and so soon as he can see the grass showing a shade of green around the fence rows, or in some sheltered ravine, turns his stock out to make their own living. This brings one of the most potent causes of unprofitable cattle raising ; namely, short pastures. The farmer who is overstocked in winter, is almost sure to turn his cattle on his pastures too early in the spring, and this generally results in short pasture all summer, and consequently the stock do not thrive as they ought, and in addition, the land which should be greatly benefited and enriched, is injured, for the development of the roots in the soil must correspond to that of the tops, and if the latter are constantly cropped short, the roots must be small. The benefit of shade is lost, and the land is trampled by the cattle in their wanderings to fill themselves, so that it is in a worse condition than if a crop of grain had been grown on it. From all these causes combined, there is a large aggregate of loss, and it is the exception to find a farm on which one or more of them does not exist, and yet without exception they may be classed as "preventable," if thought and practical common sense are brought to bear in the management.

A CRADLE FOR DRAWING A BOAT.

When it is necessary to draw a boat out of the water, a cradle should be used. This is very easily made out of some short boards and a piece of plank. The boards are cut so that when three thicknesses are bolted together, the joints shall be broken and not come opposite

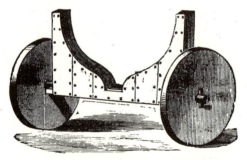

Fig. 47.—CRADLE FOR A BOAT.

each other, as shown in figure 47. The cradle should be made to fit the boat tightly, midway between stem and stern, so that when it rests upon it, the boat will be evenly balanced and firmly held. The cradle is mounted upon two wheels, which may be made of hard wood plank. A piece of two-inch plank may be sawn out for the axle, and the upper part of the cradle firmly bolted to it. Such a cradle as this may be made light or heavy, and if desired may be furnished with iron wheels, so that it will sink in the water. It can then be run down under the boat, and that be drawn upon it. By hauling upon the ring-bolt in its stern, the boat can be drawn up out of the water, and easily moved on land.

When it is desired to lift a boat out of the water, and suspend it in a boat-house, all that is necessary to be done is to fix two strong hooks, or rings, in the top of the house, and a ring-bolt at each end of the boat. A pair of double-sheaved blocks is provided for each end of the boat. The blocks are hooked to the rings in the house and to those in the boat, which is then drawn up, one end at a time, alternately, until high enough. If two persons are in the boat, both ends may be hauled up at once. The loose end of the rope is fastened to the ring of the boat, or to a ring or a cleat at the side of the boat-house. Then the boat remains suspended in the boat-house.

FEED-RACK FOR SHEEP.

The rack, figure 48, is made of poles for the bottom

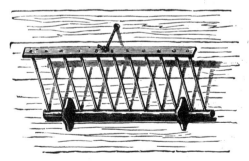

Fig. 48.—FEED-RACK FOR SHEEP.

and top, and cross-bars fitted into them. The bottom bar slides loosely in brackets, which are fixed to the wall of the shed, and the upper bar is secured by a cord, which passes over a small pulley in a hole in the wall above the rack; a weight being attached to the outside end of the rope, serves to keep the rack always against the wall. When the hay is put in the rack is drawn down, and, when filled, is pushed back against the wall, holding the hay closely, and being kept in place by the weight. This prevents the hay from being pulled out too freely by the sheep or cattle. It is recommended that the grain-trough be placed beneath a rack of this kind, so that the chaff which falls from it may be caught in the trough and saved for use, instead of being trampled under foot.

HOW TO MANAGE NIGHT-SOIL

The fertilizing properties of night-soil are well known. The principal reason why this valuable material is neglected and permitted to go to waste, is the difficulty of handling it. If improperly handled, it is disagreeable and difficult to apply to the uses to which it is best adapted. There are many cases in which it could be made use of very conveniently, if rightly managed. In country towns and villages it is difficult to dispose of it, and it becomes a serious nuisance to householders, and a detriment to the public health, when it ought to be turned to profitable uses. In some other countries this refuse matter is eagerly collected and carefully used by the farmers. The methods employed in England, Germany, and France might very well be adopted by us, and a large quantity of fertilizing material be gathered. By the methods there in use, the night-soil is easily handled and prepared for distribution upon the land, or for mixing in composts. Arrangements are made with persons in towns and villages who wish to have the soil removed, and the time being fixed (this is always in the night, from which circumstance the name given to the material is derived), wagons with tight boxes, or carts, are sent to the place. Carts are mostly used, as indeed they are in Europe for most of the farm work. The carts, or wagons, carry out a quantity of earth, chopped straw, ashes, or such other absorbent as may be conveniently procured, and some sheaves of long straw, or else the ashes or other absorbent used, which is frequently the sweepings and scrapings of streets, is prepared upon the ground or near by. This material is then disposed

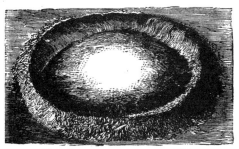

Fig. 49.—PREPARING NIGHT-SOIL.

in the form of a bank enclosing a space of sufficient size to hold the night-soil, as shown in figure 49. A reserve heap is kept to be mixed with the night-soil as it is emptied into the place prepared for it. Wheelbarrows with tight boxes are generally used to convey the soil from the cesspool. When the whole has been removed from the cesspool, the cut straw is mixed in and the banks of earth are turned over upon the pile, which can then be handled with shovels or forks, and is ready to be loaded into the wagon. Some of the long straw is laid in the bottom of the wagon-box, and the mixed mass is thrown upon it, layer after layer alternately with straw, until the top of the wagon-box is reached. It is most convenient to have a rack, or flaring side-boards, to confine the upper part of the load, but this is not necessary if the loading is properly done. The manner of loading the top is as follows: a bundle of straw is spread so that half of it projects over the side or end of the load. A quantity of the mixed stuff is forked on to the straw, the loose projecting ends of which are turned back on to the load when more is laid upon it. The doubled straw holds the loose stuff together, which might else be shaken off the load as it is carried home. In this manner the load is built up until it is completed, when it appears as

Fig. 50.—MANNER OF LOADING NIGHT-SOIL.

shown in figure 50. Loads thus made are carried many miles without losing anything on the journey, and the mass, which would seem to have no coherence, is kept solidly together. Carts are sometimes loaded to a hight of two or three feet above the side-boards, and are made to carry a load for three horses. By this management, this material is no more disagreeable than ordinary manure, and the work of moving it is rendered quite easy.

THE USE OF LIME IN BLASTING.

There are some forces, apparently insignificant, which act with irresistible power through short distances. The expansion of water in freezing is a force of this kind. The increase in bulk in changing from the liquid to the solid state of ice is only about one-tenth, yet it exercises a power sufficient to break iron vessels and rend the hardest rocks. Every one who has slaked a lump of quicklime by gradually pouring water upon it, has observed that the first effect of the contact between the water and lime is to cause a swelling of the lump. It generally expands and takes up considerable more room than before. This expansive force has recently been successfully applied to coal mining in England. Powdered quicklime is strongly compressed into cartridges about three inches in diameter, and each has running through it a perforated iron tube, through which water can be forced. These cartridges were used in a coal mine in place of the usual blasting charge, water was forced into them, and the expansion of the lime threw down a mass of coal weighing about ten tons, with little of the small coal made with the usual blast. The exemption from danger and the avoidance of smoke, have caused coal mine owners to regard this new method with favor. Some of our ingenious reapers may find a useful hint in this.

A WATER AND FEED TROUGH.

A supply of water in the cow-stable is a great convenience; a simple arrangement for furnishing it to the cows in their stalls may be made as follows: Sheets of galvanized iron are bent to form a trough, and fitted into the floor joists under the feed-box, as indicated in figure 51, making a trough three inches deep and sixteen inches wide. The flanges on each side are nailed to the joists, and the sheets of iron riveted together at the ends, and made water-tight by cement. The trough runs the entire length of the feed floor, and is supplied with water from a pipe, pump, or hose; a pipe at the other end carries away the surplus water and prevents overflow, and another pipe with a faucet is provided for emptying the trough. The feed-box is built over the

Fig. 51.—WATER AND FEED TROUGH COMBINED.

water trough, a part of its floor being a trap—indicated by dotted lines in the engraving—by which admission to the water is gained. Before opening this trap, the manger is swept clean; and if there were no other advantage than this compulsory cleansing of the mangers after each feeding, it would be sufficient to pay for the cost of constructing such a watering arrangement.

THE CONSTRUCTION OF STALLS.

It is rare, even in these days of progress, to see a well-arranged stall in a farmer's barn. No horse stall should be less than six feet in width, nor of a length less than nine feet. This affords room for the animal to lie down and rise comfortably without bruising hips and limbs, and also for the attendant to pass in and out. The partition between stalls should be of sufficient hight to prevent playing, biting, and kicking. Racks of iron are neat and serviceable. The horse eats its food from the ground, and because many first pull out a greater portion of the hay from the rack, we shall dispense with the rack as commonly used, and substitute a single manger which serves for both hay and grain.

Whatever may be the foundation of the stall, whether of brick, stone, cement, clay, or wood, it should have inclination enough to carry off all fluid. Over this place a flooring composed of strips of plank, four inches in width by two inches in thickness, with an inch intervening between each strip. This need not extend more than half the length of the stall, the upper portion being compact. The essential point is that the horse shall stand with an equal weight upon all the extremities. This custom of confining a horse to a sloping stall, in one position sometimes for days, is a cruel one, and very detrimental to the limbs and feet, as it brings about, sooner or later, serious affections in these parts. A loose box is far preferable to the stall, wherever practicable. Every stable or barn should be provided with one at least, in case of sickness or accident. By the arrangement of a floor as just described, the bedding is kept dry and the animal clean and comfortable. Litter should be always kept beneath the animal; it gives an air of comfort to the place and invites to repose of body and limbs by day and night. Stalls for both horses and cattle should be of sufficient hight, as also all door and passage ways about a barn. Formerly, it was the custom to build in such a way that no horse, and not even a man of respectable hight could enter a door-way without danger of knocking his skull, and inflicting serious injury. There are stalls in country barns so low that a horse cannot throw up his head without receiving a blow against the beams above. Animals undoubtedly acquire the trick of pulling back, or of making a sudden spring when passing a door-way, from having been obliged to run the gauntlet of some narrow, low, ill-contrived passage-way. The man who should now be guilty of building in this way would deserve to have his own brains knocked, every time he passes in and out, as a gentle reminder of his folly. All barn-doors should be high, wide, and, when practicable, always slide.

The common mode of securing cattle in the barn, especially milch cows, by placing their necks between stanchions, is not to be advocated, especially when they are confined in this way for many hours at a time without relief, as is often necessary in the winter season. A simple chain about the neck with a ring upon an upright post affords perfect security, while it gives the animal freedom of movement to head and limbs—and conduces to its comfort in various other ways. Animals should not be overcrowded, as is too often the case in large dairy establishments—a fact which will make itself evident sooner or later in the sanitary qualities of the milk, if in no other manner. We cannot deny the fact, if we would, that everything, however trifling, that contributes to the welfare of our domestic animals is a gain to the owner of them pecuniarily, and what touches a man's pocket is generally considered to be worth looking after, at all times and in all places.

HOG-KILLING IMPLEMENTS—RINGING.

The stout table on which the dead porkers are lain to be scraped and dressed after being scalded, is made with its top curving about four inches in a width of four feet, and consisting of strips of oak plank, as represented in figure 52. This curved top conforms to the form of the

Fig. 52.—A DRESSING TABLE.

carcass, and holds it in any desired position better than a flat surface. For scrapers, old-fashioned iron candlesticks are used ; the curved and sufficiently sharp edges

Fig. 53.—HANDY MEAT CLEAVER.

at either end serving as well as a scraper made for the purpose, and its small end has an advantage over the latter for working about the eyes and other sharp depressions. A cleaver for use in cutting up the pork is shown in figure 53; it has a thirteen-inch blade, three inches wide at the widest part, and one-quarter inch thick at the back. This is a convenient implement, easily and cheaply made by a good blacksmith, if it cannot be nad at the stores; any mechanic can put on the **wooden handle.** In figure 54 is represented a home-made hog-ringing apparatus. The blacksmith makes an instrument resembling a horse-shoe nail, of good iron, about three inches long, three-sixteenths of an inch wide, and one-thirty-second of an inch thick, tapering to a point; the "head" is merely the broad flat end curled up.

Fig. 54.—HOG-RINGER AND KEY.

Just before using, this needle-like instrument has its corners rubbed off on a file; it then is easily pushed through the septum of the pig's nose. A key with its tongue broken off and a slot filed in the end, is used to curl up the projecting end, and the ringing is done. The "rings" cost about seventy-five cents a hundred, and are effective and easily applied.

HOW TO MIX CEMENT.

The article to be used is the Rosendale cement. This is nearly as good as the imported Portland cement, and much cheaper. The cement is made from what is known as hydraulic lime-stone—that is a rock which contains, besides ordinary lime-stone, some clay, silica, and magnesia. Pure lime-stone contains only lime and carbonic acid, in the proportions of fifty-six parts of the former to forty-four of the latter in one hundred. When this stone is burned, the carbonic acid is driven off by the heat, and pure or quick-lime is left. When this is brought in contact with water, the two combine, forming hydrate of lime ; during the combination, heat is given out ; the operation is called slaking. When the water is just sufficient to form the combination, a fine, dry powder is produced, which we call dry slaked-lime. When the water is in excess, the surplus is mixed mechanically with the lime, and forms what is called the milk of lime, or cream of lime, according to its consistence ; it is this pasty substance which we mix with sand, to form building mortar. But when we have clay mixed in a certain proportion, either naturally or artificially, with the lime-stone, and this stone or mixture is burned in the same manner as ordinary lime-stone, we get what is known as hydraulic lime, because it combines with a much larger proportion of water than pure lime, and in combining with it, instead of falling to powder, like ordinary lime, it hardens into stone again. This hardening takes place even under water ; the hydraulic lime combines with just so much water as is required to "set" or harden, and leaves the remainder. It possesses this property, also, when mixed, with sand in proper proportions, and when so mixed, the cement will adhere very firmly to the surface of any stone to which it may be applied. This property is made available in constructing works of concrete, which consists of broken stone mixed with such a quantity of cement, that, when it is packed closely, the surfaces of all the pieces of stone are brought into contact with the cement, and the spaces between the fragments of stone are filled with it. That there may be no more cement used than is actually needed, the mixture is rammed down solidly, until the fragments of stone are brought into close contact with

Fig. 55.—BOX FOR MIXING CEMENT.

each other. The composition of the impure or hydraulic lime-stone, which behaves in this useful manner, is, in the case of some of the Kingston stone, as follows : Carbonic acid, 34.20 per cent.; lime, 25.50; magnesia, 12.35; silica, 15.37; alumina (clay), 9.13 ; and peroxide of iron (which is useless or worse), 2.25. On account of this difference in character between lime and cement, a different treatment is necessary for each, and each is put to different uses. The cement makes a much harder and more solid combination with sand, and is therefore chosen

Fig. 56.—SIDE OF CEMENT BOX.

when great strength is required. Its rapid setting, when mixed with water, also requires that it be used as soon as it is mixed, and renders a rapid mixture necessary. The cement and sand should, therefore, be mixed together dry, and very thoroughly. Four parts of sand to one part of cement are the proportions generally used. These may be mingled in a box of suitable character, and the mass is so spread as to have a hollow in the centre, into which water is poured. The sides of the heap are gradually worked into the water, with a common hoe, in such a way as to prevent the water from spreading about, and as it is absorbed more water is poured in, until the whole is brought to a thin semi-liquid condition. A box very suitable for this operation is shown in figure 55. This is made of pieces of plank, prepared as follows: The side pieces are shown at figure 56. The end pieces are made with tenons, which fit in mortises in the side pieces, and the frame thus made is held to-

Fig. 57.—MACHINE FOR MIXING CEMENT.

gether by keys driven into the holes seen in the tenons. The bottom planks are fastened together with cleats, so placed as to receive the frame and fit snugly. Iron bolts are put through holes in the cleats, and through the holes in figure 56, and by means of nuts with washers under them, the whole box is brought firmly together. Such a box, after having been used for this purpose, will be found very useful for mixing feed in the barn, or for many other purposes, and may, therefore, be well made at the first. When the mortar is mixed, the broken stone may be thrown into it, beginning at one side, and the whole is worked up thoroughly with the hoe, so that every piece of stone is coated with the cement. A machine, that is easily made, may be used for this mixing, and is also very useful for mixing ordinary mortar for building or plastering. It is shown in figure 57. It consists of a box set upon feet, with a smaller box attached at the rear end, having an opening at the bottom where the mortar is seen escaping, and a shaft, having broad, flat arms on it, placed at a somewhat acute angle with the line of the shaft, so that they will operate as a screw to force the mass along the spout and out of it at the opening. A crank handle is fitted to this shaft, and if a fly-wheel can be borrowed from a feed-cutter, or a corn-sheller, and attached to the shaft as shown, so much the better. The materials to be mixed are thrown into the box, and by turning the handle, the whole will be thoroughly incorporated with great rapidity and ease.

RINGING AND HANDLING BULLS.

Now that more attention is given to improving farm stock, a bull is kept upon nearly every large farm. The high-bred bulls are spirited animals, and are exceedingly dangerous if the utmost caution is not exercised in managing them. Experienced breeders are not unfrequently caught unawares, and unceremoniously lifted over the fence, or forced to escape ingloriously from one of their playful animals, or even seriously injured by the vicious ones. It should be made a rule, wherever a bull is kept, to have him ringed, before he is a year old, and brought under subjection and discipline at an early age, while he can be safely and easily handled. Some time ago we assisted at the ringing of a yearling bull, which severely taxed the utmost exertions of six persons with ropes and stanchions to hold him. A slip of the foot might have caused the loss of a life, or some serious injuries. To avoid such dangerous struggles, a strong frame, similar to that in figure 58, in which to confine the bull, may

Fig. 58.—STALL FOR BULL.

be used. The frame consists of four or six stout posts set deeply in the ground, with side-bars bolted to it, forming a stall in which the bull can be confined so that he cannot turn around. The frame may be placed in the barn-yard or a stable, and may be made to serve as a stall. At the front, a breast-bar should be bolted, and the upper side-bars should project beyond this for eighteen or twenty inches. The forward posts project above the side-bars some inches. The ends of these posts, and the side-bars, are bored with one-inch holes, and at the rear of the frame there should be tenons or iron straps to receive a strong cross-bar, to prevent the animal from escaping should the fastenings become broken or loosened.

Fig. 59.—STRAP.

The bull, led into the frame, is placed with his head

over the breast-bar, and the horns are tied with ropes an inch in diameter to the holes in the bars and posts. He is then secured, and his head is elevated so that the trochar and cannula can be readily used to pierce the cartilage of the nose, and the ring inserted and screwed together. Before the ring is used, it should be tested to ascertain that it is sound and safe.

When the ring is inserted, the straps shown in figure 59 should be used, for the purpose of holding it up and out of the way, so as not to interfere with the feeding of the animal until the nose has healed and become calloused. The straps may be left upon the head permanently, if desired, when the front strap will offer a convenient means of catching him by the staff, when necessary to do so in the field. The staff is a matter of the greatest importance. This should be made of the toughest ash or hickory, and not less than five feet long. With a staff of this length, the herdsman can check the wildest bull, and by resting the butt-end of it upon the ground, can throw the animal's head up, and prevent him from approaching too near. The hook of the staff is shown of two kinds in figures 60 and 61. One is furnished with a spring, by which it is closed. A metal bar attached to the spring and passing through a hole in the staff, prevents the ring from slipping along the spring. The other is provided with a screw by which it is closed.

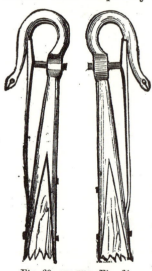

Fig. 60. STAVES. Fig. 61.

SLED FOR REMOVING CORN-SHOCKS.

A sled used for moving corn-shocks from a field which is to be sown with winter grain is shown in figure 62. It is simply a sled of the most ordinary construction, and which any farmer can build. It is made of two joists or planks of hemlock, though oak might be better; say three inches thick, a foot wide, and fourteen to sixteen feet long, rounded at one end and connected by three strong cross-pieces, being in form just

Fig. 62.—SIDE OF SLED.

such a sled as a farmer boy would make to use in the snow, with the addition of cross braces before and behind. The under edge of the runners should be rounded off to the extent of one and a half to two inches, to turn more easily. There should be also short standards before and behind. The runners may be four to five feet apart, according to the length of the corn. A side view of the runner with the standards is given in figure 62,

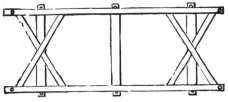

Fig. 63.—TOP OF SLED.

and a top view of the complete sled in figure 63. First, cut off the corn and put it in shocks in the usual way, making the shock smaller than usual. Let it stand thus a few days to dry, then a pair of horses are hitched to the sled, which is driven alongside the shock. The shock is pushed over on to the sled, and so one shock after another until the sled is full. The load is then driven to an adjoining field, where the shocks are set up on end again, and about four of them made into one and tied at the top, or reared against a fence.

The particular advantages of this plan are: First, that by use of the sled and method of loading and unloading the shocks, all actual lifting of the corn is avoided, and the labor and expense reduced more than one-half. Second, by permitting it to dry a few days, its weight is greatly reduced, and the handling much lighter. Third, the corn being partially dried, it can be put together in larger shocks the second time, and will keep better. By this method one man can clear two acres or more in a day, according to the weight of the crop.

A TAGGING TROUGH.

Sheep should be tagged in early spring, and a table for this purpose is shown in figure 64. The sheep is placed on this table feet upwards, in which position it is perfectly helpless, and will not struggle. Then the soiled wool about the hind parts, the belly, or the legs is clipped off with great ease, less than a minute being needed to tag a sheep. Half time will serve for some shearers to do this. In large flocks these tables will be necessary, and those who have small ones will find them very useful.

LIME AND LIME KILNS.

The periodical use of lime as a fertilizer is necessary to good culture. In the best cultivated parts of the country, lime is used once in every rotation of five crops, the usual rotation being two years, grass, corn, oats, wheat, or rye, seeded to grass or clover again. The lime is applied to the land when it is plowed for the fall grain, and is harrowed in before the seed is drilled, or it is harrowed in with the seed, sown broadcast. The quantity used is from forty to fifty bushels per acre. The effect of lime is both mechanical and chemical; it opens and

Fig. 64.—TROUGH FOR TAGGING SHEEP.

loosens heavy clays, and consolidates light, loose, sandy, or peaty vegetable soils; it has the effect of liberating potash from the soil, and of decomposing inert organic matter, and reducing it to an available condition. But while it is beneficial, it cannot be used alone without exhausting the soil of its fertile properties. This is evident from what has been said of its character; at least this is true, so far as regards its effects beyond affording directly to the crops any lime that they may appropriate from the supply thus given. All the benefits received beyond this is a direct draft on the natural stores of the soil. It is therefore necessary, to good agriculture, that either a thrifty clover sod should be plowed under, at least once in the rotation, or that a liberal dressing of manure be given, or both of these. In those localities where the benefits to be derived from the skilful use of lime are best known and appreciated, this method is practised; a heavy sod being plowed under, after having been pastured one year, for the corn, and a good coating of manure being given when the land is plowed for fall grain. Under such treatment, the soil is able to maintain itself and return profitable crops. It is not where

Fig. 65.—IMPROVED LIME KILN WITH ELEVATED TRACK.

this course is pursued that complaints are prevalent of the unprofitableness of farming. The use of lime is spreading gradually into the Western States, where the competition of the still farther and fresher western fields is being severely felt. The experience of Eastern farmers is now being repeated in what were once the Western States, and every appliance of scientific and thorough agriculture is found to be needed to maintain those Western farmers in the close contest for a living. This kiln, figure 65, is intended to stand upon level ground, and is furnished with a sloping track, upon which self-dumping cars containing fuel or lime may be drawn up by horse-power with a rope and pulleys. The body of the kiln may be twenty feet square at the bottom, and thirty feet high, with a flue above the stack of ten to twenty feet. The stack may be built of stone or brick, but should be lined with fire-brick or refractory sandstone. The arch is protected by the shed under the track. At *B, B,* are two bearing bars of cast-iron, three by two inches thick, which support the draw-bars, *C.* These are made of one and a half inch round wrought iron, having rings at the outer end, and of which there are four to the foot across the throat of the kiln, which is four or five feet in diameter. The rings serve to admit a crow-bar, by which the bars, or some of them, are drawn out to let down the charge of lime. The open space, *D,* is intended for the insertion of the bar to loosen or break the lime, should the throat become gorged. A cast-iron frame, with an aperture of three by twenty-four inches, is built into this opening. It also serves to kindle the kiln, and is closed by an iron door. The car should be made of wood, and lined with sheet-iron; it is hinged to the front axle, and hooked to the draft-rope, so that when the fore-wheels strike the block, *E,* at the mouth of the kiln, the car tips and dumps its load. The iron door, *F,* which closes the kiln, is raised or lowered by means of the rope and ring, *G,* which passes over a pulley fixed upon the side of the flue. A covered shed will be needed to protect the top of the stack, and a gallery should be made around it, for a passage-way for the workmen. This kind of kiln is suited only for the use of coal as fuel; when wood is used for burning the lime, common pits or temporary kilns are to be constructed.

FALL FALLOWING.

The old practice of summer fallowing, or working the soil for one year without a crop, for the purpose of gaining a double crop the second season, is now, very properly, obsolete. While some may question the propriety of this opinion, there can be no doubt as to the value of fall fallowing. The constant turning and working of the ground during the fall months cost nothing but time and labor, at a season when these cannot be otherwise employed, and so, in reality, cost nothing. But the benefits to the soil are very considerable. Especially is this the case with heavy clay soils, and less, in a descending ratio, through the gradations from heavy clay down to light loams—at least it is so considered by many; and it is reasonable to suppose that if the atmospheric effects upon the particles of a clay soil serve, to some extent, to dissolve the mineral particles, they may easily do the same service for a sandy soil, and help to set loose some of the potash contained in the granitic or feldspathic particles of such a soil. The mechanical effects of the fall working are certainly more useful upon clay than a light loam; but there are other purposes to serve than merely to disintegrate the soil, and mellow and loosen it. There are weeds to destroy, and the forwarding of the spring work by the preparation of the ground for early sowing. These services are as useful for a light soil as a heavy one, and as it is reasonable to look for some advantage from the working in the way of gain in fertility on light as well as heavy soils, it is advisable that owners of either kind should avail themselves of whatever benefits the practice affords. Fall fallowing consists in plowing and working the soil with the cultivator or the harrow. This may be done at such intervals as may be convenient, or which will help to start some weeds into growth, when these may be destroyed by the harrow or cultivator. Heavy soils should be left in rough ridges at the last plowing, with as deep furrows between them as possible, in order to expose the largest surface to the effects of frost and thaw. Light soils may be left in a less rough condition, but the last plowing should be so done as to throw the furrows on edge, and not flat, leaving the field somewhat ridged. A very little work in the spring will put the ground into excellent order for the early crops, and for spring wheat, especially, this better condition of the soil will be of the greatest benefit. When thus treated in the fall, the soil is remarkably mellow, and is dry enough to work much earlier than the compact stubble land which remains as it was left after the harvest. As to the time for doing this work, the sooner it is begun, and the oftener it is repeated, the better. It is not too late to finish when the ground is frozen or there is an inch of snow on the ground.

UNLOADING CORN.

Every little help that will ease the troublesome labor of transferring the corn crop from the field to the crib is

Fig. 66.—BOARD FOR UNLOADING.

gratefully accepted. We have used both of the contrivances here shown (figures 66 and 67), to help in getting the ears out of the wagon-box. At the start it is **difficult** to shovel up the corn, and until the bottom of the wagon-box is reached, the shovel or scoop cannot be made to enter the load. But if a piece of wide board is placed in a sloping position, resting upon the tail-board of the wagon (figure 66), the shovel can be used with ease

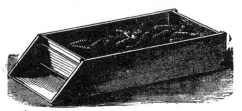

Fig. 67.—UNLOADING ARRANGEMENT.

at the commencement of the unloading. Another plan is to make the box two feet longer than usual, and place the tail-board two feet from the end, figure 67. When the tail-board is lifted, the ears slide down into this recess, from which they can be scooped with ease.

STONE BOATS.

For moving plows, harrows, etc., to and from the fields,

Fig. 68.—PLANK STONE BOAT.

and for many other purposes, a stone boat is far better than a sled or wagon, and is many times cheaper than either. Two plans of construction are illustrated. The boat shown in figure 68 is of plank, six feet in length, one foot at one end being sawed at the angle shown. Three planks, each one foot in width, will make it of about the right proportion. A railing two by three inches is pinned upon three sides, while a plank is firmly pinned at the front end, through which the drawbolt passes. That shown in figure 69 has some advan-

Fig. 69.—STONE BOAT WITH RUNNERS.

tage over the former, a cheaper quality of wood and of shorter length can be used, and when one set of runners is worn out, others can be readily attached without destroying the frame. Oak or maple plank should be used for the best boats, and when runners are used, the toughest wood at hand should be selected. Don't think because it is only a stone boat it is not worthy of being taken care of.

A DUMP-CART.

The dump-cart, figure 70, is a handy contrivance, a good deal used in some parts of this State, and is simply an ordinary ox-cart, the tongue shortened and fastened by a king bolt to the forward axle of a wagon, as shown in the engraving. It can be turned very short, as the wheels have a clear swing up to the cart-tongue, and is very convenient for hauling anything that is to be dumped: such as stones, earth, wood, manure, etc.

The seat of an old mowing machine is fastened to the

Fig. 70.—IMPROVED DUMP-CART.

cart-tongue, on which the driver sits. Horses or oxen may be used.

TO PREVENT WASHING OF HILL-SIDES.

Much damage is done by the washing of hill-sides into deep gullies by heavy rains. Where sloping ground is cultivated this is unavoidable, unless something is done to prevent it. In some cases deep plowing and loosening the subsoil will go far to prevent washing, as it enables the water to sink into the ground, and pass away without damage, by slow filtration. But where the subsoil is not very porous, and when the rain falls copiously and suddenly, the water saturates the surface soil in a few minutes, and the surplus then flows down the slope, cutting the softened earth into many channels, which by and by run together. Then the large body of water possesses a force which the soil cannot resist, and carries the earth down with it, often doing serious and irreparable damage in an hour or less. Of the many plans which have been suggested and tried to prevent this washing, the most successful is the terracing of the slope. This is done by plowing, with a swivel plow, around the hill, or back and forth on the slope, commencing at the bottom and throwing the earth downwards in such a manner that a flat terrace is formed, which has a small slope backwards from the front of the hill. When this terrace has been formed, the plowing is commenced ten or twelve feet above, and another terrace is made in the same manner. This is continued to the top of the slope. If thought desirable, the inner furrows on each terrace may be made to form a water channel, and this may be connected with the channel on the next slope lower down, in some safe manner, either by a shute of boards or of stone, to prevent washing of the soil at these points where the fall will be considerable. This, however, is a side issue, which does not necessarily belong to the main work. The arrangement of the hill-side is shown in figure 71, in which the

Fig. 71.—PROFILE OF A TERRACED HILL.

original outline of the hill, and the arrangement of the terraces, which are cut out of it, are given. When a heavy rain falls upon the terraced hill, the effect will be to throw the water backwards from the outer slope, into the channels at the rear of the terraces; and there, as well as upon the broad surface of the terraces, there is abundant means of escape by sinking into the soil. If not, and the amount of water is too great to be thus disposed of, it may be carried down the slope, by arranging the furrows as drains in the way previously indicated. Hill-sides of this character should be kept in grass, when the slope is too steep for comfortable plowing, after it has been thus arranged ; or it may be planted with fruit trees, vines, or timber, upon the slopes, leaving the terraces to be cultivated, or the slopes may be kept in grass, and the terraces cultivated. But in whatever manner the ground may be disposed of, it would be preferable to leaving it to be gullied by rains, barren, useless, and objectionable in every way.

A LOG MINK-TRAP.

A mink-trap is made by boring a two-inch or two and

Fig. 72.—MINK-TRAP.

a half inch hole in a log, four or five inches deep, and into the edges of this hole drive three sharpened nails, so that they will project half an inch or so inside, as shown in figure 72. The bait being at the bottom, the mink pushes his head in to get it, but on attempting to withdraw it is caught by the nails. Musk-rat is good bait for them, and a highly praised bait is made by cutting an eel into small bits, which are placed in a bottle and hung in the sun, and after a time become an oily and very odorous mass. A few drops of this are used. The above simple mink-trap may be made by using any block of wood, or a stump of a tree, large or small, and the same plan may be made use of to trap skunks, or, by using a small hole and some straightened fish-hooks, it will serve to catch rats or weasels, enemies of the rural poultry yard, which may be thinned off by the use of this trap.

PLOWING FROM THE INSIDE OF THE FIELD.

There is but one reason why plowing should not be done from the inside of the field, and that is, the imaginary difficulty in "coming out right." There are several points in favor of this method : When a field is plowed, beginning at the outside, there is always a dead furrow running from each corner to the centre ; besides this, the team is obliged to run out, and turn upon the plowed land at every corner, making a broad strip which is much injured by the treading, especially if the land is clayey and rather moist. By beginning at the middle, all this is avoided ; the horses turn upon unplowed land, and the soil at each plowing is thrown towards the centre of the field, as it should be. There is no difficulty in finding the centre of the field from which to begin the plowing. Suppose we have a rectangular field like the one shown in figure 73 ; any person who can measure by pacing, is able to find the middle of the ends,

A D and *B C;* the points *K* and *L.* From *K,* pace towards *L,* a distance equal to one-half *A D,* which gives the point *E.* Also the same distance from *L,* towards *K,* giving F, and the work of fixing the central point is done. Run a furrow from *A* and *D* to *E,* and from *B* and *C* to *F;* these define the corners and assist in the turning of the plow. The plowing then begins by back-

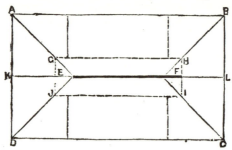

Fig. 73.—PLAN FOR RECTANGULAR FIELD.

furrowing from *E* to *F;* plowing on the ends as soon as possible. After the work has progressed for a time, as far as indicated, for example, by the dotted lines, *G, H,*

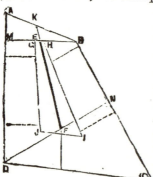

Fig. 74.—PLAN FOR IRREGULAR FIELD.

I, J, pace from the furrow to the outside (see dotted lines), at or near each end of the furrow, as a correction, and, if necessary, gauge the plow until the furrow on all sides is equally distant from the boundary. When the field is of irregular shape, it is not difficult to begin in the centre and plow outward —in fact, this system is of most importance here, because all the short turning in the middle of the field, incident to the irregularity of the field, comes on unplowed ground.

In figure 74 we have a piece of very irregular shape. From a point on *A D,* at right angles to *B,* pace the distance to *B,* and place a stake at the middle point, *E.* In the same way, determine the point *F* on the line *N D.* In a line with *E, F,* measure from *K* a distance equal to *M E* (one-half the perpendicular distance across the end of field), and also in like manner determine the point *F*—which gives the central line, *E F.* The plow should be run from the four corners, as in the first case, to make the corner lines. The plowman will use his judgment, and plow only upon the lower portion at first, until the plowed land takes the shape *G, H, I, J,* when the correction is made. From this time on the furrow runs parallel with the boundary, and the work continues smoothly to the end.

A WIRE-FENCE TIGHTENER.

Having occasion recently to tighten some wires in a trellis, we made use of the following contrivance. Into

Fig. 75.—WIRE TIGHTENER.

a small piece of wood a few inches long we put two screws about three inches apart, and near to one end one other screw, leaving the heads projecting about half an inch. By placing the wire between the two screws, and turning the piece of wood around, the wire was drawn tight; and by engaging the head of the single screw upon it, the tension was maintained. The operation of the contrivance is shown at 1, and the method of arranging the screws or pins appears as 2. By using a strong piece of wood two feet long, and strong iron bolts, fastened with nuts upon the back side, this device may be used to tighten fence wires.

PLANTING CORN—A MARKER.

What would be thought of a mechanic who should rip his boards from a log with the old-fashioned whip saw and plane them or match them by hand, or who should work out his nails on the anvil one at a time by hand labor? He would hardly earn enough to find himself in bread alone. Yet in an equally old-fashioned, costly, and unprofitable way do thousands of farmers plant and cultivate their corn crops. The ground is plowed, har-

Fig. 76.—RUNNER AND TOOTH FOR MARKER.

rowed and marked out both ways, either with the plow, or sometimes by a quicker method, with a corn marker. The seed is dropped by hand and covered by hand with a hoe; the crop is hoed by hand or plowed in the old method, leaving the ground ridged and deeply furrowed, so that in a dry season the corn suffers for want of moisture. All this costs so much that the farmer's labor brings him about fifty cents a day, upon which he lives, grumbling that "farming does not pay." This method would be ruinous in the West where corn is a staple crop, and that it is not so in the East is simply because it is not grown to a large extent. But there is no crop that may be grown so cheaply and easily in the East that produces so much feed as corn. Fifty bushels of corn and four tons of fodder per acre contain more dry nutriment than thirty tons of turnips or mangels, and may be grown with less labor and less cost, if only the best methods are employed. Now, with the excellent implements and machines that are in use for planting and cultivating corn, no farmer can afford to work this crop in the old-fashioned method. There is no longer any need to plant in squares, for the crop may be kept perfectly clean when planted in drills, if the proper implements are used. There are several corn planters by which the seed

Fig. 77.—THE MARKER AT WORK.

may be dropped and covered at the same time in single or double drills, at the rate of eight to twenty acres per day. By using the Thomas harrow a few days after planting, every young weed will be killed, and the crust, which so often gathers upon the surface, will be broken up and the surface mellowed. The harrow may be used without damage until the corn is several inches high. Then anyone of the many excellent horse hoes may be used by which the weeds may be cut out of the rows close

Old-Fashioned Labor-Saving Devices

to the corn until the crop is so high that farther working is useless. This method of cultivation may cost two dollars per acre, or less, as the ground may have been kept free from weeds in previous years, while on the old-fashioned system it may cost ten dollars per acre, or more, as the weeds may have been allowed to get further ahead.

Nevertheless, there are farmers who will still work on the hand-to-mouth plan, and will still mark out their crops by a marker and drop the seed by hand. For these it will be convenient to have at least a good marker. It will mark uneven as well as level ground; it can be set to any width between rows; any farmer or smart boy can make it, and the inventor, who is a farmer in Canada, does not propose to patent it. The marker is made of two by four scantling, one piece being eight feet long. In this five holes are bored, one for each of the runners, one and one-eighth inch in diameter. The runners are also of two by four timber, and eighteen inches long. Holes one and one-eighth inch in diameter are bored through the runners, in which are placed hard wood pins fourteen inches long. These are driven in from the bottom, the ends being left broad, so that they may not pass through the holes, and projecting an inch and a half. This is shown in figure 76. The small pin which passes through the larger one serves to connect the runner with the principal timber, and by shifting the large pin from one hole to another, the runners may be brought from four feet to one foot, or even six inches apart, and made to mark rows of widths increasing by spaces of six inches up to four feet. When one of the markers meets with an obstruction it is lifted by it, as seen in figure 77, and passes over it. A guide marker is fixed by a hinge to one of the outside runners, and carries a scraper which is held in place by a pin, by moving which the distance of the next row may be regulated. A pair of light shafts may be attached to the marker, and a pair of handles by which it may be guided.

FEED TROUGH AND HALTER.

The trough rests on the floor and is four feet long. *A, A,* are inch auger holes; a rope, four feet long, is put through them and tied. Another rope, *D,* has a ring

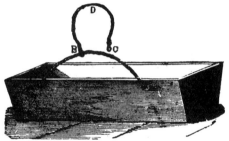

Fig. 78.—FEED TROUGH AND HALTER.

spliced on one end, and a "snap-hook" on the other. The longer rope passes through the ring, *B,* and when the rope, *D,* is put over the neck of the cow, the "snap," *C,* hooks into the ring. This allows the animal to stand or lie down with comfort.

THE HORSE-SHOE AND ITS APPLICATION.

Any excess of growth at the toe renders the pasterns more oblique, and, as a consequence, throws undue weight upon the "back sinews," whereas, too great height of heels has a similar effect upon the joints of the extremities, by rendering them too upright. Taking as our guide the foot of the animal that has never been brought to the forge, and which, in consequence, must be considered as a correct model, let the external wall of the hoof be reduced by means of the rasp to a level with the firm unpared sole. If there is no growth of the external wall beyond this level, then there is nothing to be removed.

In the selection of a shoe for the healthy foot, we must bear in mind the object in view, which is to protect the parts from excessive wear. This protection is to be found in a metallic rim of proper size and shape, securely adjusted. Almost every shoe in common use meets this end more or less satisfactorily, and we have already remarked that the proper preparation of the foot that has been previously shod is of vastly more importance than the particular kind of shoe to be adopted. At the same time, there are faults in the shoe most commonly employed, which had their origin in its particular adaptation to the foot after this had undergone more or less severe mutilation at the hands of the farrier, and which have been retained more through custom than through actual necessity, as we have reason to hope. The most prominent of these faults consists in extreme narrowness of rim with a concavity upon the upper or foot surface, in order to prevent the sole from sustaining least weight or pressure, which it is perfectly unfitted to do after being pared down to a point of sensitiveness. In a state of nature we know that every portion of the foot comes to the ground and sustains its share of weight, and in the shod state it should do the same, as far as practicable. Hence, the shoe should be constructed with its upper surface perfectly flat, and with a breadth sufficient to protect a portion of the sole, and to sustain weight. It should be bevelled upon the ground surface, in imitation of the concavity of the sole, and not upon its upper surface, where the space thus formed serves as a lodging place for small stones and other foreign bodies. In shape it should follow the exact outline of the outer wall, being narrowed at the heels, but continued of the same thickness throughout. The lateral projection at the quarters, and the posterior one at the heels are unsightly, of no benefit, and should never be allowed where speed is required

HOW TO MAKE A FISHING SCOW.

Boat-building should be done during the winter, when in-door work is more agreeable, and leisure is more ample, than in the summer. A boy who can handle tools, may make a very handsome boat or scow, such as

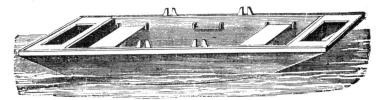

Fig. 79.—VIEW OF FISHING SCOW.

is shown at figure 79, at a cost of five dollars or less, in the following manner. Procure five three-quarter or half-inch clear pine boards, twelve feet in length and eight inches wide; four boards ten feet long, one inch thick, and one foot wide, and three strips ten feet long, one and a quarter-inch thick, and three inches wide. Plane all these smoothly on both sides, and have them all free from loose knots or shakes. Cut two of the one-inch boards sloping at each end to a straight line for two feet, and then slightly rounding the middle of the board. Cut two pieces of the one and a quarter-inch strips into lengths of two feet ten inches, and nail them to the ends of the side-boards, as shown in figure 80. If strips of soft brown paper are dipped into tar and placed between the joints, they will be made closer and more water-tight. Cut the eight-inch boards into three feet lengths, and nail them across the bottom, as shown in figure 80; where the bevel ends, the two bottom boards must be bevelled slightly upon one of their edges, so as to make a close joint. Then take two of the one and

Fig. 80.—PUTTING ON THE BOTTOM.

a quarter-inch strips, and make cuts in each on one side with the saw, one inch deep, as follows: measuring from one end, mark with a pencil across the strip three feet six inches from the end; then mark again across the strip one inch and a half from the first mark, and score between these marks with an ×. Then measure three inches and make another mark, and then an inch and a half and make still another mark, and score as before between these last two with an ×. Then do precisely the same on the same side of the strip, measuring from the other end. Then on the edges of the board score with gauge or make a line with a pencil exactly one inch from the marked side. Then make the cuts on the pencil lines down to the score on the edge, just one inch deep, but no more. Cut away the wood in the places that were marked with an ×, leaving four slots one inch and a half wide, one inch deep, and with three inches between them upon each strip. Nail these strips with the cut side inwards, to the upper edge of the side-board, on the outside of the boat, as seen in figure 81. The spaces left in the gunwales are for the rowlocks. The strips, should be well nailed near the rowlocks, and if a quarter-inch, flat-headed, counter-sunk carriage-bolt were used on each side of them, it would be very much better than so many nails. A thin washer, or burr, should be used beneath the nut of each bolt. The rowlock pins should be made of hard maple or oak, in the shape shown at *a*, figure 81. They are one inch thick, one and a half inch wide at the lower part, which fits into the slot, with a shoulder of half an inch, and the top is bevelled off neatly as shown. The seats, of which

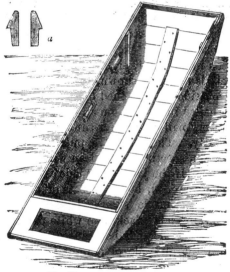

Fig. 81.—INTERIOR OF BOAT.

there are two, are made ten inches wide. The cleats for the seats, one inch thick, one and a half inch wide, and ten inches long, are nailed three inches below the upper edge of the side-board. The middle seat goes exactly in the centre of the boat, with each edge four feet seven inches from the end of the boat. The end seats are placed with the backs two feet from the ends of the boat, leaving eight inches between each seat and the edge of the rowlock nearest to it. There are cleats for three seats, but only two seats are used at once. When one seat is used, the rower sits in the centre, and he can use either of the rowlocks, the boat being double-bowed. When two seats are used, one person only rows at one time, but either can row without changing seats, and one always faces to the direction in which the boat moves. This arrangement of seats is very convenient. Eighteen inches of each end is closed in, and makes a locker for holding fish-lines, hooks, or the "painter," which is a light rope for tying up the boat when not in use. This may be fastened to a ring-bolt or a hole bored in one of the locker covers. The long bottom-board, seen in figure 81, eight inches wide and half an inch thick, is nailed as shown, by wrought nails driven from the outside and clinched on the inside. The seat cleats are nailed in the same manner, as are also the side strips. Every nail is counter-sunk and the hole filled up with putty. The seams are puttied or filled with a strip of cotton sheeting pushed in with the blade of a dinner knife. If the joints are made as well as they may be, this is not needed, but two coats of paint will make all tight. The inside should be painted lead-color, made by mixing lampblack with white paint to a proper shade. The outside may be painted white or a light-green, with the gunwale of a light-blue. A few days will be required to harden the paint before using the boat. None but seasoned boards should be used.

CROWS AND SCARECROWS.

Probably there is no point upon which a gathering of half a dozen farmers will have more positive opinions than as to the relations of the crow to agriculture. It is likely that five of these will regard the bird as totally bad, while the minority of one will claim that he is all good. As usual, the truth lies between the extremes. There is no doubt that the crow loves corn, and knows that at the base of the tender shoot there is a soft, sweet kernel. But the black-coated bird is not altogether a vegetarian. The days in which he can pull young corn are few, but the larger part of the year he is really the friend of the farmer. One of the worst insect pests with which the farmer, fruit-grower, or other cultivator has to contend is, the "White Grub," the larva of the "May Beetle," "June Bug," or "Dor-Bug." It is as well established as any fact can be, that the crow is able to detect this grub while it is at work upon the roots of grass in meadows and lawns, and will find and grub it out. For this service alone the crow should be everywhere not only spared, but encouraged. We are too apt to judge by appearances; when a crow is seen busy in a field, it is assumed that it is doing mischief, and by a constant warfare against, not only crows, but skunks, owls, and others that are hastily assumed to be wholly bad, the injurious insects, mice, etc., that do the farmer real harm have greatly increased. Shortly after corn is planted, the crows appear, and are destructive to young corn. Some assert that the crow pulls up the corn plant merely to get at the grub which would destroy it if the bird did not. How true this may be we do not know, but as the corn is destroyed in either case, it may be as well to let it go without help from the crow. The first impulse of the farmer, when he finds his corn pulled up, is to shoot the crow. This we protest against. Even admitting that the crow does mischief for a short time, it is too useful for the rest of the year to be thus cut down in active life. Let him live for the good he has done and may do. It is vastly better to keep the crows from pulling the young corn, for two or three weeks, and allow them all the rest of the year to destroy bugs and beetles in astonishing numbers. The corn may be protected by means of "scarecrows," of which there are several very effective kinds. Crows are very keen, and are not easily fooled; they quickly understand the ordinary "dummy," or straw man, which soon fails to be of service in the corn-field. It has no life, no motion, and makes no noise, and the crow soon learns this and comes and sits upon its outstretched arm, or pulls the corn vigorously at its feet. A dead crow, hung by a swinging cord to a long slender pole, is recommended as far better than a straw man—as it, in its apparent struggles to get away, appeals impressively to the living crow's sense of caution. But the crow may not be at hand to be thus employed, and if it were, the farmer cannot afford to kill it. Better than a dead crow is a glass bottle with the bottom knocked out, which may be done with an iron rod. The bottle is suspended to an elastic pole by a cord tied around its neck; the end of the cord should extend downward into the bottle, and have a nail fastened to it and within the bottle, to serve as a clapper. If a piece of bright tin be attached to the cord extending below the bottomless end of the bottle, all the better. A slight breeze will cause the tin to whirl, and, in the motion, cast bright reflections rapidly in all directions, while the nail keeps up a rattling against the inside of the bottle. An artificial "bird," to be hung in the same manner, may be made from a piece of cork—one used in a pickle-jar—into which a number of large goose or chicken feathers are fastened so as to roughly imitate a dilapidated bird. A rough head may be carved and put on, to make the deception more complete. As this "bird" catches the wind, it will "fly" here and there in a peculiar manner not at all enticing to the corn-loving crows.

FLOOD FENCE.

The weak point of a fence is where it crosses a stream; a sudden freshet washes away loose rails, and a gap is

Fig. 82.—A FLOOD GATE.

left through which trespassing cattle soon find a passage. Many devices have been used. The one shown in figure 82 is self-acting: when water rises high enough, it opens, and when the flood falls it closes again. It may be made of rails, bars, or fence strips.

CLEARING SLOUGH LAND.

In clearing up land that is covered with tussocks of coarse grass and a tough sod, and digging out ditches to drain such land, much useless labor may be given that could be spared by skilful work. The spade is commonly used for this purpose, but, as in digging dry ground, this slow tool may be replaced to very great advantage by the plow and the horse-shovel. In working in swamps these more effective tools may be made available in many cases. To cut off the tussocks with grub-hoes, while they are tough in the summer time, is very hard and slow work; but if a common horse-scraper is used they can be torn up, or cut off, with the greatest ease. The scraper should be furnished with a sharp steel-cutting blade in the front, which may be riveted on, or fastened with bolts, so that it may be taken off and ground sharp. If there are wet and soft places the scraper may be drawn by a chain of sufficient length to

Fig. 83.—THE HORSE-SHOVEL AT WORK.

keep the horse upon dry ground, as shown in figure 83. This plan has been tried by the writer with success, and with a great saving of time and expense; the digging of a pond twenty feet wide along the edge of a swamp, was performed with one man, a boy, a team, and a horse-shovel, as quickly as ten men could have done it with spades. In cutting tough swamp, the plow may be used to break up the surface when the horse-shovel will remove the snuck very fast. If the swamp is wet, and water flows in the excavation, the digging may still be done with the horse-scraper by adding to the length of the handles and using planks upon each side for the man to stand upon, and planks upon the inner side of the excavation for the scraper to slide upon with its load of muck. The muck may be thrown in heaps on the side of the pond or ditches, and it will be found convenient to leave it upon one side instead of in a continuous heap, as this will greatly facilitate its final disposal in whatever way that may be.

HOW TO DRESS A BEEF.

There is a way of slaughtering that is not butchering, and it may be done painlessly by taking the right course. The barn floor or a clean grass-plot in a convenient spot

Fig. 84.—THE PROPER PLACE TO STRIKE.

will be a suitable place for the work. To fasten the animal, put a strong rope around the horns, and secure the head in such a way that it cannot be moved to any great distance, and in a position to allow a direct blow to be easily given. The eyes may be blinded by tying a cloth around the head so that there will be no dodging to avoid the stroke. The place for the stunning blow is the centre of the forehead, between the eyes and a little above them. The right place is shown at *a,* figure 84. The best method is to fire a ball from a rifle in the exact spot, and this may be done safely when the animal is blinded, by holding the weapon near to the head, so that a miss cannot be made; otherwise a blow with the back of an axe made when the striker is on the right side of the animal, and the head is fastened down near the ground, will be equally effective. So soon as the animal falls, the throat is divided with a cut from a long, sharp knife; no jack-knife should be used, but a long, deep, sweeping stroke

Fig. 85.—RACK FOR A CARCASS OF BEEF.

which reaches to the vertebræ as the head is held back. This divides all the blood-vessels, and death is almost instantaneous, but at any rate painless. When the carcass has been freed from blood, it should be turned on its back, and the skin divided from the throat up the brisket, along the belly to the legs, and up the legs to the knees, where the joints should be severed, taking care, however, to cut off the hind feet below the hock joints about two or three inches. The skin is then stripped from the legs and belly, and as near to the back as may be by turning the carcass. The belly is then opened, and the intestines taken out; the brisket is cut through, and the lungs and gullet removed. It is now necessary to raise the carcass. This is done on the rack, the forward legs of which are placed on each side of the carcass, and the gambrels are placed upon the hooks shown in figure 85. The legs of the rack are then raised as far as possible, and as the carcass is lifted, the hinder leg is brought up to hold what is gained until the carcass is clear of the ground; the hide is then wholly removed, the carcass washed and scraped from anything adhering, and then divided down through the backbone, leaving the sides hanging. As a matter of safety from dogs or other dishonest animals, it is well to have the work done in the barn, laying down a quantity of straw to protect the floor, if thought necessary, as the beef should remain at least twelve hours to cool and set.

A FARM CART.

While there are different kinds of farm carts, we have not yet hit upon *the* cart—*i. e.*, one that meets with general approbation. The writer, having much work for a cart, has designed one which is intended to do all the work of the farm more easily than a wagon or any other cart. For the carriage of manure, of fodder-corn, green clover, or other soiling fodder, for hauling roots and such work, a cart is needed with a low body, that can be turned around in its own length to back, or even turn in a manure cellar or on a barn floor. All this can be done with this cart, and when hay, straw, or green fodder is to be loaded, the fore and hind racks may be put on, and greatly increase its capacity. With four-inch wheels, this cart can be drawn, when loaded, over plowed ground or muddy roads, and scarcely sink below the surface. The cart body consists of a frame eight feet long, three and a half feet wide, and fourteen inches deep, thus holding, when heaped, about a cubic yard and a half of manure, or as near as possible one ton. The frame is made of three by four timber for the top, and two by three for the bottom, sides, and cross-bars, and is covered with bass-wood or willow boards on the bottom, the front, and the sides near the wheels. The rear end is closed when desired by a sliding tail-board. The axles are fixed to the frame, as shown in figure 86, and pass through the middle side posts under the upper slide bar and a wide iron strap, which embraces the top of the frame, and passes under the bottom, as shown in the engraving, being screwed by bolts to the timbers. The wheel is the same size as an ordinary wagon wheel, viz., four feet; this brings the bottom of the cart body to within one foot of the ground, and in loading, the lift is only a little more than two feet from the ground. The saving of labor and the effect of work are thus greatly increased, a man being able to load twice as much with the same force, into a cart of this kind, as into a wagon-box four feet high. The rear end of the cart may be provided with a roller, fitted into the rear posts, which serves to ease the unloading of the cart when it is tipped, the rear end then easily moving over the ground as the cart is drawn over the field when unloading manure. But as the cart body is so low there will rarely be any need for tipping the cart. To enlarge its capacity, there

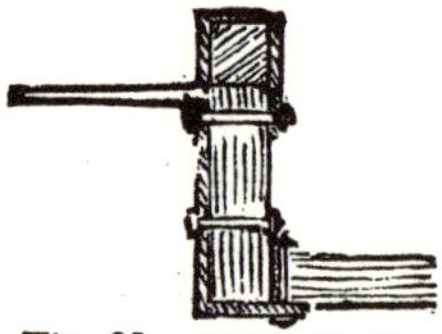

Fig. 86.—AXLE FASTENING.

are movable racks fitted before and behind, as shown in figure 87. The cost of two of these carts is not more than that of a wagon, and may be less, if economy

Fig. 87.—THE CART WITH MOVABLE RACKS.

is exercised in making them. The shafts may be bolted to the sides and so arranged that the cart can be tipped over when the load requires it.

BRACES FOR A GATE POST.

On the side of the post, and near the surface of the ground, spike an inverted bracket, made of a two-inch plank of white oak, or other hard wood. The bracket

Fig. 88.—BRACING A GATE POST.

should be not less than six inches wide, and a foot long. There should be two of these braces, one on the gate

Old-Fashioned Labor-Saving Devices

side of the post when the gate is shut, and one on the gate side when open. Under the bracket place a flat stone firmly settled in the ground, on which the bottom of the bracket is to rest; a piece of plank, as long as it lasts, will do instead of the stone.

The hang of the gate can then be exactly adjusted by putting a thin stone or piece of wood between the bottom of the bracket and the flat stone or plank. This is a simple and effective method of supporting a post, where there is no other convenient way of bracing, and even in almost all cases, it gives additional firmness. If the lower end of the post is of good size, and is well put in, this method of bracing will hold a very heavy gate.

WHIPPLE-TREES FOR PLOWING CORN SAFELY.

We have found it beneficial to cultivate our corn crop until the rows become impassable for a horse, or until it was four feet or more high. But to do this with the wide whipple-tree, the ends of which project beyond the traces, and break down the stalks, is impossible. It may, however, be done by using a whipple-tree specially provided for it. This is made as follows: a piece of oak timber, two inches thick, three wide, and twenty inches long, is rounded at the corners, and deeply grooved at the ends, so that the trace-chains may be entirely imbedded in the grooves. A small hole is bored through each end, into which a small carriage bolt is inserted, being made to pass through a link of the trace-chain, and it is then fastened beneath with a nut.

Fig. 89.—WHIPPLE-TREE.

The trace-chains should be covered with leather where they will rub against the corn, and a flap of leather should be left to cover the front corners of the whippletree, as shown in figure 89. A ring or an open link is fastened at the part of the chain which is attached to the clevis, and one at each end by which it is hooked to the traces. With this arrangement one may cultivate his corn without injury, and the same method may be applied to the whipple-trees, for plowing or cultivating amongst trees in the orchard or garden.

WHAT TREES TO PLANT FOR FUEL AND TIMBER.

The attention of our people in the older States is being very properly turned to planting rocky ridges and worn-out pastures with forest trees. This work is done by those who have no expectation of cutting the timber themselves, but with a view to improve their property for future sale, or for their heirs. These old pastures now are worth $10, or less, per acre. Forty or fifty years hence, covered with heavy timber, they would be worth three hundred dollars, or more, per acre. Two elements may safely enter into this calculation of the profit of tree planting: the steady growth of the trees, and the constant increase in the price of fuel and timber. There is great difference in the price of the varieties of wood, but still more in the rapidity of their growth. Hickory grows more rapidly than white oak, and in most markets is worth a quarter more for fuel. Chestnut grows about three times as fast as the white oak, and for many purposes makes quite as good timber. It is in great demand by ship-builders, and cabinetmakers. The chestnut, the tulip tree, and the hickory attain a good size for timber in twenty to twenty-five years, and the spruce and pine need about fifty years. The maples grow quite rapidly, and are highly prized, both for fuel and for cabinet purposes. On light sandy land, the white pine will grow rapidly, and cannot fail to be a good investment for the next generation. As a rule, the more rapid growing trees, if the wood is valuable, will pay better than the oaks.

TO STEADY PORTABLE MILLS.

Figure 90 shows a contrivance for steadying portable mills, which has been used for several years. It is an

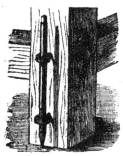

Fig. 90 —LEG OF MILL.

iron rod of suitable size, about a foot long, fastened by iron brackets to the leg, or post of the mill. Three or four inches of the rod is a screw, and fits one of the brackets through which it runs, and can be turned up or down. The lower end of the rod is pointed, and the upper end squared, that it may be turned with a wrench. The rod is fastened firmly to the side of the post (one on each of the forward posts), and turned down so that the point shall enter the floor sufficiently to hold it firmly.

SPLITTING RAILS AND POSTS.

Autumn is the best season for cutting timber, as many farmers have learned by experience. The seasoning process is much more perfect, because there is no layer of growing sap wood. Insects do not work in autumn cut timber, as in that cut in the spring or summer, and the wood does not "**powder** post." It is best to split the logs into rails or posts at once, and not wait until the timber has become seasoned in the log. The logs will split easier, the rails will season quicker, and be more durable. The splitting of rails is a work that requires good judgment, otherwise much timber will be wasted. Some persons will make rails that are large at one end, and gradually tapering to a sliver at the other, and are worthless for fencing purposes. Set the wedge at the top end of the log, after first "checking" with the axe, by driving with the beetle, so as to divide the log into two equal parts. Now drive in two wedges, as shown in figure 91, both at the same time. Next use a wooden wedge or "glut," either in the end of the log, or on the top a little back from the end. After halving the log, quarter it, and then proceed on the principle that a rail should be about three by three inches. The size of the log will determine the number of rails to be made. For example, in figure 92, six rails are made by first halving the quarter, then splitting off the inner part half-way from the centre, and afterwards halving the outer part. Should the logs be larger, twelve rails are made from each quarter, as shown in figure 93,—or forty-eight rails from the log. In splitting logs into posts, a broad and smooth side is to be sought. Suppose we have the same sized log as the one split into forty-eight rails, or twelve rails per quarter, figure 93—the splitting would be, in each case, from the centre to outside with cross splitting midway. The number of posts would be determined by the size of the posts desired. If the logs are of the size of the quarter, shown in figure 92, there is no cross splitting, unless a small piece for a

Fig. 91.—POSITION OF WEDGE.

stake is taken from the centre. When the logs are only large enough for four posts, and a broad surface is desired, as in bar posts, they may be split by first "slabbing," and afterwards splitting through the centre; all the split surfaces to be parallel. If still smaller, three

Fig. 92.

Fig. 93.

posts can be made, by splitting off two slabs on opposite sides, as in the case above, and not divide the heart, and finally when the log will make only two, it can be halved.

A MIXTURE OF GRASSES.

It is a well-known fact that mixed crops are more productive than those sown singly. Thus one acre sown to oats and barley, or oats and peas, will yield as much, or nearly as much, as two acres sown singly to either crop. So in grass lands, Clover and Timothy, mixed, will produce nearly twice as much as if the ground were seeded to one of these alone. It is also a well-known fact that our grass lands are not so productive as we could wish, and the reason of this may be, and probably is, that we have but one or two kinds of herbage in them. If we examine an old, thick, luxuriant sod, in a pasture or a meadow, it will be found to consist of a variety of grasses and other plants, each of which seems to vie with the other in occupying the soil for itself. This is the result of natural seeding, and gives us a lesson which we may well profit by. There is another reason why grasses should be mixed, this is that the periods of greatest vigor of different varieties occur at different times. We can therefore secure a succession of herbage for a long season by sowing a variety of grass seeds.

To give examples, we might mention that a mixture of Orchard Grass, Red Clover, Timothy, and Kentucky Blue-Grass will produce a pasture which will be in good condition for grazing from April, when the first mentioned grass is in fine condition, up to October, when the last is in its most vigorous state; the Clover and Timothy serving to fill up the interval. With one of these alone there would be but one month of good herbage, and that coarse, if given the whole field to itself. In like manner, a quantity of Rye Grass added to a meadow would help to furnish a quick growing herbage which rapidly and constantly recuperates after cutting or eating down.

The fact is, that we make much less of our advantages in regard to our meadows and pastures than we might. On the average, seven acres of pasture are required to keep one cow through the pasturing season, when by the best management one acre, or at the most two, ought to be sufficient. This is due in great measure to the prevalent fashion of seeding down with but one variety of grass, with clover added sometimes, a fashion which, hereafter, experience teaches us should be more honored in the breach than in the observance.

HITCHING A CRIB-BITER

Those persons who have a horse that is a crib-biter and windsucker, and which practices his vice when hitched to a post in the street, is recommended to try a hitching-rod, such as shown in figure 94 It consists of a piece of hickory, white oak, or tough ash, about twenty-four or thirty inches long, thickest in the middle, where it may be an inch in diameter. A ferule with a ring is fastened to each end; in one ring a common snap-hook is fixed, and a short leather strap is passed through the other, by which the stick is fastened to the post. The horse thus hitched cannot possibly reach the top of the post, to seize it with its teeth. In the stall such a horse should be hitched with two straps, one at each side of the stall, and of such a length that he cannot reach either side to take hold of the rail or partition of the stall. If a swinging feed-box is used, the crib-biter will be forced to suspend operations, as he cannot draw in the air or "suck wind," unless he has some projecting object that he can lay hold of with the teeth.

Fig. 94.

HOW TO INCREASE VEGETABLE MATTER IN THE SOIL.

The amount of vegetable matter in the soil may be increased by various methods; one is by large applications of barn-yard manure, say fifty cords to the acre. But this would be very expensive, and is out of the question in common farming. It may be done by putting on peat or muck, when these are near to the fields. But this involves a considerable outlay for labor in digging the peat, and a still larger expense in carting it, whether it first pass through the yards and stables, or be carted to the fields for composting or spreading upon the surface to be plowed in. On some farms this may be the cheaper method of supplying vegetable matter to the soil. But on others the most economical method is the raising of clover, to be fed off upon the land, or to be turned in. If a ton of clover may be worth nine dollars, as a fertilizer, the growing of the plant is a cheap method of improving the land. Two tons for the first crop and a ton for the second is not an uncommon yield for land in good heart. The roots of clover also add largely to the vegetable matter in the soil. The first crop may be pastured, waiting until the crop is in blossom, and then turning in cattle enough to feed it off in three or four weeks. They should be kept constantly upon the field, that the whole crop may be returned to the soil. This will, of course, help the second crop, which may be turned in with the plow soon after it is in blossom. If the equivalent of three tons of dried clover hay, and one ton of roots have been grown to the acre, about thirty-six dollars' worth of manure have been added to the soil, and it has been distributed more evenly than would have been possible by any mechanical process. There has been no expense for carting and spreading peat, or for composting. On the contrary, there has been the equivalent of two tons of clover-hay consumed upon the field, worth, as fodder, twenty-four dollars. This will more than pay the cost of seed, of plowing twice and other labor. This is generally admitted to be the cheapest method of increasing the vegetable matter and the fertility of soils in common farming. And this, it will be seen, requires some little capital.

OPEN LINKS.

An open link, shown in figure 95, is made of three-eighth inch iron rod, and when used to connect a broken chain, is simply closed by a blow from a hammer or a stone. There being no rivet, the link is not weakened in any way. Figure 96 shows another link, made of malleable cast-iron, in two parts, which are fastened together by a rivet in the centre. A few of these links may be carried in the pocket, and are ready for instant use in case of an emergency. The last-mentioned links are

Fig. 95.—COMMON LINK.   Fig. 96.

kept for sale at the hardware stores; the first named may be made in a short time by a blacksmith, or any farmer who has a workshop and a portable forge.

CARE OF THE ROOT CROPS.

Sugar beets and mangels, if early sowed, will need little care. They ought not to stand too thick, however, and it would certainly pay to go through the rows, thinning out all superfluous plants, whether beets or weeds, leaving the plants six to eight inches apart. If the leaves are not so large as to forbid horse-hoeing, this should be done and the crop "laid-by." No root crop should ever be left after horse-hoeing, without a man going through it immediately after, to lift and straighten up any plants which may have been trodden upon, covered with earth, or injured in any way. Rutabagas, and any turnips in drills, need the same general culture. One of the great advantages of the introduction of roots into the rotation is that, when properly treated, no weeds ripen seeds. Even red sorrel and snapdragon succumb to two or three years' cropping with mangels or Swedes. This advantage is often lost by careless cultivators, and nothing offers surer evidence of heedless farming. The crop itself may be very fine, but if kept clear of weeds it would be enough better to pay for the trouble, and the weeds would then be where they will make no more trouble forever.

Turnips may be sown as late as the middle of August, but the land should be in good heart, and good tilth. Swedish turnips (rutabagas) sowed as late as the first of August, will usually make a crop delicious for the table, and, though small, bring a good price. Thus they are often used to follow early potatoes by market gardeners, though by them usually regarded as a farm crop.

TRAP FOR SHEEP-KILLING DOGS.

In many places the losses by dogs are so great as to prevent the keeping of sheep altogether; thus this profitable and agreeable industry is made impracticable over the greater portion of the country; unless such precautions are taken as will add greatly to its trouble and cost. With small flocks only, this extra cost and trouble are too onerous, and it is only where sheep are kept in large flocks that it will pay to employ shepherds to constantly watch them, or take other necessary precautions. In several of the States—West Virginia and Tennessee more particularly—very stringent laws have recently been enacted for the protection of sheep against dogs, which will go far to encourage the raising of flocks. In other States, where the influence of the owners of dogs is of more weight than that of sheep-owners, these latter are obliged to look out for themselves, and protect their sheep as they may be able. For such the contrivance here described and illustrated, may be useful. It is made as follows: In the meadow or field, where sheep are pastured during the day, a small pen, eight feet square, is made, and fenced strongly with pickets or boards. This pen is divided into two parts (*A*, *B*, figure 97) by a cross-fence. The pen is wholly covered over

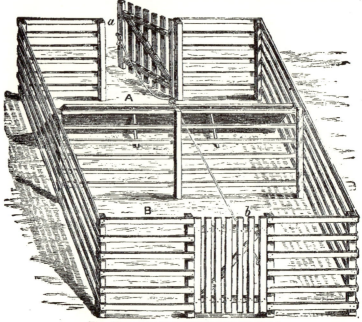

Fig. 97.—TRAP FOR SHEEP-KILLING DOGS.

on the top with strong lath. Two gates (*a*, *b*,) are made so that they will swing open of their own accord, and remain so, unless held closed or fastened. The gate, *a*, is furnished with a latch, by which it is fastened when closed. This gate is intended to admit the dog into the part of the pen, *A*, when he is attracted to it by a sheep confined for the purpose in the other part of the pen (*B*). In the part of the pen, *A*, is a heavy board, reaching across it. One edge of this board rests upon the ground against two pegs, which keep it from slipping backwards. The other edge is kept up by means of two shaky slender supports. A rope is fastened to the upper edge of this board, and to the gates, so that one half of it, when the board is propped up, allows the gate, *a*, to swing open, and the other half holds the gate, *b*, shut, and thus keeps the sheep confined. The trap is now set. A dog, prowling in search of mutton, finds the sheep, and seeks an entry into the pen. He finds the open gate, and rushes in, over the board set upon its edge, and knocks this down. This closes the gate, *a*, which is at once latched and fastened. The gate, *b*, is allowed to swing open, and the sheep is liberated, and, of course, proceeds homeward without delay, while the dog is imprisoned. We need not suggest any method of dealing with the prisoner, as there are many, more or less effective, which will suggest themselves. We think it would be an improvement upon this plan, if the sheep be confined in the pen, where it can be seen by the dogs, and an additional apartment, if not more than one, made, in which other dogs could be trapped. Sheep-hunting dogs usually go in couples, and if only one dog were trapped, the sheep escaping from the pen would be caught by the other before it could reach home. With two or three traps all the dogs could be caught, and in a short time the locality would be rid of them, or, being identified, their owners could be made responsible for their trespasses. It would be necessary to have the pen made very strong, so that the dogs should not tear their way out of the trap, or into the pen in which the sheep is confined. Stout wire-netting would make a safe fence.

So far as regards what are called dog-laws, it would be well if these should provide, amongst other things, that every dog must wear a collar, bearing its owner's name; that the owner of any dog which is caught in pursuit of sheep upon the property of any person other than the owner of the dog, should be held liable for damages for the trespass, and that any dog caught trespassing, and being without a collar bearing its owner's name, should be destroyed by the person capturing it. As any citizen has as much right to keep a dog as another has to keep a sheep, without being taxed for it, and can only be held liable for what damage his dog may do, it does not seem just that any tax should be levied upon dogs. The only just claim that can be made by a sheep-owner is that he shall be protected in the enjoyment of his property, and that the person by or through whom he is injured should recompense him. In the case of irresponsible owners of dogs, from whom no recovery can be made, the dogs should be destroyed by a proper officer. If the right of persons to keep dogs, when they wish to do so, without being taxed, is recognized in this manner, much of the opposition to the enactment of what are called "dog-laws," would be removed, and the protection of sheep made much less difficult, and productive of much greater profit.

HOW TO USE A FILE PROPERLY.

The file is very frequently used in such an imperfect manner as to greatly reduce its value as a mechanical tool. The chief difficulty in using a file is in keeping it in a perfectly horizontal position as it is moved over the work, and in maintaining an equable pressure upon the work meanwhile. Perhaps the most difficult work in filing, and that which is most frequently ill-done, is in sharpening saws. The bearing of the file upon the work is very narrow, and unable to guide its direction, and unless the file is held very carefully the direction varies continually, so that the saw tooth is filed round-

Fig. 98.—IMPROPER USE OF THE FILE.

ing instead of flat, or sloping instead of horizontal, or at exact right angles with the line of the saw, as it should be in a mill-saw or a rip-saw. When the file is held as shown in figure 98 (a very common manner of holding it), it is almost impossible to do good work upon a saw. When the file is pushed on to the tooth, the weight or pressure of the right hand is exerted upon the longer

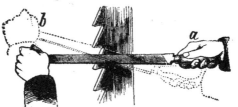

Fig. 99.—ANOTHER WRONG WAY OF FILING.

portion of the tool, making it act as if it were the longer arm of a lever, and thus depresses that portion below the horizontal, as at *a*. When pushed forward, the pressure is then exerted upon the longer portion of the file, which is carried from the horizontal in the contrary direction. The work is thus made round. Or if the pressure of the left hand is guarded against, that of the right hand is seldom altogether controlled, and the work is left sloping, as in figure 99; the position at the commencement being shown at *a*, and that at the finish of the stroke at *b*. This is a very common error with sawyers in mills, as well as with many good carpenters in filing their rip-saws.

To avoid either form of this error, the file should not

Fig. 100.—PROPER METHOD OF FILING.

be held with the ball of the thumb pressing upon the handle of the file, as in figures 98 and 99; but the end of the file should be taken lightly between the thumb and fore-finger, as in figure 100. There is no uneven pressure in this case, and the direction of the file may easily be kept perfectly level. In filing the base of the

Fig. 101.—FILING UNDERNEATH.

tooth, or the under portion of any work which cannot be turned over, the end of the file should be supported upon the ends of the fingers, as in figure 101, or be held by the end of the thumb, in an easy gentle manner. If held lightly, and not grasped too firmly, the arm or wrist will not be tired so soon as when it is held rigidly; and the motion of the file will be more even and regular.

When the arm is wearied by working in one direction, it may be rested by reversing the position of the file, taking the handle in the left hand, grasping the end be-

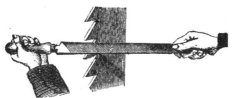

Fig. 102.—TO REST THE HAND IN FILING.

tween the fingers and thumb of the right hand, and drawing the file towards the body, instead of thrusting it away from it. The file is then held as in figure 102. This is an excellent position in which to hold the file when finishing off a saw tooth, or when touching it up at noon.

A MITRE-BOX.

A mitre-box of an improved form is shown in figure

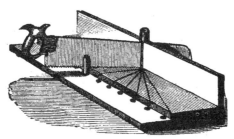

Fig. 103.—MITRE-BOX.

103. The greatly increased use of moulding in house

building renders a mitre-box very necessary in the workshop. In the one here described, a bevel of any angle may be cut. At the rear of the box is a slotted post, which works in a socket, so that it will turn readily in any direction. From the post, lines are laid out upon the bottom at various angles. At the termination of each line is a round hole, into which a pin may be fitted. The pin is used as a guide for the saw in cutting a mitre-joint, as shown in the illustration.

THE MANURE HARVEST.

In the midst of the harvest of grain, and grass, and tubers, we must not forget the compost heap, in which we garner and store the unsowed crops of a future season. The saying that "anything that grows in one summer will rot before the next," is a safe guide in collecting vegetable matter for the compost heap. When sods, muck, and weeds form a part of the heap, it is not alone the material which we are assiduous in collecting, and put into the heap, that constitutes its whole value. The fermentation induced by the dung and liquid manure, and the action of the lime or ashes added, work upon the earth, adhering to the roots of the weeds, and forming a considerable part of both sods and muck, and develop an admirable quality of plant food. Hence this element of the compost heap, which is generally overlooked as possessing any special value, should never be wanting. It has, moreover, its own offices to perform, in promoting decay, in the formation of humus, and in preserving, locking up, and holding on to valuable ingredients of plant food.

The compost heap should always be laid in even layers, and each layer should go over the entire heap, for thus only can final uniformity be had. We do not mean special-purpose composts, but those made for general farm crops. It would be well if every particle of dung, liquid manure, straw, litter, leaves, weeds, etc., could be worked together into uniform fine compost, and there is really no substantial reason why this should not be done. The gardener would plead for certain special composts. It might, perhaps, be well to make a special hen-manure compost for corn in the hill, and taking the general compost as a basis, to make one for turnips, by the addition of a large percentage of bone-dust. All this may be done—establish once the rule to compost everything of manurial value, and we have in prospect an abundance of farm-made fertilizers at all times and for all crops—victory over weeds, a good place for decomposable trash of all kinds, a sacred burial ground for all minor animals and poultry, whose precincts need never be invaded. There will besides be no stagnating pool in the barn-yard, for all liquids will go to the tank, to be pumped over the compost heaps—no nasty, slumpy barn-yard, for everything will be daily gathered for the growing compost heap, and the harvesting of the manure crop, and its increase day by day, all the year round, will be a source of constant pleasure to master and men.

FASTENING CATTLE WITH BOWS.

Everything connected with this method of fastening cattle in the stable, by means of bows, is so simple in construction, that it is within the reach of every farmer. It requires no outlay, as each one can make all the parts for himself. The bow, figure 104, passes around the animal's neck in the same manner as an ox-bow, and is made of a good piece of hickory, by bending a strip, of the right length, and three-quarter inch in diameter, into the bow form. After the bow-piece, *A*, is made of the right size and shape, with one end left with a knob, to prevent the clasp from slipping off, and the other cut

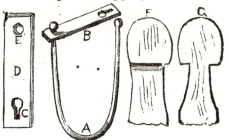

Fig. 104.—BOW AND CLASP.

as shown in front view in figure 104, *G*, and side view at *F*, to fit into the slot, in the clasp, it is carefully bent until its ends are brought together, fastened, and left so for a considerable time, when it will take its form and

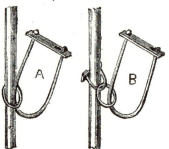

Fig. 105.—BOW AND ATTACHMENT.

be ready for use. The clasp is shown at *B*, *D*, and consists of a piece of hard-wood—hickory is best—three-quarters of an inch in thickness, and long enough to hold the top of the bow well together. A round hole is bored in one end, *E*, through which the bow passes as far as the knob, the other end is cut with a hole for the passage of the other end of the bow, and a slot, *C*, into which its narrow neck springs when the bow is secured about the creature's neck. A smooth, stout hickory pole, two and a half inches in diameter, reaching from the floor to the beam overhead, serves as a stanchion to which to attach the animal, by means of a small bow, and stationary clasp, figure 105, or an iron ring, *A*. If a little more room is desired for young stock, a link or two of chain, *B*, can be inserted between the bow and

Fig. 106.—STABLE SHOWING BOW AND STANCHIONS.

stanchion ring. In fastening the cattle, the bow is raised when it passes around the neck, and the clasp is brought on, and the end of the bow is sprung in place. When the animal is to be let loose, the end of the bow is pressed in, the clasp slips off, the bow falls, and the work is done in less time than it takes to describe it, and everything is out of the way. Figure 106 shows a stable arranged for this method of fastening; aside from the manger, there is but the stanchion poles, one for each animal. There is sufficient freedom of movement of the head, but not an excess; the animal can stand or lie down with perfect comfort, as the bow moves with ease the whole length of the stanchion. After a week's practice, the animals will take their place with their heads by the side of the stanchion, with a precision that is remarkable. Having used the method, here illustrated, for several years, the writer has found it inexpensive, easy in application, and safe.

THE PRESERVATION OF WOOD.

It is known that the decay of timber first begins through the fermentation of sap within the pores, and that it is continued after this by the absorption of water. The neutralization of the acids in the timber by the use of lime, has been made use of to preserve it from decay with success; but the most effective methods have been to saturate the pores with oils or mineral salts. Creosote and petroleum have been used successfully, but few persons are aware of the enormous absorptive capacity of timber for these liquids. Cypress wood, when dry, will absorb thirty-nine pounds, or five gallons of oil per cubic foot, and California redwood and pine absorb twice their weight when perfectly dry. But it is not necessary for perfect preservation that timber should be fully saturated. One gallon per cubic foot, for the most porous woods, will be fully effective, and a coating of one and three-quarters of a pint per square foot for weather boards, or half as much for shingles, will render them perfectly water-proof. In some careful experiments recently made, dry spruce absorbed, during two days' soaking, nearly two per cent. of its weight of water, and but one-tenth as much when treated with oil; dry pine absorbed sixteen per cent. of its weight, and oiled pine absorbed none that could be ascertained by careful weighing. Pine has proved to be the most easily waterproofed of any timber. Those who wish to preserve shingle roofs, will be able to draw their own inferences as to the usefulness of coating them with crude petroleum.

A Nest for Egg-Eating Hens

In the winter season hens frequently acquire the habit of eating eggs. Sometimes this vice becomes so confirmed that several hens may be seen waiting for another one to leave her nest, or to even drive her off, so that they may pounce upon the egg, the one that drops it being among the first to break it. In this state of affairs there is no remedy, except to find some method of protecting the egg from the depredators. The easiest way of doing this is to contrive a nest in which the egg will drop out of reach. Such a nest is shown in figure 107. It consists of a box with two sloping false half-floors; one of these being **depressed** below the other sufficiently to make a space through which the egg can roll down to the bottom floor. A door is seen in the side of the nest, through which the eggs can be removed. The sloping half-floors are shown by dotted lines. Upon the back one, close to the back of the nest, a glass or other nest-egg is fastened by a screw or by cement. The false floors may be covered with some coarse carpet or cloth, and the bottom **floor** with some chaff or moss, upon which the eggs may **roll** without danger of breaking. If the eggs do not **roll**

Fig 107.—SAFETY-NEST.

down at once, they will be pushed down by the first attempt of a hen to attack them.

PLOWING GEAR FOR A KICKING MULE.

Below is presented a plan for hitching a mule which has a habit of kicking when harnessed to a plow, but which goes very well in shafts. Kicking is a vice which sometimes belongs to horses as well as mules, and the following expedient has been found effective in

Fig. 108.—PLOWING GEAR FOR KICKING ANIMALS.

curing it. Take a pair of light shafts from a wagon, or make a pair, and fit to the end of it a bent strap of iron, as shown in figure 108. When the mule or horse is hitched into the shafts the end may trail on the ground, and the beast may be exercised with the shafts alone. When used to these, the bent bar is fastened to a plow by means of a clevis, and any difficulty there will soon be overcome. This device has been used, not only for plowing, but for drawing a stone boat, railroad cars, and other similar vehicles.

A LEAF FORK.

A useful plan for making a fork to gather leaves is shown in figure 109. The fork is made of tough ash, with ten teeth, similar to the fingers of a cradle, three feet long, and slightly turned up. The head into which the butts of the teeth are inserted, is thirty inches long. A light cross-bar of tough wood is fastened to the teeth, about eight inches from the head, by means of copper

Fig. 109.—FORK FOR GATHERING LEAVES.

wire and a light screw to each finger. A handle is provided and fixed in its proper place, being flattened somewhat to keep it from turning in the hand. The handle should be braced by two strong wires. With such a fork leaves may be loaded very easily and rapidly.

PREPARATION OF THE WHEAT GROUND.

Wheat demands for its perfect development, among other favorable conditions, besides showers and sunshine, depth and richness of soil, thorough tilth, and freedom from excess of moisture. Soil that will yield good clover will bear good wheat. Wheat follows corn very well, but this involves rather late sowing. Where there is a market for new potatoes, which, as they are intended for immediate use, may be freely manured, the potato ground —well plowed and harrowed with a dressing of bone-dust, superphosphate, or, if there is much organic matter in the soil, with a dressing of lime—forms an admirable seed-bed for wheat. One of the best rotations, including winter wheat, is corn on sod, early potatoes, wheat, clover and timothy, the grass to be mowed as long as it is profitable—the manure being applied in the hill for corn, and put on broadcast very liberally for the potatoes. Winter wheat follows none of the usual root crops well, for it ought to be sowed and up before the middle of September, although it often does well sowed nearly a month later.

When wheat follows clover, a crop of clover-hay is often taken off early, and a second crop allowed to grow, which is turned under about the first of August for wheat. In case we have very dry weather in July, the growth of clover will be meagre. If, however, the clover stubble be top-dressed at once, as soon as the early crop is cut, with a muck and manure compost, or any fine compost, "dragged in" with a smoothing harrow, the second crop will be sure to start well, while none of the manure will be lost. Lime, or ashes, if they can be obtained, are to be spread after plowing under the clover and manure, and thoroughly harrowed in. Forty bushels of ashes to the acre is about right, and where hearths of old charcoal pits are accessible—ashes, charcoal-dust, and baked earth, are all excellent—they form a good substitute for ashes and for lime. Sixty to one hundred bushels of evenly dry-slaked lime is a usual application, which, if it could have been mixed with an equal quantity of soil or sods during the slaking, would be all the better.

The soil, and particularly wheat ground, is not well enough tilled in this country. We plow fourteen to sixteen-inch furrows, and use a skim-plow; this leaves the surface so mellow, and covers the sod so perfectly, that we think it hardly needs harrowing at all, and only smooth it over with a harrow, and let it go. The skim plow is a great advantage, but we should take narrow furrows.

The following practice, on heavy land especially, is excellent: Turn under the first crop of clover as deep as possible, just before it is in full blossom; cross-plow the first or second week in August; then put on seventy-five bushels of lime, or more, and harrow it in lightly. Sow early after a soaking rain, and apply at the time of sowing two hundred and fifty pounds or more of superphosphate to the acre.

How to Drive a Horse-Shoe Nail.

Most farmers hesitate to attempt to fasten on a loose shoe for fear of injuring the foot by driving the nail in a wrong direction. It is such a saving of time and money to be able to put a shoe upon a horse in a hurried busy time, that every farmer ought to learn how to do it. He may practice upon a piece of soft pine wood in a rough way, when he will find how easy it is, by properly preparing the nails, to make the point come out in exactly the proper place. To prepare the nail it should be laid upon the anvil (which every workshop should have for such work as this), or a smooth iron block, and beaten out straight. The point should then be bevelled, slightly upon one of the flat sides, and the point also bent a very little from the side which is bevelled. It will then be of the shape shown in figure 110. In driving such a nail into a piece of soft wood, or a horse's hoof which is penetrated easily in any direction, if the bevelled side is placed towards the centre of the hoof and away from the crust, the point will be bent outwards, and will come out lower or higher on the crust as the bevel and curve is much or little. A little practice will enable one to cause the point to protrude precisely at the right place. By turning the bevel outwards, in driving the nail, the course will be towards the centre of the

Fig. 110.—Nail.

foot as shown by the line *b*, in figure 111. The nail is sometimes started in the wrong direction by careless blacksmiths, and the horse is lamed in consequence. If the mistake is discovered, and an attempt made to draw out the nail, a piece of it may be broken off, and at every concussion of the foot the fragment will penetrate further, until it reaches the sensitive parts, and great suffering will follow. Many a horse is supposed to have navicular disease (because that happens to be one of those obscure affections of the foot which has no outward sign), when the trouble is a fragment of nail broken off by a bungling shoer. We have examined the foot of a horse which was killed because of an incurable lameness, and found a piece of nail thus bedded in the centre of the foot, surrounded with an abscess which had eaten into the bone. The torture suffered by this horse must have been intense, and it was supposed to be a case of navicular disease, while the real cause was unsuspected. In driving nails into the hoof, great caution should be exercised. The hand, or the thumb, should be held over the spot where the point of the nail is expected to come out, and if it does not appear when it should do so, the nail must be withdrawn. Use no split or imperfect nail, and have the point very carefully prepared. The course taken by a nail properly pointed and driven is shown by the lines curved outwards at *a, a*, in figure 111.

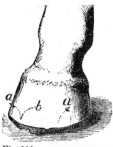

Fig. 111.—DRIVING NAILS.

SCREW-DRIVERS.

To drive a screw with a screw-driver, as it is usually pointed and handled, is a disagreeable task. If the screw goes in with difficulty, the driver **slips out** of the groove, or it cuts the edges **of** the groove so that the screw is useless. This is because the point of the tool is not ground properly. It should be ground with an even and long bevel, at least an inch long in small tools, and two inches in large ones. The sides of the bit should be kept straight, and not tapered off nor the corners ground off or rounded. There should be no sharp edge ground upon the end of the tool, and the grinding should be lengthwise, or from handle to point, and not crosswise. The edge should be slightly rounded. The degree of roundness given may be such as would make it equal to an arc of a circle ten to twelve inches in diameter; for small tools this may be lessened considerably. The shape of a well-pointed screw-driver is shown in figure 112. Flat handles should be abolished as a nuisance; after an hour's use of a driver with such a handle, the hand will be stiff and sore. The handle should be round. Screw-drivers are used more frequently than necessary. We have driven hundreds of screws in all sorts of timber, hard white oak even, with the hammer, just as nails are driven, without the use of a screw-driver, and found them to hold perfectly well. This, of course, can be done only with the sharp taper-pointed screws, and if any one uses the old blunt-pointed kind, he is **too** far behind the times to be much of a mechanic **or** farmer either.

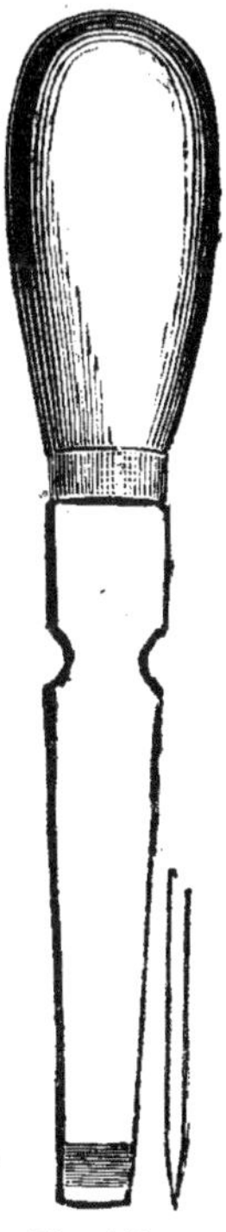

Fig. 112.— SCREW-DRIVER

TO PREVENT COWS SUCKING THEMSELVES.

There are many devices to prevent cows from sucking themselves. A spiked halter is shown in figure 113. A buckle at the upper part, behind the ears, makes it quite easy to detach it. Figure 114 shows

 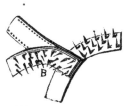

Fig. 113.—SPIKED HALTER.   Fig. 114.—MAKING THE HALTER.

how the spikes are secured. The spikes should not be over two inches in length. They are best made of wrought nails, which are sold at the hardware stores. They are placed in an iron vise and the heads flattened as much as possible by pounding with a hammer; they are then driven into a piece of thick leather, and secured by sewing or riveting it upon another piece of leather, as shown at B in figure 114.

ABUSE OF BARN CELLARS.

A great change has come over the farm during the last thirty years, in all our thrifty farming districts, in the general use of barn cellars. Formerly such an arrangement of the barn was a novelty, and farmers have slowly learned its great advantages—the greater comfort of cattle, the cheaper cleaning of stables, the more convenient watering of stock, the larger use of peat, muck, and headlands in the compost heap, and the greater value of the manure made under cover. Now the cry is raised of damage to fodder and stock from the barn cellar. Almost any good thing can be perverted and become a nuisance, and it were strange if men who do not read much, and think less, could not abuse the barn cellar, which is the stomach of the farm. The same kind of men not infrequently abuse their own stomachs, and suffer grievously in consequence. "If you make your barn cellar tight, carbonic acid gas and ammonia are thrown off and injure the quality of hay stored in the rooms above, and the health of the cattle in the stables. If you turn your pigs into the cellar to make compost, and keep them from the air and the light, they become diseased, and you put bad meat into your barrel to breed disease in your family." These are not uncommon complaints, circulating in our agricultural journals. Well, suppose we admit these things to be true, what of it? Is there any necessity for having a barn cellar without ventilation? If you leave one end open towards the south, you certainly have ventilation enough—and the gases that are evolved from fermenting manure are not going through two-inch stable plank and the tight siding of the barn when they have the wind to carry them off. If a barn cellar is properly managed, and seasonably furnished with absorbents, the ammonia will be absorbed as fast as it is formed. There will be no odor of ammonia that the nostrils can detect. If the pigs do not do the mixing fast enough, the shovel and the fork, the plow and the harrow, can be added. The making of compost under the barn is nice work for rainy days in winter, and is more likely to pay than any work exposed to the storm. The keeping of pigs under the barn is a question of two sides, and however we may decide it, barn cellars will stand upon their own merits. Any farmer who makes a business of raising pork for the market will find a well-appointed pig-sty, with conveniences for storing and cooking food, a paying investment. If he sees fit to utilize the labor of his pigs by making compost in a well-ventilated barn cellar, their health is not likely to suffer from the wholesome exercise, or that of his family from the use of the flesh. Swine, furnished with a dry sleeping-apartment and plenty of litter for a bed, will keep comfortably clean, and not suffer from overwork in the compost heap. If anything is settled in the experience of the last thirty years, it is the economy of the barn cellar. Our most intelligent farmers, who can command the capital, in-

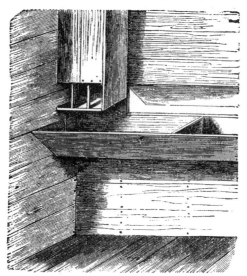

Fig. 115.—HAY RACK AND MANGER.

vest in them. A nice appendage to them is a watering trough fed by a spring or a large cistern in the embankment, to catch all the water, and bring it out by a faucet upon the stable floor above. This works admirably

HAY-RACK AND MANGER.

A cheap and convenient hay-rack and manger is shown in figure 115. The front of the manger should be of oak or other hard wood plank, two inches thick, and one foot wide, the lower edge of which is placed about two and a half feet from the floor; the bottom should be one foot wide. The side of the hay-rack is one foot wide, the front is eighteen inches wide; the top and bottom being of the same width, so that hay will not lodge. The bottom is made from one and a half inch hard board, and is placed one foot above the top of the manger. Two guards, one inch in diameter, and one foot in length, are placed in an upright position across the opening. At the front of the manger is a swinging door, which is shown partly open. This opens into the feed-passage. The manger may have one end partitioned for feeding grain. All corners should be smoothed and rounded off, and to make it durable, attach a thin, flat bar of iron to the upper edge of the manger by screws or rivets.

A BARN BASKET.

Figure 116 shows a home-made basket or box for use in the barn or in gathering crops. It is made of two pieces of light board, twelve inches square, for the ends, fastened together by laths sixteen, eighteen, or twenty inches long, for bottom and sides. These are securely nailed. The handle consists of a piece nailed to each end, and connected by a light bar. This box is quickly made, and will be found very handy for gathering many crops in the field, as it may be made to hold exactly one bushel, half a bushel, or any other definite quantity, by changing the size. To hold a bushel, which is two thousand, one hundred and fifty cubic inches, the box may be scant twenty inches long, twelve inches wide, and nine deep, or scant eighteen inches long, twelve inches wide, and eleven inches deep. For half a bushel,

Fig. 116.—CONVENIENT BARN BASKET.

scant eighteen inches long, ten inches wide, and six deep; or fifteen inches long, nine inches wide, and eight inches deep. For a peck, ten inches long, nine wide, and six deep; or eight inches square, and scant eight and a half inches deep.

THE TREATMENT OF KICKING COWS.

It is safe to say that a kicking cow is not naturally disposed to this vice, but has been made vicious by some fault of her owner. There are few men who possess sufficient patience and kindness to so manage a cow, from calfhood until she comes to the pail, that she will be kind and gentle under all circumstances. There are nervous, irritable cows, that are impatient of restraint, which are easily and quickly spoiled when they fall into the hands of an owner of a similar disposition. One who is kind and patient, and who has an affection for his animals, is never troubled with kicking cows, unless

Old-Fashioned Labor-Saving Devices

he has purchased one already made vicious. Unfortunately, few persons are gifted with these rare virtues, and, therefore, there are always cows that have to be watched carefully at milking time. Cows sometimes suffer from cracked teats, or their udders may be tender from some concealed inflammation, and they are restless when milked; so that, now and then, in the best regulated dairies, there will be cows that will kick. Many devices have been recommended to prevent such cows from exercising this disagreeable habit. Different methods of securing the legs have been tried. The best plan that we have heard of, or have tried, is shown in figure 117. This fetter is fastened to the cow's near leg, by means of the strap in the centre, the curved portions embracing the front of the leg above and below the hock. It will be perceived that, while the cow can move her leg to some extent, and is not hobbled, as when the legs are tied together, yet she cannot lift it to kick, or to put her foot in the pail. We have seen this "fetter" tried upon a cow that had very sore cracked teats, and that kicked furiously when milked, but with the fetter she was unable to kick or hinder milking.

Fig. 117.—COW-FETTER.

HOW TO BUILD A BOAT-HOUSE.

Any kind of a house that is large enough may be used, if provided with the needed fittings named below. Where the level of the water is liable to little change, the house need not be raised much above the surface of, the water, but the floor may be made so low that one can easily step out of the boat to the floor. Of course there should be a channel made in the centre of the house, deep enough to float the boat when loaded. The plan of the floor is shown in figure 118, with the boat in the centre. The floor should be protected by a light railing around it (see figure 119), to prevent accidents from slipping when the floor is wet. Where the water level changes, the house should be raised on posts, or bents, as may be necessary to keep it

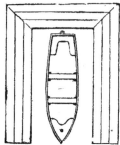

Fig. 118.—PLAN OF HOUSE.

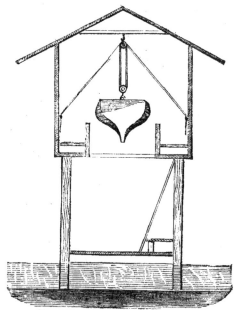

Fig. 119.—SECTION OF BOAT-HOUSE.

above high water. A hanging ladder, that may be drawn up, is provided for use at low water.

WASTE LANDS—MAKE THEM USEFUL.

Waste land abounds everywhere. It is fenced, and has the appearance of farm-land, but the owner, if a farmer, would be better off without it than he is with it. No one locality seems to be better or worse than another in this respect, unless it be that the Southern States have the most waste land, and the Eastern States come next in this respect. There are rocky fields, and fields covered with loose stones; swamps and wet ground, and land covered with wretched brush and small timber, and in the South, especially, barren and gullied hill-sides. It is true, that to clear up these lands, and make them fruitful, will cost in labor, if the labor is valued at the current rates, more than the land would bring if offered for sale. But this is not the right way to look at this matter. In reality, it will cost nothing to clear these lands, because their owners may do it by working when they would otherwise be idle. The way to do it is to set about it. To clear an acre or two at a time, of those fields that can be cleared; and to plant with timber, of some valuable sort, that ground which is too rough for the plow, instead of permitting it to grow up with useless brush. In many cases, the worst trouble that farmers suffer is, that they have more land than they can care for, under their present system of management. Hundreds of farms are worked as grain farms, that are not well suited for any other use than dairy farms, and ground is plowed that should be kept in permanent grass. In some cases, the owners of land have discovered their proper vocation, as in the dairy district of Central

New York, in the fruit and grain farms of the **western part of that State**, in the pasture farms of the **blue-grass region of Kentucky**, and in the corn-growing and pork-raising prairies of the West. If the system of culture in these places were changed, the farmers would be poor instead of being rich, and one sees very little waste land in these localities. There are districts where the surface is hilly, and not so well suited for arable purposes as for pasture, but where, instead of grass and cows, side-hill plows and poor corn fields, washed and gullied by rains, are to be seen. Here are waste lands in plenty; and their owners show every sign of poverty and want of thrift. It is not easy to change these circumstances quickly, but it is easy to begin—just as it is easier to start a stone rolling down a hill, than to throw it down bodily; and when it is once started, it goes slowly at first, and may need help, but it can soon take care of itself, and speedily reaches the bottom. It is just so with such improvements as are here referred to. They are necessarily begun slowly, but when one or two acres of these waste places are reclaimed, the product of these adds to the farmer's resources. He is richer than before by the increased value of these acres, and he is better able to reclaim more. When these in their turn are improved, the means for further improvements are greatly enlarged; the ambition of the man to excel in his vocation is excited, and he speedily becomes a neater, better farmer, and necessarily his circumstances are improved. Thus the rough waste lands, which give a disagreeable appearance to the landscape, and are a stigma upon its character and that of our farmers, in the eyes of our own citizens and of foreigners, might in a short time be improved and a source of profit.

To keep rats away from anything that is hung up, the following simple method may be used. Procure the bottoms of some old fruit-cans, by melting the solder which

Fig. 120.—GUARD AGAINST RATS.

holds them upon a hot stove. Bore holes in the centre of these disks, and string a few of them upon the cord, wire, or rope upon which the articles are hung. When a rat or mouse attempts to pass upon the rope by climbing over the tin disks, they turn and throw the animal upon the floor. This plan, shown in figure 120, will be found very effective.

A CRUPPER-PAD FOR HORSES.

Many horsemen desire a method by which to prevent a horse from carrying its tail upon one side, and from clasping the reins beneath the tail. We cannot advise the operation of "nicking," which consists in cutting the skin and muscles upon one side of the tail, and tying it over to the cut side, until the cuts heal, when the skin, being drawn together, pulls the tail permanently over to that side. A different form of the operation causes the tail to be carried up in a style that is supposed to be more graceful, and prevents the horse from clasping the reins when driven. As a preventive of both of these habits, the pad shown in figure 121 is often used by horsemen, instead of the cruel and unnecessary operation of "nicking." This appliance is made of leather, is stuffed with hair or wool, and is about three inches in diameter at the thickest part, gradually tapering toward each end, where it is fastened to the crupper straps. It should be drawn up close to the roots of the tail, and by exerting a pressure beneath it, the tail is carried in a raised position, and is not thrown over to one side. If it is, a few sharp tacks may be driven into the inside of the pad.

Fig. 121.—CRUPPER-PAD.

A DAM FOR A FISH POND.

In making a fish pond, by placing a dam across a stream, it should be borne in mind that success depends upon the proper construction of the dam, whether it be

Fig. 122.—STAKES AND BRUSH.

large or small. Any defect here will make the whole useless. The main point in the construction of a dam is, to have a complete union between the earth of the bed and that of the dam. This cannot be done by throwing the earth upon an old surface. A new surface must be made, solid and firm, to receive the new earth. In addition, there should be a central core of some strong material, that will serve to strengthen and bind the new construction. In making a dam or embankment to retain or exclude water, the beginning should be to dig a shallow ditch, removing sod or uneven ground, or if the earth is bare, to disturb it thoroughly with the pick, so as to provide binding material to unite with the bottom of the dam. A line of stakes is driven into the ground, and filled with brush woven in, or wattled, as in figure 122. In building the dam, all the sods and vegetable matter should be placed on the outside, where these will root, and bind the surface together; the rest of the earth should be well trodden, or rammed down firmly, and if the soil is puddled by admixture of water in the process of ramming, the work will be better for it. The waterway in the stream should be tightly boarded or planked. Three posts may be driven or set on each bank of the stream, and boards nailed, or planks spiked for a larger structure, so as to retain the earth of the embankments on each side, figure 123. A timber is fitted as a mudsill, to the front and rear posts, and one to the central posts; the latter at such a height as will raise the water to the desired depth. The spaces between these timbers are boarded and planked, and may be filled in with earth, well rammed, and mixed with straw and fine cedar brush, under the covering. If it is desired to raise the water to a greater depth, loose flash-boards may be fitted with cleats, on the centre of the waste-way, or a wire-gauze fence may be placed there, to prevent the escape of the fish. If freshets are apt to occur, a sufficient number of these waste-ways should be provided to carry off the surplus water, and prevent overflowing and wasting of the dam. The dam of a fish pond should always be made high enough for safety against overflow, and to guard against percolation, and washing away by undermining, it should be made three times as wide as it is high, with slopes of one and a half foot horizontal on

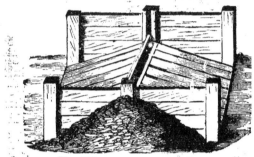

Fig. 123.—WASTE-GATE FOR POND.

each side, to one foot in perpendicular height. If any plants are set upon a dam or embankment, they should be of a small, bushy growth, such as osier willow, elders, etc., but nothing larger, lest the swaying caused by high winds should loosen and destroy the bank.

A WAGON JACK.

In figures 124 and 125 is shown a most convenient home-made wagon jack, in constant use for ten years, and has proved most satisfactory. The drawings were made with such care, the measurement being placed upon them, that the engravings tell nearly the whole story. Figure 124 shows the jack when in position to hold the axle, at *a*. When not in use, the lever falls down out of the way, and the affair can be hung up in a handy place. Figure 125 shows the "catch-board," and the dimensions proper for a jack, for an ordinary wagon, buggy, etc. It is so shaped and fastened by a din between the upright parts of the jack, that it is pushed in position, *d*, by the foot at *c*, when the axle is raised; and falls back of its own accord when the lever is raised a trifle to let the wheel down. All the parts are made

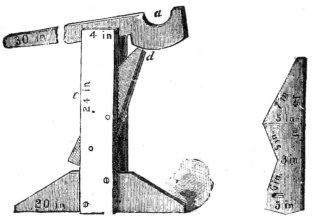

Fig. 124.—MICHIGAN WAGON JACK.   Fig. 125.—CATCH-BOARD.

of inch stuff, the foot board, catch, and lever should be of hard wood; the upright boards between which they are placed can be of pine or other soft wood. Persons who see this simple and convenient wagon jack frequently say, "Why don't you get it patented?" but the inventor thinks that such simple things, which any one can make, ought to be contributed for the common good, and in the same spirit we commend it to any who may be in need of a good wagon jack.

WILL YOU FEED HAY OR WOOD?

A great deal has been said and written about the proper time of cutting hay. The best time, all things considered, is to cut the grass just after it has come into full bloom, though many think the preferable time is just when it is coming into full blossom. As it is impossible to always mow every field just at the right moment, the general safe rule is, we think, to be all ready to begin at full bloom, and finish before it is entirely past.

There is this important fact to be kept in mind, viz., that as soon as grass of any kind has attained its growth, and is full of juices, it begins to change more and more into woody fibre, and that when fully ripe a large part of the stems or stalks differ very little in composition from dry wood. And every one knows that dry wood is neither easily digested nor nutritious. It stands to reason that a stalk of grass cut when it is full of juice containing sugar, gum, and protein compounds, and cured thus, must be more nutritious than if left standing until a part of these constituents have changed into woody fibre. Feeding hay not cut until it is thoroughly ripe, is giving the animals that which is in part only so much wood. The practical lesson is, make a good ready well in advance, now, and have the barns, mows, stacking arrangements, mowers, scythes, horse and other rakes, forks, wagon racks, in short, all things, in perfect order—and the work planned, so as not to let any hayfield get into the fully ripe condition. Head work beforehand will save hard work and worry, and secure better hay.

A BRACE FOR A KICKING HORSE.

Those so unfortunate as to own a kicking horse know something of the patience that it requires to get along with it—and will welcome anything which will prevent the kicking and finally effect a cure. The writer knew a horse, which was so bad a kicker that after various trials, and after passing through many hands, and getting worse all the time, to be perfectly cured in the course of three months by the use of the device here given. This is a simple brace, which acts upon the fact that if the head be kept up, the horse cannot kick. A kicking horse is like a balance, when one end goes up, the other must go down. The brace is shown in figure 126, and consists of a one-half inch iron rod, which may be straight, or, for the looks, bent into a graceful curve. It is forked at both ends; the two divisions of the upper end are fastened to the two rings of the bit, while the lower ends fit upon the lower portion of the collar and hames. The upper ends can best be fastened to the bit by winding with wire, which should be done smoothly, so as not to wear upon the mouth. The lower end is secured by means of a strap fastened to the upper loop, and passing around the collar is buckled through the hole in the lower part of the end of the brace. The brace need not be taken from the bit in unharnessing.

Fig. 126.—THE BRACE.

Any blacksmith can make such a brace, taking care to have it of the proper length to fit the particular horse. Keep its head at about the height as when "**checked** up," and the horse will soon be cured.

HOW TO SAVE LIQUID MANURE.

In ordinary farm practice, by far the larger part of the liquid manure of the stock kept is lost. No effort is made to save it. There is no barn cellar, no gutter behind the stabled animals, no absorbents. Analysis shows that the liquid manure is quite as valuable as the solid, or even more so. In 1,000 pounds of fresh horse dung there are 4.4 pounds of nitrogen, 3.5 of potash, and 3.5 of phosphoric acid. In horse urine there are 15.5 pounds of nitrogen, and 15.0 of potash. In 1,000 pounds of fresh cattle dung there are 2.9 pounds of nitrogen, 1.0 of potash, 1.7 of phosphoric acid. In the urine, 5.8 pounds of nitrogen, 4.9 of potash. These are the most valuable constituents of manure, and no farmer can afford to have them so generally run to waste. There is very little loss where there is a gutter well supplied with absorbents, and a barn cellar well coated with dried peat, muck, or, headlands, to absorb the liquids as fast as they fall. But barn cellars are still in the minority. Mr. Mechi had a very expensive apparatus for distributing the liquid manure over his farm, by means of tanks and pipes, and thought it paid, but failed to convince his contemporaries of the fact. However that may be, it is out of the question to apply liquid manure in this manner, economically, upon the average farm. It takes too much capital, and requires too much labor. By the use of absorbents, it can be done economically on a small or large scale, with very little waste. Some use a water-tight box, made of thick plank, covering the floor of the stall. This is a very sure way to save everything, and the only objection to it is the expense of the box, and the increased labor of keeping the stalls clean. We used for several years dried salt-marsh sod, cut in blocks eight or ten inches square, taken from the surface of the marsh in ditching. This had an enormous capacity for absorbing liquids, and a layer of these sods would keep a horse or cow comfortably dry for a fortnight. Refuse hay or **straw** was used on top for purposes of cleanliness. The **saturated** sod was thrown into the compost heap with other manure, where it made an excellent fertilizer. Later we used sawdust, purchased for the purpose at two cents a bushel, as bedding for a cow kept upon a cemented floor. A bed a foot thick would last nearly a month, when it was thrown out into the compost heap. The sawdust requires a longer time for decomposition, but saves the liquid manure. Our present experiment, covering several months, is with forest leaves, principally hickory, maple, white ash, and elm. A bushel of dried leaves, kept under a shed for the purpose, is added to the bedding of each animal, and the saturated leaves are removed with the solid manure as fast as they accumulate. The leaves become very fine by the constant treading of the animals, and by the heat of their bodies, and the manure pile grows rapidly. It is but a little additional labor to the ordinary task of keeping animals clean in their stalls, to use some good absorbent, and enough of it, to save all the liquid manure. What the absorbent shall be is a question of minor importance. Convenience will generally determine this matter. No labor upon the farm pays better than to save the urine of all farm stock by means of absorbents. These are in great variety, and, in some form, are within the reach of every man that keeps cattle or runs a farm. Stop this leak, and lift your mortgage.

AN OPEN SHED FOR FEEDING.

A feeding-trough in a yard, which can be covered to keep out snow or rain, is a desirable thing, and many devices have been contrived for the purpose, most of which are too costly. We give herewith a method of constructing a covered feeding-trough, which may be made very cheaply of the rough materials to be had on every farm. A sufficient number of stout posts are set firmly in the ground, extending about ten feet above the surface. They should be about six feet apart and in a straight line, and a plate fastened to their tops. A pair

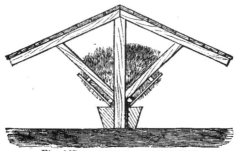

Fig. 127.—AN OPEN FEEDING-SHED.

of rafters supported by braces, as shown in figure 127, is fitted to each post. A light roof of laths is laid, and covered with bark, straw, corn-stalks, or coarse hay Strips are fastened from one brace to another, and laths or split poles nailed to them, about six inches apart, to make a feed-rack. A feed-trough for grain or roots is built upon each side. For sheep, the shed and rack may be made only eight feet high at the peak, and the eaves four feet from the ground; giving better shelter.

A SHADE FOR HORSES' EYES.

The most frequent cause of weak eyes in horses is a badly-arranged stable. Foul gases irritate and inflame the tender membranes of the eye and head, and horses brought from dark stables into bright sunlight, or onto glittering snow, are dazzled and blinded. The existing weakness or irritation is intensified, and the poor animal suffers unsuspected torments. The remedy is to purify the stable and give it sufficient light, shaded by blinds, from before and behind the horse, or from both sides, avoiding a light from only the front, rear, or one side light. A shade for weak or inflamed eyes may be constructed by fastening wires to the bridle and covering it with oiled cloth in the manner represented in figure 128. Thus a soft, subdued light reaches the eyes, while the horse can still see the ground immediately before him. It will be a timely job to prepare such a shade for use before the snow of winter comes.

Fig. 128.—TO PROTECT THE EYES.

TEST ALL SEEDS—IMPORTANT.

No one can, by merely looking at them, positively tell whether any particular lots of field, garden, or flower seeds have or have not sufficient vitality of germ to start into vigorous growth. Yet it is a severe loss, often a disastrous one, to go through with all the labor and expense of preparation and planting or sowing, and find too late that the crop is lost because the seeds are defective. All this risk can be saved by a few minutes' time all told, in making a preliminary test, and it should be done before the seed is wanted, and in time to get other seed if necessary. Seeds may not have matured the germ; it may have been destroyed by heat or moisture; minute insects may have, unobserved, punctured or eaten out the vital part of a considerable percentage.

Select from the whole mass of the seed, one hundred, or fifty, or even ten seeds, that will be a fair sample of all. For larger seeds, as wheat, corn, oats, peas, etc., take a thin, tough sod, and scatter the counted seeds upon the earth side. Put upon the seeds another similar sod, earth side down. Set this double sod by the warm side of the house or other building, or of a tight fence, moistening it occasionally as needed. If very cold, cover, or remove to the kitchen or cellar at night. The upper sod can be lifted for observation when desirable. The swelling and starting of the seeds will in a few days, according to the kind, tell what percentage of them will grow—a box of earth will answer instead of sods, both for large and small seeds. Small seeds of vegetables or

Fig. 129.—HOME-MADE ROLLER.

flowers, and even larger ones, may be put into moist cotton, to be kept slightly moist and placed in the sun or in a light warm room. For small quantities of valuable flower seeds and the like, half a dozen will suffice for a trial test. With any seed, for field or garden, however good, it is always very desirable and useful to know exactly how many or few are defective, and thus be able to decide how much seed to use on an acre, or other plot.

A FIELD ROLLER.

A very good field roller may be easily made in winter, when timber is being cut. Use a butt-log of an oak tree, in the form shown in figure 129. The log need not be a very large one, because the frame, in which it is mounted, enables it to be loaded to any reasonable extent, and the driver may ride upon it, and thus add to the weight. A roller will be found very valuable in the spring when repeated frosts have raised the ground and thrown out the stones.

A PORTABLE SLOP BARREL.

A barrel mounted upon wheels, as shown in figure 130, will be found useful for many purposes about the farm, garden, or household. The barrel is supported upon a pair of wheels, the axles of which are fastened to

Fig. 130.—PORTABLE BARREL FOR SLOPS.

a frame connected with the barrel by means of straps bolted to the sides. The frame may be made of iron bent in the form shown in figure 131, or of crooked timber having a sufficient bend to permit the barrel to be tipped for emptying. A pair of handles are provided, as shown in the engraving. When not in use, the barrel rests upon the ground, and may be raised by bearing down upon the handles. The barrel may be made to rest in notched bearings upon the frame, so that by raising the handles, the wheels may be drawn away from the barrel, and the latter left in a convenient place until it needs removal. This contrivance will be useful for feed-

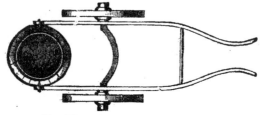

Fig. 131.—PLAN OF FRAME OF BARREL.

ing slops to pigs, or for removing the waste of the house to the barn-yard.

WHERE AND HOW TO APPLY FERTILIZERS.

It is often difficult to decide—for barn-yard or stable manures, or for any artificial fertilizer—whether to use it in the hill or broadcast it; and whether to apply it on the surface, or bury it deeply. Here is a hint or two. If not strong enough to injure the first tender roots, a little manure near at hand gives the plant a good send-off, like nourishing food to the young calf or other animal; the after-growth is much better if the young animal or plant is not dwarfed by imperfect and insufficient diet. Therefore, drilling innocuous hand fertilizers in with the seed is useful, as is putting some well-rotted manure or leached ashes into hills of corn, potatoes, indeed with all planted seeds. But there are good reasons for distributing most of the manures or fertilizers all through the soil, and as deeply as the plant roots can possibly penetrate. The growth and vigor of all plants or crops depend chiefly upon a good supply of strong roots that stretch out far, and thus gather food over the widest extent of soil. If a flourishing stalk of corn, grain or grass, be carefully washed, so as to leave all its roots or rootlets attached, there will be found a wonderful mass of hundreds and even thousands of roots to any plant, and they extend off a long distance, frequently several feet—the farther the better, to collect more food and moisture. Put some manure or fertilizer in place two feet away from a corn or potato hill, or from almost any plant, and a large mass of roots will go out in that direction. So, if we mix manures or fertilizers well through the whole soil, they attract these food-seeking roots to a greater distance; and they thus come in contact with more of the food already in the soil, and find more moisture in dry weather. A deeply-stirred soil, with manure at the bottom, develops water-pumping roots below the reach of any ordinary drouth, and the crops keep right on growing—all the more rapidly on account of the helpful sun's rays that would scorch a plant not reaching a deep reservoir of moisture.

A MILL FOR CRUSHING BONES.

To save the expense of a purchased bone-mill, one may be made as described below, which will crush them into a condition much more valuable for manure than the whole bones, if not quite as good as if finely ground. Make a circular mould of boards, six feet wide and two feet deep. Hoops of broad band-iron are fitted to the inside of the mould, and secured to it about one inch apart. The mould is then filled with a concrete of Portland cement, sand, and broken stone. Place in the concrete when filling binding pieces of flat bar-iron, to prevent the mass from cracking when in use. In the centre place squares of band-iron, as a lining for a shaft by which the crusher is turned. When the concrete is set and hardened, the frame may be taken apart; and, as in setting the concrete will expand somewhat, the iron bands around the mass will be found to have become a tight solid facing to the wheel. The wheel is then set up on edge, and a square shaft of yellow pine, six inches thick, is wedged into the central space. This shaft is fitted to an upright post by a loose band of iron and a swivel joint, so that the wheel may be made to revolve around it. Any other suitable connection may be used for this purpose. A hollow trough of broken stone and well rammed concrete is then laid in the track of the

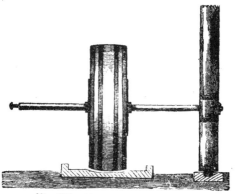

Fig. 132.—HOME-MADE BONE-MILL.

wheel as it revolves, and the crusher is complete and ready for a pair of horses to be attached to it, figure 132. A crusher of this kind may be put up at a country mill, or as a joint affair by a few farmers uniting their efforts, and thus utilizing a valuable fertilizing material, which is now wasted for want of means to render it available.

LIME AND LIMESTONE

In the first place, limestone, marble, calc-spar, chalk (of rare occurrence in this country), marl, and oyster, and other shells, are all essentially the same in composition, however they may differ in texture, form, and other particulars. They are all different forms of the carbonate of lime; that is, they consist of the alkaline earth, lime, in combination with carbonic acid, and in the case of shells, with animal matter. As a general thing, we only know carbonic acid as a gas. It has a very weak hold of the lime, for if we drop a fragment of limestone into strong vinegar, the acetic acid of the vinegar will unite with the lime (forming acetate of lime), while the carbonic acid, being set free, will be seen to pass off in small bubbles. In this case we free the lime from its carbonic acid, by presenting to it a stronger acid, that of vinegar. But if instead of using another acid to displace the carbonic acid, we place limestone in any of its forms, in a strong fire, the carbonic acid will be driven off by the heat, and there will be left, simply lime. This is called quick lime, or caustic lime, and by chemists oxide of the metal calcium, or calcium oxide. Lime, then, is limestone without its carbonic acid. All the forms of limestone are very little soluble in water; lime itself is more soluble, though but slightly so, requiring at ordinary temperatures about seven hundred times its own weight of water, yet it gives a marked alkaline taste to water in which it is dissolved. Lime in this condition, as quick lime, or when combined with water, "slaked" as it is called, is much employed in agriculture. A small portion of lime is required by plants, but the chief use of lime, when applied to the soil, is to bring the vegetable matters contained in the soil into a condition in which they can be used as plant food. This application of lime as a fertilizer has long been followed by farmers, and in many cases with the most beneficial results. Within a year or so great claims have been made for ground limestone, especially by the makers of mills for grinding it; some of these have asserted that it was superior to burned lime, and superior to nearly all other fertilizers. The question which most interests farmers is, has limestone, however fine it may be, any value as a fertilizer? To this the answer would be both "yes" and "no." Upon a heavy clay soil the carbonate of lime, or limestone in any form, appears to have a beneficial effect; it makes such soils friable and open, so that water and air may penetrate them. While its action upon the vegetable matter in the soil is far less prompt and energetic than that of quick-lime, yet its presence, affording a base with which any acid that may be present in the soil may unite, is often beneficial. To extol ground limestone as "the great fertilizer of the age," to even claim that it is equal to lime itself, is a mistake. Both have their uses. It should be borne in mind by inquirers about the value of ground limestone, that many soils already contain more lime in this form than can ever be utilized, and need no addition.

A FARM WHEELBARROW.

The wheelbarrow is an indispensable vehicle on the farm and in the garden. Applied to hard uses it needs

Fig. 133.—FARM WHEELBARROW.

to be strong and durable. A barrow of the ordinary kind, used on farms, soon becomes weak in the joints and falls to pieces. The movable sides are inconvenient, and the shape necessarily adopted when movable sides are used greatly weakens the structure. It will be noticed at first sight that the wheelbarrow, shown in figure 133, is most strongly supported and braced, that the box, instead of weakening it, greatly strengthens it, and that it is stout and substantial. It is put together at every part by strong bolts, and can be taken apart to pack for transportation, if desired, and a broken part readily replaced.

TO PREVENT THE BALLING OF HORSES.

When the snow upon the roads is cohesive and packs firmly, it collects upon the feet of horses, forming a hard, projecting mass, in a manner known as "balling." This often occurs to such an extent as to impede the motion of the horse, while it causes the animal great discomfort, and is sometimes dangerous to the rider or driver. The trouble may be prevented very easily by the use of guttapercha. For this purpose the gutta-percha should be crude, *i.e.*, not mixed with anything or manufactured in any manner, but just as imported. Its application depends upon the property which the gum has of softening and becoming plastic by heat, and hardening again when cold. To apply it, place the gutta-percha in hot water until it becomes soft, and having well cleansed the foot, removing whatever has accumulated between the shoe and hoof, take a piece of the softened gum and press it against the shoe and foot in such a manner as to fill the angle between the shoe and the hoof, taking care to force it into the crack between the two. Thus filling the crevices, and the space next the shoe, where the snow most firmly adheres, the ball of snow has nothing to hold it, and it either does not form, or drops out as soon as it is gathered. When the gutta-percha is applied, and well smoothed off with the wet fingers, it may be hardened at once, to prevent the horse from getting it out of place by stamping, by the application of snow or ice, or more slowly by a wet sponge or cloth. When it is desired to remove the gum, the application of hot water by means of a sponge or cloth will so soften it that it may be taken off. As the softening and hardening may be repeated indefinitely, the same material will last for years. For a horse of medium size, a quarter of a pound is sufficient for all the feet.

TO PREVENT CATTLE THROWING FENCES.

To prevent a cow from throwing fences or hooking other cows, make a wooden strip two and a half inches wide and three-quarters of an inch thick, and attach it to the horns by screws; to this is fastened, by a small bolt, a strip of hardwood, three inches wide, half an inch thick, and of a length sufficient to reach downward within an inch of the face, and within two or three inches of the nostrils. In the lower end of this strip are previously driven several sharp nails, which project about one-quarter of an inch. The arrangement is shown in figure 134; the strip, when properly attached, allows the animal to eat and drink with all ease, but when an attempt is made to hook or to throw a fence, the sharpened nails soon cause an abrupt cessation of that kind of mischief.

Fig. 134.—CATTLE CHECK.

FEED BOXES.

In figure 135 a box is shown firmly attached to two posts. It has a hinged cover, *p*, that folds over, and may be fastened down by inserting a wooden pin in the

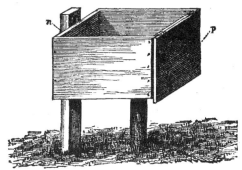

Fig. 135.—COVERED FEED BOX.

top of the post near *n*. The one given in figure 136 may be placed under shelter, along the side of a building or fence. One side of the top is hinged to the fence

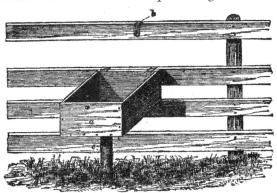

Fig. 136.—HINGED FEED BOX.

or building, the bottom resting upon a stake, *e*. When not in use, the box may be folded up, the end of the strap, *b*, hooking over the pin, *a*, at the side of the box,

A good portable box, to be placed upon the ground, is shown in figure 137. It is simply a common box, with a strip of board, *h*, nailed on one side and projecting about

Fig. 137.—PORTABLE FEED BOX.

eight inches. When not in use, it is turned bottom up, as shown in figure 138. The projecting strip prevents three sides of the box from settling into the mud or snow. The strip is also a very good handle by which to carry it.

Fig. 138.—FEED BOX INVERTED.

Those who now use portable boxes will find the attaching of this strip a decided advantage. A very serviceable portable feed box is made from a section of half a hollow

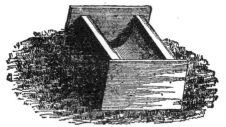

Fig. 139.—BOX FROM HOLLOW LOG.

log, with ends nailed on, as shown in figure 139. By letting the ends project above the sides four or five inches, it may be turned over when not in use, and easily turned back by grasping the sides without the hand coming in contact with earth or snow. All feed boxes and racks should be placed under shelter during summer, or when not in use.

A CATTLE TIE.

Judging from the numerous stanchions and arrangements for fastening cattle in stalls, illustrated from time to time in the public print, the perfect cattle-fastening has not yet been invented. We do not claim perfection for the arrangement given in figure 140, but it will be difficult to devise a cheaper one, and we doubt if any better or more satisfactory one is in use. The fastening consists of a three-fourth inch rope, which is run through the partitions of the stalls, one long rope being used for the tier of stalls, although short pieces may be employed if desired. This rope is knotted on either side

Fig. 140.—CATTLE TIE.

of each partition, and a good swivel snap for use with a rope, is tied in the rope in front of the centre of each stall. The rope should pass over, very neatly, the front of the manger—from the side of the cattle—and for cattle of ordinary hight, it ought to be about two feet from the floor. When put in, the rope should be drawn up tightly, as it will soon acquire considerable and sufficient slack from the constant strain from the animals. With this arrangement each cow must be provided with a strap or rope about the neck, the rope or strap being supplied with a free-moving iron ring. When the animal is put in the stalls the snap is fastened in the ring, and if the snap is a good one—none but the best swivel snaps should be used—an animal will rarely get free from it. This fastening, it will be noticed, admits of considerable fore and aft motion, and but slight lateral movement. The cost of this arrangement it is difficult to state accurately, it is so small. The rope for each stall will cost less than five cents; the snaps will cost ten cents when bought by the dozen, and the time of putting these fittings in each stall is less than fifteen minutes. The rope will wear two years at least.

A BEEF RAISER.

Two posts are set about fifteen feet high. A deep mortise is cut in the top of each to receive the roller, which is grooved at the points of turning. One end of the roller extends beyond the post, and through this end three two-inch holes are bored. Three light poles are put through these holes, and their ends connected by a light rope. In raising the beef the middle of a stout rope is thrown over the roller; the ends are drawn through the loop, and after the beef is fastened to the loose ends the roller is turned against the loop by means of the "sweep," or lever arms, figure 141. A heavy

beef can be easily raised, and may be fastened at any

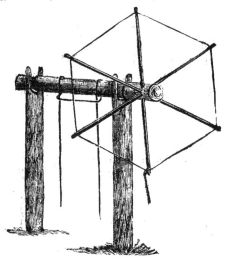

Fig. 141.—A BEEF RAISE

hight desired, by tying the end of one of the levers to the post with a short rope.

A CEDAR STEM SOIL-STIRRER.

A convenient and quickly-made implement for stirring and mixing manure and fertilizers with the soil, may be

Fig. 142.—A STIRRER MADE OF A CEDAR STEM.

made as follows: A cedar stem is cut about eight feet long, and the branches cut off several inches from the stem, leaving long spurs on all sides for its whole length, as shown in figure 142. A horse is hitched by a chain to the butt end, and the driver guides the implement by a rope fastened to the rear end of the stem. By means of the guide-rope the implement may be lifted over or around obstacles, and turned at the end of the field. Such an implement is specially useful in mixing fertilizers with the soil, when applied in drills for hoed crops.

A HINT FOR PIG KILLING.

Lay a log chain across the scalding trough, and put the pig upon it. Cross the chain over the animal, as

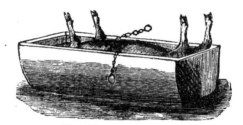

Fig. 143.—SCALDING A PIG.

shown in figure 143. A man at each end of the chain can easily turn the pig in the scald, or work it to and fro as desired.

MENDING BROKEN TOOLS.

Farming tools, such as shovels, rakes, forks, etc., that are much used, will often, through carelessness or accident, become broken, and, with most men, that means to be thrown one side, as utterly useless. By exercising a little ingenuity, they could in a short time be fitted up to do service for several years. The head of hand-rakes often becomes broken at the point where the handle enters, and not unfrequently the handle itself is broken off where it enters the head. In either case the break is easily made good by attaching a small piece of wood to

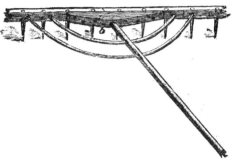

Fig. 144.—A MENDED RAKE.

the head, by small nails or screws, as shown in figure 144. Should the head be broken where one of the bows

Fig. 145.—MENDING A SHOVEL.

passes through, it may be mended in a like manner. *b.* Shovels and spades, owing to the great strain to which they are often subjected, especially by carelessly prying with them, crow-bar fashion, are frequently broken, and usually at the point where the wood enters the blade. This break, bad as it is, should not consign the broken parts to the rubbish pile, especially if the blade and the handle be otherwise in fair condition. Remove the iron straps or ferule from the handle; firmly rivet a strip of iron, *a*, figure 145, on top of the handle, and a similar one underneath, to the blade and handle, as shown in the engraving. Other broken tools may be made to do good service by proper mending.

A LARGE FEED-RACK.

The width of the rack is seven feet, but it can be any length desired; hight, ten feet; hight of manger, two and a half feet; width, one and one-half foot. Cattle can eat from both sides. The advantage of such a rack,

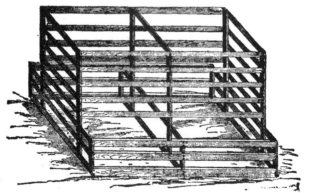

Fig. 146.—A LARGE YARD FODDER-RACK.

shown in figure 146, is that it will hold a large quantity of feed, and so securely that very little can be wasted by the feeding animals.

BARN DOOR FASTENING.

One of the best barns in the country has its large double doors fastened by a bar of iron, about six feet long, which is bolted to one of the doors at its middle point. The ends of the bar are notched, one upon the upper and the other on the under side, to fit over sockets or "hooks" that are bolted to the doors. One hook

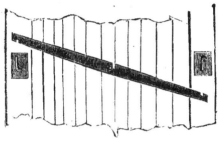

Fig. 147.—IRON BAR DOOR FASTENING.

bends upward, and the other downward, and the bar moves in the arc of a circle when the door is being unfastened or bolted. The construction of this door fastening is shown in figure 147. A wooden bar may replace the iron one, and may be of a size and length sufficient

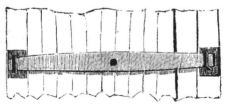

Fig. 148.—WOODEN BAR DOOR FASTENING.

to make the fastening secure. A wooden bar is shown in figure 148. Such a method of fastening could be used for a single door, provided it needs to be opened and closed only from the inside. By putting a pin in the bar near the end that passes by the door-post, so that it will reach through a slot in the door, such a "latch" might be used for any door.

A "FORK" STABLE SCRAPER.

A very handy stable scraper is made of an inch board, five inches wide, and about eight inches longer than the width of a four-tined fork. Bore a hole for each tine a quarter inch in diameter from the edge of the board to about two inches from the opposite edge, the holes passing out upon the side. The lower part of the board is bevelled behind, thus forming a good scraping edge. After the coarse manure is pitched up, the fork is in-

Fig. 149.—A "FORK" BARN SCRAPER.

serted in the holes of the board, and a scraper is at once ready for use, figure 149. To store it, nail a cleat on the floor two inches from the wall, and secure the scraper behind this cleat; place one foot upon the board and withdraw the fork. Notches may be cut in the edge of the board opposite each hole, to assist in placing the tines.

A METHOD OF CURING HAY.

A method of curing hay which has been used for several years with entire satisfaction consists in taking

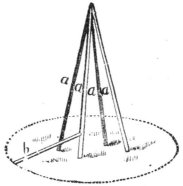

Fig. 150.—THE FRAME.

four slender stakes six feet long, *a, a, a, a* (figure 150),

Fig. 151.—THE SMALL STACK.

fastened together at the upper ends with a loose joint similar to that of an ordinary tripod. One end of the fifth stake, *b*, rests on one of the four legs about a foot from the ground, the other end resting on the ground. The hay is stacked around this frame nearly to the top of the stakes, after which the stake, *b*, is withdrawn, and then the four upright stakes are removed. This is done by two men with hay forks, who raise them directly upwards. As soon as the legs are lifted from the ground the pressure of the hay brings them together, and they can be removed with ease, leaving a small stack of hay, as shown in figure 151, with an air passage running from the bottom upwards through the centre of the small stack, as indicated by the dotted lines.

GRANARY CONVENIENCES.

The better plan for constructing grain bins is to have the upper front boards movable, that the contents may

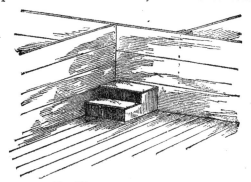

Fig. 152.—STEPS IN A GRANARY.

be more readily reached as they lessen. But as there are tens of thousands of granaries where the front bin boards are firmly nailed, a portable step, like that shown in figure 152, is almost a necessity. It should have two steps of nine inches each, and be one foot wide, and two feet long on top. It is light and is easily moved about the granary.

Every owner of a farm needs a few extra sieves, which, when not in use, are usually thrown in some corner, or

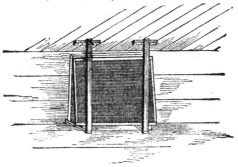

Fig. 153.—A SIEVE RACK.

laid on a box or barrel to be knocked about and often injured by this rough handling, besides being frequently in the way. A little rack, which may be readily made

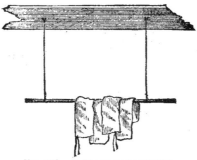

Fig. 154.—A GRAIN BAG HOLDER.

above one of the bins in the granary, as shown in figure 153, is convenient to put sieves out of the way, and keep them from injury.

Grain bags are too expensive and valuable to be scattered about the buildings. A simple mode of securing them is shown, which is at once cheap and safe. In the ceiling over the bins, staples are driven about four feet apart, to which are attached pieces of wire two feet in length. To these wires is fastened a pole five feet in length, over which the bags are thrown when not in use, and they are then out of reach of mice from the bins and wall, as shown in figure 154.

A NON-SLIPPING CHAIN FOR BOULDERS.

One great trouble in hauling boulders or large stones with team and chain is the liability of the chain to slip off, especially if the stone is nearly round. By the use of the contrivance shown in figure 155, nearly all of this trouble is avoided. It consists in passing two log chains around the stone and connecting them a few inches above the ground by a short chain or even a piece of rope or wire. Connect the chains in a similar manner near the top of the stone. The ends of the draught chains are attached to the whipple-trees in any way desired. In

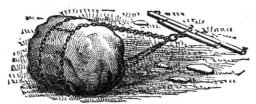

Fig. 155.—METHOD OF FASTENING CHAINS ON A BOULDER.

hauling down an incline, or where the ground is very rough, it will be best to wrap each chain clear around the stone, connecting with whipple-trees by a single chain, thereby preventing a possibility of the chains becoming detached or misplaced in any way.

A PITCHFORK HOLDER.

Having occasion to go into the barn one night, we received a very bad wound from a pitchfork which had fallen from its standing position. This led us to construct a holder, shown in the engravings. The fork-holder is made of an inch board, of a semicircular shape, with five holes large enough to admit a fork handle, bored near the curved side. This board is nailed to a standing post in the barn. A strap or curved bolt is placed some distance below to hold the handles in

Fig. 156.—FRONT VIEW. Fig. 157.—SIDE VIEW.

place, as they rest on a bottom board fixed for the purpose. Figure 156 shows the front view of the holder; figure 157 gives the side view.

A CONVENIENT HOG LOADER.

Figure 158 shows the "loader" attached to a wagon, with the rack. The bed-piece consists of two pine boards, six inches wide by nine feet long. These are fastened together by three cross-pieces of the same material, of proper length, so that the "bed" will just fit in between the sides of the wagon-box. A floor is laid on these cross-pieces, on which short strips of lath are nailed, to prevent hogs from slipping. At one end the sides are notched to fit on the bottom of the wagon-box. There are two staples on each side by which the sides are fastened on. The "rack" is made like an ordinary top-box, with the exception that each side is composed of three narrow boards about four inches apart, and nailed to three cleats (the two end cleats to be on the inside, and the middle one on the outside of the rack), and projecting down

Fig. 158.—RACK FOR LOADING HOGS.

the side of the wagon-box. End-boards are made and fastened in like those of an ordinary wagon-box. For unloading the hogs nothing but the bed-piece need be used, which, being light, may be easily thrown on and taken with the wagon.

A HOME-MADE ROLLER.

Take a log six or eight feet long, eighteen or twenty inches in diameter, and put pins in each end for journals, either of wood one and a half inch, or iron one inch. Make a frame of two by four scantlings, or flat rails three or four feet long to suit the size of the roller. Bore holes for journals a little back of centre, and also inch-holes two inches from the back end of scantlings. Fasten these ends together with a chain or rope tight enough to keep the scantlings square with the ends of

Fig. 159.—A HOME-MADE ROLLER.

the log, figure 159. Fasten the front ends together with a stiff pole or rail, and put a heavy chain across the front, with one end around each front corner. Attach the double-tree at the middle of this chain. The draft chain and the pole will keep the front ends of the frame in position, and the chain behind will prevent the rear ends from spreading. When the roller goes faster than the team, the draft chain will slacken, and the front of the frame will drop and prevent the roller from striking the team. A roller is such a valuable implement that there should be one in use on every farm. Even a rough home-made roller is better than none, whether it is used to break up clods, or to compact the soil after sowing.

A LAND SCRAPER.

In districts where land needs draining, scrapers must be used. A very good one is shown in figure 160. It has one advantage over most scrapers: the team can stay on the bank while the scraper is thrown into the ditch. When the ditch is a large one, fourteen feet or more

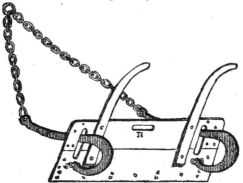

Fig. 160.—A LAND SCRAPER.

wide at the top, it is only necessary to lengthen the chain. The scraper consists of two boards, twelve inches wide and three feet long, fastened firmly together by two strong iron plates, figure 161, *p, p,* bolts, and rod-iron nails. The scraper-edge is made of an old cross-cut saw,

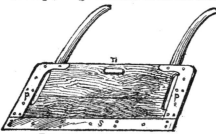

Fig. 161.—FRONT OF SCRAPER.

fastened on with rod-iron nails. Two notches are cut at *p, p,* for the hooks to pass through, also one at *n,* for a holder for lifting the scraper when necessary. To make the scraper work perfectly, the rod or hook should have the right bend, as shown at *a,* figure 162,

The hook is fastened to the scraper by two bolts, *b, b,*

Fig. 162.—THE HOOK-ROD.

figure 162, and small pins, *c,* when the land scraper is complete.

A HOME-MADE BAG-HOLDER.

This bag-holder is one of the most useful articles a man can have in his barn. It consists of a post, *a,* two by four inches, and five feet long, with six one-half inch holes near the upper end, as shown in figure 163. The bar, *b,* passes through a mortise and over the pin nearest

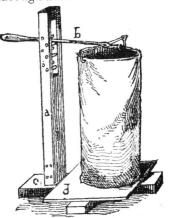

Fig. 163.—A HANDY BAG-HOLDER.

the bag, and under the other pin. This bar can be moved up or down, to suit the length of the bag. The post, *a,* sets in a bed-piece, *c,* two by three inches and two feet long. A board, *d*, eighteen inches square, fastened upon the bed-piece, furnishes the necessary rest for the bag. The mouth of the bag is held open by means of hooks placed on the ends of the cross-bar, with another beneath the main bar.

A SAFETY EGG-CARRIER.

In figure 164, *a* represents the bottom-board of the spring-box, near the edges of which are fastened six wire-coil springs or bed-springs. At *b* is represented a hole made in the board to receive the lower end of the spring, about half an inch of which is bent down for that purpose. Small staples are driven into the board to hold

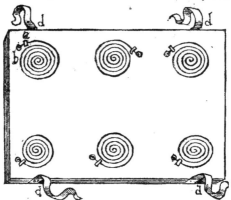

Fig. 164.—BOTTOM-BOARD OF SPRING-BOX.

the springs in place. Scraps of leather or tin might be tacked or screwed down, instead of using staples; *d, d,* are leather straps, an inch or more wide, and long enough to reach from the bottom-board, where each one is fastened by two screws, to the egg-box, after being placed on the springs. Figure 165 represents the side and end boards, which, when placed over the bottom-board holding the springs, forms the spring-box; screws fasten the side and end-boards to the bottom-board of the spring-box, pieces of tin being nailed around the corners of the box, to give it proper strength, the nails being clinched on the inside.

After securing the springs and straps to the bottom-board, the egg-box should be placed on the springs, and the points of the springs placed in holes previously made in the bottom of the egg-box to receive them. Now put a sufficient weight in the egg-box to settle it down firmly on the springs, and fasten the upper ends of the straps to the box, being careful to have the box

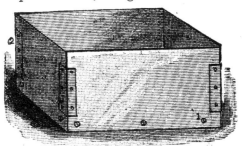

Fig. 165.—FRAME FOR HOLDING EGG-BOX.

set level. Having done this, take the part, figure 165, and put it down over the egg-box to its place, and make it fast to the bottom-board of the spring-box with heavy screws. The object of the bottom, figure 165, is to keep the springs from being strained to one side in going over rough ground. It should be made one-quarter inch or so larger than the egg-box, that the latter may have the benefit of the springs. Our former custom was to put a feeding of hay in the wagon-box, about midway from one end to the other, place the egg-box on the hay, and drive carefully over the rough places. But more or less eggs would be broken, the best we could do, whether they were packed in bran or put in paper "boxes" or

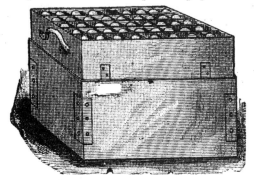

Fig. 166.—EGG-BOX COMPLETE.

cases. After setting the box on springs as described, place it on the bottom boards of the wagon-box, with one end directly over the forward axle of the wagon.

A BUSH-ROLLER.

Figure 167 shows a device which has been made for clearing sage-bush land. It consists of a roller, eight feet long and two and a half feet in diameter, coupled by a short tongue—six feet is long enough—to the forward wheels of a wagon. A standard at each end of the roller-frame supports a cross-piece just clear of the roller. Upon this cross-piece, about four feet apart, and extending to the bolster of the wagon, are bolted two pieces of one and a quarter by six-inch spruce boards. A board is placed across the centre for a seat, thus making a complete and easy-inclining "buckboard." With a span of good horses and this machine, figure 167, one can roll from eight to ten acres of sage-bush in a day; and it is so easily killed, that in two or

Fig. 167.—A HOME-MADE BUSH-ROLLER.

three weeks after such treatment, it will burn off like a prairie on fire.

BROOD-SOW PENS.

Figures 168 and 169 represent a convenient arrangement for brood sows. The pens are not equal to the

Fig. 168.—PLAN OF CHEAP PIG-PEN.

costly piggeries of wealthy breeders, but they answer a good purpose in a new country, where farmers are obliged to get along cheaply. Many who have built expensive houses say these pens answer a better purpose. First, there is a tightly-boarded pen (except in front), sixteen feet by twelve feet. This is divided into four nests, twelve by four feet. A shed roof extends eight feet from the rear. The tops of the nests are covered with boards, and the space between this room and the roof is filled with straw, making it wind-tight, except in front. When young pigs are expected during the cold weather of winter, hang a gunny sack in front of the nest. The doors, figure 169, are the most convenient. The board door is slipped in from the top, between pairs of cross-boards in the pig-pen.

Fig. 169.—DOOR TO PEN.

A RABBIT TRAP.

Rabbits are a great nuisance both in the garden and orchard, and a trap of the following kind put in a black-

Fig. 170.—A GOOD RABBIT TRAP.

berry patch, or some place where they like to hide, will thin them out wonderfully. A common salt barrel, with a notch sawed out at the top, is set in the ground level with the top. There is an entrance box, four feet long, with side pieces seven inches wide—top and bottom four and a half or five inches. The bottom board is cut in two at b, and is somewhat narrower than in front, that it may tilt easily on a pivot at c. A small washer should be placed on each side of the trap at c, that it may not bind in tilting. The distance from b to c should be somewhat longer than from c to d, that the board will fall back in place after being tipped. No bait is required, because a rabbit (hare) is always looking for a place of security. The bottom of the box should be even with the top of the ground at the entrance to the top of the barrel. The barrel should be covered closely with a board, as shown in figure 170. Remove the rabbits from the trap as fast as they are caught.

WOODEN STABLE FLOOR.

Elm makes an excellent and durable stable floor ; the fibre of the wood is tough and yielding. The planks should be secured in position by wooden pins, as they are constantly liable to warp. Any of the soft oaks make a good floor ; the hard, tough varieties are. unyielding, and, until they have been in use several months, horses are liable to slip and injure themselves in getting up. Both pine and hemlock make good floors, being soft and yielding, but they are not as durable as many other woods. Planks for a stable floor should be two and a half inches in thickness, and not laid until quite thoroughly seasoned, and then always put down lengthwise of the stall, and upon another floor laid crosswise, as shown at b, b, b, figure 171. The planks of this floor, or cross floor, should be laid one inch apart, that they may the more readily dry off, and offer a better **ventilation to** the floor above. Unless the upper floor is of material liable to warp, it should not be nailed or pinned, **but** made as close-fitting as possible. It is not profitable **or** necessary to have the stall planks more than eleven **and a** half feet in length, or extend farther back than **the** stall partition, as shown at *e, e*. This plan leaves **a**

Fig. 171.—MANNER OF LAYING A STABLE FLOOR.

wide smooth walk behind the stalls at *k*, so necessary for ease and rapidity in cleaning the manure from the stable.

Some horse-keepers prefer a slatted floor, similar to that shown in figure 172. Material of the proper length, four inches wide and two inches thick, is set upon edge, as at *h*, with a strip three-quarters of an inch thick and one and a half inch wide placed between the slats, the whole made to fit the stall as closely as possible. By this method it is quite impossible for horses to become **so** dirty as when lying upon a common plank floor, as the space between the slats form a most admirable channel

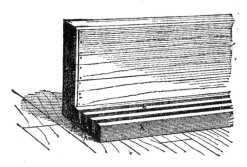

Fig. 172.—A SLATTED STABLE FLOOR.

for carrying off the urine. A few days' constant use somewhat clogs the passages, but they are readily opened by using a home-made cleaner, like that shown in figure 173. Stable floors should have at least one inch descent

Fig. 173.—A CLEANER FOR A SLATTED FLOOR.

in ten feet, and many make the descent three and even four inches in the same distance, but this is unnecessary. All stabled animals should stand upon floors as nearly level as is consistent with cleanliness.

A RAIL HOLDER OR "GRIP."

Drive two posts, *b, b*, figure 174, three feet long, firmly in the ground, four feet apart, between two parallel logs, *a, a.* A third post or "jaw," *c,* somewhat shorter, is mortised in a block placed between the logs, and out of line with, or to one side of the posts, *b, b,* so as to hold a rail, *d,* between the three. A lever, *e,* eight feet long, and heavy at the outer end, is mortised into another block, which is placed on the side of *b, b,* both blocks bearing against the posts. The lever and jaw are con-

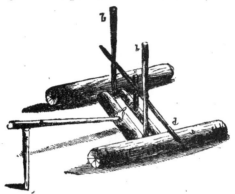

Fig. 174.—A RAIL HOLDER.

nected by a chain passing around the lever, over its block and through a hole in the jaw. An iron pin through a link couples them just enough apart to hold a rail firmly when the lever is on the ground. To remove the rail, raise the lever and rest it upon the small post, *f,* at the farther end, which slackens the chain.

A CHEAP AND DURABLE GRINDSTONE-BOX AND HANGERS.

A good grindstone, well hung, is one of the most valuable aids about the farm or workshop. Those who cannot afford to buy a very neat and handy grindstone frame of the hardware dealers, will find a frame and hangers shown in figure 175, that for convenience, cheapness, and durability is hard to excel. The frame consists of a well-seasoned "trough" of pine or other wood, fourteen inches square (or even one foot square), and from two and a half to three and a half feet in length, to which legs are nailed at *b, b*, four inches wide, an inch and a half thick, and bevelled at the top. Supports or hangers, *h, h*, are nailed firmly to the side, as indicated; they should be hard wood, and of a size to correspond with dimensions and weight of stone. The shaft may be of iron or wood; fit a piece of sheet lead, or piece of lead pipe, properly flattened out, in the top of each hanger; this will cause the shaft to turn easily, and prevent all squeaking for want of oil. The wooden plug at *r*, is for drawing off the water after each using of the stone, and should in no case be neglected. If one side of the stone is left standing in water, it softens, and

Fig. 175.—A BOX FOR A GRINDSTONE.

the surface will soon wear quite uneven. After the box is completed, give it one heavy coat of boiled oil; then in a few days apply a coat of lead and oil, and with even common care, it will last a lifetime. When the stone becomes worn, it is kept down to the water by simply deepening the groove in the top of the hangers. Always buy a long shaft for a grindstone, for in this age of reapers and mowers, the cutting apparatus of which must be ground, a long shaft for a grindstone is almost a necessity, or truly a great convenience. If the grindstone is to stand out-doors, always cover it with a closely fitting wooden box when it is not in use.

A "LADDER" FOR LOADING CORN.

Take a plank two inches thick, ten inches wide, and eight feet long. Nail upon one side of it cleats, of one-inch by two-inch stuff, at easy stepping distances apart. At the upper end nail upon the underside of the plank a cleat projecting four inches upon either side, to which

Fig. 176.—A "LADDER" FOR LOADING CORN.

attach small ropes or chains, and suspend the ladder from the hind end of the rack, so that one end of the plank will rest upon the ground. This makes a very convenient step-ladder, up which a man can carry a large armful of fodder, and thus load his wagon to its full capacity with greater ease than two men could load it from the ground. I find it of great convenience to me when hauling corn fodder alone. The "Ladder" is shown in figure 176.

One of the greatest annoyances in underdraining is the trouble arising from the outlet becoming choked or filled up by the trampling of animals, the action of frost, or even of water in times of freshets. This trouble

Fig. 177.—END OF TILE DRAIN.

is quite successfully overcome by the arrangement as shown in figure 177; it consists of a plank, ten or twelve inches in width, and five or six feet in length, with a notch cut in one side, near the centre. This plank is set upon

Fig. 178.—LOGS AT END OF DRAIN.

edge at the outlet of the drain, with the notch directly over the end of the tile, and is held in position by several stakes on the outside, with earth or stone thrown against the opposite side. This plan is best for all light soils, while for heavy clay land the one shown in figure 178 is just as good, and in most cases will prove more durable. It consists of two logs, eight or ten inches in diameter, and from three to ten feet in length, placed parallel with the drain, and about six inches apart; the whole is covered with plank twenty inches long, laid crosswise. Flat stones will answer and are more lasting than planks. The whole is covered with earth, at least eighteen inches in depth; two feet or more would be better, especially if the soil is to be plowed near the outlet.

A LOG BOAT.

A convenient boat for dragging logs is shown in figure 179. The runners, *d, d,* are two by six inches and four and a half feet long; the plank is two by nine inches, and three and a half feet long. A mortise is made at *h* for the chain to pass through. The cross-piece, *c,* is four by seven inches, and three and a half feet long, and worked down to four and a half inches in the middle. Notches are cut into the cross-piece four inches wide and two inches deep, to receive the scantlings, *e, e,* two by

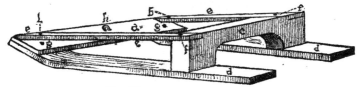

Fig. 179.—A STOUT LOG BOAT.

four inches, and three feet long, which are fastened down by strong bolts, as shown at the dotted lines, *f. f.* The two bolts in front, *b, b,* go through the scantling, plank and runner, while the bolts, *g, g,* pass only through the plank and runner.

It will be more convenient to load the logs by horses,

as shown in the illustration, figure 180. The boat is raised with its upper side against the log. The chain is fastened to the cross-piece at *a*, with the large hook, and the other end is put around the log, under the runner and cross-piece at *b*, and pulled through between the runner and scantling at *c*, when the end of the chain, *d*, is fastened to the whippletree. As the team is started, the

Fig. 180.—LOADING THE LOGS.

boat tips over, with the log on top. Loosen the chain from the two-horse evener, and pull it back through the runner and scantling at *c*, and through the hole.

CHEAP AND DURABLE WAGON SEATS.

It is tiresome to be jolted over rough roads, in a wagon without springs, with a simple board for a seat; but no farmer or cartman need adhere to this practice, when comfortable and portable seats can be so easily and cheaply made.

For a one-man seat, that shown in figure 181 is the simplest and most durable, and should be one foot longer

Fig. 181.—SPRING SEAT FOR ONE PERSON.

than the wagon-box is wide; the connecting blocks should be four inches high, and placed near the ends.

The one shown in figure 182 is arranged for two persons, the connecting block being placed in the centre, the ends being kept a uniform distance apart by bolts, with the nut upon the lower side, out of the way. The hole

Fig. 182.—A DOUBLE SPRING SEAT.

for the bolt through the lower board should be just large enough to allow the bolt to play freely.

In figure 183 is shown a seat a little more expensive, yet far more elastic. Both boards are eight inches longer than the width of the box upon which they rest. At each end of the top-board is mortised or nailed in a strip of hard wood, one inch thick, two inches wide, and about seven inches in length, which is made to pass freely up and down in a corresponding notch sawed in

Fig. 183.—A COILED SPRING SEAT.

the end of the lower board. At or near each corner of the seat is placed a coiled spring. A pin, passed through the wooden strip near the bottom, keeps the seat-boards from separating.

A BAG-HOLDER ON PLATFORM SCALES.

Figure 184 shows a contrivance which does away with the need of a second person in filling grain bags, and is both cheap and simple. It is attached to a platform scales for convenience in weighing, and consists of an iron hoop, nearly as large around as a bag. The hoop has four small hooks on it, at equal distances apart, to which the bag is fastened. Attached to the hoop is a piece of iron about six inches long, exclusive of the shank, which slips into a socket fastened to the front of the upright enclosing the rods, that run from the bottom of the scale to the weighing beam. This iron and hoop are fastened securely together. The shank should fit loosely in the socket, to let the hoop tilt down, so that the bag can be readily unhooked. There is an eyebolt in the hoop where the iron rod joins it, and a rod

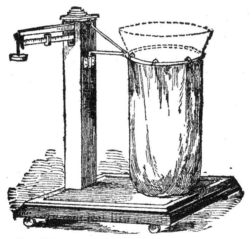

Fig. 184.—A BAG-HOLDER ON PLATFORM SCALES.

with a hook on the upper end is fastened into it. This rod reaches to a staple fastened above the socket on the upright of the scales, as shown in figure 184. When the hook on the end of this rod is slipped into the staple, it lifts the hoop to a level position, and is of sufficient strength to hold a bag of grain. The hoop should be high enough to allow a bag to clear the platform of the scales. When filled, a sharp blow of the hand removes the hook of the sustaining rod, and lets the hoop tilt downward, when the bag rests on the platform. The hoop can be swung to one side, and entirely out of the way. We have a sort of hopper made out of an old dish pan with the bottom cut out. It is very convenient to keep grain from spilling while filling the bags.

MAKING BOARD DRAINS.

On very many farms, wooden drains are used in place of tiles, but mostly in new districts where timber is cheap, and tiles cannot be purchased without much expense. They will answer the purpose well, without much expense. Wooden drains, if laid deep enough, so that the

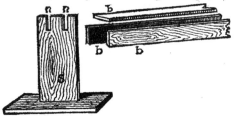

Fig. 185.—FRAME FOR HOLDING BOARDS.

frost will not affect them, will last many years. We know of an old drain that has been built twelve years, where the timber is still sound in some spots. To make wooden drains, two men are generally required—one to hold the boards, and another to nail them. This mode of constructing board drains can be improved upon by making a "standard," which consists of an upright board three feet high, having notches cut into it six inches apart, one inch wide, and several inches deep, to hold the boards firm. The boards *b, b*, figure 185, are laid into the notches, *n, n,* when the top *b*oard can be quickly and easily nailed on. Another method, shown in figure 186, consists of two posts, driven into the ground about three feet from a fence, with a board nailed across from

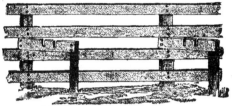

Fig. 186.—FRAME BY A FENCE.

each post to the fence. Notches are then cut into each cross-board several inches deep, when it will be ready for use.

PUT THINGS IN THEIR PLACES.

We have in mind an extensive and well-tilled farm, where a large space in the end of a wagon-shed is called a tool-room. The tools are deposited in the barn, wood-shed, crib, in the field, hung in trees, anywhere but in the right place. The tool-room floor is covered with heaps of rusty iron, old leather, broken harness, fragments of tools, and other accumulations of forty years of farm life. The old iron should be sorted over, and any bolts, nuts, rings, hooks, etc., that are good, may be put in a box by themselves, and the rest should go to the junk dealer. There may be a few straps and buckles of the old harness worth saving. If so, oil the leather and lay it aside; throw the rest out of sight. Put a light scaffold near the roof-plates, and pile many small articles upon it; they will be out of the way and within easy reach. Make a drawer in a bench for holding small tools, and a row of pigeon-holes for nails, screws, etc. Across one end of the room, in front of the plate, fasten

a long narrow board by pegs, so that a six-inch space will **be** between the plates and board. Let the pegs be a foot **apart** and stand out beyond the board some five or six **inches,** upon which to hang long-handled tools. About **four** feet from the floor make a similar rack for shovels,

Fig. 187.—SECTION OF A TOOL ROOM.

picks, chains, whippletrees, etc. Bring all the tools to **this** room, except those needed every day in the barn. **There** should be a paint-pot in the tool-house, to use on **a** rainy day for painting the tools. Figure 187 shows a **section** of a well-arranged tool-room.

Lay down this law to your man-servant and maid-**servant,** to your son and daughter, to your borrowing neighbor and your good wife, to all that in your house abide, and to yourself: "That whoever uses a tool shall, when his or her work is done, return the tool to the tool-houseand place it where it was found."

WATER-SPOUT AND STOCK-TROUGH.

The water-trough for the stock should not be immediately under the pump spout, but some ten or twelve feet distant, a spout being employed to convey the water. This spout (figure 188) is made of two good pieces of clean white pine, inch stuff. One piece is four inches and the other is three inches wide, nicely planed and jointed. If securely nailed, it will not leak for a long time, but when it does, let it dry, and then run hot pitch down the joint. The trough should be made of two-inch oak, or pine of the same thickness may do, if kept well painted, inside

Fig. 188.—WATER-TROUGH.

and out. Instead of nailing on the sides to the ends, have the ends fitted into grooves, and use rods, with burrs on them to bring the sides up tightly to their places. When the trough leaks, tighten up the burrs a little with a wrench, and the trouble generally ceases for the time. Even the best trough is by no means very lasting, and its longevity is increased by keeping it thoroughly painted, inside and out, with good paint. Where there are horses that destroy the edges of the trough with their teeth, it is a good plan to rim it all around with thin iron. The spout, where it goes under the pump, can have a strap slipped over the nozzle of the pump.

A DESIRABLE MILKING SHED.

(See Frontispiece.)

We recently observed a peculiarly constructed building used as a milking shed during the warmer portions of the year. It is a common frame structure, thirty-five feet in length and eighteen feet wide, with posts eight feet high. The sides and ends are boarded up and down with eight-inch stuff, leaving a space three inches wide between the boards for ventilation, light, etc. A row of common stanchions are placed along each side. A door is made at one end, through which the cows enter. If grain is fed, it is placed in position before the cows are admitted. A small quantity of salt is kept on the floor, immediately in front of the stanchions, thus allowing the cows to obtain a supply twice each day. This manner of salting is an inducement for the cows to enter the building and take their accustomed places; it also tends to keep them quiet while milking. This arrangement, for cleanliness, ventilation, etc., is far superior to the common basement stables, and is a great improvement over the usual plan of milking in the open yard, where broken stools, spilled milk, and irritable tempers are the rule rather than the exception. No matter how stormy it may be without, this shed always secures a dry place, with comparative quiet. A greater supply of milk is obtained with such a shed. The floor of the stable portion may be of earth, covered with coarse gravel.

WEAR PLATE FOR HARNESS TUGS AND COLLARS.

In the manufacture of improved harness trimmings, devices are employed to prevent, as much as possible, the wear and breaking of the tugs where the buckle tongue enters them. This is quite an important point with those purchasing new harness. The simple contrivance, such as is shown in figure 189, consists of a

Fig. 189.—WEAR PLATE FOR TUG.

thin iron plate a little narrower than the tug, and about two inches in length, with a hole for the reception of the buckle-tongue when placed between the tug and the buckle. The strain from the buckle upon the tug is equally distributed over the entire surface against which the plate rests. A harness thus equipped will last many years longer than those not so provided. There is another part of the harness that is the cause of much trouble— mainly, the part where the tug comes in contact with the collar. The tug and its fastenings to the hame soon wear through the collar, and compress the latter so much that during heavy pulling the horse's shoulder is often pinched, chafed, and lacerated. This is worse than carelessness on the part of the teamster, as the collar should be kept plump at this point, by re-filling when needed ; yet, very much of this trouble may be avoided by tacking to the

Fig. 190.—WEAR PLATE FOR HAMES.

underside of the hame a piece of leather, as shown in figure 190. It will be found not only to save the collar, but prevent chafing of the shoulder.

POTABLE WATER FENCE.

The water fence, shown in figure 191, is one of the best we have ever used, and those who live near or on tide-water will find such an one very useful. This fence is made usually of pine; the larger pieces, those which lie on the ground and parallel with the "run" of the fence, are three by four-inch pieces, hemlock or pine, and connected by three cross-bars, of three by four-inch pieces, mortised in, three feet apart. Into the middle

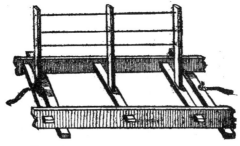

Fig. 191.—SECTION OF A WATER FENCE.

of these three cross-pieces (the upright or posts), are securely mortised, while two common boards are nailed underneath the long pieces to afford a better rest for the structure when floating on the water, or resting on the ground. Stout wires are stretched along the posts, which are four feet high.

DITCH CLEANER AND DEEPENER.

Open ditches require constant attention to prevent their being choked with weeds and accumulations of silt.

Keeping them cleaned out with a hoe is a difficult and laborious task, while drawing a log down them is unsatisfactory and ineffective. To run a plow along the bottom is not only a disagreeable task, but frequently does more harm than good. In view of these facts we devised the simple and effective implement shown in figure 192.

The centre-piece is six by eight-inch oak, eight feet long, and shaped as shown in the cut. The wings, or

Fig. 192.—A CLEANER FOR DITCHES.

scrapers, are made of oak, or other tough wood; boards ten inches wide. They are attached to the centre-piece at the forward end of an inch bolt that passes through all three pieces. They are connected at the rear end by a strong cross-bar of hard-wood. Twelve or fifteen inches back of this bar the end of the lever is attached to the centre-piece by an eye and staple. A short chain is fastened underneath the centre of the cross-bar, with an eye-bolt passing through it. The chain is attached to the lever with a hook, and may be lengthened or shortened as required.

The implement is drawn by two horses, one on each side of the ditch. A man stands on the centre-piece, and handles the lever. If the ditch is narrow and deep, the rear ends of the wings or scrapers will naturally be forced upward to a considerable height, and the lever chain should be lengthened accordingly. In wide, shallow ditches, the cross-bar will nearly rest on the centre-piece, and the chain must be short. The scrapers are forced down hard by bearing on the lever. If the bottom of the ditch is hard, two men may ride on the implement. Long weeds catching on the forward end must be removed with a fork. A strap of iron is fastened across the forward ends of the scrapers where the bolt passes through to prevent them from splitting. The horses may be kept the proper distance apart by means of a light pole fastened to the halter rings.

HOW TO BUILD A DAM.

A form of crib, shown in figure 193, is built of logs, about eight feet square for ordinary streams. The bottom should have cross-pieces pinned on the lowest logs. The stones that fill the crib rest on these cross-pieces,

Fig. 193.—A CRIB FOR A DAM.

and hold everything secure. The crib can be partly built on shore, then launched, and finished in its place in the dam. All the logs should be firmly pinned together. The velocity of the stream will determine the distance between the cribs. The intervening spaces are occupied with logs, firmly fastened in their places. Stone is filled

Fig. 194.—LOG FRAME FOR A DAM.

in between the logs, and the bottom is made water-tight with brush and clay.

A dam without cribs, built of timbers spliced together, and reaching quite across the stream, is shown in figure 194. The frame is bound together with tiers of cross-timbers about ten feet apart. The sides of this framework of spliced logs are slanting and nearly meet at the top. The interior is filled with stone and clay, and planked over tightly, both front and rear. For a small stream with an ordinary current, this is perhaps the cheapest and most durable dam made. The engravings fully illustrate the construction of the two forms.

DRIVING HOP AND OTHER POLES.

The usual method of driving stakes, etc., is to strike them on the upper end with a sledge or other heavy article; but in the case of hop or other long poles this mode is impracticable. Hop poles are usually set by making a hole with an iron bar and forcing into it the

Fig. 195.—DRIVING BLOCK.

lower end of the pole. Poles and other long stakes often need to be driven deeply in the ground, and this may be done quickly, and without a high step or platform, by using a device shown in figure 195. This consists of a block of tough wood, one foot in length, four or five inches square at the top, made tapering, as shown, with the part next the pole slightly hollowed out. Take a common trace chain, wind closely about the block and pole, and hook it in position. With an axe, sledge, or beetle, strike heavy blows upon the block. Each blow serves only to tighten the grip of the chain upon the pole. In this way, quite large poles or stakes may be quickly driven firmly in the ground. To keep the chain from falling to the ground when unfastened from the pole, it should pass through a hole bored through the block.

A CONVENIENT GRAIN BOX.

The box here represented, figure 196, is at the foot, and just outside of the bin. It serves as a step when emptying grain into the bin. The front side of it is formed by two pieces of boards, hung on hinges at the outside corners, and fastened at the middle with a hook and staple. The contrivance opens into the bin at the back, thus allowing the grain to flow into it. When a quantity of grain is to be taken from the bin, the cover is fastened up, the front pieces swung round, giving a chance to use the scoop-shovel to fill bags or measures.

The box is a foot deep and sixteen inches wide. Its length is the same as the width of the bin. The first four boards, forming the front of the bin, may be made stationary by this arrangement, as, at that convenient hight, bags may be emptied over by using the box as a step. The cost of this is about seventy-five cents. An improvement has the front piece and ends nailed together,

 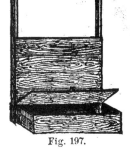

Fig. 196.   GRAIN BOXES.   Fig. 197.

and the whole fastened to the bin-posts by hooks and staples from the end-pieces, as shown in figure 197. Then the whole could be removed by unhooking the fastenings, and the cover could be let down, to form the lower board on the front of the bin, if desired.

A ROAD-SCRAPER.

A road-scraper is shown in figure 198, which consists of a heavy plank or hewn log, of oak or any other hard timber, six feet long, six inches in thickness, and ten inches wide. A scantling, *b*, two by four inches thick and six feet long, and the brace, *c*, are secured to the log, *a*, by a strong bolt. The edge of the scraper is made of an old drag-saw, and secured by rod-iron nails. The scantling serves as a reach, and is attached to the front part of a heavy wagon, when in use. When the road is very hard, it becomes necessary sometimes for the driver to stand on the scraper, to make it take better hold. The scraper should be shaped about as

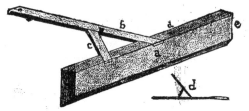

Fig 198.—A ROAD-SCRAPER.

shown at *d*, in the engraving, so as to make it run steady, and cause the loose dirt to slide to one side, and leave it in the middle of the road.

AIDS IN DIGGING ROOT CROPS.

Figure 199 shows a carrot and sugar beet lifter, made in the following manner: Take a piece of hard wood, two and a half by three inches, and six feet long, for the main piece, *a*, into which make a mortise two feet from

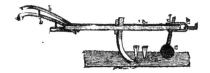

Fig. 199.—A ROOT LIFTER.

the wheel end, to receive the lifting foot (figure 200); attach two handles, *b, b*, at one end, and a wheel, *c*, at the other. This wheel can be set high or low as desired, by the set screw, *d*, in the clevis, *e*. Figure 201 shows the lifting "foot" separate from the machine. This is made of flat iron or steel, five-eighths inch thick and three inches wide, with a steel point and a small wing at the bottom. It is in the curved form seen in the engraving. The roots are first topped with a sharp hoe or sickle, two rows of tops being thrown into one, which leaves one side of the rows clear for the lifter. The horse walks between the rows and the foot of the implement enters the ground at the side of the roots in a

Fig. 200.

Fig. 201.

slanting direction, as shown in figure 201, lifting the roots so they may be rapidly picked up. The implement is very easily made to run deep or shallow, by simply changing the wheel and lifting, or pressing down upon the handles. A "foot," made in the form of figure 200, may be placed in the centre arm of a common horse hoe with sides closed, and used as above.

THE WOOD-LOT IN WINTER.

A few acres in trees is one of the most valuable of a farmer's possessions; yet no part of the farm is so mistreated, if not utterly neglected. Aside from the fuel the wood-lot affords, it is both a great saving and a great convenience to have a stick of ash, oak, or hickory on hand, to repair a break-down, or to build some kind of rack or other appliance. As a general thing, such timber as one needs is cut off, without any reference to what is left. By a proper selection in cutting, and the encouragement of the young growth, the wood-lot will not only continue to give a supply indefinitely, but even increase in value. A beginning, and often the whole, of the improvement of the wood-lot, is usually to send a man or two to "brush it," or clean away the underbrush. This is a great mistake. The average laborer will cut down everything; fine young trees, five or six years old, go into the heap with young poplars and the soft underbrush. The first point in the management of the wood-lot is, to provide for its continuance, and generally there are young trees in abundance, ready to grow on as soon as given a chance. In the bracing winter mornings one can find no more genial and profitable exercise than in the wood-lot. Hard-wooded and useful young trees should not have to struggle with a mass of useless brush, and a judicious clearing up may well be the first step. In timber, we need a clean, straight, gradually tapering and thoroughly sound trunk. In the dense forest, nature provides this. The trees are so crowded that they grow only at the upper branches. The lower branches, while young, are starved out and soon perish, the wounds soon healing over are out of sight. In our open wood-lots, the trees have often large heads, and the growth that should be forming the trunk is scattered over a great number of useless branches. Only general rules can be given in pruning neglected timber trees; the naked trunk, according to age, should be from one-third to one-half the whole hight of the tree; hence some of the lower branches may need to be cut away. All the branches are to be so shortened in or cut back as to give the head an oval or egg-shaped outline. This may sometimes remove half of the head, but its good effects will be seen in a few years. In removing branches, leave no projecting stub on the timber, and cover all large wounds with coal-tar. Whosoever works in this manner thoughtfully cannot go far astray.

SWINGING-STALL FRONTS.

The value of swinging-stall fronts is appreciated by those who have used them. They prevent the animals from putting their heads out into the alleys, and endangering themselves thereby. The "cribber," or "windsucker," has been made such by want of a contrivance like the one shown in figure 202. Anyone with a moderate knowledge of the use of tools can put it up, as the engraving shows how it is made; *a, a,*

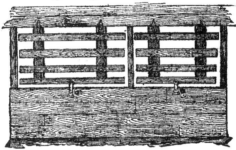

Fig. 202.—FRONT OF STALLS.

being straps to fasten the "fronts" down into place when they are not raised to feed the stock. Inch stuff constitutes the material. The cleats to which the strips are attached should be four inches wide, with the sharp, exposed edges taken off with a plane. The strips should be from two to two and a half inches wide, and attached with screws or wrought nails. The hinges can either be of wrought iron or of heavy leather. If more durable fronts are desired, oak, or yellow pine can be used, though it is much more expensive. Unplaned lumber will answer, but to make a neat, workmanlike job had better use planed lumber.

SAVE ALL CORN FODDER EVERYWHERE.

The profits of farming, as in other business, is the margin between receipts and expenditures. The receipts are largely augmented by saving wastes; these wastes in farming are enormous in the aggregate. The losses in this direction, that might be saved, would make the business very profitable, where it is now barely paying, or not doing that. Take corn stalks, for example. The leaves and a portion of the stems that produce each bushel of corn have a certain amount of nutriment that would support and increase the weight and growth of animals. Yet of our great corn crop, seventeen hundred to two thousand million bushels annually, only a very small part of the fodder is turned to much account. At the very lowest estimate, the stalks yielding one bushel of corn are on the average worth ten cents for feed, even including the great corn regions—a total of two hundred million dollars. At the South, generally, little value is attached to corn stalks as fodder. At the West, many farmers let their cattle roam in the fields, pick off some leaves, eat a little of the stalk, and trample the rest down; they pack the earth so much in trampling on it, that the damage thus done to many fields surpasses the value of the food obtained.

Nearly the whole of a corn stalk, except a very little of the thin, hard outside coating, affords nutritious fodder, if it is cut at the proper time, is well cured and judiciously fed. It needs to be cut when not so green as to mould in the shock, but not so ripe as to lose all its succulence and become woody. Experience and observation will generally indicate to every one the proper time of cutting it.

In shocking corn, the stalks should be kept straight and parallel. The shocks should be large enough to not have too many stalks exposed to the weather, yet small enough to dry and cure through. For somewhat heavy corn, twelve hills square (one hundred and forty-four hills), is abundant for one shock. A good mode of shocking is this: When the shocks are set nearly perpendicular, draw the tops together very firmly with a rope, and tie temporarily—two men working together. Bind with straw or with stalks. For the latter choose tough, nearly ripe, long, slender stalks. "Bend-break" the top with the thumb and finger every two or three inches. Thrust the butt end into the shock and towards the centre nearly two feet, and carefully bend-break it at the surface to a right angle. Insert a similar top-broken stalk two feet distant; bring the top of the first one firmly around the shock, bend it around the second stalk close to the shock, and then bend the second stalk around and over a third one; and so on, using as many stalks as required by size of shock and length of binders. Bring the end of the last one over the bend in the first, and tuck it under the binder into a loop, into which insert a stalk stub, pushing it into the shock to hold the loop. All this is more quickly done than described.

IMPROVED BRUSH RAKE.

One of the most disagreeable tasks connected with a hedge fence is gathering and burning the annual or semi-annual trimmings. It is generally done with pitchforks, and often causes pain. To have a long shoot, covered with thorns an inch long, spring out from a roll of brush and hit one square across the countenance, is exasperating in the extreme. To avoid this danger, many expedients are resorted to. Among the best of these is a long, strong rail, with a horse hitched to each end by means of ropes or chains eight or ten feet long. A boy is placed on each horse, and two men with heavy sticks, eight or ten feet long, follow. The horses walk on each side of the row of brush, and the men place one end of their sticks just in front of the rail, and hold them at an angle of about forty-five degrees, to prevent the brush from sliding over it. When a load is gathered, the horses are turned about, and the rail withdrawn from the brush.

The device shown in figure 203 is an improvement on this method. A good, heavy pole, eight to twelve feet long, has four or five two-inch hard-wood teeth set in it, as seen in the cut. These teeth may be twelve to

Fig. 203.—A BRUSH RAKE.

twenty inches long, and slide on the ground in front of the pole similar to those of a revolving hay rake. The handles are six to eight feet long, of ash or other tough wood, and fit loosely into the holes in the pole. Two horses are employed, one at each end of the rake. One man holds the handles, and raises or lowers the teeth as necessary. When a load is gathered, the handles are withdrawn, the ends of the teeth strike the ground, throw the pole up, and it passes over the heap. After a little practice, a man can handle this rake so as to gather up either large or small brush perfectly clean, and do it rapidly.

DIGGING MUCK AND PEAT.

A dry fall often furnishes the best time in the whole circle of the year for procuring the needed supply of muck or peat for absorbents in the sty and stable. The use of this article is on the increase among those farmers who have faithfully tried it, and are seeking to make the most of home resources of fertilizers. Some who have used muck only in the raw state have probably abandoned it, but this does not impeach its value. All that is claimed for it has been proved substantially correct, by the practice of thousands of our most intelligent cultivators, in all parts of the land. There is considerable difference in its value, depending somewhat upon the vegetable growth of which it is mainly composed, but almost any of it, if exposed to the atmosphere a year before use, will pay abundantly for digging. This dried article, kept under cover, should be constantly in the stables, in the sties and sinks, and in the compost heap. So long as there is the smell of ammonia from the stable or manure heap, you need more of this absorbent. Hundreds of dollars are wasted on many a farm, every year, for want of some absorbent to catch this volatile and most valuable constituent of manure. In some sections it is abundant within a short distance of the barn. The most difficult part of supplying this absorbent is the digging. In a dry fall the water has evaporated from the swamps, so that the peat bed can be excavated to a depth of four or five feet at a single digging. Oftentimes ditching, for the sake of surface draining, will give the needed supply of absorbents. It will prove a safe investment to hire extra labor for the enlargement of the muck bank. It helps right where our farming is weakest—in the manufacture of fertilizers. It is a good article not only for compost with stable manure, but to mix with other fertilizers, as butcher's offal, night soil, kainite, ashes, bones, dust, fish, rock weed, kelp, and other marine products. Dig the muck when most convenient and have it ready.

A CLEANER FOR HORSES' HOOFS.

The engraving herewith given shows a simple and convenient implement for removing stones and other substances from between the frog and the ends of a horse's shoe. Its value for this and other purposes will be quickly appreciated by every driver and horse owner. When not in use, the hook is turned within the loop of

Fig. 204.—A HOOF-CLEANER.

the handle, and the whole is easily carried in the pocket. The engraving shows the implement open, two and one-half times reduced in size. If horsemen keep this cleaner within easy reach, it will often serve a good turn, and be of greater value than a pocket corkscrew.

COLD WEATHER SHELTER FOR STOCK PROFITABLE.

Not one farmer in a hundred understands the importance of shelter for stock. This has much to do with success or failure of tens of thousands of farmers. Animals fairly sheltered consume from ten to forty per cent less food, increase more in weight, come out in spring far healthier; and working and milk-producing animals are much better able to render effective service. The loss of one or more working horses or oxen, or of cows, or other farm stock, is often a staggering blow to those scarcely able to make the ends of the year meet, and the large majority of such losses of animals are traceable to diseases due, directly or indirectly, to improper protection in autumn, winter, or spring. Of the food eaten, all the animals use up a large percentage in producing the natural heat of the body at all seasons, and heat enough to keep up ninety-eight degrees all through the body is absolutely essential. Only what food remains after this heat is provided in the system can go to increase growth and strength, and to the manufacture of milk in cows and of eggs in fowls. When heat escapes rapidly from the surface, as in cold weather, more heat must be produced within, and more food be thus consumed. In nature this is partly guarded against by thicker hair or fur in winter.

Any thinking man will see that an animal either requires less food, or has more left for other uses, if it is protected artificially against winds that carry off heat rapidly, and against storms that promote the loss of heat by evaporation of moisture from the surface of the body. A dozen cows, for example, will consume from two to six tons more of hay if left exposed from October to April, than if warmly sheltered, and in the latter case they will be in much better health and vigor, and give much more milk. Other cattle, horses, sheep and swine will be equally benefited by careful protection.

GOOD STONE TROUGHS OR TANKS.

Figure 205 shows an unpatented stone water tank, or trough, neat, effective, and readily constructed by almost any one. These troughs may be of any length, width and depth desired, according to their position, use, and the size of stones available. Here are the figures of the one shown: The two side-pieces are flagging stones, six feet long and twenty-seven inches wide. The bottom-piece is four feet ten inches long, two feet wide; and the two end-pieces, two feet long, twenty inches wide, or high. These stones were all a little under two inches thick. Five rods, of three-eighths inch round iron, have a flat head on one end, and screw and nut on the other; or there may

Fig. 205.—A STONE TROUGH.

be simply a screw and nut on each end; they must not extend out to be in the way. Five holes are bored or drilled through each side-piece, which is easily done with a brace and bit in ordinary stone. The middle hole is four to five inches above the bottom edge, so that the rod through it will fit under and partially support the bottom stone. The end rods are about four inches from the ends of the side-pieces, and stand clear of the end stones in this case so that the dipper handles hang upon them; but they may run against the end stones. When setting up, the stones being placed nearly in position, newly-mixed hydraulic cement is placed in all the joints, and the rods screwed up firmly. The mortar squeezed out in tightening the rods is smoothed off neatly, so that when hardened the whole is almost compact solid stone-work—if good water-lime be used. Almost any flat stones will answer, if the edges of the bottom and end-pieces be dressed and a somewhat smooth groove be cut in the side-pieces for them to fit into or against. The mortar will fill up any irregularities. A little grooving will give a better support to the bottom-piece and the ends than the simple cement and small rods. It will be noted that the side-pieces extend down, like sleigh runners, leaving an open space below. A hole can be drilled in a lower edge to let out the water in hard freezing weather, and be stopped with a wooden plug. Such tanks will keep water purer than wood, and last a century or longer, if not allowed to be broken by freezing. Any leakage can be quickly stopped by draining off the water and applying a little cement mortar where needed. When flagging or other flat stones are plentiful, the work and cost would be little, if any, more than for wooden tanks. They can be set in the ground if desired. The iron rods need painting, or covering with asphalt, to prevent rusting.

ARTIFICIAL FEEDING OF LAMBS.

It frequently happens that artificial feeding of lambs is necessary, and to do it successfully good judgment is required. The point is to promote a healthy and rapid growth, and not allow the lambs to scour. The milk of some cows, especially Jerseys, is too rich, and should be diluted with a little warm water. Farrow cows' milk, alone, is not a good feed, since it frequently causes constipation. It may be given by adding a little cane molasses. Milk, when fed, should be at about its natural temperature, and not scalded. Lambs, and especially "pet" lambs, are often "killed with kindness." Feed only about a gill to a half pint at first. After the lamb has become accustomed to the milk, it may be fed to the extent of its appetite. When old enough, feed a little flax seed and oats, or oil-meal if early fattening is desired.

There are various methods of feeding young lambs artificially. A satisfactory way is to use a one-quart kerosene oil can with the spout fixed so as to attach a nipple ; the milk flows more freely from this than from a bottle, on account of the vent. Let ewes and lambs have clean, well-ventilated apartments. When the weather is mild and warm turn them out into the yard. If it is not convenient to let the ewes out, arrange partitions and pens, so that the lambs may enjoy the outside air and sunlight.

A CONVENIENT BAILED BOX.

The common box with a bail, or handle, is a useful farm appliance ; it answers the purpose of a basket, is much more durable, and a great deal cheaper. Instead of a flat bail, we would suggest, for heavy work, a green hickory or other tough stick, to be chamfered off where it is nailed to the sides of the box, the portion for the

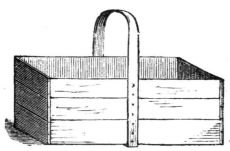

Fig. 206.—A BAILED BOX.

hand being, of course, left round. It will be found useful to have these boxes of a definite size, to hold a half-bushel or a bushel. A legal bushel is two thousand one hundred and fifty (and a fraction) cubic inches. A box may be made of this capacity of any desired shape. Ends a foot square, and side-pieces and the bottom eighteen and a half-inches long, will make a bushel box. If desired narrower, make the ends eight inches high and fourteen inches wide, with the sides and bottom two feet long. Such a box, shown in figure 206, holds a very little more than an even bushel. It is inexpensive.

SAWDUST FOR BEDDING.

We have tried for two years dry sawdust in the cows stable, and on the whole like it better than any bedding we have ever tried. It makes a more comfortable bed, completely absorbs the urine, and the cow is kept clean with less labor than when any other is used. The objection to salt-marsh sods, dried, or to headlands, and dry muck, is that they soil the cow, and make it necessary to wash the bag before milking. Straw, of all sorts, soon becomes foul, and, without more care than the ordinary hired man is likely to bestow, soils the cow's bag also. Dry sawdust is clean, and makes a soft, spongy bed, and is an excellent absorbent. The bag is kept clean with the aid of a coarse brush without washing. A charge of fifteen bushels in a common box-stall, or cow stable, will last a month, if the manure, dropped upon the surface, is removed daily. The porous nature of the material admits of perfect drainage, and of rapid evaporation, of the liquid part of the manure. The sawdust is not so perfect an absorbent of ammonia as muck, but it is a much better one than straw, that needs to be dried daily, in the sun and wind, to keep it in comfortable condition for the animals. In the vicinity of saw and shingle mills, and of ship-yards, the sawdust accumulates rapidly, and is a troublesome waste that mill-owners are glad to be rid of. It can be had for the carting. But even where it is sold at one or two cents a bushel, a common price, it makes a very cheap and substantial bedding. The saturated sawdust makes an excellent manure, and is so fine that it can be used to advantage in drills. It is valuable to loosen compact clay soils, and will help to retain moisture on thin, sandy and gravelly soils. There is a choice in the varieties of sawdust for manure, but not much for bedding. The hard woods make a much better fertilizer than the resinous timber. To keep a milch cow in clean, comfortable condition, we have not found its equal.

A CHEAP ENSILAGE CART.

The adoption by many farmers of the silo method of preserving fodder, has made it necessary to change the manner of feeding live stock. When the ensilage is removed twenty feet or more from the silo to the feeding rack, it is best to have some means of conveying it in

Fig. 207.—AN ENSILAGE CART.

quantities of from one to two hundred pounds at a time. This can be done cheaply and quickly by a small handcart, one of which any farmer having the tools can make in half a day. A good form of ensilage cart is shown in figure 207, and is simply a box eighteen inches wide, three feet long, and two and a half feet in hight. A wooden axle, of some tough fibre, is nailed to the bottom, ten inches from the end, and wheels from one to two feet in diameter are placed upon the axle. Suitable wheels can be made from planks, with cleats nailed on to keep them from splitting. Handles and legs are attached as shown in the engraving. The axle being near the centre, throws nearly the whole weight of the load upon it while being moved. It will be found easier to handle than a barrow, and not so liable to upset when unequally loaded. It is a cheap arrangement, and may be used for various other purposes as well as for moving ensilage.

MILKING AND MILKING TIME.

Any one who has had to do with dairy farming knows that there are a great many poor milkers, against a few who understand and practice the proper method of removing the milk from a cow. It is a well-known fact that some persons can obtain more milk from a cow with greater ease and in quicker time than others. In the first place, there must be an air and spirit of gentleness about the milker, which the cow is quick to comprehend and appreciate. It is not to be expected that a cow, and especially a nervous one, will have that easy, quiet condition so necessary to insure an unrestrained flow of milk, when she is approached in a rough way, and has a person at her teats that she justly dislikes. There must be a kindness of treatment which begets a confidence before the cow will do her best at the pail. She should know that the milker comes not as a thief to rob her, but simply to relieve her of her burden, and do it in the quickest, quietest, and kindest way possible. The next point in proper milking is cleanliness: and it is of the greatest importance if first-class milk and butter are the ends to be gained in keeping cows. No substance is so easily tainted and spoiled as milk; it is particularly sensitive to bad odors or dirt of any kind, and unless the proper neatness is observed in the milking, the products of the dairy will be faulty and second-class. Those persons who can and will practice cleanliness at the cow, are the only ones who should do the milking. It matters not how much care is taken to be neat in all the operations of the dairy, if the milk is made filthy at the start; no strainer will take out the bad flavor. Three all-essential points are to be strictly observed in milking: kindness, quickness, and neatness. Aside from these three is the matter of the time of milking. It should be done at the same hour each and every day, Sundays not excepted. It is both cruel and unprofitable to keep the cows with their udders distended and aching an hour over their time. We will add another *ness* to the essentials already given, namely: promptness.

A REVOLVING SHEEP HURDLE.

An easily moved feeding hurdle is shown in figure 208. It consists of a stout pole or scantling of any convenient length, bored with two series of holes, alternating in nearly opposite directions, and twelve inches apart. Small poles five or six feet long are so placed in the holes that each adjoining pair makes the form of the letter X. These hurdles are arranged in a row across the field, and the sheep feed through the spaces between the slanting poles. The hurdles are moved forward by revolving them, as shown in the engraving. By using two rows of these hurdles, sheep may be kept on a narrow strip of land, and given a fresh pasture daily by advancing the lines of hurdles. This method of feeding off a forage crop is one of the most effective and inexpensive for en-

Fig. 208.—A REVOLVING HURDLE FENCE.

riching worn-out land, especially if a daily ration of grain or oil-cake is given to the sheep.

LIGHTS IN THE BARN.

It is estimated that nine-tenths of all fires are caused by carelessness. Winter is the season when the lantern is frequently used in the barn, and we give a word of caution. Never light a lamp or lantern of any kind in the barn. Smokers may include their pipes and cigars in the above. The lantern should be lighted in the house or some out-building where no combustibles are stored. A lantern which does not burn well should never be put in order in the hay-mow. There is a great temptation to strike a match and re-light an extinguished lantern, wherever it may be. It is best to even feel one's way out to a safe place, than to run any risks. If the light is not kept in the hand, it should be hung up. Provide hooks in the various rooms where the lights are used. A wire running the whole length of the horse stable, at the rear of the stalls, and furnished with a sliding hook, is very convenient for night work with the horses. Some farmers are so careless as to keep the lamp oil in the barn, and fill the lantern there while the wick is burning. Such risks are too great, even if the buildings are insured.

A NEST FOR SITTING HENS.

The nest box shown in figure 209 can be made to contain as many nests as desired, and be placed in the poultry house or any other convenient place. When a hen is set in one of the nests, the end of the lever is slid from under the catch on top of the box, and the door falls over the entrance to keep out other hens. They rarely molest the sitting hen after she has held exclusive possession three or four days, and the drop may be raised

Fig. 209.—BOX OF HENS' NEST.

again. The box legs should not be over six inches long. The step in front of the nests, four to six inches wide, is a continuation of the bottom of the box. It is a vast improvement on old barrels, broken boxes, and other makeshift hens' nests so generally employed.

BARN-YARD ECONOMY.

A dark stream, often of golden color, always of golden value, flows to waste from many an American barn-yard. This liquid fertility often enters the side ditch of the farm lane, sometimes of the highway, and empties into a brook, which removes it beyond the reach of plants that would greatly profit by it. Mice may gnaw a hole into the granary and daily abstract a small quantity of grain, or the skunks may reduce the profits of the poultry yards, but these leaks are small in comparison with that from the poorly-constructed and ill-kept barn-yard. The most valuable part of manure is that which is very soluble, and unless it is retained by some absorbent, or kept from the drenching rains, it will be quickly out of reach. Manure is a manufactured product, and the success of all farm operations in the older States depends upon the quantity and quality of this product. Other things being equal, the farmer who comes out in the spring with the largest amount of the best quality of manure will be the one who finds farming pays the best. A barn-yard, whether on a side-hill or on a level, with all the rains free to fall upon the manure heap, should be so arranged as to lose none of the drainage. Side-hill barn-yards are common, because the barns thus located furnish a convenient cellar. A barrier of earth on the lower side of the yard can be quickly thrown up with a team and road-scraper, which will catch and hold the drenchings of the yard above, and the coarse, newly-made manure will absorb the liquid and be benefited by it. It would be better to have the manure made and kept under cover, always well protected from rains and melting snows. Only enough moisture should be present to keep it from fermenting too rapidly. An old farmer who let his manure take care of itself, once kept some of his sheep under cover, and was greatly surprised at the increased value of the manure thus made. In fact, it was so "strong" that when scattered as thickly as the leached dung of the yard, it made a distinct belt of better grain in the field. The testimony was so much in favor of the stall-made manure that this farmer is now keeping all his live stock under cover, and the farm is yielding larger crops and growing richer year by year. If it pays to stop any leak in the granary, it is all the more important to look well to the manure that furnishes the food, that feeds the plants, that grow the grain, that fills the grain bin. At this season the living mills are all grinding the hay and grain, and yielding the by-products of the manure heap. Much may be saved in spring work by letting this heap be as small as out-door yard feeding and the winds and rains can make it, but such saving is like that of the economic sportsman who went out with the idea of using as little powder and lead as possible. In farming, grow the largest possible crops, even though it takes a week or more of steady hard work to get the rich, heavy, well-prepared manure upon the fields. More than this, enrich the land by throwing every stream of fertility back upon the acres which have yielded it. Watch the manure heap as you would a mine of gold.

A CHEAP MANURE SHED.

Many farmers waste much of their stable manure by throwing it out of doors to be acted upon by sun and

rain. We recently saw a very cheap, sensible method of almost wholly preventing such loss. A board roof, **ten** feet square, is supported by posts eight feet long **above** ground, which are connected inside by a wall of planks (or of poles, as the one examined was). Near the post at each end, stakes *a, a* (figure 210), are set, against which one end of the end-planks rest. This allows the

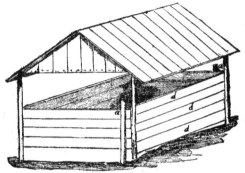

Fig. 210.—A SHED FOR MANURE.

front planks, *d, d,* to be removed in filling or loading. It is placed near the stable, preferably, so that the manure from the stable can be thrown directly into one corner, whence it is forked to the opposite corner in a few days, to prevent too violent fermentation. A frequent addition of sods, leaves, and other materials that will decompose, will increase the heap, and improve its value, supplying a manure superior to many of the commercial fertilizers, at less cost.

A SHEEP RACK.

The dimensions of the rack (fig. 211) are: length **twelve** feet, width two feet nine inches, and hight three **feet.** The materials are: ten boards twelve feet long, eight of them ten inches wide, one seven inches wide, and one eight inches wide; four boards, two feet nine inches long and twelve inches wide; six posts three by four inches, three feet long; sixty-four slats, sixteen inches long and one inch square; and two strips, twelve feet long and two and a half inches wide. Nail the two narrower boards in the shape of a trough, turn it bottom up, and draw a line through the middle of each side. Set the dividers to four and a half inches, and mark along the lines for holes with a three-quarter-inch bit, and bore the narrow strips to match. Set the slats into the trough, and fasten the strips on their upper ends. Nail two of the boards to the posts on each side, as seen in the sketch, and also the short boards on the ends.

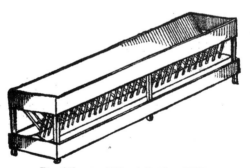

Fig. 211.—FODDER RACK FOR SHEEP.

Lay in a floor one foot from the ground, and set in the trough as shown in the engraving. Fit a board from the slats up to the top of the outside of the frame. The floor need not cover the middle under the trough.

A GOOD PICKET POINTER.

Fig. 212.—
FRONT VIEW.

On many farms a picket pointer might never be of use but anyone wishing to put up a picket fence a hundred or more feet long would save time by making one for the occasion. Pickets may be purchased ready pointed, but true economy consists in doing as much of the work as possible at home. This arrangement does not concern the fancy-topped pickets sometimes seen, but simply the popular square picket with pyramidal point, which makes, after all, one of the neatest fences that can be found for the yard. The waste material from building or fence-making, and an hour's time, will suffice for its making.

A bit of studding material, 30 inches long, has a hardwood strip three inches wide nailed on each side so as to project half of its width forward, thus forming a groove in which the picket is held, as will be seen later. They extend lower down than the central piece and with it form the front leg. The left strip, instead of extending to the top, however, is there replaced by a broader bit of hardwood board five or six inches long and projecting forward three inches, after which the projecting edges on both sides are sawed off at the proper angle for the picket points, say a little lower than 45 degrees.

Fig. 213.—SIDE VIEW.

The two rear legs are strips of lath five feet long, **fastened** near the top of the front leg and braced so that the forward part is not quite vertical. A block or seat 18 inches long is fastened across them 32 inches from the lower end, and so adjusted as to hold them one foot apart at the ground. The clamp by which the pickets are held in place consists of a half cylindrical block suspended by short lengths of strap iron and connected by a wire on each side to a foot lever, the action of which need be but slight.

Measure from the bevel at the top, down just the length the pickets are to be made, and place a block transversely in the groove at that point, for the stick to rest on. The groove should be at least one-fourth inch wider than the pickets, but a small wedge is inserted at the bottom on the left, so that as they fall into position they are crowded over to the right side.

To do the pointing, first cut all the pickets in a miter box to the right length, and at the proper angle to fit the water ledge over the baseboard, then place one in the groove of the pointer, thrust it down past the clamp, which it will push out, till it reaches the block at the bottom. Apply a little pressure on the foot lever to hold it in place, and then, with a sharp drawing knife, bevel the top, keeping the blade flat on the guides of hardwood; lift the picket, turn one quarter to the right, thrust down and cut again, and so on until it is finished. With poplar pickets one and one-fourth inches square, I have seen them pointed at a little more than one per minute, which is certainly much better than to lay off each one and cut with a chisel, as I have known a carpenter to do.

STERILIZING OVEN AND BOTTLE TRUCK.

Both oven and truck for milk can be made by any carpenter and tinner. Fig 214 represents the sterilizing oven. It is made on a light frame, of matched lumber; the inside is lined with zinc soldered at the joints. The door should be double, with beveled edges fitting loosely and having felt, rubber or asbestos packing all around the outside. No threshold or extra floor is required. Drainage must be supplied, preferably through the floor.

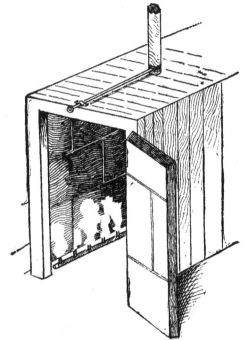

Fig. 214.—STERILIZING OVEN.

Steam is introduced by a row of jets eight to 12 inches apart in a steam pipe laid on or near the floor on the two sides and back and connected with steam supply. A valve just outside regulates the amount to be used. The pipes at the end just inside the door are capped so that no steam escapes except at the short nipples, or simply holes drilled in pipe, which will answer very well. A flue opens out of the top of the oven, made of tin, three or four inches in diameter and long enough to go out at the roof. This flue is closed by a damper just above the oven; except after sterilizing it is opened to hasten the cooling and assist in drying off the bottles which are inside. Such an oven is never to be used for the heating of milk, but in it may profitably be placed not only bottles, but tinware, stirrers, faucets, dishcloths, in fact, anything movable that comes in contact with the milk.

A convenient method of handling a large number of bottles is illustrated by fig. 215. This consists of shelves

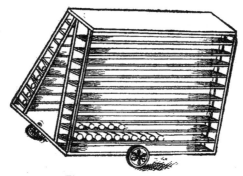

Fig. 215.—BOTTLE TRUCK.

so arranged that when the bottles are placed on them, necks inside, they are inclined sufficiently for the water to drain out of them readily, and the dust does not as readily enter them as it would if they were in an upright position.

The truck is of such a size that when loaded it will readily enter the oven and admit of the door being closed. A good way to mount such a truck is to place it on two wheels in the center, which bear the entire weight. The little wheels, one each at the front and rear, do not quite touch the floor when the truck is level; these latter are also fixed so as to turn around in a socket like a table caster. Thus rigged, the truck may be pushed around wherever wanted to load or unload and saves a vast amount of handling and inevitable breakage.

INEXPENSIVE BUILDING CONSTRUCTION.

Many farmers would like to put up a small building for some purpose or other but are deterred by the expense, the shingling or clapboarding of walls and the shingling of the roof being a large item in the expense account, both for labor and materials. The cut shows a

Fig. 216.—BATTENED BUILDING.

simple and inexpensive plan that will give good satisfaction. The frame of the building is put up and covered, roof and sides, with red resin-sized building paper stretched tightly and lapping so as to shed water if any should ever reach the paper. This costs only $1 per 500 square feet. The boarding is then put on, "up-and-down," and the cracks battened, as shown. Cover the boards and battens with a cheap stain or paint, and they will last for many years. Such a building will not only be inexpensive but it will be very warm, and in later years can, if desired, be clapboarded and shingled by simply removing the old battens.

COVER FOR SAP BUCKETS.

A good cover for sap buckets may be made at a cost of less than one cent by taking a wide shingle (*a*), sawing off four inches of the tip end and fastening to it a small spring wire, as shown in the illustration. The wire can

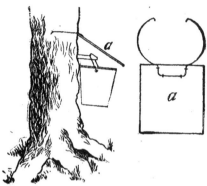

Fig. 217.—COVER FOR SAP BUCKETS.

be made fast to the shingle by little staples, or by using a narrow cleat like a piece of lath. The wire should be about 30 inches long and will cost less than half a cent. When done, spring the ends of wire apart and it will hug the tree firmly.

A HANDY TROUGH.

For watering or feeding cattle in the barn a handy trough is illustrated, gotten up by a practical farmer. It may be of any desired dimensions, but is usually about four feet long and one and one-half feet wide. If built slanting, stock can eat up clean any feed in it, or the trough can be readily cleaned. It is very handy for watering cattle in winter, as the trough full of water can be rolled down in front of the cattle, and from one to another as soon as they are through drinking. Where running water is handy, it can be let into this tub and quickly rolled in front of the cattle. With wheels made

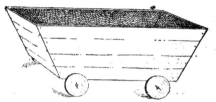

Fig. 218.—A HANDY TROUGH.

of hard wood this device will last for years, and can also be used for a variety of other purposes about the barn. It is one of those handy contrivances that save labor and add to the pleasure and profit of farming.

SUBSTITUTE FOR FLOOD GATE.

When a flood gate cannot be used, the device shown in the illustration is very desirable; *a* represents the posts or trees to which the device is attached; *b* is a piece of iron

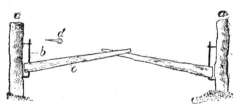

Fig. 219.—FLOOD GATE SUBSTITUTE.

in the shape of a capital L, the lower end of which is driven into the post. Further up is a small iron with an eye which fits over the upper end of this iron. This is driven in or turned in after the poles, *c*, have been placed in position. It is best to make the poles or rails, *c*, of some good timber. Use enough of these to make the fence or gate sufficiently high. These swing around on the rods as the water forces them apart. When the water recedes these can be again placed in position, and there is no loss of fence material. The ends are laid on each other, as in building up a rail fence.

HOOKS FOR SHOP OR STORE HOUSE.

A handy arrangement for hanging up articles, as for instance, tools in the shop, or meats and other eatables in the storeroom, is shown in the accompanying sketch. This plan is particularly to be commended where it is desired to get the articles up out of the reach of mice, rats

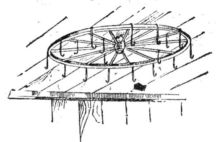

Fig. 220.—CHEAP SUPPORT FOR HOOKS.

or cats. Suspend a worn-out buggy wheel to the ceiling by an iron bolt, with a screw thread on one end and a nut or head upon the other. The wheel can be hung as high or as low as desired. Hooks can be placed all about the rim and upon the spokes, in the manner shown, giving room in a small space for the hanging up of a great many articles. This arrangement is convenient, also, from the fact that one can swing the wheel about and bring all articles within reach without moving.

IMPROVING A PASTURE SPRING.

The average pasture spring is apt to be a **mud** hole because not protected from the cattle's **feet**. Where a spring is to furnish the sole supply of water for a pasture year after year, it is worth while to make the most of it. If there is an old iron kettle with a break in the bottom, it can be utilized after the fashion shown in

Fig. 221.—A SPRING WALLED UP.

the cut, provided the source of the spring is a little higher than the point where it issues from the ground. With rough stones and cement, build a water-tight wall about the spring, setting the rocks well down into the ground. Set the kettle with the opening in the bottom, so that the water will rise to its top. A pure supply will thus always be at hand for the stock and a permanent improvement made to the pasture.

A GENERAL FARM BARN.

The ground plan shown in the illustration, fig. 222, provides sufficient stable room for ten cows, three horses, and a box stall, besides a corn crib and a tool house. These are all on the first floor. The building is 40x30, with a feed way running through the middle four feet wide. The building can be made any desired hight, but 20-foot posts are usually most desirable. On the second floor is space for hay, sheaf oats, corn fodder or other coarse food. There should also be on the second floor a bin for oats or ground feed. This is spouted down to the feed way, where it can be easily given out.

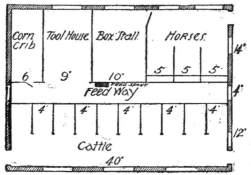

Fig. 222.—GROUND PLAN OF BARN.

The corn crib, of course, can be divided, if it is thought necessary, so that ground feed can be kept in a portion of it. There are plenty of windows in front and back, so that the building is well lighted. This barn can be built cheaply, and is large enough for a small dairy farm.

HANDY CLOD CRUSHER AND LEVELER.

One who has not tried it would be surprised to find how much execution the device shown in the cut will ac-

Fig. 223.—CLOD CRUSHER.

complish. Insert a narrow plank in front of the rear teeth of an A harrow, and the land will be harrowed, the lumps crushed and the surface leveled, at one operation. One can also, by stepping on and off the crosspiece, drag earth from knolls and deposit it in depressions, thus grading the land very nicely.

GIVING SEEDS AN EARLY START IN THE GARDEN.

The ground is often cold when the seed is put into the garden plot. To get the earliest vegetables, have a few boxes without bottoms and with a sliding pane of glass

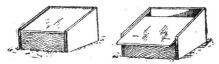

Fig. 224.—FORCING BOXES.

for a top, as shown in the cut. Let the top slope toward the sun. Shut the slide entirely until the plant breaks ground, then ventilate as one would in a hotbed, as suggested in the right-hand sketch. A few such boxes will make some of the garden products ten days earlier—worth trying for.

A POST ANCHOR.

Where temporary wire fences are used to any considerable extent, the corner or end posts may be anchored, as shown in the illustration. The large rock, *a*, is sunk into the ground as deep as the post is placed and the earth is solidly trampled above it. Place the wire around the stone before it is put into the ground, then pass it around the top of the post. By using a stick, *b*, the wire can be tightened if there is any tendency to become loose. To move the fence, loosen the lower strand from the posts. Begin at one end and make a coil about two feet across. Roll this on the ground, crossing and recrossing the strand of wire with the roll, about every foot of length on the strand. The barbs will hold it and keep the roll together. When the roll is as large as is convenient to handle, cut the wire and begin again. When replacing, fasten one end to the post

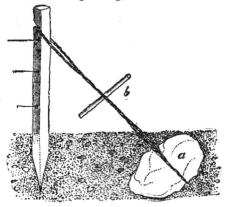

Fig. 225.—ANCHOR FOR END POST.

where the top wire is to stay and roll along the ground close to the posts. Follow with the second one a little further off, and then the third. Experience has proved to me that this is the easiest, quickest and best plan to remove wire fence, as after some practice it can be done quickly.

STONEBOAT FROM TWO BOARDS.

Most of the stoneboats in use are made with runners. I prefer to secure two boards the length desired for the boat, about 15 inches wide and three inches thick. I then measure 12 inches on top of the board and 18 inches on the opposite side, as shown in fig. 1. Saw through on the dotted line, turn the end of the board over and with four bolts fasten it as shown in fig. 2.

Do this with both boards, place them side by side and **fasten** with strong crosspieces. This makes a good boat,

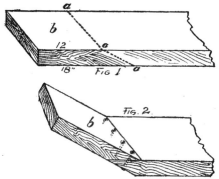

Fig. 226.—EASILY-MADE DRAG.

and in my experience is more desirable than any other kind. They can not only be used for hauling about the place, but are excellent for breaking roads during the winter.

A HANDY GARDEN BARROW.

A great improvement on the ordinary garden wheelbarrow is shown in the cut. The wheels have broad

Fig. 227.—IMPROVED BARROW.

tires, are light and run beneath the body—just in the position to balance the load when the handles are raised.

This barrow can be dumped from the side, as in the case of the ordinary barrow. It is thus possible to make over one of the old-fashioned wheelbarrows into the style shown, and that, too, at but small trouble and expense.

HOMEMADE TRUCKS AND WHEELS.

Low trucks are constantly of service on the farm. Now it is a feed car for the barn, or a two-wheel barrow

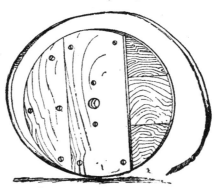

Fig. 228.—HOMEMADE WHEEL.

for the garden, or it may be that low wheels are needed for one end of a crate for moving sheep or hogs. The cut shows how to make any of them. With a "keyhole" saw cut circles from inch boards and screw them together with the grain at right angles, as shown. Two-inch hoop iron binds the edges and keeps them from splitting. Large iron washers help to hold such wheels firmly in place on the axles.

A ROLLER FROM MOWING MACHINE WHEELS.

Cast-off mowing machine wheels may be utilized very readily for making a land roller. Use narrow strips of plank with slightly beveled edges, putting them around the wheels in the manner shown in the cut,

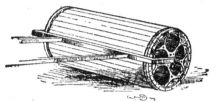

Fig. 229.—SIDE VIEW.

making slots in the planks to fit the cogs on the rims of the wheels. These strips are held firmly in place by "shrinking on" two iron hoops at the ends, as shown. The frame is attached in the usual manner.

MAKING A PICKET FENCE HEN-TIGHT.

On many farms the hens could be given free range if the garden fence were a sufficient barrier to the fowls. The cut shows a picket fence with a picket extending upward for fifteen inches every twelve feet. To these extended ends of the pickets is stretched a twelve-inch

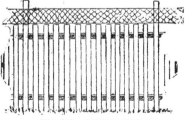

Fig. 230.—PICKET FENCE.

strip of wire netting, as shown in the sketch. In the prominence of the pickets the fowls do not clearly notice the netting until they fly against it. After a few trials they will give up the attempt to fly over. Poultry yard fence can be constructed in this way, using ordinary pickets, and above them any needed width of netting, according as the fowls are Brahmas, Plymouth Rocks or

---

BARREL STRAWBERRY CULTURE.

Probably many readers have heard of the plan of raising strawberries on the outside of a barrel. If one has only a small city or village lot, or "back yard," the experiment is well worth trying. The accompanying illustration shows one or two wrinkles that may help make the experiment a success. First bore the holes all about the barrel, then put inside a drain pipe made of four strips of board, reaching from the top to the bottom. The joints should not be tight. Now fill in earth about the pipe and set out the strawberry plants in all the holes and over the top. Put the barrel on a bit of plank, on the bottom of which wide casters have been screwed. The barrel can then turned about every few days to bring the sun to all the plants. An ordinary flour barrel will answer very well for trying this interesting experiment.

Fig. 231.—VIEW OF BARREL.

II.
FARM APPLIANCES

Old-Fashioned Labor-Saving Devices

FARM APPLIANCES.

CHAPTER I.

RACKS, MANGERS, STANCHIONS AND TROUGHS.

RACKS AND FEED-BOXES FOR HORSES.

There are various forms of racks, mangers and feed-boxes for horses. One of the worst devices is the old-

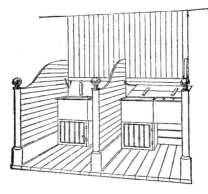

Fig. 1.—FEEDING RACK FOR HORSES.

fashioned hay-rack, extending from the manger high above the head of the horses, which are compelled to reach up for their hay. This is a most unnatural position for a horse, which does not, when out of the stable, take its food like a giraffe from trees, but from the ground. Aside from this, a high rack causes the double peril of getting dust into the lungs and other objects into the eyes of the horses. The above engraving shows an arrangement for hay and cut feed, or dry grain, which prevents waste, and is very convenient for the horse and its owner. The manger extends across the whole stall (a single one) and is reached through a falling door in the feeding passage. The hay box goes to the bottom, and has a barred door, through which the waste chaff may be removed, if it does not work out. The feed-box is protected by a barred cover, made of half-inch round iron, having spaces through which the horse can feed; but the bars prevent him from throwing out the feed or grain, in the attempt to pick out the best. The halter is run through a hole in the top of the manger, or a ring bolt in the side of the stall, and has a block of wood at the end, by the weight of which it is kept drawn tight, leaving no slack for the horse to get entangled with. When the horses are fed, the feeding door is shut and fastened by a button.

COVERED HORSE MANGER.

Horses will get their heads to the bottom of the hay

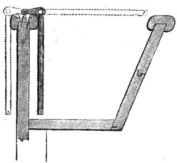

Fig. 2.—IMPROVED HORSE MANGER.

manger if they can, and will often throw the hay out, if not prevented. The illustration, figure 2, is taken from a stable, in which such annoyance is easily and simply prevented. A rack of iron rods, or of wood, is made and hinged to the top of the manger in front, so that it may be thrown up and over the front when the manger is filled, and then turned down upon the hay. The bars or rods are just far enough apart for the horse to get his nose through to the hay, but of course, he cannot get his head through. Iron is better than wood, because the horse cannot gnaw upon it. The bottom of every manger should be slatted, to let the hay seed and dust fall through—thus averting a frequent source of cough and heaves in horses.

FEEDING TROUGH AND HAY SHUTE.

To prevent waste of grain and hay, the trough and hay manger may be made as shown in the engravings here

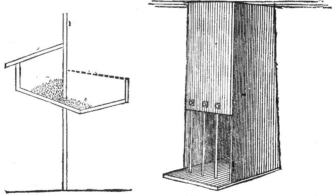

Fig. 3.—FEED BOX FOR OATS.   Fig. 4.—HAY FEED BOX.

given. The grain box (figure 3) is fixed in the front of the stall, a part of it projecting through the partition, into the feed passage, where there is a lifting hinged cover. The trough, of course, opens into the stall. In the center of the trough there is an upright division, open only for an inch or two, through which the grain or meal slides down little by little into the front division.

The hay shute is shown at figure 4. It comes from the floor above, where it has a hinged cover, which, if desired, is left open for ventilation. It increases in width downwards, to prevent the hay from lodging. The front is provided with small iron bars, to prevent the horse from pulling out the hay and thus causing loss. The bottom should be slatted, to allow the escape of dust.

DEVICE FOR BOX STALL.

For valuable animals it is best to have loose box-stalls. A range of such stalls can be built very cheaply, and as

Fig. 5.—FEED BOX AND HAY RACK IN BOX STALL.

the occupants need not be fastened, they can be quickly let out of the building in case of fire. The feeding arrangement for such stalls is shown at figure 5. It consists of a hay-rack in the corner, with a feed box near it. At the front of the feed box there is a falling door in the partition, through which, when it is half let down in a sloping position, the feed of grain, or the cut feed, may be placed in the box. The same arrangement may be used for the hay-rack, if the front is boarded up to the top; but if it is boarded only for five feet, the hay may be lifted over the top of it from the feeding passage.

There are times when the arrival of friends or other event calls for an extra stall. To provide for such emergencies, a feed box, and the way to use it, are shown in the engravings, figures 6 and 7. The trough, figure 6, is useful anywhere, it being a "fencetrough" or feed box. Upright pieces with mortises are made of inch stuff, and nailed on each side of the passage-way. Two by three-inch bars are used, entering into mortises on one side and dropping into slots on the other, the middle bar being keyed in. The upper bar is kept in

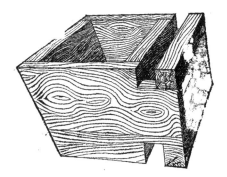

Fig. 6.—FENCE FEED BOX.

place by a swinging key put on the partition with a stout screw, and given a little play, so that it will drop by its own weight into its proper position. The feed box is made as in figure 6, with elongated sides extending through and beyond the rails or bars, with notches to receive the bars as indicated, made by nailing the pieces at the extreme ends across from side to side, as shown. The box being put on the lowest bar, close to the end of it, and the middle bar being placed in position and keyed, secures it. When the box is not in use, it is kept in the harness closet with the two lower bars. The top bar is

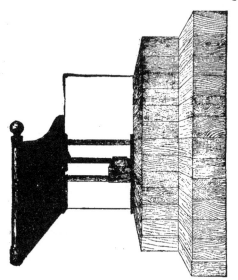

Fig. 7.—STALL IN PASSAGE-WAY.

generally left in place, to prevent horses, that might get loose, going into the carriage house.

VARIOUS CATTLE STANCHIONS.

In the engraving figure 8, one of the stanchions is shown open, and the other two closed. The pieces d, e, f, g, and h, are immovable, a, b, c, being the movable stanchions. The device consists of three strips, two inches wide, and three quarter inch thick, fastened to one upright piece by means of two bolts, d and b; the length of the strip is regulated by the distance between the stanchions. Bolts are also used at a and c, the bolt at *c* passing through a small block, two inches thick, which assists in moving the upright piece. A similar block, *e*, is also placed on the movable stanchion, upon which the block at *c* rests when the stanchion is closed.

The fastening *f*, and the piece *c*, are so arranged as to fall in place at the same time. It will be seen that the animal not only fastens herself in place, but she is doubly secured by the pieces *f* and *c*. (The block at *e* may be omitted if desired, and the device be used with the

Fig. 8.—SELF-CLOSING CATTLE STANCHION.

fastening *f* only). A badly hooked cow is often the result of careless hired men, and such carelessness is obviated by the use of the above arrangement. A cow takes her place in the open stanchion, and in trying to get at the feed below, presses against the lever *a*, brings *c* to place, and closes the stanchion.

The engraving, figure 9, shows how every farmer who uses stanchions can arrange to close all the cows in at the same time. The two-inch strip *g*, is planed on all sides, and made to move easily in the loops *e*, *d*, which are of heavy galvanized iron, bent below so as to allow the strip to slide, and are attached to the immovable stanchions by screws. The hard wood pins *a*, *b*, *c*, extend about two inches through, so as to catch the movable stanchions. A lever is fixed at *h*, and attached to the movable strip. This device is comparatively inexpensive, and can be attached to all kinds of **movable stanchions,** generally used for fastening cows. Even after it is put on the stanchions, it need not be used unless desired. It has the advantage in being separate from every stanchion. One, two, or more animals may be closed in by hand and the balance with this device. It in no way interferes

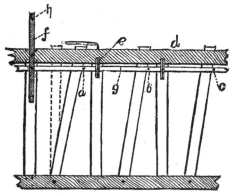

Fig. 9.—DEVICE FOR CLOSING CATTLE STANCHIONS.

with the necks of the cows, and saves a great many steps. If a person reaches over in front of the cows, to close them in by hand, he is in danger of being struck in the face with a horn. The above device removes this danger. It is simple and cheap.

The use of permanent neck-chains, locked on around the necks of breeding animals and young blooded stock, affords an excellent means of fastening the animals in their stalls. A chain and snap are attached to the stall, by which, the snap being caught into the ring of the neck chain, the animals are fastened. A better way is shown in the accompanying sketch of a cow stable. Two round stanchions are placed three feet apart for each stall, and are the only indications of subdivisions or stalls in the stable. A chain about eighteen inches long having a snap at one end, is attached by a ring to each stanchion. Both chains are made fast to the ring in the "necklace," and should have very little slack. If the stanchions are of hard wood, and smooth, the rings will slide easily up and down, but should not come within a

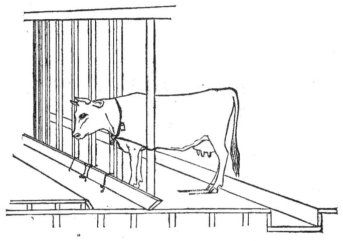

Fig. 10.—CHAIN CATTLE STANCHION.

foot of the floor. The cows will have free motion of the head to either side, can lie down and get up easily, but have very little motion forward and back, hence will keep on the platform and keep clean. They are besides kept perfectly devoted each to her own affairs, as she cannot reach over to either neighbor, to quarrel or to steal her forage.

The chief objection to the stanchion comes from its rigidity and vice-like grip, and any improvement in it should be in the direction of comfort to the animal, rather than in handier ways of fastening. The accompanying engraving shows how the rigid plan of the neck latches can be in part avoided. The greatest discomfort to stock, when stanchioned, comes when lying down. When standing, there is freedom of movement, but when the animal is down and attempts to rise, it is held fast. Stanchions made as here shown, avoid this. The neck-latches *a*, *b*, are not fastened at the bottom, but pass through the side block *c*, which rests on the lower stringer. By making this side block about eight inches shorter than the space between the uprights *d* and *c*, a swinging motion is obtained that gives considerable freedom. The bolt through the neck latch *a*, in the upper stringer,

Fig. 11.—STANCHION FOR DAIRY COWS.

should not be screwed up snug, but leave the latch a chance to play. It is usually the plan to set stanchions in a perpendicular position, and if the upper stringer is pitched over against the manger about eight inches, a great gain is made in the ease afforded the animal when it gets up, as its shoulder by this plan does not strike squarely against the latches, and avoids the necessity of "hitching back," to clear the stanchions, and thus prevents the extra strain and exertion often noticed in perfectly rigid, and upright stanchions.

FEEDING CRIB FOR PORK-PRODUCING SECTIONS.

To construct the crib shown in the illustration, four forked posts are set in the ground at the corners of a nine foot square. In the forks are placed stout poles and on these are laid the floor and is built the crib. The posts make the pen high enough for the swine to pass under it; hence, any corn that falls through it is eaten. The feeding floor is laid under and around the pen. In the greatest pork producing sections, nearly all the hogs are fattened from October 1st to January 1st, the corn

Fig. 12.—CRIB FOR FEEDING LOT.

being fed to the hogs as it is husked. In the pen shown fifty to one hundred bushels can be thrown—enough to feed for two or three days—when it is desired to do other work. It is an easy matter to throw the corn from the crib to the feeding floor, and as the corn will never remain in the crib longer than a week, no roof is required. Set the posts solidly in the ground, for if the weight of the corn should cause the crib to fall, it would kill any fat hogs that might be under it. The hogs cannot possibly get into this crib. Rats cannot infest it. The materials exist on nearly every farm, and any farmer can make this crib and in a short time.

It is often inconvenient to go among the sheep in feeding them, and there is always trouble from scattering hay or feed about the enclosure or from the animals getting out by the open doors or gates. Figure 13 shows how to feed from outside. The boarding of the pen for about eighteen inches in width, and about six

Fig. 13.—FEED-BOX FOR SHEEP.

inches from the floor is removed, leaving the bottom board in place. Then upright slats are nailed across this aperture inside the fold, allowing twenty to twenty-four inches for each sheep. The slats should be nailed so that an opening eight inches wide is left in the centre of this space for the sheep to thrust their heads through. If much narrower they will rub the wool off their necks.

A tight feed-box with flat bottom and upright sides is made of boards, and placed on the floor outside of and against the slats, and fastened in place. A horizontal swing door, two feet wide and the length of the feed trough, is attached with hinges to the outside upper edge of the feed box. Chains keep it from falling below a proper angle, and a button at the top secures it when closed. The swing door will keep the hay always in reach. With this arrangement one can feed either hay, turnips or grain without going among the sheep, distributing it much more easily than when they are crowding round him. He can also clean out the rack and feed box conveniently from the outside. The sheep cannot crowd each other when eating. When they are through eating, or when the rack is not in use, it may be closed up, shutting off drafts or keeping out dogs. It is desirable to have such an arrangement open under a shed, building or other protected spot, which can generally be provided. It will be found that sheep waste much less fodder and feed than when fed off the ground. The feed trough may be changed so as to come inside the fold, and the rack

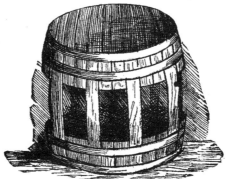

Fig. 14.—BARREL RACK.

made so the sheep can put only their noses through, but it makes the trough inconvenient to reach, and will tend to increase the waste of hay and grain in feeding.

A BARREL RACK.

The illustration, figure 14, shows a rack for feeding hay or straw to calves or sheep. Procure a crockery cask and cut two thirds of the staves, making holes from which the feed can be obtained. If calves are to feed from it, the holes are made slightly larger than for sheep. The animals feeding from this rack waste no food, and the strong cannot so easily drive the weak from it, as from the ordinary rack or manger. Lambs or calves are disposed to fight over their food, and it may be necessary to drive a stake about a foot from the hogshead and opposite the whole staves; this will effectually prevent the weaker ones being driven from their feed. The rack is easily filled, and the fodder, hay or straw may be fed from it without waste; and if moistened bran or meal are mixed with it, forming a complete ration, it may be fed in an economical manner, and be easily reached.

IMPROVEMENTS IN PIG TROUGHS.

One of the simplest troughs is shown in figure 15. The end pieces may be as long on one side as on the other, or

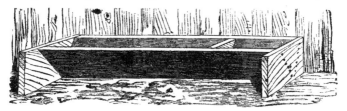

Fig. 15.—SIMPLE PIG TROUGH.

long on one side and shorter on the other, so that the pigs cannot turn the trough over. They may have crosspieces fastened in strongly every two feet, to make it less easy for the pigs to stand in the trough, and the trough may stand in the open lot or in positions near the fence.

Where the hogs are confined in pens, a trough is set in the pen as shown in figure 16. This is a fixture, must be strongly made, and be set at the bottom, on a level with the floor of the pen. A pig of one hundred

Fig. 16.—TROUGH INSIDE OF PEN.

pounds weight cannot stand in the trough; the latter can be cleaned out and the feed can be put into it from the

Fig. 17.—GOOD FORM OF PIG TROUGH.

outside. A good form of trough is shown in figure 17.

Here the swinging shutter keeps the pigs away from the trough, or admits them to it, at the will of the attendant, and the trough may be conveniently cleaned out or filled, without any interference by the ravenous herd. Figure 18, shows an improved shutter for the trough last described. The improvement consists of strong bent irons

Fig. 18.—IMPROVED TROUGH WITH SHUTTER.

securely screwed or bolted to the swinging shutter on the inside above the trough, so that a strong pig can neither get into the trough, nor push others away, and get the lion's share. Assuming that ground, soaked or cooked food can only be fed out of troughs with advantage, that pigs will eat and digest well a great deal more cooked food than they will raw, and that the more food a pig eats and digests the more profit there is in feeding him, it is easy to see the importance of good pig troughs.

The engraving, figure 19, represents a good trough for

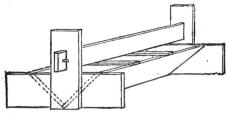

Fig. 19.—DOUBLE FEEDING TROUGH FOR PIGS.

pigs. The sides of the trough are firmly nailed to the end boards. An upright board, which runs lengthwise of the trough, divides it into two parts, and keeps the pigs from getting into the trough. Strips, four inches wide, nailed to the edges of the trough, divide the length into spaces for each pig to feed in, and prevent one pig from crowding the next one. There must always be more spaces provided than there are pigs to feed, in order to avoid fighting among the animals. These troughs may be made of various lengths, according to the number of pigs to be fed.

A PLANK TROUGH.

The common V-shaped trough, as ordinarily constructed, is a short-lived affair. How it may be strengthened and made durable is shown in the engraving, figure 20. The

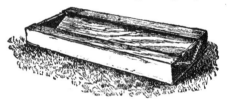

Fig. 20.—DURABLE TROUGH.

trough is made of two-inch pine planks, one six and the other eight inches wide, the end-pieces two inches longer than the extreme width of the trough. Side-pieces of inch pine are nailed at each end, with the upper edge flush and level with the top edge of the ends. A strip of inch pine is nailed from the inside edges of the trough to the outside edges of the end-pieces. When the upper strips become worn, they can be quickly replaced, and there is a hog-trough that will stand very rough usage. The trough should be put together with large wood screws, as these hold better than nails. Place white lead on the joints before fastening the trough together, to prevent leakage. Good tar, applied hot, will answer the same purpose. Some farmers paint the entire trough with hot pitch or tar, which acts as a preservative.

A PROTECTED TROUGH.

Pouring the slop into a trough, with forty hogs crowding and squealing about, is behind the times. When the

Fig. 21.—DEVICE FOR FEEDING HOGS.

slop is thrown into a trough, which passes through the fence to that from which the hogs drink, the stronger ones will crowd together at the conducting trough and get most of the slop. And about every other day a new conducting trough must be made, as the hogs will break it up in crowding for the slop. If it is made to terminate so high that they will not do this, when the slop is poured in, the biggest hog will get directly under it, and the slop, striking on his head and shoulders, will be deflected off to the ground. These evils are avoided by having a separate pen for the trough, filling it, and then letting the hogs in. But it costs something to have an extra pen, and often the space cannot be conveniently made use of.

This device, shown in figure 21, is a rack or screen, made so it will revolve on pins driven through the end-pieces and into the posts, as shown by the dotted line. The trough should be just long enough to fit in between the posts, where it is firmly secured. The most of the trough projects into the hog-yard, leaving merely enough projecting on the other side, to allow of the slop being poured in readily. The illustration represents the frame as it is when the pigs are feeding, and should be hooked into place until they are through. Before pouring in the slop, reverse the rack, so it covers the trough, the extra weight of slats on the hog-yard side keeping it in place until the trough is filled, when the rack is raised and hooked into place, giving the pigs access to their food.

TROUGHS FOR THE PASTURE.

Figure 22, shows a closing trough, nailed against a fence, that is very convenient for feeding bran, oats, corn,

Fig. 22.—FENCE TROUGH.

etc., to cows, calves, sheep and horses. The bottom is made three inches wide, and the outer side stands away from the other, both being set on the bottom. The end pieces of the trough are hinged to the side next to the fence, and the outer side is hinged at the bottom. Strips of leather answer for hinges. A bolt, or strap, passing through the trough at each end allows the outer side to come back just enough to receive the end-pieces, which are held in place by a pin passed through a hole bored vertically through the outer corner of each, and down into the slanting side. To fold the trough up, remove

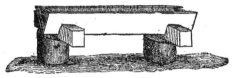

Fig. 23.—A LOW TROUGH.

these pins, and fold the end-pieces inward, bring the outer side up against these, and secure it in place with a strap. This trough is very convenient along the side of a shed, as it can be folded up out of the way. Another closing trough is shown in figure 23. The triangular end-pieces are held in place by cleats on each side. It is

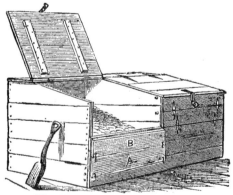

Fig. 24.—CONVENIENT GRAIN BIN.

not necessary to fasten the sides together, but they may be hinged at the bottom. To close the trough, the end-pieces are taken out and laid against one side, while the other side is closed against them. The sides are kept from spreading apart, when the trough is open, by the notches cut in the cross-pieces, upon which the trough rests. These cross-pieces rest upon large blocks.

IMPROVED GRAIN BIN.

A very convenient grain-bin is illustrated in figure 24. The lid or top is raised as usual ; then, when desirable, the front top board, which is hinged at the bottom, and hooked inside at the top, is unlocked and let down. This gives convenient access to the bin both in filling and in emptying—enabling one to take out the last remnants of grain or meal.

STRAW BALER.

Good, clean oat straw finds a ready market in cities for filling beds, and other purposes. But its quality and

Fig. 25.—BOX FOR BALING STRAW.

texture are greatly impaired by baling in powerful hay presses, and it is much better, therefore, put up by the aid of a hand press, which preserves the fibre of the straw unimpaired. Figure 25 shows the box and the method of construction. The binding cords are laid cross-wise of the box, resting upon the bottom, as seen in figure 25, and the ends extending through the notches, *B*, *B*, *B*, as shown in figure 26. A small forkful of straw is then

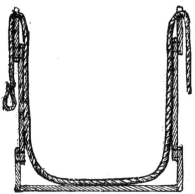

Fig. 26.—MODE OF ARRANGING THE CORD.

placed at each end, and one in the middle, and so on, until the box is filled and the straw packed down compactly. The cords are then brought together around the bundle and securely fastened.

WATERING TROUGHS FOR STOCK.

A good substantial water trough is an absolute necessity on every farm, and we here give illustrations of several useful forms. Figure 27 shows one made of planks or boards. The sides should be of one piece, and also the ends and bottom if possible. If made of two pieces each, joint the edges and join them with dowel pins, using the best white lead between the joints before driving the pieces together snugly. The end pieces should be let into the sides about half an inch, and both the sides and ends should be slightly sloping, so that the form secures freedom from danger of bursting in winter. In putting together, always use white lead on the joints. Use no nails, but draw the parts together with stout iron rods, having large heads on one end and screw threads on the

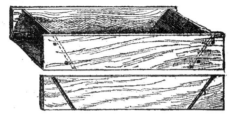

Fig. 27.—A PLANK WATER TROUGH.

other. When this is done, make the bottom edge true, coat well with white lead and securely fasten on with large wood screws. Give the trough a couple of coats of good paint, and when dry, the trough is ready for use. A convenient size is as follows, all inside measurements at the top : six feet long, fourteen to sixteen inches wide and twelve inches deep.

This form of trough will be found useful where water is continually running from water logs, and is designed to prevent freezing and overflow. At one end, as in figure

Fig. 28.—WATERING TROUGH.

28, a board is fitted across the trough, and goes to within about one inch of the bottom. The water must flow under this to reach the outlet. This portion of the trough has a cover with a hinge. It will be seen that with this construction no straw or rubbish can get into this covered portion to clog the outlet, and thus cause overflow. This protection is usually sufficient in the winter to prevent the outlet from freezing. But a plug is inserted in the bottom of the trough, which can be taken out when the trough needs cleaning, or in very severe weather.

Farmers who have never used a covered water trough, and who have not been able to keep the water free from leaves and mud in summer, and to prevent the trough

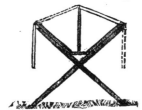

Fig. 29.—COVERED WATER TROUGH.

becoming filled with snow and ice, will be glad of the illustration (figure 29) of a covered trough, which can be used on both sides. It should stand in the middle of a yard, and the best way of supplying it is by a pipe carried underground from a pump. It is supported on crossed posts set in the ground and pinned together. The trough has a central division, upon the top of which the covers rest. When in use, the covers are let down, and when not in use they rest upon the dividing plank, as shown by the dotted lines, and as soon as the stock is watered, the plug is drawn to let the water off.

This non-freezing trough should be made two feet deep, eighteen inches wide, and fourteen feet long, and constructed out of two-inch oak plank. Figure 30 is a sectional side view of the trough. Over it is fitted a double cover, with four-inch space, which extends to within fourteen inches of the outer end. This part is

covered with a single hinged cover, which can be raised
and fastened up. The trough rests on the ground, and
a bank of earth three feet wide is raised around it even

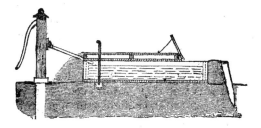

Fig. 30.—SECTIONAL VIEW OF TROUGH.

with the top. At the open end of the trough this bank
is eighteen inches thick, and is held up with boards as
shown in figure 30. Over all, except the open end, is
placed a layer of chaff a foot deep. On the north, west,
and south of the well and trough is a tight board fence,
one end and side of which are shown in figure 31.

Fig. 31.—THE TROUGH AND SURROUNDINGS.

Across the open end, just back of the opening in the
trough, barbed wires are stretched across to keep stock
off the well and trough. Under the end of the trough
nearest the well is placed a drain, made of fence boards,

leading to lower ground. Over this drain is a hole in the bottom of the trough, closed by a plug, which extends through the cover as seen in figure 30, and by which the trough may be emptied into the drain. The trough is filled in the morning, and the natural warmth of so much water having so small a surface exposed, prevents it from freezing during the day, even in the coldest weather. At night the open end is closed. In summer the water in this trough is always cool, and vastly superior for live stock to that standing in open troughs.

A GUARDED HORSE TROUGH.

Chickens have a way of leaving their drinking pens and "fountains," and seeking the more abundant and fresher water of the horse trough. It is all very well so long as

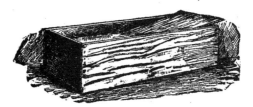

Fig. 32.—FLOATING BOARD IN HORSE TROUGH.

the trough is overflowing, but when the water is low, they lose their balance, fall in and drown. Figure 32 shows a board which floats at one end in the water, and rests at the other upon the end of the trough, being held in place by a twenty-penny nail driven through it. The board, being two inches narrower than the trough, floats freely, and there are no more drowned chickens, for, if they fall in, they can get out again unassisted.

BOX FOR WATERING PAILS.

Figure 33 shows an arrangement for keeping the pails used for watering the horse and cow, assuming that many keep but one or two cows or horses, and that the water is carried to them, from being filled with snow in winter, and from standing in the hot sun in the summer. This plan, as shown in the illustration, is as follows: Have a box standing near the well pump. The size

Fig. 33.—BOX FOR WATERING PAILS.

of the box for a single pail should be about sixteen inches square, or twenty inches would be no disadvantage. Have a cover fastened on with either leather or strap hinges; the latter can be bought cheaply at the hardware store, and are better than leather ones. For two pails, the box should be two and one-half or three feet long. In this way, the pails are always in place and much trouble and annoyance is avoided. The best way to arrange the cover is, to have a strip of board some two or three inches in width to go across the top of the box, forming part of the covering, to which the hinges can be securely fastened. Use a smaller box in the hen-house.

HOME-MADE HEATING VAT.

Vats or tanks with wooden sides and metallic bottom, have long been used for heating and evaporating fluids. Figure 34 shows an improved method of construction, which gives greater strength and simplifies the matter of securing water-tight joints. The sides are of pine, two inches thick, ten inches wide, and six feet long. The lower angles are rounded off, as shown in the engraving. Four inches from each end grooves are cut half an inch deep and two inches wide. Into these are fitted and nailed two pieces of pine, two by eight inches, and twenty-five inches long. They are flush with the top, leaving a space of two inches at the bottom. Two rods of half-inch round iron, each with a head at one end and a screw-thread and bolt at the other, are inserted through holes made for the purpose, near the top

Fig. 34.—VAT FOR HEATING WATER.

of the cross-pieces and screwed firmly in place. The bottom is of galvanized iron, seven feet eight inches long and twenty-eight inches wide. This is fastened by a double row of three-penny nails to the lower edge of the side pieces, extending around the curves to the top. If desired, it may be cut long enough to turn over at the top, and nailed to the upper edge of the wooden cross-pieces. This would give sufficient strength without the iron brace-rods. This vat is set upon an arch of brick or stone two feet wide, so that the wooden sides will project over it. For scalding hogs, a scraping bench is erected close to one side of the vat, and level with the top.

CHAPTER II.

VEHICLES, ROLLERS, HARROWS AND MARKERS.

A CART FOR BREAKING COLTS.

Most colts, if taken young enough, and gently, though firmly handled, can be driven as soon as they can be made to know what is wanted of them. Now and then a spirited fellow feels his oats, or is very nervous about the harness, and still more about the wagon, or cart, and rears, and kicks, and pulls side-ways, trips himself up, and goes down in spite our best efforts to prevent it. For such a good, strong breaking-rig is essential. The cart, figure 35, is home-made, except the wheels; for these a pair of strong wagon wheels—either front or hind—will do. The shafts are a pair of seasoned hickory poles, extending about two feet behind the wheels. They are bolted upon the axle-tree, and underneath these is a lighter pair of poles, attached to the shaft in front, and bolted also to the axle-tree by the same clamps that are used to hold the shafts. These extend back as braces, and are mortised into pieces, which are themselves mortised into the shaft-poles near the end. The object of this arrangement is to keep a colt from rearing. The ends of these pieces will bear upon the ground, the moment he lifts himself up. The same result would be accomplished by having the poles extend far out behind, but this makes turning exceedingly awkward, so that rigs of this kind can only be comfortably used in an open lot. The box, or body of the vehicle, is made with reference to strength, so that it cannot easily be kicked to pieces, nor broken by overturning or being run away with. A strong plank is bolted to the poles in front; uprights, and cross-boards of three-quarter-inch spruce, form the dashboard, which is well braced. The back and seat are similarly attached. It is important that the seat should

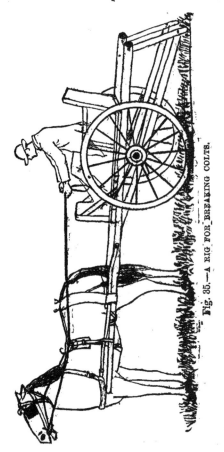

Fig. 35.—A RIG FOR BREAKING COLTS.

be so placed that the driver may at will throw his full weight forward, to bring the bearing of the shafts upon the saddle, or backward, to lift up on the girth or belly-band. The harness should always be sufficiently strong, and before using the breaking-cart, the colt must be well harness-broken.

A HOME-MADE CART.

Figure 36 shows a serviceable farm cart, which can be made by any one who understands the use of a saw and hammer. The sides of the box, which is six feet long and four feet wide, are of plank a foot wide, the bottom of inch boards; the end-board is fastened with hooks, so that it can be readily removed when loading the cart.

Fig. 36.—HOME-MADE CART.

The wheels are those of an old, worn-out reaper, and the axle consists of a piece of gas-pipe, large enough to fit the hub of the wheels. Pins put in holes drilled through the ends of the axle, keep the wheels in their places. The axle is fastened to the wagon by wooden blocks, hollowed out to proper shape; these blocks are firmly screwed to the side-pieces. The thills pass through the front board and are bolted to the sides of the box. A single-tree is fastened to a cross-piece bolted to the thills close to the box. Such a cart is very convenient on every farm, and being low, it is easily loaded.

APPARATUS FOR LIFTING A WAGON-BODY.

To lift a heavy wagon-body from its truck is tedious work, if to be done by main force only. The use of pulleys facilitates the operation materially, but not as much as the apparatus shown in figure 37. It is simple, and may be easily made by any farmer handy with tools. *b*, in the engraving, is a wooden roller, about three inches in diameter, and resting on the

Fig. 37.—APPARATUS FOR HOISTING A WAGON-BODY.

joists *a*, which are over the wagon in its shed. *d* is a rope which winds around the roller, and is fastened at its lower end to the cross-piece *e*. Through each end of the cross-piece passes a half-inch round iron bar, *f*, with bar on top of *e*. The lower ends terminate with square bends of three inches, which hook under the box, and when turned half round will slip off, and may be hoisted up and put out of the way. The handles, *c*, are four feet long and are mortised into the roller. A man or boy standing on the ground can turn the handles with ease, and raise the box from its bed in half the time four men could do it by hand.

JACK FOR WAGON BOX.

A cheap method of removing a wagon box is shown in figure 38. A platform to receive the box is made by driving stout stakes into the ground and nailing crosspieces to them. The platform should be as high as the top of the wagon standards. The lifter consists of a stout piece of timber, which will reach two feet above the wagon box, the top rounded, and a pin, driven into it, which passes through a slot in the lever. Two chains, provided with hooks, are fastened at the short end of the lever, and a rope at the other. One arm of the lever is

Fig. 38.—JACK FOR WAGON BOX.

three feet long, and the other nine feet. The wagon is driven close against the side of the platform. The lifter is placed, as shown in the engraving, on a line midway between the wagon and the platform. The hooks on the end of the chains are caught under the box, or the rod which passes through the rear end of the box, and by pulling on the rope, the box is easily lifted out and swung around on the platform. Then lift the front end over. The jack can be used to return the box to the wagon. The pieces need not be large, and when made of seasoned wood, the jack is easily handled.

SERVICEABLE WAGON-JACKS.

Take a scantling two and a half feet long, one inch thick, two and a half inches wide; rip it with a saw from top, to within five or six inches of the bottom, like a

Fig. 39.—WAGON-JACK.

tuning fork, figure 39. One prong is the lever, saw the other prong off at top, one inch higher than the bottom of the hind axle; then saw it off at the shoulder five or six inches from bottom; fasten it on again with a hinge exactly where it was sawed off, and it is ready for use.

Fig. 40.—HOME-MADE WAGON-JACK.

Set it under the axle, lowering the lever enough to allow it to go there; then raise the lever past the balance, and it will go together of its own weight, and stay there. At the left of the engraving it is seen as lowered, at the right as raised. This jack is very cheaply made, and varies in dimensions according to the weights to be raised. In the one shown in figure 40, the lever *a* is made of one-inch stuff, and the post *b* and the bearing-piece *c* of two and a half by two and a half. The latter two are slotted to admit of the lever working freely in them. The bearing-piece is held to the lever with an iron or a wooden pin, a little behind the post or fulcrum, so that when in use the jack will support the wagon without any other fastening.

ADJUSTABLE WAGON SEAT.

A six-inch board has slots cut in each end, so as to go  between the stakes of the wagon. Another board, one foot wide and three feet long, is fastened to the first in the position shown in the engraving, figure 41. An old seat, from a harvester or mower, is fastened upon the boards, when an easy and satisfactory seat is provided for a wagon when in use for purposes of drawing wood, lumber, etc.

Fig. 41.—A WAGON SEAT.

LUBRICATING AXLES.

Many lubricate axles only to prevent wear; they overlook the fact that by reducing the friction they lessen the draft. A well-oiled axle lightens the load. Oil to axles is best governed by the rule of "little and often." If too much is used it exudes at the ends, gathers dust, and thus the lessening of the friction is not so great, while oil is wasted. In nearly every case where the lubricant is wasted it is because it is stuff not fit to be used, for a good lubricator costs enough to keep the average man from allowing it to waste. Oil that "gums" much is unfit to be used. Castor oil is a splendid lubricator for axles, but used alone may gum too much. This is corrected by the addition of refined coal-oil (that used for lamps), or lard; the coal-oil is the better. Some wagons are yet made unprovided with metal shields or "thimbles," being banded with steel; for these some tallow may be used, as it is one of the best of lubricants when iron and wood are brought together. Pine-tar is a good addition to the lubricant for wagon axles, and is a part of most of the "axle greases" sold. Plumbago is another good addition; its fine particles fill the small irregularities in the opposing surfaces, thus making them smoother. A mixture of lard and plumbago is good for the journals of reapers, mowers, etc.; we have found castor oil and refined coal oil also good for this use, particularly for use on the "sickle-driver." For carriages nothing is better than castor oil and a very little lard oil or refined coal oil. Lard oil alone has not "body" enough for the journals of reapers, mowers, etc.; add a little castor oil, or tallow or plumbago. While the axles of reapers, grain-drills, hay-rakes, etc., will not need lubricating so often during the year as the axles of the wagon, oiling them must not be neglected, as the rough ground the wheels pass over makes the wear on unoiled axles quite rapid. The axles of corn-cultivators require frequent lubricating. For these the best lubricants are those recommended for wagon axles.

A LIGHT SLEIGH OR "JUMPER."

A light sleigh may be made of hard-wood poles cut and bent into shape, a few bolts, and a light body or box. Figures 42 and 43, made from sketches of a recently constructed "jumper," will serve as a guide to any one who wishes to provide himself a light sleigh at a trifling cost. Two hickory poles, for the runners, are dressed down, and the small ends bent to the proper curve and fastened until they will retain the bent shape. The posts are mortised into these runners and the bench pieces, which latter are firmly fastened together with bolts. The braces and their positions are shown in the engravings.

Fig. 42.—A JUMPER.   Fig. 43.—REAR VIEW OF JUMPER.

A floor is laid upon the bench pieces, and extends beyond the sides of the box or body. The box may be plain or ornamented in various ways. The one shown in the engraving has the sides and back flaring. The shafts are fastened to the curved end of the runners with eye-bolts.

A SUBSTANTIAL SLED.

Figure 44 shows a sled which is principally used in the pineries of Michigan, where a single team will draw on it from two to five thousand feet of lumber in the log. Special roads are kept open to accommodate these broad-track sleds, and when a load of a dozen or more logs is under way, it would be perilous for any who should venture to block the road.

Figure 44 shows the general construction of the sled. The bunks, *a, a,* are eight by ten inches and ten feet in length; the sway bars *b, b,* are four by four inches; the reach, *c,* is ten feet between the bunks, the beams, *d, d,*

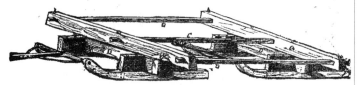

Fig. 44.—MICHIGAN SLED.

are ten by twelve inches, and the track is four feet eight inches long.

The particular feature of this sled is the concaves, *x,x,* made in the beam, *F,* which fit two convexes in the block, *E,* as shown in figure 45. These taper from the top to the bottom, fitting snugly at the bottom, and open one-sixth of an inch on each side at the top. By this

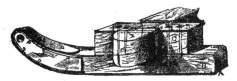

Fig. 45.—SLED RUNNER.

means slight play is allowed to the runners, which eases the motion considerably on rough ground. *A,* in figure 45, shows one of the steel shoes which are four by five-eighth inches; the runners, *B,* are four by six inches, and four feet long; the blocks, *C,* are four by twelve inches, and three feet in length. The iron plates are shown at *D,* the bolts at *C;* the beam, which is ten by twelve inches, at *F.*

A DUMP-SLED.

A method of constructing a dump-sled for hauling manure, earth and other substances, is shown in figure 46, and it will be appreciated by many northern

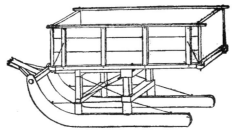

Fig. 46.—A SLED ARRANGED FOR DUMPING.

farmers. The front bog of a double sled has the framework raised by means of a trestle, and upon this the box is secured by eye-bolts, and a staple and pin.

A TRIPLE LAND ROLLER.

A great objection to the use of the roller is, that it tears up the ground for a considerable space when it is turned around. Another is, that the weight of the tongue and frame bears heavily upon the necks of the horses, and often causes sores. The roller shown in figure 47 has neither of these objections. It is made in three sections, and the hinder section balances the weight of the frame and tongue. In turning, the whole implement moves easily with the side roller as a pivot, and avoids all disturbance of the soil. The center roller is made a little longer than the side ones, and thus secures the complete pulverization of the soil. The rollers are easily made, either of solid logs, or of round discs, to which narrow bars are spiked. The best roller is the heaviest, and cast iron is the best material; although much cheaper ones may be made of artificial stone molded in wooden cylinders. The material may be mixed as follows: One barrel of good hydraulic cement is well mixed dry with three barrels of coarse, sharp sand. A sufficient quantity of the mixed cement and sand for one section is then wetted and worked up into a thin mortar, and is at once put into the mold; broken stone, first wetted, may

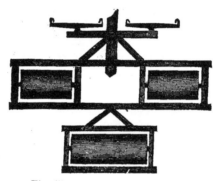

Fig. 47.—A TRIPLE LAND ROLLER.

be worked into the center, around a square shaft of oak timber, carefully centered. The whole is well rammed down, and more is added and rammed as it is put in, until the mold is filled. The ends of the roller should be of clear cement and sand for a few inches, only the interior being filled in with stone for the sake of economy and for weight as well. When the mass is dry and solid, the mold is taken apart. Wing gudgeons are fitted into the oak shaft. They run in wooden boxes, bolted to the under side of the frame. In this way a most excellent and useful roller, equal to a cast iron one and quite as durable, may be made for a cash outlay of about three dollars only.

A CHEAPER TRIPLE ROLLER.

Figure 48 shows a much simpler form of triple farm roller, made chiefly of wood. It is in three sections, each about two feet long, such a one being much easier on the team than when made solid or in merely two sections. A good oak or maple log, as nearly cylindrical as possible for ten or twelve feet, can be cut in the woods, the bark peeled off, and the log sunk under water for several weeks, when it is to be dried out under cover.

Fig. 48.—FARM ROLLER.

If seasoned with the bark on, the worms are apt to work on it. Saw off the pieces the required length, strike a center and work them to a uniform size, and then bore holes for the journals. The best way is to have a pump-maker bore entirely through the pieces an inch and three-quarter hole. Then hang them on a round bar of iron or steel, an inch and a half in diameter, as a loose spindle. The brace-irons can be made of stout old tire by the nearest blacksmith, and four of them, securely bolted into place, will be sufficient. Keep under cover when not in use

A DOUBLE LAND ROLLER.

The cheap home-made roller shown in figure 49 consists of two sections of a round log, dressed smooth, and fitted in a frame. The frame is made of four by four oak, bolted together firmly. The logs are each eighteen inches in diameter, and three and one-half feet long, one being set three inches ahead of the other in the frame. The pins for the rollers are one and a quarter inch thick, round for four inches at one end, and square

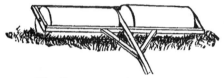

Fig. 49.—A HOME-MADE ROLLER.

for twelve inches; this end is pointed, and is driven into an inch hole, bored in the end of the log. The tongue is braced with strong iron braces, and a seat may be fitted partly over the rear of the frame, and balance the weight of the tongue, and relieve the horses' necks.

STALK LEVELER.

The frame, figure 50, is of two pieces six inches wide and two inches thick. They are joined together with

Fig. 50.—STALK LEVELER.

pieces of old wagon tire, which has been straightened out, and two holes punched or drilled in each end, to hold the spikes. The front ends of this tire-iron are bent or curved, to hold the chain to which the horses are attached. By using this contrivance when the stalks are stiff and hard with frost, they will break off clear and clean near to the ground, and can then be gathered up and burned, or made into manure.

USEFUL CLOD CRUSHER.

The illustrations, figures 51 to 53, present different views of a home-made implement to be used as a clod crusher

Fig. 51.—CLOD CRUSHER IN OPERATION.

or for other purposes. The runners are of oak plank, two inches thick, six feet long and eight inches wide, each rounded off at one end, and notched on the upper edge, as shown in the engravings. The cross-pieces are of similar material, three feet long and seven inches wide, spiked in place. The outer edges of the cross-

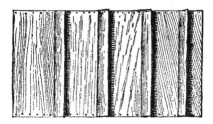

Fig. 52.—BOTTOM OF CLOD CRUSHER.

pieces are faced with band-iron. A staple with ring is driven from the inside of each runner, near the front, and the chain by which it is drawn is run through the ring. In this form it serves a very good purpose as a clod crusher. If additional weight is desired, large stones may be placed between the runners.

To fit it for use as a sled, it is inverted, a box of inch boards made five feet ten inches long, three feet broad, and nine inches deep. The lower edges of the sideboards are notched to fit the projections of the crosspieces. Inch boards are nailed across the bottom to close the spaces between the latter. Staples are driven into

Fig. 53.—CLOD CRUSHER AND SLED.

the sides of the runners to receive hickory stakes, which hold the box in place. For use in winter the thills are attached by iron straps bolted on, as shown in figure 53. When the runners become worn, the bottoms are planed off and strips of oak pinned on. The box may be replaced by a rack for drawing hay or other bulky stuff.

A BRUSH HARROW.

For the cultivation of various kinds of crops, one of the most useful implements made on the farm, and one which properly constructed, lasts a lifetime, is a smoothing and brush harrow, figure 54. It should be made of rather heavy stuff, so that the weight, as it is dragged along, will be sufficient to break the lumps and level the soil. This harrow can be used with good effect in covering newly planted seed, and in all cases where a disc or tooth harrow would be too heavy or wide-spread, a brush

Fig. 54.—BRUSH HARROW.

harrow like that herewith represented, will be found to be a good substitute.

AN IMPROVED HARROW FRAME.

Figure 55 shows a very cheap and excellent harrow frame intended for grass seeding; also for working

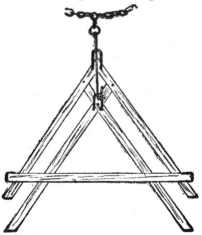

Fig. 55.—IMPROVED HARROW FRAME.

corn and potato land while the crop is young and small. For this purpose, a harrow should be light, broad, have a large number of fine teeth sloping backward, and should be so arranged that it will draw level and not lift at the front. The owner and inventor of this harrow claims that he has secured all these. The special point of this harrow is the hitching device. This consists of a hooked bar which works in two stirrups, one to draw by and the other to permit the draw-bar or chain to rise and fall, as the harrow passes over the ground that is not quite level. This is an important end to secure. The harrow is not patented, and any farmer is free to make one.

LAND-MARKERS.

Figure 56 represents a one-horse land-marker, such as is used among the gravel and cobblestone soils of some

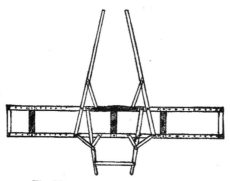

Fig. 56.—LAND-MARKER COMPLETE.

sections, where it does good service. The lumber should be of well seasoned oak; the long rails, two by three stuff in pairs; the cross-bar and end pieces the same; the cross bars, in which the teeth are set, three by three inches square; the thills one and a half by two inches at the large ends and tapering beyond the braces. The handles are common straight plow handles, that is, bent only at the grip. Three-eighths bolts are large enough for the frame.

The center tooth should be permanently framed in, the outside teeth being adjustable, work in the slot between

Fig. 57.—END VIEW OF LAND-MARKER.

the long rails, and are held in place by two three-eighths iron pins. They can be moved so as to mark from two feet six to five feet. The rails should have seven-sixteenth holes bored through them every three inches, commencing at two feet six from center of middle tooth. For shares use old points of shovel plows. The whiffletree is held by a bolt which passes through the center cross-bar.

Figure 56 shows the adjustment of the teeth, one being set at two feet six, the other four feet, also the position of the thills, the whiffletree, the handles. The cross-rail tenons at ends should fit in the end of slots and be bolted

Fig. 58.—MOVABLE TOOTH OF LAND-MARKER.

fast with three-eighths bolts. The braces on thills and handles are of iron, a quarter of an inch thick and an inch wide, held by quarter-inch bolts. Figure 57 is an end view, showing the pitch of handles and thills, a tooth also, and the mode of fastening the same. Figure 58 shows one end of the pair of long rails which form the slot for a movable tooth; also the shape of share. This

Fig. 59.—A HORSE LAND-MARKER.

implement is not patented, and can be made by any one with common tools and knowledge and ingenuity enough to use them.

Figure 59 shows a marker with plank runners, so simple in its construction and so clearly shown in the engraving that no description is needed.

Figure 60 shows an excellent marker for "checking" corn ground. The runners are of hard-wood plank two by six inches, and four feet long. They are usually placed three feet ten inches apart. The cross-pieces, of two by four inch stuff, are laid on top of the runners, and fastened in place with square pieces; or better yet, let into the runners. Pieces of two by four inch stuff run diagonally from the rear corners and meet in front, forming bases of attachment for the pole tongue. Bows of pieces of hoop-poles are fastened in these, through which the rear end of the tongue passes. This is much superior to bolting the tongue across the top of the marker, for then every irregularity in the walk of the horses is communicated to the marker, making short crooks in the checks and where the marker dips in a depression, its weight is

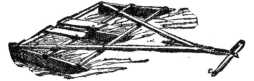

Fig. 60.—SERVICEABLE MARKER.

thrown on the horses' necks. When the tongue is attached, as shown in the cut, no short crooks are made in the checks, there is neither lateral or horizontal strain on the horses' shoulders, while the hoops make the marker manageable in crossing deep furrows, etc. The tongue is held in place by a round iron bolt passing through it and the end of the diagonals. The double trees are fastened just in front of this point of attachment. The driver stands on the two boards on the rear center of the marker.

COMBINED MARKER AND CLOD-CRUSHER.

In figure 61 is a very clear illustration of a useful marker and clod-crusher, which is made as follows:

Fig. 61.—COMBINED MARKER AND CLOD CRUSHER.

Three runners are provided, four feet long, eight inches wide and two inches thick; four two-inch planks of strong, hard wood, eight feet long and eight inches wide, are let into the runners four and one-half inches deep; these slope from top to bottom edge backwards, forty-five degrees, so as to draw over the rough ground, and break clods by pressing on them. These runners are let into the cross-pieces one inch, and are fastened together by large screws. A strip of two by four is halved down on the runners in the front, for a draw-bar. The tongue is fitted with hooks, which are attached to rings on the draw-bar, so that it can be removed when the sled is turned over to be used as a clod-crusher.

A LAND LEVELER.

For preparing land for grass seeding, or for corn-planting the three plank leveler and clod-crusher is useful.

Fig. 62.—LAND LEVELER.

The planks are held together by a chain, and both with large washers, which pass through links. If short pieces of heavy chain are fastened to the holes in the rear plank they will mark sufficiently plain for corn or potato planting.

CHAPTER III.

SMALL TOOLS AND APPLIANCES.

BAG HOLDERS.

There is an endless variety of devices for holding a bag upright, with the mouth open. One of the simplest, figure 63, consists of a piece of hickory or white oak bent into a half-circle, and the ends passed through a

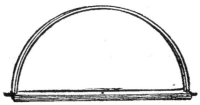

Fig. 63.—CHEAP BAG HOLDER.

somewhat larger rod of the same kind of wood, and wedged fast. A screw is driven into each end of the rod, and filed to a point. To use it, the mouth of the bag is put through the half circle, and the edge is turned down over the holder, and over the sharp points, which hold it firmly. The bag is then held while it is filled, or it may be hung upon two hooks, or the holder may be fitted in a frame on a stand, so that one can use it without any help to hold the bags.

A very good form is shown in figure 64 for farmers who sack their grain in the granary, one side of the room being used as a passage-way. It is swung by staples to the posts, and can be changed readily from one post to another by having staples arranged in each post. Three-quarter inch round iron is used, all in one piece, the rod being bent or welded to make the circular shaped opening for the hopper. The hopper is made of common sheet iron, funnel-shaped, turned and wired on the upper

Fig. 64.—GRANARY BAG HOLDER.

side to add to its strength and to reduce the sharpness of the edge. Four small hooks can be riveted to the hopper, to attach the sack when filling it. When not in use, the holder can be swung back out of the way. If desired, the hopper can be permanently attached to the iron rim or holder by a couple of small rivets passing

Fig. 65.—A BETTER BAG HOLDER.

through both. This will prevent the hopper from being displaced by the weight of the bag.

The holder illustrated in figure 65, has the advantage

of being built almost wholly of wood, and can be made by any ingenious farmer. It can also be adjusted to various heights by moving it up or down a notch. The back is of inch board, about one foot wide and of any desired length, from fifteen to thirty inches. The arms are an inch thick and an inch and a half wide, fastened by screws into the notches in the back and supported by wire rods which may be held by screws through the flattened ends, or may pass through the back and arms and clinch. The cross-piece is of tough wood, three-fourths

Fig. 66.—PORTABLE SACK HOLDER.

of an inch square. For holding the bag there is one hook on the back piece, two on each arm, and one under the cross-piece. The whole is supported on two strong spikes driven into the wall of the barn or other building, and projecting far enough to fit the notches on the side.

The bag holder shown at figure 66, is portable and may be taken wherever it is to be used. The sack to be filled is brought up inside of the frame and turned over and hooked on the underside of it. The hooks are put here because they are not in the way and the sack is not torn by the weight of the grain, as would be the case if the hooks were put on the top of the frame. The frame must be somewhat smaller than the sack. The sack can be filled to the top of the frame, as the part drawn over will be enough to tie by. The material used is inch stuff. The length of the legs must be such that when the sack is put on the hooks the bottom will rest on the floor.

Another form of portable holder, shown in figure 67, is so compact and light that it can be carried into the

Fig. 67.—A SIMPLE BAG HOLDER.

field if desired. The apparatus consists simply of three light poles about six feet long, and loosely fastened together at one end with a small carriage bolt, and three screw-hooks at the proper height for holding the bag when stretched out, as seen in the illustration.

HANDLING POTATOES.

Potatoes are best stored in a dry, cool cellar, where the temperature can be kept by ventilation at about forty degrees. The floor should be of planks, raised three inches from the ground, and laid with one-inch spaces between them for ventilation. The bins should be about eight feet long, four feet wide and deep, made of loose-barred partitions (figure 68), wired together at the corners. A bin of this size will hold one hundred bushels, and with such a one it is very easy to know precisely how much the crop amounts to.

The box shown at figure 69 will be found a great convenience in gathering and storing the potatoes. It is made eighteen inches long, fifteen inches deep in the clear at the sides, and ten inches wide, all inside measurements; thus holding two thousand and seven hundred

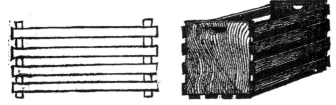

Fig. 68.—PANEL OF POTATO BIN.   Fig. 69.—SLATTED BOX FOR POTATOES.

cubic inches, or thirteen cubic inches (about two good-sized potatoes) over a heaped bushel, which is two thousand and six hundred and eighty-seven inches. These boxes can be set one upon another, and then have a space left between the potatoes, and are thus well adapted for use in storing a part of the crop, or a small quantity for domestic use. The barred sides and bottom secure abundant ventilation. The bins in the cellar should have a space of four inches between the end and the wall, and between the sides; this is easily made by placing a short rail between them, or a piece of four by four scantling, and this will relieve the sides from the bulging pressure of the potatoes. It is advisable to have a well-built root cellar, or a cellar under the barn, for storing potatoes; a house cellar should never be used for this purpose.

GRINDSTONES AND FRAMES.

A grindstone, to do good service, should be at least three feet in diameter and two and one-half to three inches in thickness, having a bevel on each side of the face for grinding on. It should be quite free from hard spots of iron pyrites, which are injurious to tools, although they may be taken out with a sharp-pointed punch. If it is not centered truly it will work out of shape and soon require trueing up. It should run as fast

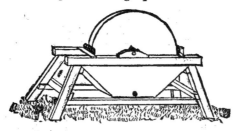

Fig. 70.—GRINDSTONE SET.

as possible, as it does its work better and more quickly. To prevent it from throwing water, a piece of bagging should be fastened to a staple fixed across the frame on each end (as shown in figure 70), but not so close as to grind it out; this will catch the excess of water and yet keep the stone wet enough and clean it. The stone should be kept in the shade and never in water, which softens it and makes one side wear faster than the other. The water box should have a hole in it to let out the water and keep the stone dry when not in use. In grinding, it should mostly turn from the tool, and if used otherwise, great care should be taken by the one who holds the tool, not to gouge the stone.

Figure 71 shows a novel style of frame for a grindstone. The frame proper consists of the iron part or bearing of a reaper reel. The arms to which the reel sticks were fastened, are all broken off but one. To this one the crank is bolted, as seen in figure 71. Four holes are drilled through the rim of the reel-wheel, to which

Fig. 71.—GRINDSTONE FRAME.

is bolted a hard wood board one inch thick, and having a square hole half way through, in which the center block fits. A bolt passes through a board block to a strip of iron, which may be bent to form a crank for

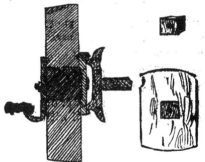

Fig. 72.—CROSS-SECTION.   Fig. 73.—CENTER BLOCK.

foot-power. A cross-section of the stone as hung is shown in figure 72; the center block and board to which it is fastened are seen in figure 73. This frame should be bolted to a post or tree.

TOOL HOLDER.

Many a boy, and his father as well, who has toiled over the grindstone to sharpen tools, will be pleased with the device shown in figure 74, for giving a smooth, even edge to tools, which can be held by the hands, while the stone is turned by a treadle or a horse-power. It is a triangle of wooden bars, put together as shown, having a sharp pin at the point, a clamp for holding the tool at the center, and holes at the sides for tying an axle helve with cords, to keep it firm. The grindstone is near a wall or a post,

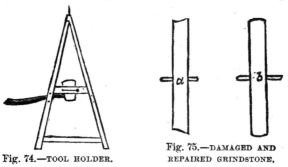

Fig. 74.—TOOL HOLDER.

Fig. 75.—DAMAGED AND REPAIRED GRINDSTONE.

and the pin is pushed into this to hold the frame. The frame is then held in its proper position by the hands, and if held firmly, will grind an even bevel on any tool. A scythe, or a cutting-bar of a mower or reaper, or a chisel, can thus be ground perfectly and with little labor.

HOW TO REPAIR A GRINDSTONE.

Usually a grindstone is worn out of level, and very irregularly. This is scarcely to be avoided when such a large variety of tools, including scythes, mower sections, axes, hoes, and many other tools are ground. After ordinary use, those who are not careful to preserve the stone true, with smooth and slightly rounded face, the stone appears as at *a*, in figure 75. It is then beyond the power of the owner to repair the damage, unless he is an expert mechanic, when he takes a piece of old stoveplate and grinds the stone down to a slightly rounded or beveled face, like that shown at *b*. The best way to do this is to take a spade or a shovel, and turning it back upwards, to grind it sharp against the turning of the stone. This will bring the stone into the right shape, and in sharpening the spade, do a useful job at the same time.

A WOODEN MANGER FORK.

The common method of pitching fodder into mangers with a steel-tined fork, is often accompanied with harm

Fig. 76.—A MANGER FORK.

to animals. They will crowd around the rack or manger, and frequently receive an accidental thrust in the head or body with the sharp fork. Not infrequently an eye is lost, and with a horse this is a serious matter. The wooden manger fork shown in figure 76 avoids this danger. It is made of a piece of hickory or oak six feet long, an inch and a half wide, and an inch thick.

Four feet of its length is shaped round for a handle. The other end is sawed or split into three equal parts, to within a few inches of the rounded portion, where an iron band is placed. The "tines" are spread apart, and held in position by a wooden brace between them.

The tines are rounded, smoothed, and slightly sharpened at their points.

HOME-MADE AND USEFUL CHAFF FORKS.

Figure 77 represents a home-made fork with tines about two feet long, and having a spread of twenty inches. The teeth are straight above, and curved towards the point. They are fastened by screws to the three-inch

Fig. 77.—LARGE CHAFF FORK.   Fig. 78.—SIMPLE CHAFF FORK.

hard-wood head, and strengthened by an iron rod near the head, and by a round wooden rod, which passes through them and to which they are tacked fast. The head is strengthened by a similar piece of oak or ash, half an inch thick, screwed upon its edge, and through which the handle passes. This is of ash or hickory, large enough around to give the hand a good hold, and is fastened by wiring to the top side of the head. Such a fork may be made quite light, and the six tines being only four inches apart, will handle either chaff or light straw to good advantage. We give, by way of comparison, a simple chaff fork, figure 78, made by first binding and then carefully splitting a single piece of hickory or ash, handles and tines being formed of the same stick. A ring-ferule or band of wire is placed at the point beyond which the splits may not go, and after the splits are made, the tines are spread apart by wedge-shaped pieces of wood. These forks are easily made and are the very best stable forks that can be used. There is no danger of pricking horses or cattle with them, and if one be carelessly left in the stable, or falls down, neither man nor beast is likely to be hurt.

STABLE SCRAPER AND BROOM.

The manure gutter is easily cleaned out with the scraper and broom shown below. The scraper, figure 79, is made

Fig. 79.   Fig. 80.

to fit the width of the gutter, and brings the manure to the trap-door. The broom, figure 80, is then used to sweep the waste matter from the floors into the gutter, and from the gutters into the trap-doors, leaving the floor clean and clear for a new supply of litter.

A STRAW OR HAY HOOK.

A convenient hook for pulling straw or hay out of a stack for distribution amon sheep or cattle, is shown in figure 81. It consists of a s ut pole pointed at one end; a slit is cut through it and t hook is pivoted as shown in

Fig. 81.—STRAW OR HAY HOOK.

the engraving, so that it will be pushed back when it is thrust into the stack, and drawn forward, when it is pulled out. A strong cord helps to strengthen the hook, When the hook is pulled out of the stack, it brings a quantity of straw or hay with it.

FORK FOR HANDLING STONES.

The fork, figure 82, for lifting stones will prevent many a back-ache. It should have four prongs, which are

Fig. 82.

curved so as to hold the stones, and a strong handle. By a knack in giving a quick jerk, a heavy stone can be lifted and thrown into a wagon, and without stooping. Having used one of these contrivances to pick up stones, we can speak with knowledge of its usefulness. It is made of prongs of horse-shoe iron, welded to a heavier cross-bar, which has two strong straps to receive the handle.

SALT BOX FOR STOCK.

Salt should be given regularly to horses, cattle, and sheep, but it is rarely so given, because a supply is not kept handy for use. The box shown in figure 83 may

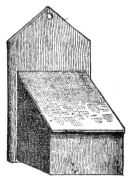

Fig. 83.

be hung in a stable or shed, or to a tree or post in the pasture. The salt is protected from the rain, and if replenished when necessary, the stock will be supplied with it regularly.

SAFETY SINGLE-TREE.

In plowing among fruit trees or in corn, single-trees having the traces arranged the usual way, will do much injury to the trees or corn. There is a method in arranging the traces which will avoid all this, as can be seen in the illustration, figure 84. A knot is made on the end of the trace rope, when the rope is passed through the hole made for the purpose, and brought around in the grooved end of the single-tree. To prevent the rope from getting out of place, it is wired or tied with strong cord. If the tree is struck by the end of the single-tree, thus guarded, it slides off without doing much injury. If the trees are young and small, with smooth and tender

Fig. 84.—SAFETY SINGLE-TREE.

bark, it is well to wrap the end of the traces, for about eighteen inches from the single-tree, with old cloth, to prevent the rough, twisted rope from chafing the trees. Always use a shorter single-tree in plowing and cultivating an orchard than in ordinary plowing, and also use a small horse or mule to do the work, as this allows of more thorough work, and with less liability of injury to the low branches or the trunks of the trees.

ROOT PULPERS AND CUTTERS.

Those who feed beets, turnips, carrots and other roots,

Fig. 85.—ROOT PULPER.

find it necessary to reduce them by some cheaper method than cutting by hand with a knife. An excellent machine for pulping roots is shown in figure 85. It may be made by any carpenter in two days, at a cost of about six dollars. The plan of the machine is given in the engraving. It is simply a square or oblong box, with a spiked cylinder fitted in it, the cylinder having a square gudgeon at one end, to which a handle is fitted. To save expense the heavy wheel and handle attached, of a fodder cutter, may be taken off and used on the root pulper, as the two will rarely be used at the same time. The cylinder is closely studded with sharp, chisel-pointed spikes. These teeth are made of one-quarter inch square bar iron, and are three inches long; the sharp edges are worked out on an anvil, and are chilled by immersion in

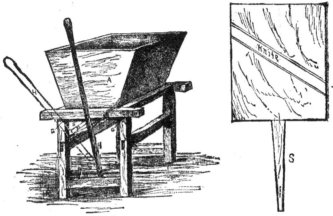

Fig. 86.—HOME-MADE ROOT-CUTTER.   Fig. 87.—ROOT-CUTTER SLIDE.

cold salt water when red hot, the other end being cut with a screw thread. To secure strength, and to make the machine work with more ease, the cutters are screwed in so far as to leave only half an inch or a little more projecting. A still cheaper form is illustrated in figure 86. At A is seen the hopper which is without a bottom. The slide, figure 87, contains a two-edged knife, and runs in the grooves, G G, in the top of the frame, close to the bottom of the hopper. Near the bottom of the frame is a roller, R, into which is fitted the handle, H. This is connected with the slide by the rod, R. The knife should be about four inches wide and one-quarter inch thick, be placed diagonally in the slide, leaving half an inch space between it and the bottom of the slide. When using the apparatus all that is necessary is to move the handle to and from the hopper. It works easily and quickly, is durable, and with fair usuage is not likely to get out of order. A ready way of chopping a few roots, is to use a spade ground to a sharp edge, and a box in which the roots are quickly reduced to slices. A basket of turnips or apples, can be sliced in this way in one minute. For a larger quantity, a chopper may be made as in the engraving, figure 88. It has two long blades. and the roots are hashed up rapidly, and all danger of choking is avoided. A common cast-iron winged gudgeon, having steel strips riveted on the edges, answers as well as one forged out by a blacksmith, at several times its cost. The roots, so cut, may be mixed with meal, and fed to the cows. Apples are excellent for dairy cows when fed in this way, and largely increase the flow of milk, besides being healthy for them.

Fig. 88. ROOT CUTTER.

ROOT WASHERS.

A convenient washer for potatoes and roots, consists of a kerosene barrel hung in a frame, as shown in figure 89, on next page. Two openings are made in one side of the barrel—a large one, two staves wide, and a small one only one inch wide. The pieces cut out are used for lids, both of which are fastened with hinges and buttons, and are made to fit tight by having thick cloth tacked around their edges. A bushel of potatoes or roots are placed in the barrel, with two or three buckets of water, the lids are closed and buttoned, and the barrel is slowly turned. If they are very dirty, open the small aperture, and by turning the barrel back and forth allow the water and mud to run out. Add clean water and

Fig. 89.—ROOT WASHER.

turn again. They will soon be cleansed, when the large aperture may be opened, and the roots or tubers emptied into a basket. The fastenings at each end of the barrel can be made by any blacksmith, and they should be bolted on with one-quarter or three-eighths inch bolts. With this simple contrivance a man can wash a large

Fig. 90.—VEGETABLE WASHER.

quantity of roots in a day without catching cold or a chill. If kept out of the sun, such a contrivance will last a lifetime. In figure 90 is shown a potato and vegetable washer for household use. The ends of the cylinders are cut out of inch board and are twelve inches in diameter. The shaft runs through and has collars, to which the ends of the cylinders are fastened to hold them firm. Strong, tinned wires are fastened from end to end, as seen in the engraving. Five of these are fastened together, and form the lid to the aperture through which articles are admitted. The end of the lid is fastened by means of a loop, which springs over a button. The vegetables to be washed are placed in the cylinder, the box is half filled with water, and by turning

Fig. 91.—TUB FOR WASHER.

the crank, or by moving it back and forth, they are quickly cleansed. Narrow wooden slats may be used instead of wire, if desired. An ordinary tub, or a half barrel, arranged as seen in figure 91, may be used instead of the box.

CLAMPS AND STOOL FOR REPAIRING HARNESS.

The device shown in figure 92 combines a stool and a clamp for holding harness work. The bench or stool, *b*, of any desired size, is supported by two legs near one end. The other end is held up by the foot of the long claw, extending to a convenient height for the operator. A shorter claw, *c*, is fastened to it by a cross-piece, *p*, about an inch thick and three inches wide, passing through a slot in the jaws, in which it works easily but firmly on two iron pins, a little more than half-way up from the bench. In the lower end of the short jaw an eccentric works on a pivot and against a projection on the larger

Fig. 92.—A HARNESS STOOL AND CLAMP. Fig. 93 HARNESS HOLDER.

jaw. Depressing the handle to this eccentric or cam, closes the jaws at the top with all the force desired.

A simple holder without the stool is shown in figure 93. Two staves of a flour barrel are sawed off at a convenient length for holding between the knees, while sitting on a chair. The sawed ends of the pieces are securely nailed to the opposite sides of a block of wood. A hole is cut through the middle of one side piece, in which a lever is placed for opening and closing the holder. The lever may be readily made of such shape that it will always remain in the hole, ready for use.

The curves of the staves will furnish sufficient spring to hold the harness.

A BOX SAW-HORSE.

The novel saw-horse shown in figure 94 is made of a dry-goods box, of inch pine boards, thirteen inches long, eighteen inches wide, and twenty-four inches in height. Upon the outside of one end are nailed two cleats, and on the inner side three cleats, the position of which is

Fig. 94.—NOVEL SAW-HORSE.

shown in figure 94. The curved lever above the box is intended to do the hard work usually imposed upon the sawyer's left knee, viz., holding the stick sawed in place. The necessary pressure of the lever is effected by means of the treadle and the small rope or sash cord connecting the two. The lever should be so attached to the side of the box that the loose or curved end rests upon the stick, held in place by it, about midway between the center and left diagonal cleats. The treadle should extend, when horizontal, eight inches beyond the left side of the box. In using the horse, raise the lever with the left hand, with the right place the stick to be sawed so that the point where it is to be cut is over the U; the lever is dropped or pulled down upon the stick; the left foot is placed upon the treadle; a slight pressure will hold the stick securely. The sawyer, thus using both limbs for support, and standing nearly erect, will find wood sawing an easy though vigorous exercise, quite exempt from many of the old-time aches and pains. If the horse is to be used in a wood-house—a room having a floor—it is well to secure it by screws to the floor; if out of doors, it may be ballasted with a few bricks or stones, or be fastened to a frame.

LONG SAW-BUCKS.

In cutting fire-wood from long timber or sawing lumber, it is convenient to have a long saw-horse. Two patterns are illustrated herewith. To make the one shown in figure 95, an oak stick averaging half a foot in

Fig. 95.—A LONG SAW-BUCK.

diameter, was selected from the wood pile, and a piece five foot long cut off. Two one-and-a-half-inch auger holes were bored near each end, not quite opposite each other, to avoid weakening the timber at one point, and

Fig. 96.—A LIGHTER HORSE.

four strong sticks from the same wood pile were driven in for legs—a little under two feet long, and standing well slanting outward. Six one-inch auger holes were bored in the top, and split-out pegs, eight or ten inches long, were driven in, in a position to firmly hold the wood to be sawed. The two pegs of each pair are not directly opposite, but separated far enough for the saw-cut to run down between them. Of the first pair one is four inches from the end, and the other seven inches back. The second pair is fifteen inches back of these, and the other in the farther end of the horse, these last answering as a support to the long end of the wood to be cut, the other two pairs being used as the saw-horse. When a stick is reduced to five feet or so in length, it is drawn forward and wholly supported on the two pairs of pins nearest together.

The other horse, shown in figure 96, consists of an ordinary saw-horse having a block nailed across its legs on one side, forming a rest for the end of a long stick, which at the other end is fastened into half a saw-horse, *a*. The piece to be sawed is laid on the three rests thus formed, the end to be sawed being placed at *a*. As each length is sawed off, *a* is shoved toward *b*, the proper distance. It will be seen that this saw-horse can be lengthened out or shortened up, to suit the length of the stick.

HOW TO TIE A BAG.

Figure 97 shows a simple and easily made bag-tie which effectually prevents any slipping, if properly ad-

Fig. 97.—BAG TIE.

justed. Take any strong cord about eighteen inches long and double it as herewith seen, passing the ends through, making a loop around the mouth of the bag. Now pull as tightly as possible; then take an end of the string in each hand and pull again in opposite directions; pass the string completely around, make a knot, and double or single bow-knot, and the work is done. A very little experience will make one expert, and he can then make sure the bag will not come untied.

A HOME-MADE RAKE HEAD.

Figure 98 shows the end view of a hand-rake with the tooth inserted. The head-block should be made of green hickory, free from knots and curls, while the rake-teeth must be of dry, well-seasoned oak or hickory, and having grooved places in them, as is seen in the illustration. The teeth are rounded and are driven snugly into the green head-piece, which latter, in drying, will hold the seasoned teeth so firmly as to effectually prevent them from ever coming out. In fact, so tightly will they be held, that they can scarcely be driven out when the head-block has become thoroughly seasoned, the shrinkage of the green wood acting as a permanent vise.

Fig. 98.—A DURABLE RAKE.

The same principle might be utilized in other small implements.

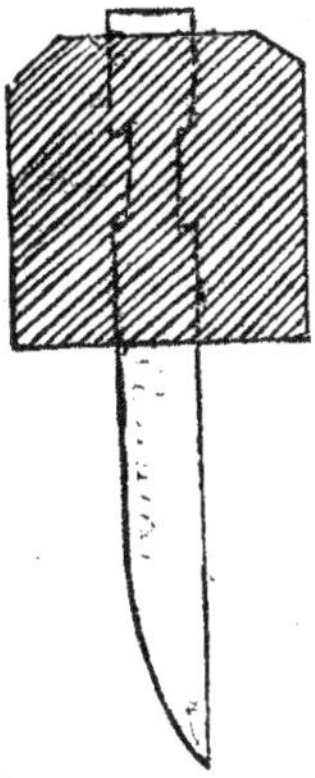

WORKING BUILDING STONE.

Stone is the most durable and the cheapest building material where it is plentiful on the farm. By a little management the stone can be brought to a convenient shape for use. The tools required, shown in figure 99, are: a chipping hammer, a wedge and steel feathers, striking hammer, drill and a bar for opening cracks in the stone. The clipping hammer has a broad, sharp edge, and acts as a chisel for dressing the faces; and the sharp edges of the rectangular head, two by four inches, serve

Fig. 99.—TOOLS FOR STONE WORK.

to dress down the edges and corners of the stones. The wedge is three by one and a half inches, and the feathers are plates of steel as wide as the wedge, which they serve to protect. The striking hammer is three inches square, and six inches long, with a beveled edge around the face. The drill is of one and a quarter inch octagonal steel, and is eighteen inches long, or if there be two, one is twelve inches long. The bar is four and a half feet long, and has a sharp-edged steel point for striking into cracks and splitting the stone, which it is usually easy to

Fig. 100.—BREAKING A LARGE STONE.

do. A large stone is broken by drilling a few holes in it with a one-inch drill, and chipping a groove across the face along the line of holes, as shown in figure 100. Small round wedges, with small feathers, are placed in each hole, and they are struck one after the other, in rotation.

By this method very large blocks are split with an even face. A small stone is easily split by chipping grooves across it, and then repeatedly striking along upon the groove with the face of the hammer.

BLOCK FOR SAND-PAPER.

Sand-paper is put up by the manufacturers in quires of sheets nine by eleven inches in size. As used by many workmen, nearly a fourth of each sheet is wasted by folding and crumpling over improperly shaped blocks. A convenient block, figure 101, which permits the use

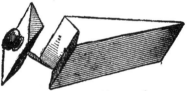

Fig. 101.

of all the sand-paper, is here described. Make a wedge-shaped piece of hard wood, one and a half inch thick, three inches wide, and five and one-quarter inches long, tapering from the head to a sharp edge. Cut a V-shaped hollow across the head. Fit a piece three inches

Fig. 102.

long, of hard-wood, exactly to this hollow. Insert in the head a wood or porcelain drawer knob seven-eighths of an inch in diameter, fastening it securely by a long screw. Cut a sheet of sand-paper into three equal parts, three by eleven inches. Fold one-fourth of an inch at each end of a strip of sand-paper, and slip under the head-piece by loosening the screw. Tightening it will hold the paper fast and smooth for work. A common wood screw may be used in place of the knob, but is not as convenient, as it must be turned by a screw-driver.

CHAPTER IV.

APPLIANCES FOR THE BARN, PASTURE AND DAIRY.

CONVENIENT STABLE VENTILATOR.

It must not be supposed that fresh air in the winter is to be excluded from stables for the purpose of keeping the animals warm. Warmth alone is not comfort. An animal may suffer from cold in a close, damp, impure air, which is really warm, while it will be quite comfort-

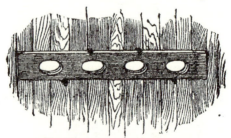

Fig. 103.—STABLE VENTILATOR.

able in fresh, pure air, which is much below freezing temperature. The absence of oxygen in the one case reduces the vital warmth, while its abundance in the other case maintains an agreeable and comfortable feeling. Consequently, ventilation of stables is necessary, even in the coldest weather, to keep the animals in good health and in comfort. But it should be regulated judiciously by a suitable provision of openings at the upper part of the stable, and these should be made so as to be readily opened and closed. A row of holes cut in the wall near the upper floor, figure 103, and covered with a sliding-board, having precisely the same kind and number of holes to match those in the wall, will afford suitable ventilation for the stable at all seasons. The covering board slides back and forth on the pins shown, and covers or opens the holes as may be desirable, according to the condition of the weather.

LIGHT NEEDED IN BARNS.

Here and there we see an old-style barn, built by our grandfathers, the only window being a single row of panes over the large door. Through this comes all of the light admitted to the barn, except what comes through the open cracks between the boards. When a barn of this kind is filled with hay it is comfortably warm, but very dark; by midwinter the hay, being half consumed, leaves the walls unprotected. With the light come in also the cold wintry winds to chill the cattle. Our fathers built some barns warmer, covering the walls with shingles or the cracks with narrow battens. The light being thus shut out, it was necessary to have windows; so they put in just enough to enable them to see to feed their cattle. It was left for our generation to build barns that are tight, comfortable, and well-lighted. But even at present many farmers do not realize the importance of light in a cattle barn. Experiments show that a herd of milch cows not only keep in better health and condition by having plenty of light, but they give more milk. Every barn should be provided with abundant light and sunshine on the side where the cattle stand. The practice, which is far too prevalent, of keeping cows in a dark and

damp basement is not a good one. They can not have the sunshine and pure air so necessary for good health. Windows that are exposed may be protected for a trifling sum by covering them with wire netting. The day of **windowless** barns has passed; but some of our new barns would be improved by a few more windows.

LANTERNS IN THE BARN.

It is estimated that nine-tenths of all fires are caused by carelessness. Never light a lamp or lantern of any kind in a barn. Smokers may include their pipes and cigars in the above. The lantern should be lighted in the house or some out-building, where no combustibles are stored. A lantern which does not burn well, should never be put in order in the hay mow. There is a great temptation to strike a match and re-light an extinguished lantern, wherever it may be. It is best to even feel one's way out to a safe place, than to run any risks. If the light is not kept in the hand, it should be hung up. Provide hooks in the various rooms where the lights are used. A wire running the whole length of the horse stable, at the rear of the stalls, and furnished with a sliding hook, is very convenient for night work with the horses. Some farmers are so careless, as to keep the lamp oil in the barn, and fill the lantern there, while the wick is burning. Such risks are too great, even if the buildings are insured.

SAFETY STICK FOR MARE'S HALTER.

Figure 104 shows a simple method of preventing colts from getting tangled in the mare's halter, and so becoming strangled. A piece of wood, eighteen inches long and two inches wide, is bored with a half-inch hole at each end, as shown in the engraving. The halter is passed through these holes and fastened in the usual

Fig. 104.—HALTER STICK FOR MARE WITH FOAL AT FOOT.

manner. The wood should be of tough oak or hickory, so that it will not break. It entirely prevents the formation of loops in the halter.

TO KEEP A HORSE FROM JUMPING.

Figure 105 shows a hopple to restrain a horse from jumping. It consists of a surcingle about the body of the horse, together with two short straps that pass through

Fig. 105.—HOPPLE FOR A HORSE.

the surcingle and around each foreleg, being buckled so that when the horse stands upright, the strap will fall about half-way to the knees. This arrangement, which allows the horse to walk quite freely, prevents its running as well as jumping. A similar plan is to connect the forelegs of a horse by straps secured just above the knee, but those who have tried both plans prefer the one herewith illustrated. Some horses are difficult to catch when at pasture, and this device will prove valuable in such cases.

COUPLING HORSES IN THE PASTURE.

Cut a piece of tough wood two feet six inches long, two inches in diameter; shave off the bark and bore a three-quarter or a one-inch hole near each end; tie a piece of half-inch rope around each animal's neck,

Fig. 106.—COUPLING FOR HORSES.

making a loose collar that will not slip over his head; take a loop of the rope and pass it through a hole in the bar, and into the loop insert the key, made of a piece of a half-inch oak board, two by three inches, shaped as in figure 106. The board being rounded at the top, will allow the rope to turn easily in the yoke and prevent choking. Always couple the animal that is likely to stray with the one that is not. This contrivance, used frequently on Southern and Western ranges, is approved by some as safe and convenient, and condemned by others as dangerous and uncomfortable for the animals. We give the illustration and description for what they are worth.

A SIMPLE TETHER.

Figure 107 shows a tether for a horse or cow which obviates the danger of an animal becoming entangled as when staked out in the usual way. It is made as follows: Take a stout piece of timber, *a*, *b*, three and one-half feet

Fig. 107.—TETHER FOR HORSE.

long; fasten a ring at *a*, and one at *c*, six inches from the lower end. Take a pole, *c*, *d*, making it long enough to extend back of the animal's heels three or four feet, and fasten a ring to each end. An iron spike, *f*, with a ring, *e*, in the end, is driven in the ground. The irregular line represents a cord of wire of any desired length.

Fasten the rod, *a*, *b*, to the halter at *a*, with a leather strap, also *c*, *d* to *a*, *b*, in the same way at *c*; tie one end of the cord in the ring at *d*, and the other in the ring in the end of the iron spike. The ring at *c*, six inches from the lower end, prevents taking up the cord, and thus entangling the animal. The end, *b*, will slide over it as the animal grazes.

CHAIN CATTLE TIE.

Various methods have been devised for coupling cattle in their stalls in a more humane manner than by stanchions. The common chain tie passes about the animal's neck, and slides up or down upon a post or iron rod, attached to the stall or manger. The tie, figure 108, is similar, except that the neck-chain is connected with two posts or rods, upon which it slides. The improvement consists in using **rings** upon the posts, and con-

Fig. 108.—AN IMPROVED TIE FOR CATTLE.

necting the side-chain with the neck chain by means of snap-hooks, attached to the central ring as shown in the engraving. This enables one to adjust the tie to any width of stall, say from three to four feet, and have it reasonably taut. The advantage of this method of fastening cattle over any other is, that while great freedom is given the head, so that a cow can lick both sides and lie down with her head upon either side, she has no more backward and forward motion than if she stood in stanchions, hence must leave her droppings in the gutter—if the stall is of the proper length. There is a constant tendency to give cow stalls too long a floor. Every cow should lie with her rump four to eight inches beyond the floor. The only objection to this is that the cows' tail will sometimes become wet from lying in the gutter. If, however, this is given a pretty sharp fall and considerable breadth, water will not accumulate, and there will be no inconvenience experienced on this score.

AN UNPATENTED CALF FEEDER.

Undoubtedly calves which take nourishment directly from the cow, do better than those which take it from the pail, unless care is taken to feed them slowly. An

Fig. 109.—CALF FEEDER.

artificial udder is shown in figure 109, made of strong water-proof duck in the shape of a cow's udder, and furnished with teats, each filled with a piece of sponge. The mouth of the bag may be closed by means of clamps, figure 110, and the bag hung up in the calf pen. The calf will get its milk slowly and along with plenty of

Fig. 110.—CLAMPS FOR CALF FEEDER.

saliva, which is an indispensable aid to digestion. It is the want of an adequate quantity of saliva with the milk, which causes so much indigestion in calves that are allowed to drink milk from a pail.

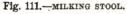

TWO KINDS OF MILKING STOOLS.

The construction of a very good milking stool is readily seen in figure 111. Upon a hard-wood board,

Fig. 111.—MILKING STOOL.   Fig. 112.—MILKING STOOL.

twelve inches wide, one inch thick, and thirty inches long, fasten at right angles a board to serve as a rest. This should be eight inches wide, and as long as the width of the back-board. Strengthen the seat with stout braces. Cut a narrow opening in the long board, to admit the fingers, by which to carry the stool, or hang it up when not in use.

The other stool, figure 112, is designed for a man who has a good many cows to milk, and desires to carry his stool around with him, while his hands are left free. The seat consists of the bottom of a peach basket; the single leg is made of a round piece of wood securely fastened to the center of the seat. The latter may be padded and covered as one chooses. Leather straps to reach up and around the waist of the milker, as shown in the illustration, should be firmly attached to the seat.

VAT FOR DEEP SETTING MILK

The advantages of the deep setting of milk at a low temperature can be enjoyed by means of the simple cooler, figure 113. To make the cooler take six pine planks, two inches thick, twelve inches wide, and six

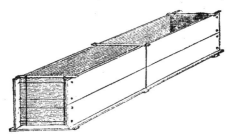

Fig. 113.—A COOLER FOR SETTING MILK.

feet long, four boards sixteen and a half inches long and twelve inches wide, and construct a box with the ends gained in with a groove a quarter of an inch deep. Place a rubber strip between the boards, and clamp with rods and bolts, to make it as tight as possible. Provide a lid to keep out dust and to shade from the sun. Place a faucet at the bottom, by which to run off the water when it has become warm. Set the cooler near the well whence cold water can easily be drawn, and keep the cans of milk submerged in the water. If there is a supply of ice, the temperature of the water may be still further reduced, and the cooler rendered more efficient. A box of the size given above will have room for twelve three gallon cans.

HOME-MADE BUTTER-WORKER.

The butter worker, figure 114, is made to stand upon a table or low bench, or when of large size, upon the floor. The lever works upon a rod and can be moved sidewise, an arrangement which we have seen in no other butter-

Fig. 114.—A SERVICEABLE BUTTER-WORKER.

worker, but which is very desirable. The table slopes forward, and has several grooves to carry the liquid down to a pail or a dish placed to receive it. The lever at the under side is leveled to a round or sharp edge, as may be wished. The cost of the worker is a mere trifle; it should be made of maple, ash or chestnut.

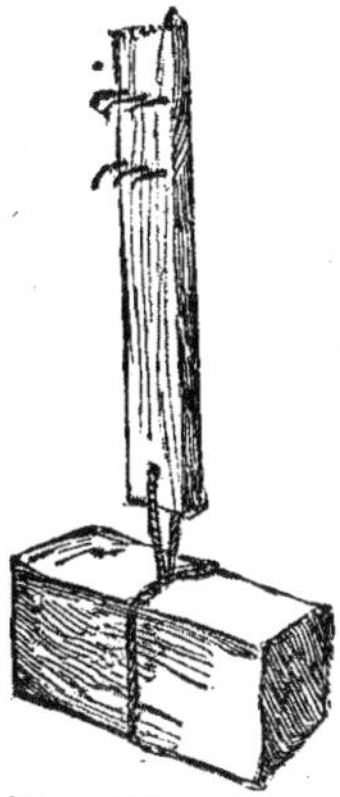

The comfort which a cow seems to derive **from a free** use of her tail during fly time, is **not** shared in any degree by the milker, **and** various means have been devised **to hold** the troublesome appendage in place. **One** of the latest is illustrated in figure **115.** Half a dozen six-penny wire nails **are** driven through a piece of lath, and **each** point bent to a hook. A brick is suspended by a string from the lower end of the stick. As the milker sits down beside the cow, the hooks are thrust into the brush of her tail, leaving the brick resting in part on the ground or barn floor. After the first futile efforts to swing the brick by tail power, the cows learn to **give it** up, and the milker is free from a very great annoyance.

Fig. 115. — TAIL-HOLDER.

REINS FOR DRIVING OXEN.

Figure 116 shows a method of arranging the reins **for** a yoke of oxen. Each ox has a spring bull-ring placed **in**

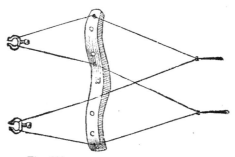

Fig. 116.—DRIVING OXEN WITH REINS.

his nose and from these rings small ropes run back as seen in the illustrations. Staples are driven into the top of the yoke through which the cords pass. It is claimed that with these reins a yoke of oxen can be guided and controlled with ease. The rings are quickly removed from the noses when work hours are over.

VAT FOR DIPPING SHEEP.

Sheep should be dipped twice a year. They suffer a great deal from vermin, which are destroyed by the dipping. After shearing, the ticks greatly annoy the lambs, upon which they gather from the shorn sheep and prevent

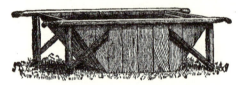

Fig. 117.—PORTABLE VAT.

their growth. The lambs, at least, should be dipped, to free them from these pests, but it is well to dip the whole flock, as a safeguard against the prevalent scab, and other skin diseases. A very good dipping vat is shown in figure 117. It is made of one and a quarter inch tongue and grooved boards, put together at the joints with pitch, and is furnished with handles, with which it can be moved from place to place. It may be six feet long, three feet wide, and three feet deep. The sloping ends have cleats nailed across them on the inside, by which the sheep are assisted to get out of the vat, upon a draining floor placed to receive them. A good dip is made of one pound coarse tobacco, and one pound of sulphur, steeped in five gallons of boiling water. It is most effective when used at a temperature of one hundred and twenty degrees, and the sheep should be left in the dip long enough to have the wool saturated, and the skin well soaked by the fluid. A quantity of fresh dip should be kept in a boiler, to renew the old dip as it is diminished by use.

SHEEP-SHEARING BENCH.

Shearing benches will be found desirable, as they save the wearisome stooping over the sheep. A bench of this kind is shown in figure 118. It is made of stout strips nailed to curved cross-pieces. These are best bent by

Fig. 118.—SHEARING BENCH.

steaming them, or soaking them in hot water for some hours, or sponging them frequently beside a hot fire, by which the fiber is much softened and the wood is warped permanently. The legs are about twenty inches long. Any dust on the wool falls through the bars.

EAR TAG PUNCH FOR MARKING ANIMALS.

A punch, which is struck with a hammer, and even the new belt-punch pattern, now so generally used, inflict considerable pain; the blow in one case, and the very considerable pressure needful in the other, are both productive of suffering which can just as well be avoided. Some breeders have used with entire satisfaction a very simple contrivance, figure 119, which any machine shop can furnish from the engraving and description herewith. Take a piece of steel rod, say five inches long and about five-sixteenths of an inch in diameter. Fix this in a chuck and drill a hole endwise from a to b in the engraving, which leaves that end a hollow tube, the walls of which are about one-thirty-second of an inch thick, supposing a one-quarter inch drill has been used. Possibly a little smaller hole would be better. Then file a notch in one side at b, so that it will clear readily. Drill a small hole, c, near the one end, in which to fit a short piece of smaller wire, d, which forms a convenient gimlet-like handle. When finished, have it nicely filed to a taper at the hollow end, so as to form a thin cutting edge, which must be kept quite sharp. After being tempered it forms the best tool for its work ever invented. To use the punch, hold in the left hand a large cork, or a small block of wood, and carefully selecting the proper place between the ribs or ridges of the ear, press the punch snugly down, give it a quick, sharp twist, just as one would a gimlet, and the animal scarcely flinches at all, so slight is the pain.

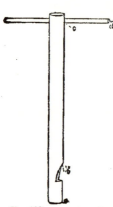

Fig. 119.—EAR PUNCH.

SEWING UP WOUNDS IN ANIMALS.

The winter season is always prolific of accidents, chiefly among horses, which are often badly blemished by cuts which are left to heal imperfectly, without any assistance.

When a horse with sharp calks kicks another, or when an animal falls upon ice, the skin is usually cut in an angu-

Fig. 120.—NEEDLE FOR SEWING UP WOUNDS.

lar shape and the flap of skin hangs over in an unsightly manner, or in a torn cut the skin gapes open and makes a wound difficult to heal. As a rule, a horse's wound

Fig. 121.—WOUND SEWED TOGETHER.

heals very rapidly under the simplest treatment. A curved needle, figure 120, is used to sew up severe wounds as shown in figure 121.

CHAPTER V.

WELLS, PUMPS, CISTERNS, AND FILTERS.

WINDLASS AND TILTING BUCKET.

As ordinary pumps draw water only thirty-three feet perpendicularly, and practically only about thirty feet from the water surface, force-pumps or windlasses are required, for wells thirty or more feet deep. The common windlass with stop ratchet serves a fair purpose, but requires the bucket to be let all the way down by turning the crank backward. Various forms of brakes have been devised. Figure 122 shows the construction and operation of one. Two opposite corner pieces, *p*, extend six feet high above the platform, and a diagonal piece connect-

Fig. 122.—IMPROVED WINDLASS.

ing their upper ends supports a grooved pulley carrying the lifting rope. A hook, *h*, turning on a pivot, is thrown over the lever *b*, and slid along it far enough to hold the brake against the windlass firmly, when the hand is removed. A swinging iron rod catches in the small pin on the top of the bucket as it rises, and tips the water into the spout. With these little additions, a windlass and bucket are better than a pump, as the water is drawn fresh, with no tainting from the pump log. The actual force required to raise the same water is less with the windlass than with the pump, as less power is required than is wasted in the friction of the close fitting valves of the pump, and the friction of the water against the side of the tube.

WELL-CURB OF STAVES.

Figure 123 is a very strong and durable curb made of staves. A cooper can make it, setting up the staves, which are one and one-quarter inch thick, as for a barrel, using three iron hoops. The shaft of the windlass is also of iron, to which a wooden cylinder is fastened by a

Fig. 123.—A "BARREL" WELL-CURB.

couple of bolts driven through the wood and iron. In making the windlass, fashion the wood to the right size, and then split open the cylinder, cut a place for the shaft, fit it in, and then drive bands over the ends.

HEMLOCK FOR WELL-CURBS.

In many sections of country stone is scarce, and plank is used for curbing wells. Pine lumber gives a disagreeable taste to water. Hemlock lumber is usually cheaper than pine, and can be obtained at most lumber yards. Five hundred feet of lumber are sufficient for a well fourteen feet deep, three by four feet outside measurement. The four posts should be four by four inches, and the planks two inches thick, fastened on with heavy spikes. Dig down until there is danger of caving, and then put in the curb, with planks enough on to reach the surface of the ground. Afterwards dig the earth from the inside of the curb, and put on the planks as fast as needed. In some soils that are loose, the weight of the curb will settle it down as the work progresses; should it not, drive on the posts. Such a curb, made of sound hemlock, will last for years, and give pleasant water from the first.

SECURING THE WELL-BUCKET.

Fig. 124.

One who has much experience with well-buckets, will find they are often set down outside of the curb, and not always in a clean place. In this manner the water in the well may be fouled with clay, if with nothing worse. Every person should be very careful to avoid anything that may in any degree tend to impair the purity of the water in a well. One way to secure this end is to have the bucket always in a safe place. This may be done by fixing a cord or a chain to the beam over the pulley, or to the stirrup of the pulley, and fastening a hook to its lower end, upon which the bucket should always be hung when not in use. This arrangement for the well-bucket is made plain by figure 124.

CURB WITH A BUCKET SHELF.

Another device for keeping the bucket clean is shown in figure 125. An iron plate of suitable size is held on the end of an arm fastened at right angles to an upright iron rod. The bottom of this rod rests upon an iron projecting from the corner of the curb, and the top is held in place by an eye-rod. The filled bucket is raised high

enough so that the plate is placed directly under it. Let
up on the windlass when the bucket is secure on the

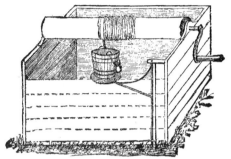

Fig. 125.—A BUCKET SHELF.

plate, and it may be swung to one side without straining
the back, or danger of slipping when it is icy.

COVERED WELL-CURBS.

Figure 126 is a desirable covering for a well-curb. The
upper part of the curb is floored over, except about a foot
and a half in the center. Cleats, *r, r*, are nailed along
two opposite sides of the bucket-holes and upon these, at

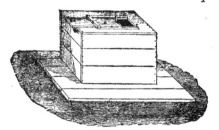

Fig. 126.—A WELL-CURB COVERING.

one end, is placed a strip, *g*. A wide board is made to
fit and slide in the grooves formed by the cleats. The

wooden pins, *a, a*, project above the cover, and answer as handles for sliding it as desired.

Figure 127 shows a covered well curb, which is safe against worms, frogs and other vermin; and also against the entrance of surface water, leaves and other objects. The wall of the well is carried up to the surface of the

Fig.—127.—A SAFE WELL CURB.

ground, and clean gravel is spread around it and beaten down firmly. A frame of four by four-inch chestnut is then bedded down level with this surface, and a floor of two-inch planks, with matched edges, is laid down, projecting a little over the raised gravel, as shown in the engraving. The ground slopes from the floor in all directions, and should be neatly sodded. The best covering, being indestructible, is a large flagstone; or, it may be made with several pieces and bedded in mortar. The curb is built around the well, large enough to give standing room for the bucket at one corner; it should be no higher than is convenient to reach over it to use the bucket. A spout is fixed to the front, into which the bucket is emptied without lifting it over the curb. The curb is protected on top with one fixed and one hinged wire gauze covered frame. The hinged one is thrown back and rests against a support, if desired, as shown, or it may fall entirely back upon the other one. This wire gauze admits air, but keeps out leaves and other trash, which is blown about by the winds. An open curb like this keeps the air in the well pure, the water clean, and in some respects it is preferable to a pump.

IMPURE WATER IN WELLS.

It becomes more and more evident each year that much of the sickness prevalent in the country is directly attributable to the quality of the water. By carefully studying the matter, it is found that in nine cases out of ten typhoid fevers originate in families whose water supply is from a well, into which impure water comes. This may be from the farm yard, and quite generally such is the case. For some years the water in a well near the house may be pure and wholesome, but by-and-bye the soil between it and the barn-yard will become so impregnated with pollution that an unhealthful quality will be imparted to it, and disease will result from its use. This is almost sure to be the case when the distance between the two is not great, because, as a general thing, the bottom of the well is lower than the yard, and the drainage from the latter will extend in all directions through the most porous strata of soil, and when it reaches the well, it will naturally flow into it as a reservoir. No matter how pure the water may have been when the well was first dug, sooner or later it will be contaminated by water flowing through the soil from barn-yards and cesspools located anywhere near it. A case is on record in which four children died from diphtheria. An examination by the physician proved that the slops from the kitchen had so filled the soil for a distance of twenty feet between the back door, out of which they were thrown, and the well, that the water in the latter was polluted by foul gases, and from the use of it **diphtheria** had certainly resulted. When making a **well, have it,** if possible, above the barn-yard, and let the drainage be from it rather than into it. Arrange a place for slops with a cement bottom and sides, from which **glazed pipes,** cemented together, allow the unhealthy **matter to** flow off and away from the well.

HOOK FOR CLEANING WELLS.

Every farmer who has open wells, knows how difficult and tiresome a task it is, to extricate articles which have **fallen** into them, but figure 128 shows a contrivance **which** has been used successfully. Find the depth of the

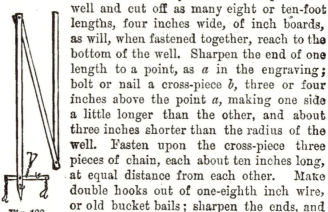

Fig. 128.

well and cut off as many eight or ten-foot lengths, four inches wide, of inch boards, as will, when fastened together, reach to the bottom of the well. Sharpen the end of one length to a point, as a in the engraving; bolt or nail a cross-piece b, three or four inches above the point a, making one side a little longer than the other, and about three inches shorter than the radius of the well. Fasten upon the cross-piece three pieces of chain, each about ten inches long, at equal distance from each other. Make double hooks out of one-eighth inch wire, or old bucket bails; sharpen the ends, and attach them to the chains. Bolt the lengths **of** boards together closely; let the cross-piece and hooks **down** into the well, tightening the bolt at the end of each length as it passes, until the point reaches the bottom. Now turn the contrivance, causing the hook to describe several circles at the bottom of the well. The article sought for will probably be caught by the hooks;

besides a good many other things not looked for will perhaps be brought up.

A NON-FREEZING PUMP.

One of the simplest methods of preventing a pump from freezing is shown in figure 129. The pump is boxed from the platform to six inches or more above the spout, the box being made large enough to admit of a

Fig. 129.—PUMP PROTECTOR.

packing of sawdust or spent tan bark between it and the pump-stock; or the pump-stock can be well wrapped with heavy hardware paper and then boxed tightly, which will effectually keep out almost any ordinary degree of cold. It is well to have the platform double-boarded, running each layer of boards in opposite directions, and mounding up well around the platform with earth, to still further protect against cold.

AGITATION OF AIR IN WELLS.

One great objection to the old style of log pump is the non-ventilation of the well. The platform is made as tight and close-fitting as possible, to prevent dirt, vermin etc., from getting into the water. By the use of a chain pump there is enough to agitate the air and water and to prevent stagnation in either. By means of a cheap, simple contrivance, shown in figure 130, all wells may

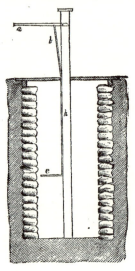

Fig. 130.—AGITATOR FOR WELL.

have an abundant supply of fresh air. In the illustration, h is the wooden or metal tube of a common lift or force pump; a, is the handle to which is attached, three or four inches from where it is hinged to the pump, a small wooden or metal rod, b. If this rod is of wood, it need not be over three-quarters of an inch in diameter, and if a metal one three-eights of an inch will answer. It runs from the handle downward to and along side of the pump-tube, shown at h, passing through two or more closely-fitting staples, and extends to within two feet of the high water mark. It is provided at the lower end with an arm, or more properly speaking, a fan, e, which should be of some light material, such as a thin board or piece of sheet iron or tin, eight or nine inches square. It is evident that the act of pumping will move this fan up and down, from three to five inches at each stroke of the handle, producing a movement of the air within the well. By continuing the rod downward for a few feet, and attaching to the end a block of wood two or three inches square, the water will also be sufficiently agitated to prevent stagnation.

DEEPENING WELLS.

Many wells which fail during long drouths, could be made, by deepening a few feet, to yield an abundant and unfailing supply of water. But it is difficult to accomplish this by ordinary means, without endangering the wall with which the well is lined. Figures 131 to 135 show a set of appliances by which the work may be safely done without danger to the wall, even in sandy or gravelly soil. Figure 131 is a sort of well-auger of galvanized iron, five inches in diameter, and of any desired length, from fourteen to twenty inches. Before it is bent in shape, a bias strip is cut from its lower edge, giving it the shape shown in the engraving. The rod by which it is worked is of wrought iron pipe one inch in diameter. A T is screwed on its summit, to receive the handle, of ash, or other tough wood. Figure 132 is a cylinder, also of galvanized sheet-iron, six inches in diameter and two feet long. It is reinforced at each end by iron bands riveted on, and is perforated throughout with thin slits for the admission of water when in position. Figure 133 is the head of the auger. It is of inch board, upon which is screwed a flange with a thread, to receive the lower end of the hollow rod. Figure 135 represents a cross-section of this head-piece. At the lower end of the auger-tube is the piece shown in figure 134. This is a circular piece of galvanized iron, cut five inches in diameter, slitted from one side to the center, and the cut edges bent to spiral or screw-shape. This is soldered

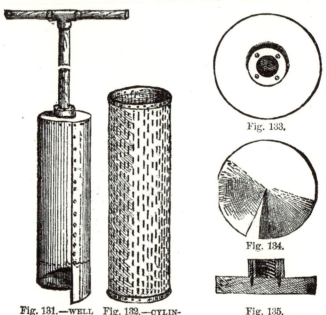

Fig. 131.—WELL AUGER. Fig. 132.—CYLINDER. Fig. 133. Fig. 134. Fig. 135.

into the lower end of the auger-tube, as shown by dotted lines in figure 131. A large hole on one side near the top, not shown in the engraving, serves to empty the tube of sand and dirt. To operate this, the cylinder is first pushed down as far as practicable into the bottom of the well. With the auger the earth is removed from inside the cylinder. As the work of excavation proceeds, the cylinder is pushed down until its upper edge is level with the bottom of the well. If a sufficient vein of water is not then reached, the boring goes on, and a second cylinder follows the first. This makes an additional depth of four feet, which is generally sufficient. If not, the process can be continued by providing additional cylinders, and splicing the auger-stem until a permanent water-vein is found.

DIGGING A WELL.

A hole is dug down and the earth thrown out as far as could be done, and then a ladder is rigged up on three stakes as shown in figure 136. A pulley is attached to one round, a cord thrown over it and fastened

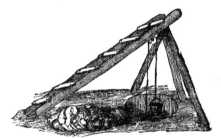

Fig. 136.—DIGGING A DAKOTA WELL.

to a pail, the other end of the rope reaching into the well. The pail is filled and drawn to the surface, where it is swung to one side, emptied and returned for another load. The upper end of the ladder should be elevated about six feet above the ground.

HOW TO BUILD A CISTERN.

Every part around the surface of a cistern should be made close. The beams which support the floor should be bedded in the wall, or shoulder of the cistern, and covered with lime or cement mortar, leaving a smooth surface all around the first floor. This should then be covered with a second floor, raised eight or ten inches on a frame of two by ten joists, made of cedar or chestnut.

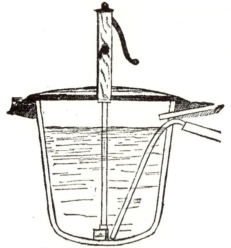

Fig. 137.—FROST-PROOF CISTERN.

The earth should be packed closely against this frame, and the top floor should extend a few inches beyond the frame all around. The cistern is then frost and vermin proof. Another important point is to get rid of the sediment that gathers at the bottom of every cistern. This is done by carrying the overflow pipe to the bottom of the cistern on a line with the inlet pipe, and thus forming a current which disturbs the sediment and carries it into the overflow. This is shown in figure 137, also the arrangement of the draw-pipe, which should have a fine wire strainer on the end, and should rest upon a support near the bottom of a fine strainer, at least two feet high. A piece of one-quarter inch mesh of galvanized wire gauze, bent into a pipe a foot in diameter, and covered with thick flannel cloth, doubled, makes a filter for the water.

WATER IN THE BARN YARD.

Water in the barn yard is a great economy and convenience; by a little management it can be secured with ease. The difficulties in the way, are chiefly in bringing the water down hill, over an elevation midway, and

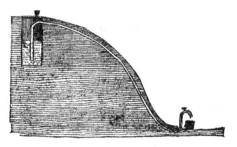

Fig. 138.—CONVEYING WATER BY SIPHON.

in bringing it up hill, from a spring or well below the level. In the former case, a siphon must be used, as shown in figure 138. It consists of a pipe, one end of which is under the surface of the water in a well or spring, and carried over a ridge, and down a slope, to a lower level. This method is open to one objection, which nearly always gives trouble. There is more or less air dissolved in water; this dissolved air escapes, as the water is flowing through the pipe, and gathers at the highest point, where it stops the flow. To remove this air, the following arrangement is made. A short pipe, furnished with a stop cock and a funnel, is fitted to the highest point of the siphon. When the flow begins to be obstructed by air, the stop cock at the lower end of the pipe is shut, and that at the top is opened.

The pipe is then filled with water through the funnel. The water is held in the pipe by a check valve at the bottom of the well pipe. The air is thus driven out of the siphon, and the top stop-cock is shut. The flow is started by opening the lower stop-cock, and all goes

Fig. 139.—RAISING WATER BY FORCE PUMP.

on again, until the air gathers in the pipe once more, when the remedy is repeated. To draw water up hill, by a pump, the method seen in figure 139 is used: The pipe, having a check valve at the bottom, is laid from the spring, up the incline, and connected with a force pump, in a dry well, at the top. Water can be raised in this manner, from about twenty-eight or thirty feet below the bottom of the dry well, and for a distance of two hundred and fifty, or three hundred feet, or more. The linear distance is not an obstacle, except for the friction in the pipes; it is the perpendicular height alone, which gives serious trouble, and about twenty-eight or thirty feet, is all that can be overcome by means of a suction pump. A force pump is useful to raise the water eight or ten feet more than this, when necessary. This method is shown in the engraving.

WOODEN WATER PIPES.

For conveying water any distances less than fifteen rods, and where the amount desired is greater than can be supplied by a half-inch pipe, wooden tubing will be found cheaper than iron, lead, or other metallic pipes. Wooden tubing, of from one and a quarter to two-inch bore, may be obtained of all hardware dealers. In purchasing observe that the ends are iron-banded, to prevent splitting when placed together, and to prevent the tubes from bursting when under a heavy head of water. Before the pipe is laid, it is best to give it one or two coats of oil; even crude petroleum will do; this adds greatly to the durability. In pipes through which there is a constant flow of water, there is little danger of decay; in fact, some old-fashioned pump logs which have been removed after nearly fifty years of use, were found sound on the inside. Wooden, as well as other pipes conveying water, should be laid below the frost line. If the water is intended for drinking purposes, place the pipe at least three feet under ground, and if in sandy, porous soils, to a still greater depth. After the pipe is in position, and before the water is admitted, pour hot coal-tar over it, especially at each joint, which is readily done by using a watering pot or an old tea or coffee-pot. Always test wooden and other pipes after they are laid, by admitting water before covering them with soil, in order that a leak, if found, may be easily stopped.

FILTERS FOR FAMILY USE.

Almost every country store is in more or less direct communication with some pottery, where salt-glazed ware is made. Lead-glazed ware should be avoided, but the salt-glazed is both cheap and safe. Any pottery will furnish to order, or they may have them on hand, five or six gallon cylindrical jars of glazed ware, having a spigot hole in the side close to the bottom, and the usual jar lid. A common flower pot of large size should be selected, which will just fit in the top of the jar, as shown in figure 140. This pot is the filter, and it is thus arranged: The bottom is covered by a circular piece of

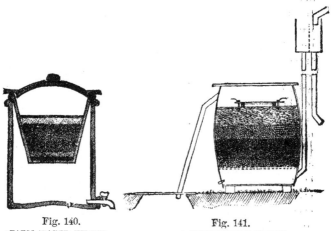

Fig. 140.
FARM WATER FILTER.

Fig. 141.
A SERVICEABLE FILTER.

thick woolen felt, or two or three pieces of blanket, upon this is placed a layer an inch thick of well-washed sand. Note that the sand, being well washed, the felt or blanket pieces should be so also. Now upon the sand, freshly burned, soft wood charcoal, which should be freshly heated, free from all dust, and about the size of grains of wheat, should be laid in to the depth of six inches more, and upon this an inch of sand, and another pad of felt or blanket to top off with. Fit up two flower pots for each filter, and keep those not in use covered and clean. The water is poured into the flower pot. A clean lump of clear ice, whole or broken up, may be placed in the jar below the pot, and then the water is fit for anybody's use.

The filter shown in figure 141 is made of a stout oak barrel with iron hoops. The head is taken out carefully and a number of holes are bored through it with a half-inch auger, then five or six oaken blocks, about three inches long, are nailed to the under side. It is then placed in the barrel for a false bottom. On this spread a layer of coarse gravel about two inches thick, then another of finer gravel; on this spread eight inches of charcoal; then add a six-inch layer of gravel, and on top place washed sand up to within an inch of the overflow pipe. Over this sand fit in the barrel a cover made of inch pine boards. In the center of this cut an opening ten inches square. Then make a low frame a little larger than the opening, cover both sides with cheese cloth, and fasten securely over the open space in the head, but in such a manner that it can be easily removed again. The object of this covering being to prevent sand from escaping into the cistern, it becomes sometimes necessary, after heavy rains, to take up the frame and wash the cloth.

The rain water flows into the barrel through a pipe between the real and the false bottom. About four feet above the cask the leader from the roof should enter a tin box, with a partition in the middle that comes within about two inches of the top. This partition separates the pipe that flows into the cask from the waste pipe, and the leader from the roof can be made to discharge on either side, as may be desired. Near the bottom of the barrel should be a large faucet or bung-hole, through which all the water may be drawn off and the filter cleaned. By pulling out the bung or opening the faucet, and, after the water has run out, pouring several bucketfuls of water on the sand at the top, all impurities are washed out and carried off; in fact, it is best to let out the water after every rain. If this filter is well made, and the cask painted, it will last many years and do good service.

When it is desired to connect a new cistern with an old one without loss of water, it can be done as shown in figure 142. Whatever the distance apart, provide a two-

Fig. 142.—CONNECTING TWO CISTERNS.

inch iron pipe, *a*, long enough to extend from the inside of the new well to the outside of the old one, and fit upon the right end of it by screw thread the pipe, *b*, long enough to extend well through the old wall. Build *a* into the new well, and close its left end with a wooden plug, *p*. When ready, pump or syphon the water from the old to the new cistern. Then open the old wall, screw *b* on to *a*, and cement around *b*. When ready, with a rod or bar, knock out the plug, which will float to the top, and the water will stand at a level in both cisterns. A connecting five or six-inch glaze ware or iron pipe, *c*, should be put in on a level with the overflow pipe, *o*. One pump and one overflow pipe answer for both cisterns.

BUILD AND DIMENSION OF CISTERNS.

In a stiff clay soil a small cistern of twenty to forty barrels capacity might be safely cemented directly to the earth, but in ordinary soils and for larger cisterns, a good four-inch-wall of hard brick is on the whole the cheapest. It is important to make the excavation smooth, so that the bricks can be pressed firmly against the earth; otherwise these will be pushed out and the cement cracked, causing a leak. As to the dimensions, a cistern should be about one-fourth deeper below the spring of the arch, than its width inside. By this rule a cistern eight feet wide will be ten feet deep below the arch. At the top is a cast iron ring, twenty inches in diameter, for the manhole, covered with a tight fitting cast iron lid. The ring has a flange two inches wide extending out over the brick. The capacity of a cistern needed to save all the water from a given extent of roof, will depend on the total annual rainfall, its distribution throughout the year, and the regularity with which it is used. A roof ninety feet by twenty feet contains eighteen hundred square feet. This is supposed to be the measure of the building on the ground and not the shingled surface. In the vicinity of New York the average annual rainfall is about forty-two inches, or three and a half feet. This would give sixty-three hundred cubic feet of water (1,800 ft. $\times 3^{1}/_{2}=6,300$). Since in that climate the rain is distributed pretty regularly through the year, it would only be necessary to provide storage capacity for about one-third of the rainfall of the year, or twenty-one hundred cubic feet. This divided by four and one-fifth (the approximate number of cubic feet in a barrel of thirty-one and a half gallons) gives five hundred barrels, and this quantity of water demands a cistern, thirteen feet diameter, to be nearly sixteen feet deep below the arch, or a square one, thirteen feet across, to be nearly twelve and a half feet deep; or a round one, fifteen feet in diameter, would need to be about twelve feet deep. In the far West—in fact, in most places west of the Missouri—the rainfall is largely during the six months beginning with March, and cisterns need a greater storage capacity.

CISTERNS WITH FILTERS.

Complaints are frequent of the impure water of cisterns. This is inevitable under the careless management of these useful additions to the water supply, and is a fruitful source of what are called "malarial dis-

Fig. 143.—A COMPLETE CISTERN.

eases." A roof gathers a large quantity of impure matter, dead insects, droppings of birds, dust, dead leaves, pollen from trees, etc., etc., all of which are washed into the cistern, unless some means are taken to prevent it. Even then the water should be filtered before it is used for culinary purposes. One way of preventing foul matter from entering the cistern, is to have the leader movable, and swing from a waste pipe to the cistern pipe, shown on the left side of figure 143. In dry weather the pipe

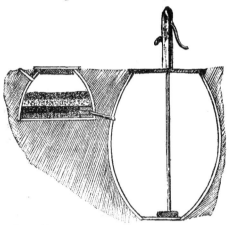

Fig. 144.—COMPLETE CISTERN AND FILTER.

is turned over the waste, and after the rain has fallen for a sufficient time to wash off the roofs and gutters, it is turned into the cistern pipe. The cistern, figure 143 is provided with a soft brick wall laid in cement, through which the water filters, coming out by the pump perfectly pure, and free from unpleasant odors. Rain water

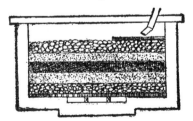

Fig. 145.—FILTER FOR A BARN CISTERN.

standing for months in impurities and filth, cannot always be purified by simply soaking through a brick wall, but should be filtered as soon as it falls. The main cistern, figure 144, is made egg-shaped, to hold one hundred barrels. The filter is flat-bottomed. The end of the pipe from the filter to the cistern is built solid

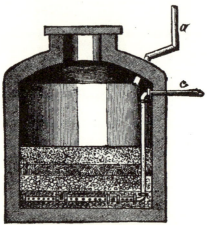

Fig. 146.—A HOUSE FILTERING CISTERN.

around the end with brick. All water has to pass through the brick. The filter is filled half full with charcoal, sand and gravel in layers—one layer of each—the charcoal covering the bricks, then sand and gravel on top. The water, as soon as it falls, begins to filter and passes into the cistern, where it stands free from impurities. The filter is built to hold twenty-five barrels of water, but is half full of the filtering material.

Figure 145 shows a good filter for a barn cistern. The top of it consists of broken stones, with a flat stone to receive the influx, so placed as to prevent heavy rains from disturbing the broken stones. This has a cover, movable in part, to permit it to be cleaned out occasionally. Figure 146 is a filtering cistern for a house. The inlet pipe is at *a*, the draw pipe is at *c*, and this is connected with a set of cross-pipes, laid in the coarse gravel in the bottom, and pierced with a number of small holes,

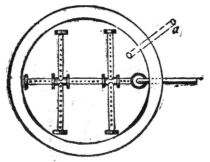

Fig. 147.—PIPES FOR HOUSE CISTERN.

as seen in figure 147, by which the outflow is made quite easy and abundant.

CHAPTER VI.

APPLIANCES FOR HANDLING HAY AND CORN FODDER.

REVOLVING HORSE RAKE.

Figure 148 shows a strong, cheap and efficient horse rake. It is especially useful in raking corn-stalks that have been cut by a mower or otherwise, and tall reeds and other rubbish, which it is desirous to rake into windrows preparatory to burning. It can also be adapted to the raking of hay and straw, by making the teeth lighter and placing them six inches or less apart.

Figure 149 represents the rake and shafts, *a* being a six by six-inch beam, ten feet long. This revolving rake can be made longer or shorter as desired, but when more than nine or ten feet long, it is not easily drawn through ordinary farm gates. The teeth are made of some kind of tough wood, well seasoned, two inches square, and the

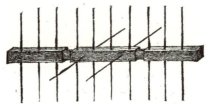

Fig. 148.—BODY OF RAKE.

pieces cut about four feet long. They are then tapered slightly toward the ends, and trimmed in the middle to fit in holes bored with a two-inch auger; thus prepared, they are inserted one foot apart, and secured in place with light bolts. At b, b, the beam is rounded to form journals, and around these the ends of the shafts can be

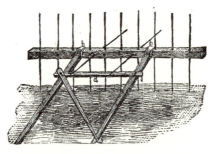

Fig. 149.—RAKE WITH SHAFTS.

bent, as seen in figure 149, or pieces of old iron, as the tire of an old wheel, may be curved round and secured to the shafts. Two stout pieces of the same length as the teeth, and at right angle to those, are inserted between the shafts. These rest on the lever, d, when the rake is moving, and serve to hold it in position with the teeth pointed toward the ground. The lever is hinged to a shaft at *e* by a bolt, and by pulling the handle, *f*, when in motion, the support is taken from the check teeth,

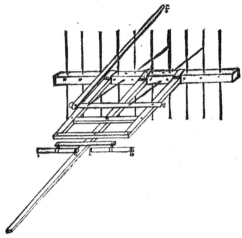

Fig. 150.—RAKE FOR TWO HORSES.

and the rake turns, depositing its load, and bringing the other row of teeth to the ground.

An implement of the above dimensions is too heavy for one horse; hence the shafts are intended to be hooked to the hind axle of a naked wagon, and thus worked by a team, the driver riding on the wagon and operating the lever whenever the rake is full.

The rake can also be made with a pole, so as to hitch a team directly to it, as shown in figure 150. The beam should then have three journals instead of two, and the number of teeth even, so that the pole can be attached at the middle.

CARE OF MOWING MACHINES.

Take up the wear of the boxes by removing the stuffing. If the journals have too much play they cut fast. But if the boxes fit too closely, they will heat. The thickness of newspaper all around each is sufficient play. Examine all the nuts and tighten any that are loose. A loose nut will cause the machine to wear or break; and will lose off in the field, causing a vexatious delay at the least. If any nut is very loose, place a leather washer under it, and sink the nut in. Make quite sure that there is no weak place in the whiffletrees. They always break at the wrong time, and may allow the machine and the team to mire down in a muddy spot. Mind the sickles. Every mower should have three sickles, so that as soon as one becomes dulled, another may be put in its place. A dull sickle does "ragged" cutting, and will increase the wear and draft of the machine one half. Observe if the sickle bar is not warped; and if the points of the sections are in a perfectly straight line. A section out of line will wear fast and increase the draft. Try the sections and tighten any that are loose. A loose section is apt to cause a breakage. A loose guard will produce the same result. See that the tool-box contains claw-hammer, pincers, file, sections, rivets, bolts, wire and nails; the lack of these will often require a trip from the field to the toolhouse. If any journals have rusted, use coal oil, every few minutes, for the first half hour, driving slowly; and it is well to use coal oil on the track of the sickle, to clear off the gum that gathers from the grass. The machine oil often sold is poor stuff; it is frequently necessary to add castor oil to give it body. If too much of the latter is used, however, it will gum. There is nothing more satisfactory than lard (unsalted) with castor oil added to give it a little body. If the lard is taken to the field hot, in the morning, the sun will keep it liquified during the day. It is not economy to be sparing in the use of oil; it should be applied quite often, and but little at a time. When much of it is applied at once, it runs from the journals, and holds dust, increasing instead of diminishing the wear. When stopping at noon, throw some grass over the sickle and the driver journals, if you cannot drive the machine into the shade. Do not mow too close. It dulls and wears the sickle, and gains nothing—what is gained in hay is more than lost in the aftermath. Drive slowly, but steadily, and thus get the most done with least wear of team and machine. Driving "in spurts" for half a day will wear the machine more than steady driving for two days. Keep the edges of the grass straight; in other words, cut the full width of the sickle, for otherwise you cannot do economical work. Using a mower properly lengthens its life and increases the amount of work it will do in a day.

SWEEP FOR GATHERING HAY.

The implement shown in figure 151 is made by having two by four inch pieces of twelve feet long for teeth,

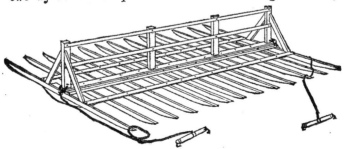

Fig. 151.—HAY SWEEP.

held together by a piece of two by six inch stuff, sixteen feet long, with a bolt through each tooth; two fence strips of inch stuff, six inches wide, keep them from spreading. Three or four upright two by four posts, four feet high, with cross fence strips, are set on the main beam. This holds the hay, and is braced at each end, as shown in the engraving. There is on the bottom of each end runner, a shoe one foot wide, two inches thick, and two or three feet long, to give the teeth a downward inclination. The teeth are tapered from the underside at each end, so as not to run into the ground. There is an iron ring at the bottom of each end post, to which ropes are fastened. These ropes are sixteen feet long or more, and a whiffletree is attached to the end of each. This contrivance takes up the hay to the stack, and picks up any dropped hay going back.

HAULING HAY OR STALKS.

Figure 152 shows a device for hauling an entire cock of hay. It is made thus: First, get a pole, elm if possible, ten or eleven feet long, and about four inches through at the butt. Peel off the bark, trim smooth,

Fig. 152.—DEVICE FOR HAULING HAY OR STALKS.

and sharpen to a point. Bore two holes near each other at the butt; pass a short piece of rope through the pole, and tie to the link on a single tree. Bore another hole a foot from the end, and pass through it a long one-inch rope, shorter on one side, and tie a knot on the rope on each side of the pole. When ready to commence hauling push the pole under the hay-cock, then take the long end of the rope, and pass it along side the hay-cock, and under the point of the pole, then through a loop in the short end, and draw tight and tie. By this method, no hay is lost on the way; it cannot roll over, nor get tangled. There is no waste, no time is lost, and the hay is laid at the feet of the pitcher just as it stood in the field. This device may also be used for hauling corn fodder or unhusked tools.

DERRICK FOR STACKING.

Figure 135 shows a derrick, which is very convenient in staking hay out-doors. The two side-pieces are mor-

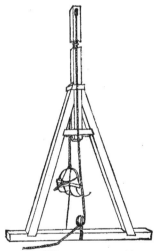

Fig. 153.—HAY DERRICK.

tised into the sill; the mast, or top stick, is not fastened, hence it can be taken out when moving any great distance. When moving only a few feet, hitch a horse to the sill, and drag it endways without taking it down, to where another stack is to be. The derrick and horse are on one side of the stack, and the load of hay on the other. The derrick stands at almost forty-five degrees, and is held in place by guy ropes—two opposite to the load, and one on the same side as the load. A solid piece of plank is used for the foot of the mast, which is mortised into it. It is best to put it together with bolts.

HAY CARRIER FOR HORSE FORK.

Figure 154 shows an ingenious device for returning a horse hay-fork from the hay-mow to the loaded wagon. It consists of a wire rope, C, stretched from the end of the track. A. to a wooden cylinder, B, four inches in

Fig. 154.—IMPROVED HAY-CARRIER.

diameter and sixteen inches long, around which a few turns are given. Two short stakes, D, D, cut from a four-by-four-inch scantling and driven slantingly into the ground, hold the roller in position. A grooved pulley, E, runs freely on the wire, and from its axis is suspended a fifty pound weight, F. The rope, G. runs over the pulley, H, which is firmly attached to the lower side of the track. The wire-rope is made of three wire clothes-lines twisted together. When in use, the upper end of the cord is attached to the rope which carries the fork. It is thus carried up with the loaded fork, and brings it back by gravitation when empty.

HAY BARRACKS.

Figure 155 shows barracks constructed by setting four posts, of chestnut, or white oak, twenty or twenty-five feet long, straight, partly squared to eight inches through, either three feet in the ground or upon sills. If upon sills, these are hewed upon one side and at the

Fig. 155.—BARRACK WITH BOARD ROOF.

ends, where they are halved together. In doing this, it is well to pin the ends with two inch oak tree-nails, which should stand up three or four inches above the sills when in place. Then when the posts are set at the corners, the pins will enter holes bored in the center of each post, and hold them in position. They will last as long as the posts and sills. For a temporary purpose, the posts may be simply set in the ground, twelve feet apart; but if permanency is desired, it is best to use sills, set level upon a flat stone at each corner, and supported in the middle. The posts must, moreover, be braced to the sills, either by diagonal braces, or straight rails, roughly squared, two by four, mortised into the posts at a height of four feet above the sills, or at a height of six feet, in case the barrack may be intended to be boarded up to make a stable. They make very good

Fig. 156.
BARRACK WITH THATCHED ROOF.

Fig. 157.
MANNER OF RAISING.

shelter for young cattle or horses, the inside between the sills being filled up level with stones, and finished with a layer of cement concrete. The cover, or roof, must be as light as is consistent with strength and efficacy, and may be of boards, or thatch, the latter being by far the most picturesque, and being lighter, it is easier to raise and lower. Before the posts are set, they are bored with inch holes, either twelve or fourteen inches apart, from the top down, exactly in the middle line, each set perfectly level, and pass through the posts in the same direction. Four pins of three-quarter inch iron, fourteen inches long, turned up a little at one end, and bent slightly downward to prevent rolling, are the roof supports. They are put into a set of low holes on the outsides of the posts, and two straight oak rails, sixteen to twenty inches longer than the space between the posts, are laid upon them. Then across the ends of these, and outside the posts, two similar rails are laid, the ends being temporarily bound together at the corners. These form the plates for the roof. One-third pitch is usually given, and the ends extend ten inches, or a foot, beyond the plates. A good coat of paint will make the roof quite durable, and prevent the boards from warping. To make a thatched roof, figure 156, nice, straight, light hoop poles are selected, which, if too heavy, must be split. These are for rafters. If binding poles are used, they must be mere rods, like light whip stocks. The rafter poles are laid up and bound at the ends, and to the cross-poles with tarred rope-yarn, but nailed to the plates. They are placed about eighteen inches apart, but the light split cross poles, about a foot to fourteen inches apart. The straw is laid on in handfuls, beginning at the eaves, and bound with rope yarn to the cross poles, or in courses, and bound down by tying the tough, slender maple rods, to the cross poles. Of course, the straw is kept even, and in courses, butts outward, and trimmed evenly with shears. When laid, the straw must be well evened at the butts, and dampened so as to pack nicely and not break in handling. These covers should be as light as possible, and be consistent with strength. They are raised and lowered one corner at a time, which may usually be done by one man, though more conveniently by two. To raise the roof, a ladder of suitable length is set under the lower plate pole of one corner, as shown in figure 157, the end of the pole being allowed to pass through between the rounds of the ladder, which is then lifted either by main strength, or by a rail used as a lever, and held in position until some one going up another ladder, can lift the pin which supports it. This is, of course, done at each corner, and thus the roof is raised, one peg at a time. It is lowered in the same manner by **reversing** the operation.

SUPPORTS FOR STACKS.

In stacking straw or hay, when stock is permitted to feed upon it during the winter, it is unsafe to leave the stack without support. The danger is that the stacks may be undermined, and fall over upon the animals.

Fig. 158.—FRAME FOR STRAW OR HAY STACK.

This will not happen if a stout support is made, as shown in figure 158. A few strong posts are set firmly in the ground, and planks spiked on the side as shown; the cattle can eat the straw from between the planks, and may eat the stack entirely through without danger of its being buried by over-turning. When the crib thus made is filled, the stack is topped off in the usual manner, being well spread over the eaves to shed the rain, and, as it is eaten out below, the straw settles down gradually. It is quite easy to cover a stack so made with a roof, so as to form a very cheap barrack. In the summer, by a little change, this will make a good calf or sheep pen.

HOME-MADE HAY PRESS.

The press shown in figures 159, 160, and 161 may be made wholly of wood, hewn to the right size, and put together with wooden pins. The frame, figure 159, is four feet long inside of the posts, and three feet wide. The

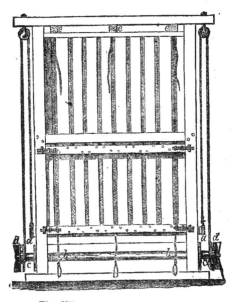

Fig. 159.—FRAME OF HAY PRESS.

height is eight feet. The movable bottom is raised by ropes which pass over pulleys or rollers, if no iron is to be used, and are wound upon the rollers at the bottom. This roller is moved by bars to be inserted in mortises cut in the roller, similar to the manner used in moving a windlass, or a capstan on shipboard. A movable door is made to fit the bottom of the press on one side, for the purpose of removing the bale after it is passed. The bale is bound with a strong cord, pieces of which are placed on the bottom and others on the top, as shown in

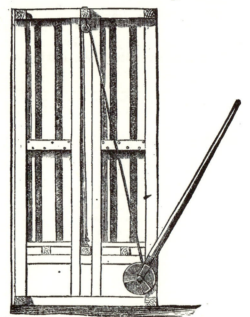

Fig. 160.—END VIEW OF HAY PRESS.

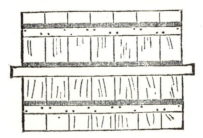

Fig. 161.—MOVABLE BOTTOM.

figure 159, and the ends are fastened when the bale is pressed as tightly as possible. It is then reduced to two and one-half feet in thickness, and eight of these bales will make a ton. The hay is easily transported in wagons when baled, and the press can be moved from one meadow to another as the hay is cut and pressed, or it will

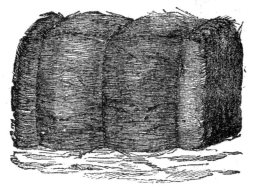

Fig. 162.—HAY BALE.

be more convenient at times to drive the cattle to the hay rather than move the hay to the cattle. Figure 160 shows the end view of the press, figure 161, the movable bottom, and figure 162, the pressed bale. When the iron can be procured without great expense, it might be well to use the pulleys and slotted wheels as here shown, but otherwise these parts may be made of wood.

TWISTING HAY AND STRAW.

The machine figures 163 to 167, consists of two two-by four bars, nine feet long, figure 163, straight and true, and of even thickness and width. They are bolted together at each end, and separated by a block four inches square and two inches thick, at one end a, and a piece of two-by-four stuff, three feet long, at b. A pulley is set at c, about thirty-nine inches from the end a. Figure 164 shows frame of back end (*A*, figure 167), *a* being a piece of two-by-four, four feet long; *b*, *b*, two uprights, one-by-four, six feet long; *c*, a two-by-four, three feet long; *d*, a one-by-four, three feet long; they are firmly

Fig. 163.—THE BARS, OR WAYS.

nailed together as shown, the upper edge of *c*, being half way up from bottom. Figure 165 is the same as figure 164, except the lower piece *a* is only three feet long. The five converging pieces are of some springy wood. They are attached by screws, three to the upper cross-pieces and two to the middle one, and prevent the hay going too fast out of the rack. Figure 166 shows a "follower" (*f*, figure 164), *a* being two-by-four, twelve inches long, *b*, two-by-four, twenty-six inches long, framed or halved on *a* ; *c* is a brace of one-inch board ; *d*, *d*, two pieces of board, the lower one eight inches wide, six inches long,

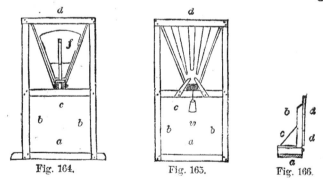

Fig. 164.   Fig. 165.   Fig. 166.

the upper twelve inches wide, sixteen inches long ; they are firmly attached to *b* by nails and screws as shown, and the brace *c* is then nailed in place. The "twister" is made of seven-sixteenths round iron, nine inches long from crank to hook, five inch crank, three and a half inch handle. The hook is turned so as to have a twist like a corkscrew, so that it will work in and catch the hay up of itself; two washers are put on that fit the rod snugly and four inches apart, by placing shaft in a vice; a nick with a cold chisel on each side of shaft on outside of each washer, will keep them in place. This is made fast upon a piece of two-by-four, twelve inches long, the upper end grooved out so that the shaft will set in about half way, then beveled off as shown; the shaft is fastened in place by a couple of strips of hoop

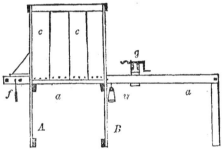

Fig. 167.—THE COMPLETE MACHINE (STRAW-TWISTER).

iron, bent over it and nailed or screwed in place; two strips are screwed on the sides, and a piece of board on the bottom end, as shown, leaving space between the two so that it will work freely on the ways, figure 163, when in place as shown in figure 167. Figure 167 shows the machine complete, *A* being figure 164, *B*, figure 165, in their places, *c*, showing boarding of rack, the edges of which show in figure 164 and 165; it is nailed to the upper piece and to the ways. *W* is a weight to bring the follower, figure 166, forward as fast as hay is used out, and keeps the hay firm and in its place against the wooden springs; the weight may be a stone, or box filled with iron or scraps. In use, draw the follower back, and run the

OLD-FASHIONED LABOR-SAVING DEVICES

pin, *f*, in hole bored through ways and follower, fill in the rack from top with hay, just mowed or slightly damp, pressing it in snugly, then draw out pin *f*, slide carriage *g* up to rack; by turning crank the hook will catch up a lock of the hay, then keep turning and drawing carriage away at the same time, and it will twist out a rope of hay, this is doubled, and ends fastened by crowding through loops. If you can get some drawer rollers to set in the follower and on the carriage, it will work much easier.

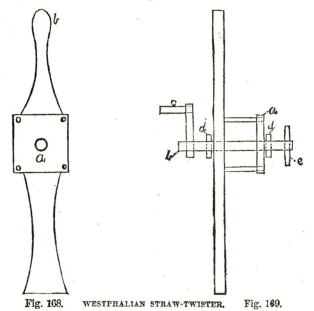

Fig. 168.   WESTPHALIAN STRAW-TWISTER.   Fig. 169.

Figures 168 and 169 show a form of **straw-twister** which has long been in use in Westphalia, Germany. A board of hard wood, half an inch thick, four and a half inches wide and five feet long, is shaped as in figure 168, and has an inch hole in the center. A piece of the same stuff, five inches square, also with an inch hole (*a* in the engravings), is attached to the large piece by means of long wooden pins, and stands three inches from it, the holes in the two exactly corresponding. A shaft of hard wood, *b*, figure 169, is square at the end, where the crank *c*, is attached, and round where it passes through the two holes. This shaft is held in place by the pins, *d, d*, which should be so set as to allow it to turn freely. Another wooden pin, *e*, passes through the shaft and projects an inch and a half on each side. In making the rope, two men are required. The straw having been slightly moistened by sprinkling from a watering can, one takes a bunch and fastens it to the pin *e*. The other operator takes the machine with his left hand, at *b*, figure 168, and with the lower end against his foot, turns the crank; he gradually moves away from the other, pushing the machine along with his foot, while keeping the crank in motion, and the other supplies straw as required. The latter sits upon a low stool, and his right hand should be protected by a stout leather glove or a piece of leather. When the rope is about a hundred feet long, or it becomes difficult to turn the crank, it is rolled into a ball, and a new one begun. The rope is finally made into balls of convenient size.

STANDARD FOR CORN SHOCKS.

The best standard is made by bending four hills together—two diagonal hills being lapped and twisted together. But to such a standard it can be objected, that a knife must be carried along to cut the stalks loose when the fodder is brought in from the fields, and that these stalks cannot be stood straight in the rick. Some prefer a movable wooden standard, of which a very good sort is shown in figure 170. A light pole, twelve or fifteen feet long, is provided with two upright supports; holes are bored through the pole about five feet from one end, through the ends of the uprights, and a bolt passed through the holes and secured by a nut. The holes should be so large that the uprights can be spread a foot apart at the bottom. Midway between the uprights and the end of the pole, another hole is bored, through which a cross-bar is put. In the four angles formed by

Fig. 170.—FODDER CORN STANDARD.

the intersection of the pole and the cross-bar, the fodder is set. When the shock reaches out to the support, the cross-bar is pulled out, and the pole can be removed. Some prefer to have the supports and cross-bar near together, about four feet from the pole. The shock is built around the supports. When done, the cross-bar is pulled out, and as the pole is removed, the supports are brought close together, and do not hinder.

VENTILATOR FOR STACKS.

A large quantity of corn fodder is spoiled for want of proper care in drying and stacking. It is not easy to hit the happy mean, between the sufficient drying of the stalks, and the over-drying of the leaves. But it can be done perfectly in the stack, by the use of the ventilator, figure 171. This consists of three or four poles or bars, fastened together with cross-slats, and made to fit one upon another. Such a ventilator, which may be four or six feet long, is set on the foundation for the stack, and passes upward through it, leaving a perfect chimney and air passage in the center of the fodder. More than

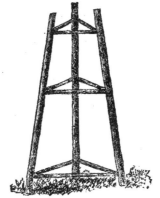

Fig. 171.—VENTILATOR FOR STACK.

one can be used if desired. These ventilators are useful in stacks of hay or grain, which may be a little damp.

BENCH FOR HUSKING.

Figure 172 represents a very comfortable and light husking stool; it is made long and wide enough to hold

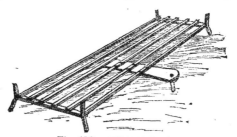

Fig. 172.—HUSKING STOOL.

a sheaf of stalk, and is provided with a seat, or may have one on both sides, if desired. If one can procure

some crooks of cedar or other light wood, such as is used in rustic work, they will serve very well for the ends. The seats may be removed when the stools are not required, and may then serve for benches in the dairy or for household purposes.

CORN-STALK BAND.

Stalks altogether dry or altogether green are not to be selected, as they will break when it is attempted to twist them. Long, slender stalks are desirable. The first stalk is broken at a right angle about two feet from the but; the but is then forced into the shock as far as the break, when the remainder of the stalk is passed

Fig. 173.—CORN-STALK BAND.

around the shock, breaking it carefully every eight or ten inches, until the tassel point is almost reached. Then another stalk is inserted in the shock. The top of the first stalk is broken every three inches between the thumb and fingers, and twisted around the second stalk, which is then broken and passed around the shock as in the case of the first one. This is continued until the last stalk reaches the first one, when it is secured by twisting it as in the case of the others, or by drawing it down between the shock and the first stalk, just in front of the break, forming a loop below, through which a piece of stalk, two feet long, is passed and driven into the shock. In figure 173 is shown the appearance of the band as it would be, if the shock could be removed after the band is completed.

CONVENIENT FODDER CARRIER.

On farms where the corn-stalks are left in the field to be carted to the yard as wanted, the use of a convenient carrier saves much work and time. Such a one is shown

Fig. 174.—FODDER CARRIER.

in figure 174. It consists of the front wheels, aı ster and pole of a common farm-wagon, with the ends of two poles, or a common cord-wood rack fastened to the bolster. The other ends of the poles drag on the ground. A cross-piece, three feet long, is securely fastened to the poles about three feet from their lower ends, and two upright stakes, four or five feet long, complete the arrangement of this farm convenience.

CHAPTER VII.

STUMP-PULLERS, DERRICKS AND SLINGS.

STUMP-PULLERS.

Figure 175 shows a very powerful machine for pulling stumps. The woodwork is made of well-seasoned oak, the winding shaft being eight inches in diameter and five feet long. The lower block, in which it revolves, is sixteen inches square and three inches thick, having a hole cut just large enough to receive the winding shaft, and is fastened securely to the middle brace at the bottom. To prevent the splitting of the winding shaft, two stout iron bands are shrunk immediately above and below where the lever or sweep is inserted. An old gear-wheel, with the spokes knocked out, is fastened to the top cross-piece or head-block, to receive the traveling ratchet attached to the shaft. The upright pieces of the frame are of two by eight inch oak, three and a half feet high; the top cross-piece or head-block two by sixteen inch oak, narrowing to twelve inches at the ends, and three feet long. The frame is set on runners four feet long, two by ten inch oak, so the implement can be quickly moved from place to place; the entire frame is mortised together. The anchor is of one-inch round iron, and attached as shown in the illustration, and a strong iron pulley-block is used on the opposite side. In pulling large stumps, a chain is more reliable than a rope. A single horse furnishes the motive power at the end of the lever or sweep, which is ten feet long.

Figure 176 shows a cheaper and lighter stump-puller. The only expense is for the chain, links of one and a half to two inch tough iron, or tough-tempered steel; ring, ten to twelve inches in diameter, and the hook, all of

Fig. 175.—HOME-MADE STUMP-PULLER.

which any blacksmith can make. The point of the hook must be formed so that it will strike in toward the heart of the stump and not tear loose on partially decayed wood. The lever may be twelve to twenty feet long, its size depending on the quality of the wood and the force to han-

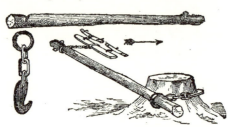

Fig. 176.—A SIMPLE STUMP-PULLER.

dle it. A lever twenty feet long on a stump two feet in diameter, would exert a force of ten tons for each one thousand pounds of direct pull by the team. Though many durable, long-rooted stumps would not yield to this, the large majority of ordinary stumps, after decaying a year or two, can thus be cleared out, with most of the roots.

Figure 177 shows a stump-puller used in New Zealand. The thread of the screw works both ways and gradually draws each chain nearer the center, where the screw is

Fig. 177.—NEW ZEALAND STUMP-PULLER.

turned by a movable bar. One end of the chain is fastened around one stump, and the other around a second; then when the screw is turned, whichever stump is the less firm in the ground is bound to be pulled out. The screw is readily worked by a man, though it will, as a rule, require two persons to work it on heavy land.

DERRICKS FOR FARM USE.

Where there is much handling of heavy barrels or sacks, one man, with some simple, mechanical contrivance, can easily do the work of two or three, working by main strength. A boom derrick, figure 178, hung high, so that the weight shall be lifted from the ground ordinarily, when the derrick swings horizontally, is very convenient. A post is banded, and has a strong dowel at each end. The lower dowel is set in a stone fixed in the ground, close to the building where it is to be used, the

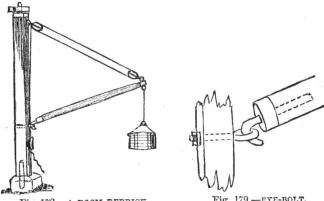

Fig. 178.—A BOOM DERRICK.   Fig. 179.—EYE-BOLT.

upper one in a strong oak cleat, bolted to the building. At the height of about five or six feet from the ground, an eye-bolt passes through the post, and another is fixed at the top. The boom is fastened to the lower eye-bolt by a three-quarter inch hooked iron, attached as shown in figure 179, while the other end of the boom has a band with two eyes. This boom is a spar or pole, stiff enough to bear the strain without doubling up or breaking, and may be ten or fifteen feet long. The end of the boom is raised or lowered by a pair of single pulleys, or by a double block tackle, which will exert much greater power. When the weight is lifted, as out of a cellar-way, it may be swung around over a wagon and lowered into it.

A convenient derrick for raising slaughtered animals, for suspending heavy hogs in scalding, and dressing beeves, and for sundry other purposes, can be cheaply and quickly made thus: Take three scantlings two by six inches, and fourteen feet long, or any other desired length and strength. Round poles will answer, by hewing flat on two sides a small portion of the upper ends. Bore corresponding holes in the top of each, and insert a strong iron bolt, with large head on one end, and large nut and screw on the other. Let the bolt fit loosely, to allow a little play. These pieces can fold together for storage, and be raised to any desired height short of perpendicular. Bore a series of small holes along the upper sides of two poles, for movable iron pins, or larger ones for wooden pins. These may be fastened in, or better, have two loose pins for moving to higher or lower holes. By placing the feet of these two poles against firmly driven stakes, and drawing the third and rear pole inward, the center will be elevated with considerable force, the power required decreasing as the timbers approach a perpendicular, when a beef carcass, for instance, is nearly lifted from the ground, and hangs more heavily. If desired or necessary, horse power can be applied by using a rope with a clevis or otherwise, attaching it to a double-tree or to a whiffletree. A single horse will be sufficient for raising a large carcass by means of this tripod derrick.

SLINGS FOR HOISTING HEAVY OBJECTS.

When one has bags to hoist by a block, or simply by a fall, from the barn floor to the loft, rope or chain slings are almost essential. The simplest sling to operate is formed on the end of the fall-rope, as shown in figure 180. This consists simply of an oak stick, half an inch

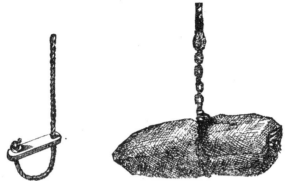

Fig. 180.   Fig. 181.—CHAIN-SLING.

thick, two inches wide and six inches long, having **two** three-quarter inch holes bored, one near each **end.** **Through** one of these the end of the rope passes, then **it**

Fig. 182.—ENDLESS ROPE-SLING.

is drawn through the other and knotted strongly. The mouth of the bag being caught in the bight of the loop, it may be safely hoisted, for the greater the weight the tighter will be the hold.

Next to this, and still more convenient, is the chain-sling, figure 181. The fall-rope is terminated by a chain with twisted links, which ends in a ring, and so a loop is made to take the bag, or simply the bag's mouth. Like the rope-sling, it will hold fast all the bags that it can be made to surround. For hoisting many bags at a time, nothing is more convenient and safe than an endless rope, figure 182, cut eighteen to twenty feet long, and the ends spliced together. This is laid upon the floor, forming a long, narrow loop; the bags are laid upon it, resting evenly on both side ropes, then the ends are brought together, one is passed through the other, so as to act like a noose, and hooked over the fall-rope, which should terminate in a strong hook, as shown in the engraving.

DERRICK FOR A CELLAR.

The carrier shown in figure 183 is similar to those used for hay, but more simple in construction. Four iron wheels are attached with bolts, which serve as axles, to two-by-four-inch oak blocks. The connecting bars holding the blocks together are made of old wagon-wheel tire, and joined together below the carrier, by a cross-bar of the same material, bearing a hook. The track is made of a bent two-by-four-inch scantling, to each side of which are bolted oak strips one inch thick, forming a roadway for the wheels. To the outer end of the track is fastened a pulley, over which passes the rope attached to the carrier. When the lead runs into the cellar the rope moves along in the groove under the track. In removing heavy articles from the cellar, the end of the rope is attached to a windlass, set a short distance from the cellar door. When not in use, the carrier may be taken down and laid aside out of the way. This device has

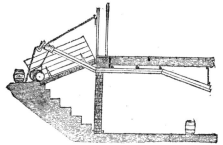

Fig. 183.—A CELLAR CARRIER.

been used in a cellar, where four hundred bushels of apples and potatoes were stored, and the owner would not part with it, if he could not obtain another. With it one man can place a hundred barrels of apples in a cellar, or remove them, as easily as he could as many pecks with his hands alone.

LEVER APPARATUS FOR LIFTING.

The implement shown in figure 184 is very useful for many purposes on the farm. Mortise a post of three of

Fig. 184.—CONVENIENT LIFTING APPARATUS.

three-inch stuff into a piece of two-inch plank. **In the top of** this saw a slot, one and a half inch wide, to receive the lever of the same thickness, four inches wide, and with the short arm, three feet long, and the long arm, six feet long. To the long arm is fastened a piece of chain, and to the short arm another piece, provided with a hook at the free end. Having the long arm of the lever twice as long as the short arm, one can easily lift a weight twice his own. It is surprising how often there is use for this. It can be used to lift sacks of grain into the wagon; logs on the sled or saw-horse; the bed off the wagon; the mower over an obstruction when putting

Fig. 185.—IMPROVED LIFTING APPARATUS.

it in the barn; and for some other things nearly every other day. By making the chain on the short lever long enough, it can be passed around a log or sack, and hooked very quickly.

The improvement shown in figure 185 consists in having the long arm of the lever longer and the short arm a very little shorter, giving a greater advantage. As the short arm of the lever is brought up, the free end of the chain is shortened; hence, it will lift the weight a greater height. With the first device one can lift a weight only three feet conveniently.

A HOME-MADE HORSE-POWER.

The worst disposition which can be made of a worn-out farm machine of any kind, is to lay it up by the fence in the dooryard or barnyard, to be an eyesore for years, and a possible source of danger to domestic animals, or even to persons passing hastily or carelessly near it. The better plan is to take the machine to pieces, set aside any unsound or broken wood for fuel, sell whatever iron is not likely to be useful in its present shape, and carefully store away in a suitable place the remaining parts, whether of wood or iron, particularly bolts, gearing, etc. With a little ingenuity, and perhaps a slight outlay of money, wheels and shafts from disabled reapers, mowers or other machines may be put together to form a light horse-power, which will be found very serviceable in driving feed-cutter, corn-sheller, or farm-mill. In the construction of a horse-power certain general principles must be kept in mind, otherwise failure, more or less complete, will be the result. The different parts must be sufficiently strong to bear the strain to which they will be subjected; the bearings need to be true, and the whole so securely braced and held together, that any slipping of cogs will be impossible. The rate of speed must be from seventy-two to one hundred and sixty revolutions of the cutting-box shaft for every one of the horse, the first being rather low for a six-foot, and the second rather high for an eight-foot sweep. Since some portion of the force employed is always lost through friction, the fewer wheels to secure the required speed and direction, the better. Hard-wood boxes are cheaper and are more easily adjusted than those made of metal, and, if they are kept properly greased, last, perhaps, quite as long.

An excellent portable-power can be made by taking a bevel-gearing from an old discarded brick-machine, a pair of spur-wheels from an ancient reaper, two or three shafts and a band-wheel from other sources—all odds and ends picked up cheaply here and there—arranging them to suit the purpose, and fitting all but the band-wheel and one shaft in a stout frame. The odd shaft extends from the end of the frame some distance, and carries the band-wheel at its further end, above which a feed-cutter stands on a loft, and is run by a belt. From a pulley on the same shaft, power is conveyed to a grindstone and corn-sheller, which require a much lower rate of speed than the cutter. The crown wheel has fifty-four cogs, its pinion, eighteen; the spur-wheel has seventy-two cogs, its pinion, fifteen; the band-wheel is thirty-six inches in diameter, and the pulleys on the cutting box, six inches. The number of revolutions of the cutter-shaft to one of the horse are, therefore, eighty-six and two-fifths. A six-inch leather belt will seldom or never slip; a four-inch belt is quite too light. Two horses, attached to this power, cut cornstalks very rapidly. The crown-wheel has a tendency to rise and allow the cogs to slip. It must be kept down by friction wheels placed above the rim, or by a collar on the axle, working against the underside of the upper cross-piece, which, in turn, must be kept in place by a bolt or rod at each end, running up through the bed-piece, and secured at the top by means of a broad washer and stout nut.

CHAPTER VIII.

PREPARING AND HANDLING FERTILIZERS.

HAULING BARNYARD MANURE.

When hauling manure it is usual to drop it in heaps, and leave it to be spread by a man who follows soon after. There are several methods of dumping the manure, but the most satisfactory is to use a manure hook, as shown in figure 186. The bottom of the sled or wagon should be formed of loose planks, each with its end shaved

Fig. 186.—A MANURE HOOK.

down to form handles. The side and end pieces of the box, though closely fitting, are not fastened together, so that they can be removed one at a time. One side or an end board is first taken out, and with a manure hook a sufficient amount of the load removed for the first heap. The manner of unloading the manure from the box

Fig. 187.—A MANURE WAGON BOX.

above described, is shown in figure 187. The other side and ends are afterwards taken off, and finally the bottom pieces are raised and the sled or wagon is soon **emptied.** In dropping the heaps, they should be left, as nearly as may be, in straight rows, and of a size and distance apart determined by the amount of manure to be spread. **If** they are placed regularly one rod from another each **way,** and eight heaps are made from a load, there will **be** twenty loads per acre. In spreading such heaps **the** manure is thrown eight feet each way, and the **whole** ground is covered. It is important that the spreading be done in a careful and thorough manner, each portion of the surface getting its proper share of the manure. It is important also that all lumps be broken up.

IMPLEMENT FOR FINING MANURE.

It is often desirable to have fine manure for use in hills and drills; and it is also at times necessary, when artificial fertilizers are lumpy, to pulverize them for use. A tool for this purpose is shown in figure 188. This is

Fig. 188.—IMPLEMENTS FOR FINING MANURE.

especially useful in preparing .the mixture of poultry manure and plaster. The implement is made of a piece of three-inch hard-wood plank, twelve inches wide, sawed and cut across into notches, and surrounded on three sides as shown, with a strip of sheet iron, or broad hoop-iron band. It is rubbed back and forth over the manure on a floor, and can be used as a shovel, by raising the handle, for turning over and mixing the mass.

MUCK AND PEAT.

Fresh muck contains valuable plant-food, but usually in an unavailable form. There are many instances where muck, applied to land, has proved positively injurious. Muck needs to be exposed to the action of the frost, rain and sun, or, as it is termed, "weathered," for a season, before it is fit to be used as a fertilizer. Even after it has thus been subjected to the elements, it is usually best to employ the finely divided muck as an absorbent of liquid manure in the stable or shed, or even the barnyard. In this way the food elements are brought into a better state for the plants to feed upon. If the "weathered" muck and manure can be composted together for a time, a still more valuable fertilizer is obtained.

When one has peat or muck in any form upon his farm, it should, of course, be dug when the water is low in the swamps, and the task of getting out muck may

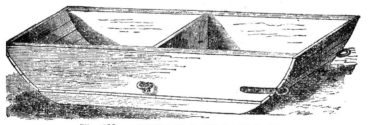

Fig. 189.—A BOAT FOR GETTING OUT MUCK.

aid essentially the work of reclaiming the swamps. Thus the main ditch may be dug the width of a cart track. By making a narrow preliminary ditch to carry off the water and dry the ground, a horse and cart may be brought into the ditch and the muck carted directly off to dry ground, where it can dry, and perhaps be exposed to a winter's freezing and thawing, before using in the compost heaps or barn-yard. In all such ditching we must begin at the lowest end of the ditch, so that there shall always be a free outlet for the water. A boat, to be used in removing muck from the bed through a water channel to a hill-side, is shown in figure 189. It is of pine boards, nailed firmly to side planks, braced by a cross plank at the middle. If made nine feet long, four feet wide, and sixteen inches deep, it will float a ton of muck. A runner is placed under each side, so that the boat can be drawn upon the land. A hook or eye should be placed on each side, and others at one end, by which the boat may be drawn. While floating, the boat is moved by handspikes. The place where the muck is heaped to dry, should be as near as possible to the bed from which it is dug.

The muck may be very peaty, or the material really may be *peat*—that is, consisting almost entirely of vegetable matter and ash—whereas *muck*, as the word is applied in the United States, is used to mean such as would be of little or no value as fuel, from the amount of soil or sand or calcareous matter in it; but it is useful as manure. The peaty mucks are greatly benefited by being treated with lime—in fact it is only by acting upon them with lime or ashes that they can be made rapidly fit for composts or for application to the land. The old rule to slake stone-lime with strong brine, adding only brine enough to dry-slake the lime, is a very good one. Such lime may be depended upon for the best results when composted with muck.

HOW TO BURN LIME.

The application of lime improves the mechanical texture of heavy soils, and this will frequently compensate for its use, if the lime can be obtained cheaply. In many localities, the farmer can burn the lime he needs, and thus obtain it at a much less cost than the market price. It is not necessary to build a kiln of masonry. The cheapest kiln is made by digging an excavation in a bank, as shown in figure 190. If much lime is to be burned, it will pay to line this excavation with brick, and place an iron grating across near the bottom, beneath which the fire is made. Whether the kiln is so made, or constructed only in a temporary manner, it must be banked up in front with earth, after the limestone is placed in it. Where the iron grating is used, it should

Fig. 190.—A LIME KILN.

project out in front as far as the bank of earth will permit, while under it is used a sheet iron door, to close the furnace and regulate the draft. A platform is built just above the projection of the grating, to support the earth banked against the rock. The top of the heap is covered with earth, leaving a hole in the center for a chimney. When the kiln is only temporary, an arch of large rocks takes the place of the iron grating, and the sides of the kiln are lined, as the rocks are laid in, with large stones instead of brick. It will take four or five days, with a good fire, to burn the kiln sufficiently.

Lime may also be burned by piling the stones in a

conical heap above ground. Large stones are used to make an arch under the heap, and the cavity below the arch is filled with fuel. Immediately above the arch is placed a layer of dry wood, then a layer of lime-stones, next a layer of wood, and so on until the heap is completed. The stones are laid rather loosely, and the entire heap is covered with earth to the depth of at least a foot, to retain the heat, leaving an opening at the top for the escape of smoke. It will pay to insert a short sheet-iron chimney in this opening, to increase the draft, as a hot fire is needed. The draft is regulated by opening or closing the doorway under the arch. Do not disturb the heap until it is perfectly cool, and if the lime is not to be used at once, it should be protected from rain by a roof, and from surface water by erecting a low bank about it. Where limestone boulders can be gathered in sufficient quantities, the cost of lime will be very little, and even when the rock must be quarried, burning lime will frequently yield handsome returns when the weather does not admit of regular farm work.

VALUE OF GAS LIME.

Gas lime, as its name indicates, is a product of gas works. Quick lime is spread in large boxes, called purifiers; the gas passes through these, and coming in contact with the lime is deprived of its impurities, especially the sulphur it contains. When the lime ceases to act, it is thrown out and replaced by a fresh supply. Gas lime smells strongly of sulphur, and contains the sulphides of ammonia and of lime. These are fatal to plant life, and before it can be used as a fertilizer, the lime must be exposed to the air for some weeks. When unpleasant odors are no longer perceptible, the gas lime may be used in the same manner as ordinary lime. It still consists largely of quick lime, and contains more or less sulphate of lime (gypsum or plaster), formed by the conversion of the dangerous suiphide into sulphate of lime. It may be used after exposure to mix with muck, but cannot safely be used in its fresh state. It is an easy matter to expose it before adding it to the muck, and thus be on the safe side.

BURNING CLAY AND SODS.

Burning clay for manurial purposes, is an old fashion, which deserves renewed notice and practice. Along with the clay or with ordinary soil or swamp muck, may be mingled coarse sods, the scrapings of road-side ditches,

Fig. 191.—BURNING CLAY AND SODS.

the mossy surface and hard tussocks of swamp meadows, rough "waste wood," coarse weeds, and other similar matters which slowly decay, and are of no value until they are decomposed. These combustible matters are placed in small heaps over an old meadow, which needs renewal, or any other piece of land. The rough waste matters being gathered, placed, and covered with earth, so that they will burn slowly, in the manner shown in figure 191; care being taken to so arrange them, as to distribute the heat all through the mass and the earth with which it is covered. These heaps are fired and left to burn slowly for several days, when the dust and ashes are spread over the surface. The lime and potash thus made available, both from the waste material and the earth covering, furnish considerable fertilizing matter.

CONVERTING STRAW INTO MANURE.

In the West the object is to feed one-third of the **straw stack,** and convert the balance into manure as rapidly as possible. The straw trampled under foot by the cattle will not thoroughly rot within a year, if left to itself. To rot and fine, it must be stirred about, and the swine can be made to do this work. If the hogs are fed on the straw twice a week, they will move the entire mass, unless quite deep, rooting after stray grains. If their noses do not get to the bottom of the heap, sharpen a heavy stake and prod it through the straw; then withdraw it and drop shelled corn or oats into the hole. · In this way a hole can be made every few feet over the pile, and the hogs will turn the manure thoroughly. A hog's snout is a very cheap and effective manure hook. The hogs must not be allowed to lie on the rotting straw, as this is almost sure to produce disease among them. They become too warm, and then when they come into the open air contract colds, catarrhal or pulmonary diseases. If the hogs are used as above recommended, straw can be converted into well rotted and fined manure within six months; and if the straw stack is put on level ground, not much will be lost during this rapid conversion. When from twelve to eighteen months are required for the rotting of the manure—and this time will be required when deep masses are not disturbed—and the straw is on a side hill, not a little of the value of the manure is lost by being washed down hill.

Marl is quite abundant in some localities, and in others oyster shells can be had for the hauling. These may be profitably burned into lime for use as a fertilizer. In regard to this use of lime, it should be remembered that the

Fig. 192.—PIT FOR BURNING MARL.

larger part of the ash of agricultural plants consists of lime, and that it is thus an indispensable plant food. It is rarely used without benefit, but is most useful when applied in a caustic state, or when it is freshly burned. Enquiries are often made about burning marl and shells. An easy way of doing this is in piles, commonly called "pits," made as shown in figure 192. A level spot is chosen, and a quantity of small wood is spread over it, either in a square, or better, in a circle. Two or three double rows of stones, covered with other flat stones, are laid as at a, a, to form flues. A layer of shells or marl is thrown upon the fuel, and other alternate layers are added, until a conical heap is made. Chimneys of small wood or chips are made over the flues as the heap is built, and carried to the top.

MAKING FERTILIZER FROM BONES.

It is well enough known that bone, when ground fine, makes one of the best and cheapest manures, especially on lands long in use. The needs of farmers with abundant capital are well enough met in the commercial fertilizers. With the Experiment Stations to analyze the samples, there is not much danger of adulteration. The high price of this comminuted bone, two cents a pound and upward, deters many farmers from using it on a large scale, even where there is no doubt that the investment would pay. In a limited way, the small farmer has the means within his reach, of reducing several barrels of bones to a fine powder every year. A solution of potash will reduce bone to a fine condition, and make it available for plant food. Most farmers still use wood for fuel, and the ashes from the fifteen or twenty cords used in a year, if saved, would reduce all the bones ordinarily within reach of the farmer. The old-fashioned leach that used to stand at almost every farmer's backdoor for soap-making, was a good contrivance for reducing the bones. But any tight, strong cask or box, will answer quite as well for this purpose. Water poured upon the ashes makes a lye, or solution of potash, strong enough to decompose the bones. The casks should stand under cover, so that the quantity of water applied to the bone and ashes will be under control. The time it will take to reduce the bone to a powder, will depend upon the amount of potash in the ashes, and attention bestowed upon the process. It is essential that the ashes and bone should be closely packed in the mass, and that they be kept in a moist state, adding water as it evaporates from the surface. The finer the bone before it is packed in the ashes, the sooner will it be reduced. The process can be hastened by putting into the mass a few pounds of common potash. But this is only necessary to save time. Ashes from hickory or any other hard wood contain sufficient potash to decompose the bone. When the mass is soft enough to break down with a spade or shovel, it can be mixed with land plaster, dried peat, or loam, to make it convenient for handling. It is a concentrated fertilizer, to be used with discretion in the hill, or applied as a top dressing to growing crops in the garden or field. We are quite sure that any one who uses this preparation of bone and wood ashes, and sees the vigorous push it gives to garden and other crops, will be likely to continue it. But many farmers near seaports and railroad stations, use coal mainly for fuel, and will have to resort to a hand or horse-mill to use up the waste bones. Small mills are extensively used by poultry-men, for crushing oyster shells as well as bone, and the machine can be adjusted to break the bone coarsely for hen feed. The oil and gelatine of the bones have an alimentary value, and, turned into eggs, pay much better than when used as a fertilizer for the soil.

CHAPTER IX.

APPLIANCES FOR THE GARDEN AND ORCHARD.

PAPER PLANT PROTECTOR.

The most effectual means for protecting young melon and cucumber plants against some of their injurious

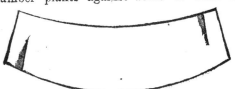

Fig. 193.—PATTERN FOR PLANT PROTECTOR.

enemies, is to inclose the young vines in bottomless boxes of some kind. Various more or less expensive and elaborate forms have been invented and are offered for sale. The principal objection to most of these is their cost.

Figures 193 and 194 represent a device which is free from this objection. It consists simply of a piece of card-board

Fig. 194.—PLANT PROTECTOR.

or stiff paper of any kind, as seen in figure 193. When the ends are brought together, and the slits, indicated in the engraving, made to interlock, a cone, as seen in figure 194, is produced which, when put around a plant, furnishes as complete a protector against insects as the most expensive device.

MUSLIN-COVERED PLANT SCREEN.

To make the device, figure 195, take four strips, one-half inch thick and one inch wide, and twelve

Fig. 195.—PLANT PROTECTOR.

inches long; bore a hole in one end of these, through which pass a wire, the ends of which are twisted together, but not so tightly as to prevent the opposite ends of the pieces from being spread apart from eight inches to a foot, making a tent-shaped frame. Cheap muslin is tacked on the frame, spreading the pieces before doing so. The muslin should be brought down to within about two inches of the ends of the sticks, so as to allow them to be run into the ground that distance, when in use. When not in use, the protectors can be closed up and take but little room, and if properly cared for, they will last several seasons.

PROTECTED PLANT LABEL.

Various devices to prevent the washing off of the names written on plant labels have been invented from time to

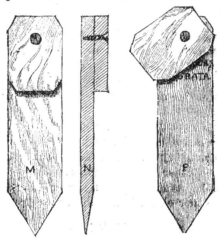

Fig. 196.—IMPROVED PLANT LABEL.

time. A novel one is shown in figure 196. It consists in fastening, with a small screw, a short piece of label over the name, as seen at M; a cross-section of the label is shown at N, and at P the cover is partly raised. This arrangement may be applied to any size of labels. The great difficulty with wooden labels is not that the name becomes obliterated, but that the portion in the ground decays. This may be avoided by using Locust, which is expensive.

POLES FOR BEANS AND OTHER CLIMBERS.

White birches and alders, so commonly used for bean poles, are about the poorest, for they last only one season at the best, and sometimes break off at the surface of the ground and let down the beautiful pyramid of green before the pods are ripe. White Cedar from the swamps is durable, and the rough bark enables the vines to climb without any help from strings, but these are not always accessible. Red Cedar is much more widely distributed, and on the whole makes the best bean pole. The wood is as durable as the White Cedar, and young trees, from which poles are made, grow quite stout at the ground, and, if well set, will resist very strong winds. A set of these poles will last for a generation. For bean poles, all the side branches are trimmed off, but for a support for ornamental climbers, these may be left on. A Cedar, six or eight feet high, with the branches gradually shortened from below upwards, makes an excellent support for ornamental vines. One of these, covered with a clematis, or other showy climber, makes a pyramid of great beauty. It is well to prepare a supply of poles for beans and other plants before the work is pressing.

POTTING STRAWBERRY PLANTS.

Figure 197 shows a simple method of turning old tin cans into contrivances for potting strawberries. Unsolder the cans, and cut into pieces of about three by seven inches. Turn back one quarter of an inch of each end, so that when the strips are bent around, they will clasp together, as shown in the engraving. In potting, the contrivance is placed on the ground with the sole of the foot. The sharp edges allow it to push through the soil easily. A runner is placed in the center of the cylinder, and held by a stick or stone, which also serves to mark the place. When the plants are well rooted, the tin pots are taken up, unclasped, and the ball of earth placed in the new bed provided for it.

Fig. 197. PLANT POTTER.

STAND FOR BERRY BASKETS.

During the berry picking season much time is lost in the field, through the lack of a suitable box or stand for

Fig. 198.—BERRY PICKING STAND.

transferring the filled baskets to the packing house. Figure 198 illustrates a very convenient and simple stand for this purpose. It may be made to contain either nine, twelve, sixteen, or twenty baskets, as may be desired. The handle is made of a barrel hoop nailed firmly to the sides. Suitable legs are attached to the stand to raise it from the ground.

TUBE FOR WATERING PLANTS.

Figure 199 shows an implement for watering garden plants. It is a tin tube, one-half inch in diameter, eight inches long, perforated near the bottom, and with a conical end. The upper end, b, is in the form of a funnel. In using this device, insert the conical end of the tube in the ground as near the plant as convenient, without disturbing the roots, and turn the water into the funnel. The water will pass out into the soil through the perforations at the bottom. The soil is not baked on the surface when watered in this manner, and the operation is very quickly done. Any local tinsmith can make the tube at a slight expense. A small flower pot is sometimes sunk in the soil near the plant, and the water, when poured into it, will gradually soak away.

Fig. 199.

MOVABLE TRELLIS FOR GRAPES.

A grape trellis, possessing several good points, is shown in figure 200. The wooden posts, which need not be fastened together, are of 3 by 4 stuff. If leant against each other, their own weight and that of the vines will hold them in place. They are joined by smooth galvanized fencing wire. The posts must be braced inside, as seen in the illustration. If it is desired to lay down the vines in the fall, the staples can be drawn and the wires pulled out, greatly simplifying the work. The trellis being double, a row of vines may be planted on each side. Another point in its favor is that it allows the picker to get at the bunches on the under sides of the vines easily and without disturbing the vines. The trellis is as cheap as any, is strong and durable, and does not require the

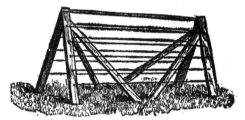

Fig. 200.—MOVABLE GRAPE TRELLIS.

digging of holes, while it may be taken out of the way when the vines are laid down, and stored under shelter in a small space until needed again.

TOOL FOR CUTTING EDGINGS.

No grass-plot, walk, or flower-bed, set in turf, is complete, unless its edges are kept neatly trimmed. The work may be done with a sharpened spade, but it is better to use a regular edging-tool. An old hoe can be taken to the blacksmith, who will straighten out the shank, and round off the corners of the blade with a file, and the tool is an excellent sod-trimmer, and very light to handle. For cutting sods, this makes much easier work than the spade, though that is needed for lifting the turf when cut. Using a board as a guide, the cutting will be rapidly done.

Fig. 201.

SUBSTITUTE FOR PEA BRUSH.

The best substitute for pea brush is a trellis of galvanized iron wire. The peas are sown in double rows, six inches apart. A post, six inches in diameter, is set firmly at each end of the row; it may be round, set three feet in the ground, and of a hight suited to the variety of pea. As soon as the vines are large enough, the wire is made fast to the post, about six inches from the ground, carried to and passed around the post at the other end, and back to the starting point. Here it is made fast; it may be cut off, but still better, two or three turns are taken around the post and another double wire stretched about eight inches above the first, and so on until as many wires as needed are put in place. No. 18 wire, which measures 150 feet to the pound, is suitable. If over 200 feet long, a similar post should be set mid-way of the row. Stakes (plasterers' laths will answer) are set every ten or fifteen feet along the row, to keep the wires from sagging. These have notches cut in them, in which the wires rest; or the wires may be attached to them by means of staples or cord. When no longer needed, the wire is wound up on a reel, and, with the posts, stored away for another year. Pea-growers for market allow the vines to lie upon the ground, and claim that the crop is not enough larger when brushed, to pay the cost of cutting and placing the sticks. In the garden, neatness, and especially the greater ease of picking, make it necessary to use brush, or a substitute. The chief precaution to be observed is, to have the wires of this trellis so near together that the vines can reach them as soon as a support is needed.

TRELLIS FOR TOMATOES.

A tomato trellis, which never fails to give satisfaction, is shown in figures 202 and 203. The standards or legs are made of one by one and a half inch stuff, three feet long, and tapering slightly toward the top. The slats are selected lath. Figure 202 is an end view of the trellis in position; figure 203 shows the trellis folded. Wires

Fig. 202.—END VIEW OF TRELLIS.

extend across the top of the trellis, and when in position, they loop over the ends of the stands, and hold it at the proper width. The standards are fastened together where they cross with one-quarter inch bolts, two inches long. Two lengths of the trellis are sufficient for three tomato plants. It may be placed in position when the plants have attained a hight of six or eight inches. At the end

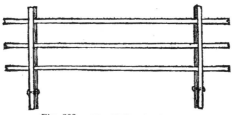

Fig. 203.—THE TRELLIS FOLDED.

of each season, after the crop is gathered, the trellises are taken up, given a coat of paint or crude petroleum, folded and packed away in a dry place. This form of trellis has the advantages of strength, lightness and portability.

TOOLS FOR KILLING WEEDS.

Weeds are easily killed when they are first seen, and more easily still, before they are seen at all. A heavy rake is better than a hoe for this work, and will do more in ten minutes, than can be done with a hoe in an hour. An implement made as in figure 204, will do this work of

Fig. 204.—RAKE FOR WEEDING.

weeding in an excellent manner. This is made of a heavy rake head, with a handle attached as shown, and furnished with a number of teeth placed about an inch apart. The teeth may be made of forty-penny nails, or one-quarter inch round iron, the weight of which will bury them in the soil without any effort. It is much more easy to work with this implement, than with a lighter rake. The beds may be cleaned close to the plants, and it should be used as soon as the weeds begin to appear.

For killing perennial weeds, a spud is a convenient implement with which to cut off the roots below the surface.

Fig. 205.—SPUD FOR KILLING WEEDS.

A good spud may be made from a carpenter's chisel of large size. This should be attached to a handle sufficiently long to allow it to be used without stooping. By thrusting this diagonally against the root, that may be cut off as far below the surface as desired. Some weeds, however, such as dandelion, plantain, etc., are not killed by merely cutting them, but need the application of some destructive liquid to make complete work. In England, oil of vitroil (sulphuric acid) is used for this purpose, but that is dangerous to handle, and must be kept in glass. Strong brine or coal-oil is sometimes applied to the roots to destroy them. We give an illustration of a vessel for the application of liquids, which is attached to the spud, and allows the cutting and killing to be done at one operation. Figure 205 shows the spud, *a*, with its attachment, a tin vessel with a tapering nozzle and holding about a quart, at *b*. At *c*, is a valve, which covers a small air-hole, against which it is pressed by a spring, and which may be raised by the cord, *e*. After cutting the root, a pull of the cord will raise the valve, allow air to enter the vessel, and a small quantity of the liquid will pass out and come in contact with the root.

VARIOUS FRUIT PICKERS.

A good picker is shown in figures 206, 207 and 208. Figure 206 is the picker. The pieces, *a* and *b*, are iron, shaped as seen in the cut. They work on a rivet, and are fastened securely to the end of the pole. Holes are punched through *a* and *b*, and stiff wires inserted, forming a cage for the fruit. The toothed end of piece *b* is sharp, and slides over the end of *a*, which may be sharp or not. A small hole is bored through the pole, and a notch cut in the front edge for a small pulley, *d*. A strong cord is attached to the lower end of *b*, and passes through the hole over the pulley, and down the pole through screw-eyes placed a short distance apart. Figure 207 is a section of the lower end of the pole. Eighteen inches from the end, the pole is squared for about fifteen inches. Over this squared portion is fitted a sliding-box handle. A thumb-stop is fastened to the upper end, as shown in figure 208. The thumb end is held up by a small spring, which presses the upper end into notches in an iron rachet-bar fitted into the pole. A screw-eye is inserted in the upper end, and a cord attached. The pole may be of any desired length.

To pick apples, grasp the pole at the lower end with

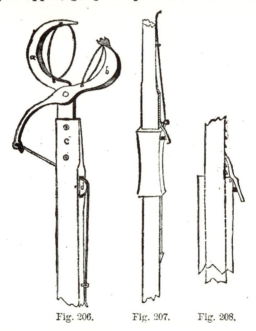

Fig. 206.   Fig. 207.   Fig. 208.

one hand, and by the sliding-box handle with the other. Press the thumb-piece and slide it up, and the weight of piece *b* opens the jaws of the picker. When the apple is in the cage, draw the slides down until the points of the picker meet on the apple stem. The thumb-stop will hold it secure. Turn the pole slowly without pulling, pushing, or shaking the limb, and the apple will come off easily. The cage of the picker should be large enough to contain the largest apple, and enough wires may be attached to hold the smallest. The jaws should not be over one-eighth of an inch thick, flattened on the inside, to prevent bruising the ripe fruit. They may be wrapped with cloth, if thought necessary.

A cheap and simple picker may be made by bending a

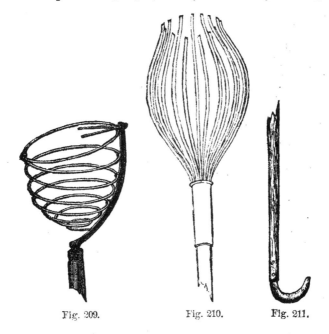

Fig. 209.   Fig. 210.   Fig. 211.

stiff wire into the form of a circle six inches in diameter, with one side of the circle prolonged three inches into a V-shaped projection. Upon this wire sew a cloth bag a foot or so deep, and fasten it on to a pole by the end opposite the V-shaped extremity. This V-shaped projection will serve as a corner, in which to catch the apple and pull it off, allowing it to fall into the bag. An excellent picker, as shown in figure 210, can be made from stiff wire by a tinner. The span across the top should be about six inches, and the depth from eight to ten inches. The wires should not be more than a half-inch apart at their tips. The wires being more or less flexible, the apple is apt to draw through them, if they are not close together. Care should also be taken to have the implement made as light as possible. A bungling mechanic will probably use too much solder. Another good picker is pictured in figure 209. It is light, durable and pleasant to handle. When, however, an apple, being very short stemmed, lies close to a limb, it is much more easily removed by the former device than by this. A simple, flattened hook, with a thin, almost cutting edge, secured on the end of a pole, figure 211, is often handy for pulling off stray apples. This is the best implement for thinning apples.

FRUIT LADDERS.

The construction is easily understood from the engraving. The method of using deep fruit baskets with a hook attached is also shown in figure 112. The use of a common grain bag as a receptacle for picking fruit has some important advantages. One side of the mouth of the bag is tied to the corresponding corner at the bottom, first putting an apple in the corner to hold the string from slipping off. The bag is then hung over the shoulder with the mouth in front. The picker has both hands free and can empty the bag by lowering it into the barrel, without bruising the fruit.

Another form is shown in figure 213. To make it, select a chestnut pole, eighteen feet long, or of the desired length. At about four feet from the top, or smaller end of the pole, nail on a band of hoop iron, to prevent splitting, and rip up the pole in the center as far as the band. The halves of the pole are spread apart three and a half feet at the base, and secured. The places for the rungs are then laid out, and the holes bored; those for the lower rungs should be one and three-eighths inch, the upper one inch; drive them in place and wedge fast.

Fig. 212.—A HANDY FRUIT LADDER.　　Fig. 213.—FRUIT LADDER.

The distance between the rungs is usually a foot; when farther apart, they are fatiguing in use. A ladder of this kind, on account of its small width above, is easily thrust in among the branches, without breaking them, and is more convenient to use on large trees, than those of the ordinary shape.

The Japanese use a pull saw instead of a push saw. One of these is quite handy, especially for pruning. The teeth are like those of a rip saw, reversed, and cut when the saw is pulled towards one. One of these saws, made

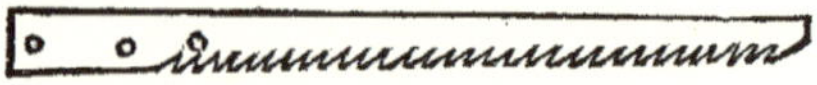

Fig. 214.—PRUNING SAW.

as shown in figure 214, and fixed to a pole of convenient size, will be found very useful in cutting branches of tall trees, as in pulling there is no tendency to bend the saw or the pole.

RABBITS AND MICE IN THE ORCHARD.

Not the least of the enemies of young orchard trees is the rabbit. He will not injure the trees in summer, when he has an abundance of succulent food; but in winter the tender bark is to him a dainty that he will partake of, if it is not made distasteful to him, or he is not kept away. Making the snow into a solid mound about the tree will keep away mice, but not rabbits, though it is often said it would. The rabbits will get on the mound and nibble away. Besides, we don't have snow half the time during the winter. The best way is to make the bark distasteful to the rabbit. He likes neither blood, nor grease, nor the odor of flesh. When you butcher, take the waste parts of the animals, and with these parts rub the trunks as far up as the rabbits can reach. The rabbits never nibble a tree so treated, while the grease or blood remains.

If the rabbits "bark" a tree, the first thing to be done is to examine the extent of the injury. Frequently it is not so bad as it looks, and the inner bark is not entirely removed. If this covers even a fourth of the wounded portion, and connects the bark above the wound with that below it, the chances are that the wound will heal, if drying can be prevented. The ordinary grafting wax, applied on old, worn cotton cloth, or on paper, as used in grafting, should be applied over the injured portion. This, especially on quite small trees, will prevent all evaporation. Another application is the old grafting clay, made by

Fig. 215.—MANNER OF INSERTING THE CIONS.

thoroughly mixing and beating together stiff clay with half as much cow manure. Apply this over the wound quite thickly, and fasten it in place by wrapping with an old cloth and tying with strings. If the inner bark is completely gone, nothing remains but to bridge over the wound with cions, and thus restore the communication between the roots and top. The cions may be taken from the same tree, if they can be spared, or those from another of the same kind will answer as well. The methods of cutting the cions and inserting them are so plainly shown in figure 215 that description is unnecessary. A small chisel may be used to aid in setting the cions. This method of cutting the ends is better than making the slope on the opposite side. If the wound is low enough, it may be covered with a mound of earth; if not, employ one of the methods suggested above.

IMPLEMENTS USED IN CRANBERRY CULTURE.

A turfing axe, shown figure 216, consists of a thin steel blade, hatchet-faced, and about six inches square.

Fig. 216.—TURFING AXE.

This blade is made fast to a stout hickory handle, some two feet and a half long, in the same manner as a common wood axe. In expert hands, this axe does wonderful

Fig. 217.—HAULING RAKE.

execution upon the tough, interlacing roots, with which the surface of the bog is filled.

A hoe, shaped like a grubbing hoe, is the implement used for grading. Every farmer knows what that is; but the grading hoe, figure 218, should be made of the best steel, and ground to an edge like an axe—the object being to cut all the fine roots to pieces, and get out such

Fig. 218.—GRADING HOE.

of them as escaped when the trees, stumps, shoots, and larger wood were removed.

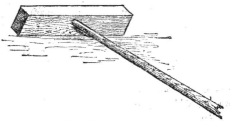

Fig. 219.—SPREADER.

The sand is spread by means of a "Spreader," figure 219, made of a piece of one-inch white oak board,

Fig. 220.—MARKER.

about fifteen inches long by three inches wide, and fastened to a handle.

A "Marker," shown in figure 220, is made of a piece of two by four inch joist, about nine feet long, having teeth eighteen inches apart, and a handle the length of a rake-handle. The teeth are eight inches long, made of white oak, driven through holes bored in the joist for the purpose. The implement is made similar to a common rake with teeth far apart, and the whole made stronger to stand harder usage, by having stays running from the handle to the head, which holds the teeth.

CHAPTER X.

APPLIANCES FOR SLAUGHTERING HOGS AND CURING THE MEAT.

STICKING HOGS.

The usual method of killing hogs on the farm is to thrust a sticking knife into the throat, severing the large veins. It requires experience, nerve, and skill to do this properly. The hog should be thrown on its back, and held there by an assistant, while the operator gives the fatal thrust. With a keen double-edged knife in his right hand, he feels with his left for the proper place to insert the knife. Having found it, he sticks in the knife, aiming directly toward the base of the tail. If properly done, the large veins are severed, and the hog soon bleeds to death. If the knife veers to either side, a gash is made in one shoulder, the death is slow and painful, and the blood settles in the flesh.

A BETTER WAY.

With a view to avoiding all mishaps, saving pain, and leaving the operator free to sever the veins without embarrassment from the squealing and struggling victim, the design called "The Stunner," figure 221 has been invented. It fits over the head of the intended victim, as seen in figures 222 and 223, and a sharp blow on the plate over the forehead drives the pin into the brain,

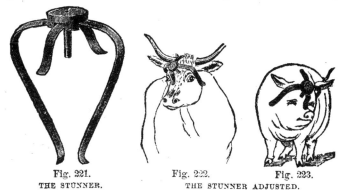

Fig. 221.
THE STUNNER.

Fig. 222.
THE STUNNER ADJUSTED.

Fig. 223.

causing insensibility instantly, and death will not be long delayed. The use of such a mask is made compulsory in many countries of Europe. Such a contrivance is not only convenient, but humane, and appeals to the better nature of every man who is under the necessity of killing a dumb beast. As soon as the animal is struck, the throat is cut to insure free bleeding.

HEATING THE WATER FOR SCALDING.

For heating scalding water and rendering lard, when one has not kettles or cauldrons ready to set in brick or stone, a simple method is to put down two forked stakes firmly, as shown in figure 224, lay in them a pole to support the kettles, and build a wood fire around them on the ground. A more elaborate arrangement is shown in figure 225, which serves not only to heat the water, but as a scalding tub as well. It is made of two-inch pine boards, six feet long, and two feet wide, rounded at the ends. A heavy plate of sheet iron is nailed with rod nails on the bottom and ends. Let the iron project

Fig. 224.—HEATING THE WATER.

about one inch on each side. The ends, being rounded, will prevent the fire from burning the wood-work. They also make it handier for dipping sheep, scalding hogs, or

Fig. 225.—HEATING AND SCALDING VAT.

for taking out the boiled food. The box is set on two walls eighteen inches high, and the hind end of the brick-work is built into a short chimney.

SCALDING TUBS AND VATS.

Various devices are employed for scalding hogs, without lifting them by main force. For heavy hogs one may use three strong poles, fastened at the top with a log chain, which supports a simple tackle, figure 226. A very good arrangement is shown in figure 227. A sled is made firm with driven stakes, and covered with planks or boards. At the rear end the scalding cask is set in the ground, its upper edge on a level with the platform, and inclined as much as it can be and hold sufficient water. A large, long hog is scalded one end at a time. The more the cask is inclined, the easier will be the lifting.

Fig. 226.—TACKLE FOR HEAVY HOGS.

A modification of the above device is shown in figure 228. A lever is rigged like a well sweep, using a crotched stick for the post, and a strong pole for the sweep, a white oak stick—such as every farmer who can do so, should have laid up to season. The iron rod on which the sweep moves must be strong and stiff. A trace chain is attached to the upper end, and if the end of the chain has a ring instead of a hook, it will be quite convenient. In use, a table is improvised, unless a strong one for the purpose is at hand, and this is set near the barrel. A noose is made with the chain about the leg of the pig,

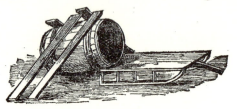

Fig. 227.—SCALDING CASK ON A SLED.

and he is soused in, going entirely under water, lifted out when the bristles start easily, and laid upon the table, while another is made ready.

Figure 229 shows a more permanent arrangement. It is a trough of plank, with a sheet iron bottom, which can be set over a temporary fire-place made in the ground.

Fig. 228.—SCALDING PIGS IN A HOGSHEAD.

The vat may be six feet long, three feet wide, and two and one-half feet deep, so as to be large enough for a good-sized hog. Three ropes are fastened on one side, for the purpose of rolling the hog over into the vat, and rolling it out on the other side when it is scalded. A number of slanting cross-pieces are fitted in, crossing each other, so as to form a hollow bed in which the carcass lies, with the ropes under it, by which it can be

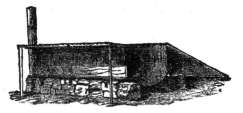

Fig. 229.—SCALDING VAT.

moved and drawn out. These cross-pieces protect the sheet-iron bottom, and keep the carcass from resting upon it. A large, narrow fire-place is built up in the ground, with stoned sides, and the trough is set over it. A stove-pipe is fitted at one end, and room is made at the front by which wood may be supplied to the fire, to heat the water. A sloping table is fitted at one side for the purpose of rolling up the carcass, when too large to handle otherwise, by means of the rope previously mentioned. On the other side is a frame made of hollowed boards set on edge, upon which the hog is scraped and cleaned. The right temperature for scalding a hog is one hundred and eighty degrees; and with a thermometer there need be no fear of overscalding, or a failure from the lack of

Fig. 230.—A GAMBREL.

sufficient heat; while the water can be kept at the right temperature by regulating the fuel under the vat. If a spot of hair is obstinate, cover it with some of the removed hair, and dip on hot water. Always pull out hair and bristles, shaving any off leaves unpleasant stubs in the skin.

Gambrels should be provided of different lengths, if the hogs vary much in size, like figure 230, or in other convenient shapes. These should be of hickory or other tough wood, for safety, and to be so small as to require little gashing of the legs to receive them.

HANGING AND CLEANING THE HOGS.

Figure 231 shows a very cheap and convenient device for hanging either hogs or beeves. The device is in shape much like an old fashioned "saw-buck," with the lower rounds between the legs omitted. The legs, of which

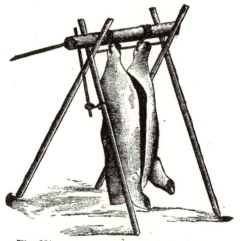

Fig. 231.—RAISING A SLAUGHTERED ANIMAL.

there are two pairs, should be about ten feet long, and set bracing, in the manner shown in the engraving. The two pairs of legs are held together by an inch iron rod, five or six feet in length, provided with threads at both ends. The whole is made secure by means of two pairs of nuts, which fasten the legs to the connecting iron rod. A straight and smooth wooden roller rests in the forks made by the crossing of the legs, and one end projects about sixteen inches. In this two auger holes are bored, in which levers may be inserted for turning the roller. The rope, by means of which the carcass is raised, passes over the roller in such a way that in turning, by means of the levers, the animal is raised free from the ground. When sufficiently elevated, the roller is fastened by one of the levers to the nearest leg.

Skill and practice are needed to take out the intestines neatly, without cutting or breaking them and soiling the flesh. Run the knife lightly down, marking the belly straight, cut to the bone between the thighs, and in front of the ribs and below, and split the rear bones with an axe carefully, not to cut beyond them; open the abdomen by running the hand or two fingers behind the knife with its edge turned outward. Little use of the knife is required to loosen the entrails. The fingers, rightly used, will do most of the severing. Small strong strings, cut in proper lengths, should be always at hand to quickly tie the severed ends of any small intestines cut or broken by chance. An expert will catch the entire offal in a large tin pan or wooden vessel, holding it between himself and the hog. Unskilled operators, and those opening very large hogs, need an assistant to hold this. The entrails, and then the liver, heart, etc., being all removed, thoroughly rinse out any blood or filth that may have escaped inside. Spread the cut edges apart by inserting a short stick between them, to admit free circulation of cool air. When dripping is over, or the hanging posts are wanted for other carcasses, remove the dressed ones, and hang them in a cool cellar or other safe place, until the whole flesh is thoroughly cooled through. Removing the lard from the long intestines requires expertness that can only be learned by practice. The fingers do most of this cleaner, safer and better than a knife. A light feed the night before killing leaves the intestines less distended and less likely to be broken.

PACKING PORK.

Pack closely in the barrel, first rubbing salt well into all exposed ends of bones, and sprinkle well between each layer, using no brine until forty-eight hours after, and then let the brine be strong enough to bear an egg. After six weeks take out the hams and bacon and hang in the smoke-house. When warm weather brings danger of flies, smoke a week with hickory chips, avoiding heating the air much. If one has a dark, close smoke-house, as the writer has, the meat can hang in all the summer; otherwise pack in boxes, putting layers of sweet, dry hay between. Long experience has convinced me that this method of packing is preferable to packing in dry salt or ashes. Much lard is injured or spoiled by overheating and burning some portions; the smallest quantity scorched gives a bad flavor to the whole. A bucket of water in the rendering kettle prevents this, if the fire is kept from rising too high around the sides. The water is easily separated at the bottom, if not slowly evaporated off during the rendering. Cutting the leaf, etc., fine with a sharp hatchet or cleaver, facilitates the free extraction of the lard.

III.

FENCES, GATES AND BRIDGES.

Old-Fashioned Labor-Saving Devices

FENCES, GATES AND BRIDGES.

CHAPTER I.

RAIL AND OTHER PRIMITIVE WOOD FENCES.

VIRGINIA RAIL FENCE.

The zigzag rail fence was almost universally adopted by the settlers in the heavily timbered portions of the country, and countless thousands of miles of it still exist, though the increasing scarcity of timber has brought other styles of fencing largely into use. Properly built, of good material, on a clear, solid bed, kept free from bushes and other growth to shade it and cause it to rot, the rail fence is as cheap as any, and as effective and durable as can reasonably be desired. Good chestnut, oak, cedar, or juniper rails, or original growth heart pine, will last from fifty to a hundred years, so that material of this sort, once in hand, will serve one or two generations. This fence, ten rails high, and propped with two rails at each corner, requires twelve rails to the panel. If the fence bed is five feet wide, and the rails are eleven feet long, and are lapped about a foot at the locks, one takes seven thousand nine hundred and twenty rails, or about eight thousand rails to the mile. For a temporary fence, one that can be put up and taken down in a short time, for making stock pens and division fences, not intended to remain long in place, nothing is cheaper or better. The bed for a fence of this kind should not be less than five feet across, to enable it to stand before the wind. The rails are best cut eleven feet long, as this makes a lock neither too long nor too short; and the forward end of each rail should come under the next one that is laid. The corners, or locks, as they are called, should also be well propped with strong, whole rails, not with pieces of rails, as is often done. The props should be set firmly on the ground about two feet from the panel, and crossed at the lock so as to hold each other, and the top course of the fence firmly in place. They thus act as braces to the fence, supporting it

Fig. 1.—VIRGINIA ZIGZAG FENCE COMPLETE.

against the wind. Both sides of the fence should be propped. The top course of rails should be the strongest and heaviest of any, for the double purpose of weighting the fence down, and to prevent breaking of rails by persons getting upon it. The four courses of rails nearest the ground should be of the smallest pieces, to prevent making the cracks, or spaces between the rails, too large. They should also be straight, and of nearly even sizes at both ends. This last precaution is only necessary where small pigs have to be fenced out or in, as the case may be. The fence, after it is finished, will have the appearance of figure 1, will be six rails high, two props at each lock, and the worm will be crooked enough to stand any wind, that will not prostrate crops, fruit trees, etc. A straighter worm than this will be easy to blow down or push over. The stability of this sort of fence depends very largely on the manner of placing the **props**, both as to the distance of the foot of the prop rail from the fence panel, and the way it is locked at the corner.

LAYING A RAIL FENCE.

It is much better, both for good looks and economy, to have the corners of a rail fence on each side in line with each other. This may be accomplished by means of a very simple implement, shown in figure 2. It consists of a small pole, eight feet long, sharpened at the lower end. A horizontal arm of a length equal to half the width of the fence from extreme outside of corners, is fastened to the long pole at right angles, near the lower end. Sometimes a sapling may be found with a limb growing nearly at right angles, which will serve the purpose. Before beginning the fence, stakes are set at intervals along the middle of the line it is to occupy. To begin, the gauge, as shown in figure 2, is set in line with the stakes, and the horizontal arm is swung outwardly at

Fig. 2.

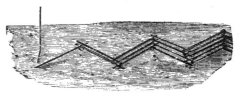

Fig. 3.—THE FENCE BEGUN.

right angles to the line of fence. A stone or block to support the first corner is laid directly under the end of the horizontal arm, and the first rail laid with one end resting on the support. In the same way the next corner and all others are laid, the gauge being moved from corner to corner, set in the line of fence, and the arm swung alternately to the right and left.

STAKING AND WIRING.

A neater and more substantial method of securing the corners of a worm fence is by vertical stakes and wires, as shown in the accompanying illustrations. When the lower three rails are laid, the stakes are driven in the

Fig. 4.—STAKES IN "LOCK."   Fig. 5.—STAKES IN ANGLES.

angles close to the rails, and secured by a band of annealed wire. The work of laying the rails proceeds, and when within one rail of the top, a second wire band is put in place. Or the upper wire may be put on above the top rail. Annealed wire is plentiful and cheap.

A very common method with the "worm" or "Virginia" rail fence is to drive slanting stakes over the corner in saw-horse style, and lay the top rail into the angle

Fig. 6.—A STAKE AND RIDER FENCE.

thus formed. The stakes, resting on the rails and standing at angle, brace the fence firmly. But the feet of the stakes extending beyond the jagged corners formed by the ends of the rail are objectionable. This is remedied in part by putting the stakes over the middle of the panel —at considerable distance apart—and laying in them long poles horizontally. In this case the stakes should be set at such an angle as to prevent their moving sidewise along the top rail, which should be a strong one. These stakes and long riders are frequently used to raise the hight of low stone walls. Figure 6 shows a fence nearly all composed of stakes and riders, which is straight and requires fewer rails than a worm fence. First, crotched stakes, formed by the forks of a branching tree limb, a foot or more long, are driven a foot or so into the ground at a distance apart corresponding to the length of poles used. The bottom poles are laid into these, and two stakes, split or round poles, are driven over these and the next poles laid in. Then two more stakes and another pole, and so on as high as the fence is required. This will answer for larger animals, and be strong and

Fig. 7.—A POLE FENCE.

not expensive. For swine, and other small live-stock, the crotch stakes may be replaced by blocks or stones, and the lower poles be small and begin close to the ground.

A POLE FENCE.

A fence which is cheaply constructed in a timbered region, and calls for no outlay whatever, besides labor, is

Fig. 8.—WITHE. Fig. 9.—WITHE IN PLACE.

illustrated at figure 7. The posts are set in a straight line, having previously been bored with an inch augur to receive the pins. When they are set, the pins are driven diagonally into the posts, and the poles laid in place. It would add much to its strength, if the poles were laid so as to "break joints." A modification of this fence is sometimes made by using withes instead of pins to hold the poles in place. The withe is made of a young sapling or slender limb of beech, iron-wood, or similar tough fibrous wood, with the twigs left on. This is twisted upon itself, a strong loop made at the top, through which the butt is slipped. When in place, the butt end is tucked under the body of the withe.

FENCES FOR SOIL LIABLE TO HEAVE.

The main point in such a fence is either to set the posts

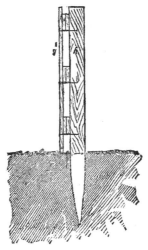

Fig. 10.—END VIEW OF FENCE.

and place a pin through them near the bottom, so that the frost may not throw them out, or to so attach the boards that the posts may be re-driven, without splitting them, or removing the rails from the fence. The latter is, perhaps, the best plan, and may be accomplished in

Fig. 11.—SIDE VIEW OF FENCE.

several ways, the most desirable of which is shown in figures 10 and 11. The post, h, is driven in the usual manner, when a strip of board, g, is fastened to it by three or four spikes, depending upon the hight of the

Fig. 12.—FENCE WITH IRON HOOKS.

fence. A space just sufficient to insert the ends of boards a, e, figure 11, is left between the post and outside strip, the ends of the boards resting upon the spikes. Many miles of this fence are in use. It looks neat; besides any portion is easily removed, making a passage to and from the field. A new post is easily put in when required, and any may be re-driven when heaved by the frost.

Where iron is cheap, a rod about three-eighths of an inch in diameter is cut in lengths of about seven and a half inches; one end is sharpened, while the opposite end, for three inches, is bent at right angles. After the boards are placed in position, the hooks should be driven in so that they will firmly grasp the boards and hold them in place. The general appearance of the finished fence is shown in figure 12, and is one adapted to almost any locality.

A much better method is to fasten the boards temporarily in place, and then bore a half inch hole through

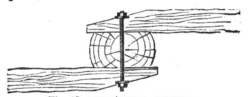

Fig. 13.—HORIZONTAL SECTION.

both boards and the post, into which a common screw bolt is then inserted and the nut screwed on firmly. The two ends should, however, be put on opposite sides of the post. One bolt thus holds the ends of both boards firmly to the post, as shown in figure 13. With this style of fence, old rails or round poles may be used instead of boards.

OTHER PRIMITIVE FENCES.

In the heavily timbered parts of the country, where the settlers a few years ago were making farms by felling and burning the huge pine trees, a fence was constructed like the one shown in figure 14. Sections of trees, about four and a half feet long and often as thick, were placed in line and morticed to receive from three to five rails.

Fig. 14.—LOG POSTS.

This style of fence could be used by the landscape gardener with fine effect for enclosing a park or shrubbery.

In the same regions, when a farmer has pulled all the stumps from a pasture that slopes toward the highway,

Fig. 15.—STUMP FENCE.

the stumps may be placed in line along the road with the top ends inside of the field. The gaps between where the stumps can not be rolled close together, are

Fig. 16.—WICKER FENCE.

filled with brushwood. A portion of this fence is shown in figure 15.

Where other material is costly, or not to be obtained,

the wicker fence, constructed of stakes and willows, is much used. In the far West it is to be seen in every town, generally built on a small embankment of earth from one to two feet deep. In this climate, with occasional repairs, it lasts from ten to fifteen years. Figure 16 shows the style of construction.

Throughout the forest regions is found the staked and ridered brush growing on the line where the fence is

Fig. 17.—BRUSH FENCE.

constructed. Figure 17 illustrates a few rods of brush fence—such fencing being met with in our Southern States.

CHAPTER II.

STONE AND SOD FENCES.

HOW A STONE WALL SHOULD BE BUILT.

To build a stone wall, some skill is required. The foundation should be dug out a foot deep, and the earth

Fig. 18.—WELL LAID WALL.

thrown upon each side, which serves to turn water from the wall. Large stones are bedded in the trench, and long stones placed crosswise upon them. As many whole stones as possible should be used in this place. The stones are then arranged as shown in the engraving, breaking joints, and distributing the weight equally. Any small spaces should be filled with chips broken off in dressing the larger stones, so as to make them fit snugly. As it is a work that will last a century, it is worth doing well.

BUILDING A STONE FENCE.

A permanent stone fence should be built from four to five feet high, two feet wide at the base and one foot at the top, if the kind of stones available allow this construction. If a higher fence is desired, the width should be correspondingly increased. The surface of the soil along the line of the fence should be made smooth and as nearly level as possible. The hight will depend upon the situation, the animals, the smoothness of the wall (whether sheep can get foot-holds to climb over), and the character of the ground along each side. If the earth foundation be rounded up previously, sloping off to an open depression or gully, less hight will be needed. Such

Fig. 19.—LAYING UP A STONE FENCE.

an elevation will furnish a dry base not heaved by frost like a wet one. Without this, or a drain alongside or under the wall, to keep the soil always dry, the base must be sunk deeply enough to be proof against heavy frosts, which will tilt and loosen the best laid wall on wet soil. The foundation stones should be the largest; smaller stones packed between them are necessary to firmness. The mistake is sometimes made of placing all the larger stones on the outside of the wall, filling the center with small ones. Long bind-stones placed at frequent intervals through the wall add greatly to its strength. The top of the fence is most secure when covered with larger close-fitting, flat stones. The engraving shows a **wooden frame** and cords used as a guide in building a **substantial stone fence.** Two men can work together with **mutual advantage** on opposite sides of the stone wall.

TRUCK FOR MOVING STONES.

The small truck (figure 20) is not expensive, and **may** be made to save a great amount of hard lifting in building a stone wall. It is a low barrow, the side bars **forming**

Fig. 20.—TRUCK FOR STONE.

the handles like a wheelbarrow. It rests upon four **low** iron wheels. A broad plank, or two narrow ones, **are** laid with one end against the wall and the other **resting** on the ground. A groove is cut at the upper end for **the** wheels to rest in. The stone is loaded on the truck, moved to the place, and pushed up the plank until **the** wheels fall into the groove, when, by lifting on the handles, the stone is unloaded.

REINFORCING A STONE WALL.

A stone wall which affords ample protection **against sheep** and hogs, may be quite insufficient for horses **and cattle.** The deficiency is cheaply supplied in the **manner** indicated by the illustration, figure 21. Round poles or

Fig. 21.—STONE WALL REINFORCED.

rails are used, and if the work is properly performed, **the fence** is very effective.

A COMPOSITE FENCE.

The fence illustrated at figure 22 is quite common **in** some parts of New England. A ridge is thrown up

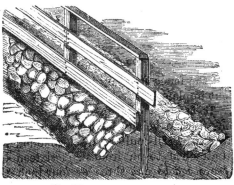

Fig. 22.—COMPOSITE FENCE.

back-furrowing with a plow, and both that and **the ditches** finished by hand with a shovel. Light posts **are**

easily driven through the soft earth, and a board fence, only three boards high, made in the usual manner. Then the stones, as they are picked up in the field, are hauled to the fence and thrown upon the ridge. This clears the field, strengthens the ridge, prevents the growth of weeds, and assists in packing the earth firmly around the bottom of the posts.

A PRAIRIE SOD FENCE.

A sod fence, beside its other value, is a double barrier against the prairie fires which are so sweeping and destructive to new settlers, if unobstructed, for a wide strip is

Fig. 23.—SOD CUTTER.

cleared of sods, the fence standing in the middle of it. A very convenient implement for cutting the sod is shown at figure 23. It is made of planks and scantling, the method of construction being clearly shown. The cutting disks are four wheel-coulters from common breaking plows, all attached to an iron shaft sixteen inches apart. They are set to cut three or four inches deep. This is run three times along the line of the fence, making nine cuts, the cutters being held down by a man riding on the rear of the apparatus. Then with a breaking plow one furrow is turned directly in the line of the fence, completely inverting the sod, the team turned to the right, and a second or back furrow is inverted on top of the first. Additional furrows are cut, diminishing in width to five or six inches on the outer side, as shown in the diagram, figure 24. After the two inner sods are turned, the rest are carried by hand, wheelbarrow or a truck, (figure 20), and laid on the sod wall, care being used to "break joints" and to taper gradually to the

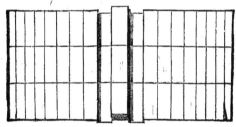

Fig. 24.—THE SOD CUT.

top. If a more substantial fence is wanted, a strip thirty-two inches wide may be left as a part for the fence, the first two furrows inverted upon the uncut portion, so that their edges just touch. The sod fence is then continued to the summit just twice as thick as it would be by the process just described. After the fence is laid, a deep furrow should be run on each side, throwing the earth against the base of the fence. A very effective and cheap fence is made by laying up a sod "dyke," as above described, three feet high, then driving light stakes along the summit, and stringing two strands of barbed wire to them.

CHAPTER III.

BOARD FENCES.

BUILDING BOARD FENCES.

In building a board fence, always start right, and it will be little trouble to continue in the same way. Much of the board fencing erected is put together very carelessly, and the result is a very insecure protection to the field or crops. A fence-post should be set two and a half or three feet in the ground, and the earth should be packed around it as firmly as possible. For packing the

Fig. 25.—PROPERLY CONSTRUCTED BOARD FENCE.

soil there is nothing better than a piece of oak, about three inches square on the lower end, and about six feet long, rounded off on the upper part to fit the hands easily. Properly used, this instrument will pack the soil around a post as it was before the hole was dug. In putting on fence boards, most builders use two nails on the ends of each board, and one in the middle. Each board should have at least *three* nails at the ends, and *two* in the middle, and these nails should never be less than tenpennys. Smaller nails will hold the boards in place for awhile, but when they begin to warp, the nails are drawn out or loosened, and the boards drop off. This will rarely be the case where large nails are used, and a much stiffer fence is secured. Many fence builders do not cut off the tops of the posts evenly, but this should always be done, not only for the improvement that it makes in the looks of the fence; but also for the reason that there should always be a cap put on, and to do this, the posts must be evened. The joints should always be "broken," as is shown in the engraving, figure 25, so that in a four-board fence but two joints should come on each post. By this means more firmness and durability is secured, there being always two unbroken boards on each post to hold it in place, preventing sagging. On the face of the post immediately over where the rails have been nailed on, nail a flat piece of board the width of the post and extending from the upper part of the top rail to the ground.

Figure 26 shows a slight modification, which consists in setting the posts on alternate sides of the boards, securing additional stability. The posts are seven feet long, of

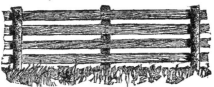

Fig. 26.—A DURABLE BOARD FENCE.

well seasoned red cedar, white oak, chestnut, or black locust, preference being accorded to order named. The boards are sixteen feet long, fastened with ten-penny steel fence nails. The posts for a space of two and a half feet from the lower end are given a good coat of boiled linseed oil and pulverized charcoal, mixed to the consistency of ordinary paint, which is allowed to dry before they are set. When the materials are all ready, stretch a line eighteen inches above the ground, where it is proposed to build the fence. Dig the post holes, eight feet apart from centers, on alternate sides of the line. The posts are set with the faces inward, each half an inch from the line, to allow space for the boards. Having set the posts, the boards of the lower course are nailed on. Then, for the first length, the second board from the bottom and the top board are only eight feet long, reaching to the first post. For all the rest the boards are of the full length, sixteen feet. By this means they " break joints." After the boards are nailed on, the top of the posts are sawed off slanting, capped, if desired,

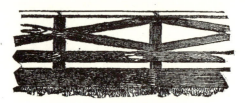

Fig. 27.—A NEAT FARM FENCE.

and the whole thing painted. A good coat of crude petroleum, applied before painting, will help preserve the fence, and save more than its cost in the paint needed.

We see another style of board fence now and then that is rather preferable to the ordinary one; it looks better than the old straight fence. It saves one board to each length; and by nailing on the two upper boards, as shown in the illustration, figure 27, great extra strength is given. These boards not only act as braces, but ties also, and a fence built on well set posts, and thoroughly nailed, will never sag or get out of line until the posts rot off.

FENCES FOR LAND SUBJECT TO OVERFLOW.

The fence illustrated in figures 28, 29 and 30 has posts the usual distance apart, which are hewed on the front side, and on this are nailed three blocks, three by four inches thick and six inches long; the first one, with its top just level with the ground, the second one, ten inches in the clear above, and the third one, four inches less than the desired height of the fence, measuring from

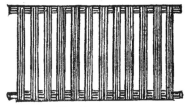

Fig. 28.—PANEL.

the top of the first block. After the panel is put in place, the rounded ends resting on the bottom blocks, nail a piece of board one and one-half by six inches on the blocks, as shown in the illustrations. This board must project four inches above the upper block, forming with it the rest and catch for the top framing piece of the panel. The panel is made of a top and bottom piece of three

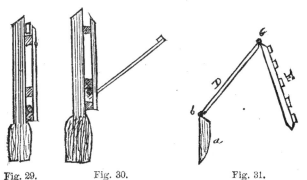

Fig. 29.   Fig. 30.   Fig. 31.

by four scantling, on which are nailed palings. The top piece is left square, and projects three inches on each side, but on the bottom piece the projections are cut round, so as to turn in the slot. The water will raise the panel up out of the upper catch, allowing it to fall down.

as seen at figure 30, so as to offer no obstruction to the water, nor will it catch drift, as fences hung from the top

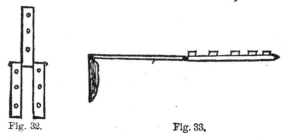

Fig. 32.   Fig. 33.

do. Figures 31 to 35 represent a fence made somewhat like the trestle used for drying clothes. The posts are

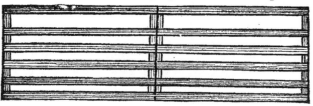

Fig. 34.

the usual distance apart, but only extend a few inches out of the ground, just sufficient to nail a hinge upon.

Fig. 35.

They must, however, be wide enough to admit of nailing two hinges on each post. The fence consists of two parts—*E* in figure 31 represents a cross-section of the fence proper, two panels of which are seen in figure 34; *D* represents the back part of the fence, a section of which is shown in figure 35; *a* in figure 31 is the post and *b b* the hinges. The panel, *E*, should always slope with the current of the stream, that the water rushing against it will place it in the position shown by figure 33, lying flat on the ground, and out of the way of both water and drift. The hinges may be ordinary strap kind, which can be bought very cheap by the dozen, or they may be made of heavy iron hoop doubled, as shown at figure 32, which can be made in any blacksmith shop.

A FENCE BOARD HOLDER.

Figure 36 shows a contrivance for holding fence boards against the posts, at the right distances apart when nail-

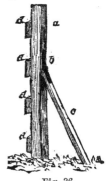
Fig. 36.

Fig. 37.—FENCE BOARD HOLDER.

ing. A two and a half by two and a half inch piece of the desired length is taken for the upright, *a*. About its center is hinged the brace, *c*. A strap hinge, *b*, or a stout piece of leather for a hinge, will answer. Blocks or stops, *d, d, d, d,* are nailed on the upright *a*, at the required distances, according to the space between the boards on the fence. The bottom boards of the fence are nailed on first. The bottom block of the board holder rests upon the bottom board, and is held in position by the brace c. The boards can be placed in the holder like putting up bars, and are guided to their places on the post by the blocks, d, d. The boards can now be nailed on the posts, and the holding devices moved for another length. When the boards are too long, they can be pulled forward a little, and the end sawed, and pushed back to place. One man using the contrivance, can nail on nearly as many boards in a day, as two persons with one to hold the boards in the old way. Figure 37 shows the manner of using the fence board holders.

REINFORCING A BOARD FENCE.

The old method of topping out a low board fence is shown at figure 38. Since barbed wire has become

Fig. 38.—STRENGTHENING A BOARD FENCE.

plenty, it is more usual to increase the height of the fence by stringing one or two strands of that on vertical slats nailed to the tops of the posts. Yet, in cases where there are plenty of sound rails left from some old fence, or plenty of straight saplings, the old method is still a very cheap and convenient one.

CHAPTER IV.

PICKET FENCES.

A GOOD GARDEN FENCE.

The engraving, figure 39, represents a good, substantial garden fence, that, while somewhat more serviceable than the ordinary kind, may be constructed at less cost. It does not materially differ from the common picket

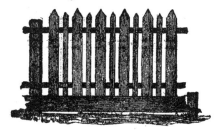

Fig. 39.—A LATH AND PICKET FENCE.

fence, further than that the pickets are put five inches apart, with strips of lath nailed between. The pickets give the necessary strength, while the lath, as a shield against poultry, or rabbits and other vermin, is equally as good at one-sixth the cost. An old picket fence surrounding a garden or yard, may be "lathed" in the manner here indicated at little expense.

A SOUTHERN PICKET FENCE.

The picket fence in very general use in the Southern States, is shown in figure 40. It will be observed that the pickets, instead of terminating in an equal-sided point, have but one slanting side, while the other is straight. Such a fence looks quite as well as one with the other style of points, and is exceedingly neat and

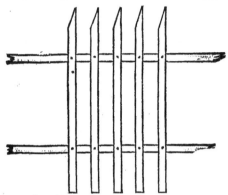

Fig. 40.—SOUTHERN PICKET FENCE.

serviceable along the line of the street, or to mark the boundary between two estates. To facilitate the sawing of the pickets, the bench or horse represented in figure

Fig. 41.—BENCH FOR SAWING PICKETS.

41 is employed. This has a stop at one end, while near the other end are two upright pieces to serve as guides in sawing. The edge of one of these is far enough in the rear of the other to give the desired slope. In saw-

ing, the saw rests against these guides, as shown by the dotted lines. In a picket fence, the point where decay commences, is where the pickets cross the string pieces. Water enters between the two, and decay takes place which is unsuspected until the breaking of a picket reveals the state of affairs. The string pieces and the pickets, at least upon one side, should be painted before putting them together, and nailed while the paint is fresh.

FENCES OF SPLIT PICKETS.

In localities where sawed timber is expensive, and split timber is readily obtained, a very neat picket fence may

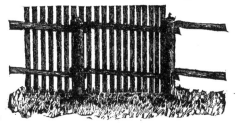

Fig. 42.—A FENCE OF SPLIT STUFF.

be made with very little outlay, by using round posts, split stringers, and rived pickets, as shown in the engraving, figure 42. The stringers are eight to twelve feet in length, and usually one of the flat sides is sufficiently smooth for receiving the pickets. Let the stringers project a few inches beyond each post, adding strength to the fence, and should the posts decay, new ones may be driven in on either side, and the stringers readily attached by heavy nails or spikes. With timber that splits freely, a man can rive out five or six hundred pickets in a day. The construction of the fence is plainly shown in the above engraving.

Figure 43 represents a fence made entirely of split timber, the only cash outlay being for nails. This may be made so as to turn, not only all kinds of stock, but rabbits, etc. The pickets are sharpened, and driven six

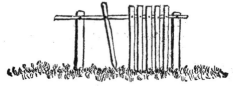

Fig. 43.—CHEAP FENCE OF SPLIT TIMBER.

or eight inches into the ground, and firmly nailed to a strong string-piece at top.

Another good substantial fence is represented by figure 44, which, though somewhat expensive, is especially

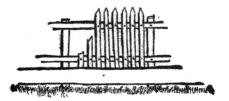

Fig. 44.—COMMON PICKET FENCE.

adapted for yard, orchard and vineyard enclosure. This needs no explanation. The posts should not be set further than eight feet apart; two by four inch scantlings should be used to nail to, and split palings should be nailed on with annealed steel nails.

ORNAMENTAL PICKET FENCES.

The fence shown in figure 45 may be constructed with flat pickets, three inches wide and three feet five inches long. The notches in the pickets are easily made with a compass saw, or a foot-power scroll-saw. The top and bottom pieces between the pickets may be

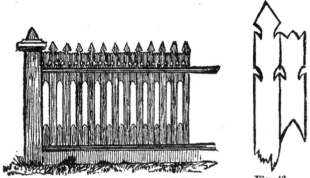

Fig. 45.—ORNAMENTAL PICKET FENCE.   Fig. 46.

painted some other color than the fence, if so desired. Any carpenter should be able to construct it at a small advance over a fence made from plain pickets, making the pattern as in figure 46.

A plainer, but still very neat form of picket fence is

Fig. 47.—A PLAINER PICKET FENCE.

illustrated at figure 47. The intermediate pieces are notched at one end and square at the other.

When the farmers on the prairies prevent the spreading of the prairie fires, young oak and hickory saplings spring up as if by magic near all the wooded streams. These saplings come from huge roots whose tops have

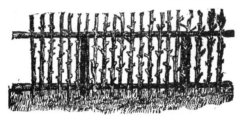

Fig. 48.—RUSTIC SAPLING FENCE.

yearly been destroyed by fire. In that section farmers often construct a very neat rustic fence from two or three year old saplings, having the appearance of figure 48. The rustic pickets are trimmed so as to leave the branches projecting about two inches, and are nailed on with four-penny nails. A fence of this kind would not last long, unless the pickets, posts, and rails were free of bark, or saturated with crude petroleum.

A very neat and picturesque fence for a garden or

Fig. 49.—RUSTIC PICKET FENCE.

a lawn is shown at figure 49. It is made of round poles, with the bark on, the posts being of similar mater-rial. Three horizontal bars are nailed to the posts at equal intervals, the slats or pickets woven into them and then nailed in place. One or two coats of crude petroleum, applied to this and other rustic work at first, and renewed every year, adds to its appearance and greatly increases its durability.

LIGHT PICKET FENCES.

For enclosing poultry yards, garden and grounds, a cheap fence with pickets of lath often serves a good purpose. If not very durable, the cost of repair or renewal is light. Figure 50 shows one of this kind, which is sufficiently high for the Asiatic and other heavy and quiet fowls. The panels are sixteen feet long, and are

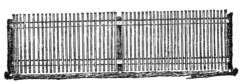

Fig. 50.—PANEL OF PICKET FENCE.

composed of two pieces of ordinary six-inch fencing, for top and bottom rails, with lath nailed across two and a half inches apart; the top ends of the lath extending ten inches above the upper edge of the top rail. Posts, three or four inches through at the top end, are large enough, and, after sharpening well, can be driven into the ground by first thrusting a crow-bar down and wrenching it back and forth. A post is necessary at the middle of each panel. Both rails of the panel should be well nailed to the posts. These panels may be neatly and rapidly made in a frame, constructed for that purpose. This frame, shown in figure 51, consists simply of three cross-pieces of six by six, four feet long, upon which are spiked two planks one foot wide and three feet apart, from outside to outside. Four inches from the inner edge of each plank is nailed a straight strip of inch stuff, to keep the rails of the panel in place while the

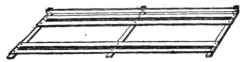

Fig. 51.—FRAME FOR MAKING FENCE.

lath are being nailed on. Against the projecting ends of the cross-pieces, spike two by six posts twelve inches long; on the inside of these posts nail a piece of six inch fencing, to serve as a stop, for the top ends of the laths to touch, when nailing them to the rails. These panels can be made in the shop or on the barn floor at odd times, and piled away for future use. Nail a wide bottom board around on the inside of the enclosure after the fence is in position.

Figures 52 and 53 show lath fences high enough for all kinds of poultry. The posts in figure 52 are eight feet apart. A horizontal bar is nailed to the posts six

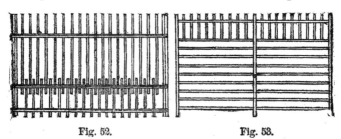

Fig. 52. Fig. 53.

inches above the ground, a second one eighteen inches, and a third four and a half feet. To two lower strips nail laths that have been cut to half length, first driving the lower part of the laths two inches into the ground.

One advantage of this fence is, that the two strips near the bottom, being so close together, sustain pressure from dogs or outside intruders better than any other fence constructed of lath, and dispenses with a foot-wide board, so generally used.

The cheapest lath fence is made with the posts four feet apart, first sawing them in two lengthwise at a sawmill, and nailing the lath directly to the posts without the use of strips. The two upper laths have short vertical pieces fastened to them with cleat nails, and present points to prevent fowls alighting on the fence. Such a fence (figure 53) will cost, for four feet, one-half post, three cents; twenty laths, eight cents; and the nails, three cents, per running foot, six feet high, or one-half cent per square foot.

HAND-MADE WIRE AND PICKET FENCES.

A very desirable and popular fence is made of pickets or slats woven into horizontal strands of plain wire. Sev-

Fig. 54.—SIDE VIEW OF BENCH.

eral machines have been invented and patented for doing this work, but it can be done by hand with the aid of the bench illustrated herewith. The wire should be a little larger than that used on harvesting machines, and annealed like it. The bench, of which figure 54 is a side view, and figure 55 a top view, should be about sixteen feet long and have a screw at each corner for raising and lowering the holding bars. For the screws at the ends of the frame one-half to three-fourth-inch iron rod will answer. The wire is twisted close and tight to the slats, and given two or three twists between them. If the

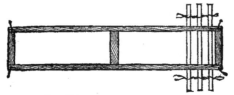

Fig. 55.—TOP VIEW OF BENCH.

slats are of green stuff, fasten the wire to them with small staples, to prevent their slipping when they shrink. The fence is fastened to the post with common fence staples.

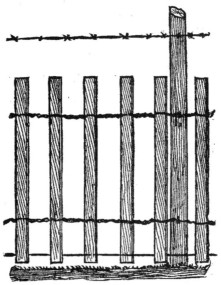

Fig. 56.—PORTION OF THE FENCE.

When this style of fence is used on one side of a pasture or highway, its effectiveness may be increased by a single strand of barbed wire stapled to the posts above the pickets, and a strand of plain wire strung along the bottom to stiffen it. The fence will then be as in figure 56. Such a fence will last many years, and for most sections of the country is the best and cheapest combined cattle and hog fence that can be made. For a garden fence it is equal to the best picket, and at one third of the cost. By having the slats sawed about one-half-inch thick, two inches wide, and five to six feet long, it makes an excellent fence for a chicken yard, as it can be readily taken down, moved, and put up again without injuring it in the least. For situations where appearances are secondary importance, round slats are equally as good as pickets. A farmer in Wisconsin planted a few white willow trees the year that he made some fences of this kind. When the fence began to need repairs, the willows had attained such a growth that their trimmings furnished all the material needed then and each year thereafter.

FENCE OF WIRE AND PICKETS.

The fence shown in figure 57 has been introduced in some sections, and is becoming more popular every

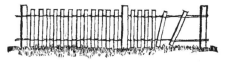

Fig. 57.—FENCE OF WIRE AND PICKETS.

year. The posts are set ten feet apart, and are so placed that they will come on the right and left side of the fence, alternately. The pickets are split from oak, or any other hard wood, and are four or five feet long, and an inch and a half or two inches wide. When the posts are set, brace the one at the end of the line, and fasten the ends of two number nine, unannealed wires to it. Stretch the wires along to the other end of the line, and a few feet beyond the last post. One pair is to be stretched near the top of the posts and one near the ground. When the wires are stretched taut, fasten them to some posts or other weight that will drag on the ground; the upper and lower wires should be fastened to separate weights, and these should be heavy enough to keep the wires at a great tension. Having done this, you are ready to commence building the fence. One man spreads the strands, while another places the picket between them; the other end of the picket is then raised up and placed between the upper wires, and then driven up with an axe or mallet. In inserting the pickets, the wires are to be crossed alternately, as shown in the engraving. The pickets should be dry and should be about three inches apart. It takes two persons to build this fence successfully, but it can be built more rapidly by three; one to spread the wires, one to place the picket in position, and one to drive it home. This is especially adapted for a line or other fence which is not required to be often moved. It is fastened to the post by nailing one of the pickets to it with common fencing nails. Fences of this kind are also made with straight, round limbs of willow or other trees in place of the split pickets. Several different machines have been patented for making this style of fence.

CHAPTER V.

BARB-WIRE FENCE.

The invention of barb wire was the most important event in the solution of the fence problem. The question of providing fencing material had become serious, even in the timbered portions of the country, while the great prairie region was almost wholly without resource, save the slow and expensive process of hedging. At this juncture came barb wire, which was at once seen to make a cheap, effective, and durable fence, rapidly built and easily moved. The original patent for barb wire was taken out in 1868, but it was not until six years later that an attempt was made to introduce it into general use, and more than ten years elapsed before the industry attained any considerable magnitude. The rapidity and extent of its subsequent growth will be seen by the following table, showing the estimated amount of barb wire manufactured and in use during the years named, the estimated length being in miles of single strand:

YEAR.	TONS.	MILES.	YEAR.	TONS.	MILES.
1874	5	10	1881	60,000	120,000
1875	300	600	1882	80,000	160,000
1876	1,500	3,000	1883	100,000	200,000
1877	7,000	14,000	1884	125,000	250,000
1878	13,000	26,000	1885	130,000	260,000
1879	25,000	50,000	1886	135,000	270,000
1880	40,000	80,000			
			TOTALS	716,805	1,433,610

There are now fifty establishments engaged in the manufacture, and the output for 1887 is estimated at 140,000 tons.

Barb wire is not without its drawbacks as a fencing material, the most common one being the liability of serious injury to valuable domestic animals coming in contact with the sharp barbs. Many means have been devised for overcoming this evil. Some of them are illustrated in the next chapter. The direct advantages

Fig. 58.—THE KELLY BARB WIRE.

of barb wire are: First—economy, not only in the comparative cheapness of its first cost, but also in the small amount of land covered by it. Second—effectiveness as a barrier against all kinds of stock, and a protection against dogs and wild beasts. Third—rapidity of construction and ease of moving. Fourth—freedom from harboring weeds, and creating snow drifts. Fifth—durability.

Barb wire, like the harvester, the sowing machine, and

Fig. 59.—HORSE-NAIL BARB.

most other valuable inventions, has attained its present form from very crude beginnings. The original barb wire consisted of double-pointed metallic discs, strung loosely upon plain wire. The next step was to twist this with another wire, as shown in figure 58.

Another crude beginning was the "horse-nail barb,"

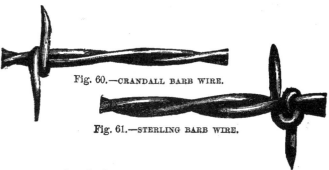

Fig. 60.—CRANDALL BARB WIRE.

Fig. 61.—STERLING BARB WIRE.

which consisted of a common horse-shoe nail bent around a plain wire, and the whole wrapped spirally with a smaller wire, as shown in figure 59. Various forms of two-pointed and four-pointed barb wire are manufactured, the principal difference being the shape of the barbs and

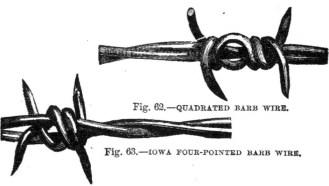

Fig. 62.—QUADRATED BARB WIRE.

Fig. 63.—IOWA FOUR-POINTED BARB WIRE.

the manner of coiling them around one or both of the strands. A few of the leading styles are illustrated herewith. Figures 60 and 61 show two varieties of two-pointed barb wire.

Of the numerous styles of four-pointed wire, three typical forms are illustrated in figures 62, 63, and 64. The Glidden patent steel barb wire is made in three

Fig. 64.—LYMAN BARB WIRE.

styles, as shown in figures 65, 66, and 67. Figure 65 shows the two-point wire, in which, like the others, the barb is twisted around only one of the wires. Figure

Fig. 65.—GLIDDEN PATENT STEEL TWO-POINT.

66 shows the "thick-set" which has barbs like the other, but set closer together for such purposes as sheep folds, gardens, or other places, which require extra protection.

Fig. 66.—GLIDDEN PATENT STEEL "THICK SET."

The four-point barb wire, figure 67, has barbs of the same form as the two other styles, that is a sharply pricking barb attached to one of the wires of the fence strand, upon which the other wire is twisted, holding the barb firmly in place. The barb is at right angles to the wire, and does not form a hook, but a straight short steel thorn. A sharp point which inflict an instantaneous prick repels an animal more safely than a longer and duller barb.

Barb wire of nearly, if not quite all the popular kinds, is shipped from the factory on strong spools, each holding

Fig. 67.—GLIDDEN PATENT FOUR-POINT.

one hundred pounds in weight, or eighty rods in length. These spools are bored through the center to admit a stick or bar, which can be used as an axle in unreeling the wire. The following table shows the weight of wire required for fencing the respective areas named :

AREA.	LENGTH OF BOUNDARY.	WEIGHT OF WIRE.	
		1 Strand. LBS.	3 Strand. LBS.
1 Acre	60 Rods.	67	202
5 Acres	³/₈ Mile.	167	400
10 Acres	½ Mile.	183	548
20 Acres	¾ Mile.	273	820
40 Acres	1 Mile.	365	1095
80 Acres	1½ Mile.	547	1642
160 Acres	2 Miles.	730	2190

It will be observed that the larger the area enclosed, the smaller is the amount of fence required per acre. The cost of fence complete can be estimated by adding to the amount of wire indicated in the last column, the cost of sixty posts, and three and three quarter pounds of staples, for every sixty rods. To ascertain the weight of wire required for any desired number of strands, multiply the

Fig. 68.—BRINKERHOFF STEEL STRAP AND BARB.

figures of the first column of "weight of wire" by the number of strands proposed to be used.

There is a kind of barb fencing in which flat steel straps are employed instead of wire. In the form shown in figure 68, the barbs are bent around a plain strap and the whole is then galvanized, which firmly fixes the barb.

Fig. 69.—ALLIS PATENT BARB.

Another form shown at figure 69 consists of a solid piece of steel, ribbed through the middle, and with barbs cut on both edges. These and similar forms are more expensive than wire, and are employed only in limited quan-

Fig. 70.—BRINKERHOFF FENCING TWISTED.

tities for enclosing lawns, paddocks, etc. Still another form is like that shown in figure 70, without barbs, and twisted. This is much used to enclose lawns and ornamental grounds. It is light, neat and strong, does not harbor weeds or make snow drifts, but is comparatively expensive, as five or six strands are required to make an effective fence.

Still another form of unarmed fencing is shown in figure 71. It is simply the ordinary wire without barbs,

Fig. 71.—TWO STRAND TWISTED WIRE FENCING.

and is used in limited quantities for fencing ornamental grounds, barnyards, etc.

STEEL FENCE STAPLES.

For fastening barb wires to the post nothing has been found so satisfactory as staples made for the purpose from No. 9 steel wire. They are cut with sharp points

Fig. 72.—1¼-INCH STAPLE.   Fig. 73.—1¾-INCH STAPLE.

Fig. 74.—SQUARE TOP STAPLE FOR BRINKERHOFF FENCING.

to drive easily into the posts, and are of different lengths, from one inch and a quarter to one and three-quarters. Figures 72 and 73 show the usual staples for wire, and figure 74 a staple made specially for strap fencing.

HOW TO SET BARB WIRE FENCE.

The timber for posts should be cut when the **sap is** dormant. Midwinter or August is a good time to cut post timber. They should be split and the bark **taken off** as soon as possible after cutting the timber. For end posts, select some of the best trees, about sixteen **inches in** diameter, from which take cuts eight and a half **feet in** length, splitting them in quarters for brace posts. They should be set three feet in the ground, which is easily done with a post-hole digger. When setting the brace posts, take a stone eighteen inches to two feet long, twelve inches wide, and six inches thick, which is put down against the post edgewise, on the opposite

Fig. 75.—WELL-BRACED BARB-WIRE FENCE.

side to the brace, as seen in figure 75, putting **it** down about even with the surface of the ground. **This** holds the post solid against the brace. A heart-rail, **ten feet in** length makes a good brace. Put one of the long posts every sixteen or twenty rods along the line of fence, as they help to strengthen it, and set lighter and shorter posts along the line about sixteen feet apart. After the posts are set, two or three furrows should be turned against them on each side, as it helps to keep stock from the wire. Such a fence should be built of a good height. It is better to buy an extra wire than have stock injured. There is no pulling over end posts or sagging wire.

To make an extra solid wire fence, brace the posts, as shown in figure 76, on both sides, in order to resist the tension in either direction. Every eighth post should be thus braced, and it makes a mark for measuring the length of the fence, for eight posts set one rod apart, make eight rods, or a fortieth of a mile for each braced post. The braces are notched into the top of

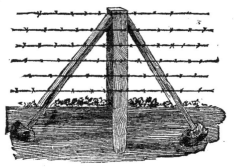

Fig. 76.—A WIRE FENCE WELL BRACED.

the posts, just below the top wire, and a spike is driven through both the brace and the post. The braces abut upon large stones which give them great firmness.

UNREELING AND STRETCHING BARB WIRE.

The general introduction of barb wire fencing has brought out a great variety of devices for handling the wire. One of these is shown in the illustrations. Two pieces of scantling are attached to the rear end of a wagon from which the box has been removed, as shown in figure 77. A slot near the end of each admits the round stick thrust through the reel of barb wire, to serve as an axle. The end of the barb wire is fastened to the fence post, the team in front of the wagon started up, and some three yards of wire unreeled. Then the **hind axle of the wagon** is made fast by a chain or rope to the **nearest fence** post, the hind wheel nearest the fence **lifted** from the ground and held there by a wagon-jack **or piece**

Fig. 77.—DEVICE FOR UNROLLING WIRE.

of board. One turn is then made in the barb **wire, as shown** at *A*, figure 78, to which is attached one end **of a piece of** smooth wire, some ten feet long. The other **end** is placed between two screws, *b b*, in the end of the

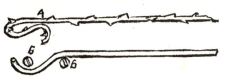

Fig. 78.—FASTENING THE WIRE.

hub, as shown in the illustration. The wire thus **fastened** is coiled around the hub, and the operator **can tighten** it and the barb wire to which it is attached, by **employing** the leverage of the spokes and felloes.

A lighter form of reel holder is shown at figure 79. It

Fig. 79.—A SULKY WIRE-HOLDER.

is made of two pieces of two by four scantlings **fastened to** the axle of a sulky corn plow. They must be **placed**

far enough apart to allow the reel or spool to run between them. Make a square axle, figure 80, of some hard tough wood, rounding it where it runs in the slots of the

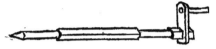

Fig. 80.—THE AXLE.

scantling; drive it through the hole in the spool, and attach the crank. In moving fence, place the spool on the frame; remove one end of the wire from the post, fasten it to the spool, and while one man holds the pole and steers and steadies the sulky—he will have to pull back a little—another turns the spool and winds up the wire. When a corner is reached, the wire is loosened, the sulky turned, and the winding continued. When the end of the wire is reached, it is carefully loosened from the post, and firmly fastened to the spool.

It is best to have a separate spool for each wire, especially if they are of great length. The same contrivance may be used for unreeling the wire. Attach a gentle horse to the sulky, fasten the pole securely to the hames,

Fig. 81.—A SLED WIRE-HOLDER.

and have a boy lead him slowly along the fence line. once in fifty yards stop the horse, grasp the handle, move forward very slowly, and draw the wire straight and taut. If no sulky plow is at hand, a light "double-ended" sled, shown in figure 81, may be used. A man holds the short pole extending from one end, steadying and pushing a little, while the other winds the reel. The sled is drawn forward by the wire as it is wound on the reel. To unreel, attach a slow horse to a chain or

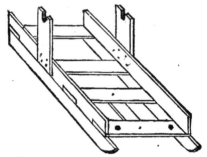

Fig. 82.—ANOTHER SLED FOR WIRE.

rope fastened to the opposite end of the sled. A man must walk behind the horse and hold the pole to steady the sled. Managed in this way, the removal of a barbed wire fence is not at all the formidable operation that has been supposed; it can be taken down and set up again, easily, safely, and quite rapidly. Figure 82 shows an-

Fig. 83.—TIGHTENING THE WIRE.

other form of home-made sled, which is very useful for carrying rolls of wire for making a fence. The roll is supported on a rod, which has round ends to fit into the uprights, and which turns in the slots. When the wire is run out, the end is fastened to the clevis on the centre beam, and a notched stake, figure 83, being put under the wire, the sled is drawn up to tighten the wire, which is then stapled. This sled is useful for many other purposes, and is large enough to carry five rolls of the wire, so that by going back and forth, the whole of the fence can be put up very quickly. It is drawn by one horse, the draft chain being fastened to the front beam.

WIRE STRETCHERS.

For stretching barb wire there are various implements in the market, and other quite simple and effective devices can be made on the farm. Figure 84 shows the

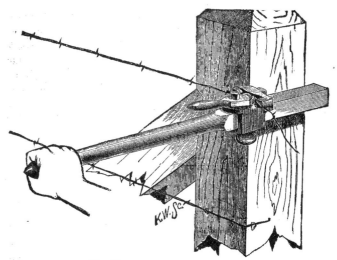

Fig. 84.—THE CLARK STRETCHER.

Clark stretcher and the manner of using it. Another stretcher, called the "Come Along" stretcher, figure 85, is used not only for tightening the wires, but also for handling it, in building or moving fences.

The useful wire stretcher, figure 86, consists of a mowing machine knife-guard, bolted to a stout stick;

Fig. 85.—THE "COME ALONG" STRETCHER.

one curved, as shown in the lower engraving, is preferable to a straight one, as it will not turn in the hand. When using it, the wire is held firmly in the slot, and may be easily stretched by applying the stick as a lever.

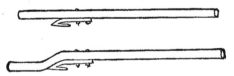

Fig. 86.—HOME-MADE WIRE STRETCHERS.

Another kind of a wire-stretcher may be made of hard wood or of iron or steel bars. It consists of three pieces, two arms and a splicer, fastened together in the manner shown in figure 87, leaving a slot near one end to hold the wire. The longer arm is made immovable upon the splice by means of two or more heavy bolts, while the shorter arm is pivoted by one bolt. This allows the slot to be opened to receive the wire. The short arm is sharpened so that it may be stuck into a post, or the side of a building, if convenient. By placing this lever behind a post, one man can stretch thoroughly a long string of wire. When one man is doing the work alone, he can stretch the wire, fasten the lever back by means of a stick

Fig. 87.

driven into the ground before it, and then go back and drive the staples. The short end of the lever should be about twelve inches long, and the long arm three or four feet, or even longer.

The stretcher shown in figure 88 is made of hard tough wood or iron. The wire is passed through the slot, the barbs preventing it from slipping. The arm at right angles to the lever is used to measure the distance of the strands. When the lever is set against the post, the arm

Fig. 88.—STRETCHER AND GAUGE.

rests on the strand below. By sliding it up or down, the distance between the strands is regulated.

Figure 89 shows another stretcher, that can be made by any blacksmith. The toothed cam holds the wire so that it will not slip. A block and tackle are often found useful to draw the wires with. The rolls of wire are paid out of a wagon body, and when the wire is to be drawn up, the grip is put on at any point, the tackle is attached, and one horse draws it as tight as it needs be.

A wire fence needs frequent drawing up or it sags and

becomes useless. The alternate contraction and expansion caused by change of temperature soon stretch the wire, to say nothing of other causes. The cheap and ef-

Fig. 89.—GRIP FOR FENCE WIRE.

fective method employed by telegraph companies is illustrated in figure 90. It consists of a pair of grip tongs and a set of small tackle-blocks. The tongs may be made by any blacksmith, and the blocks are sold at all hardware and tool stores. An iron hook is used to cou-

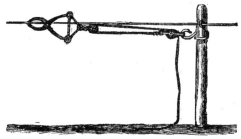

Fig. 90.

ple the tongs to the block, and as the wire is drawn up, the free end of the rope may be given a turn around the same post, to hold it while the staple is tightened to hold the wire.

SPLICING BARB WIRES.

The accompanying engravings show an iron implement for splicing wire and the manner of using it. To make this splicer take a bar of half inch round iron, nine inches long. Heat about three inches of one end and hammer it flat until it is one inch wide. With a cold chisel cut a one-fourth inch slot a quarter of an inch from the right side and an inch deep, as seen in figure

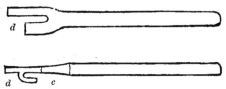

Figs. 91 and 92.—THE SPLICER.

91. Bend the part marked d, so that it will be a quarter inch from the flat part, as shown in figure 92. The lower part of the slot c should be about a half inch from the bend at d. Smooth with a file. To use it let e and

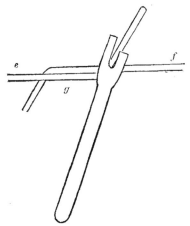

Fig. 93.—MAKING THE SPLICE.

f, figure 93 represent two wires to be joined. Bend the ends so they are nearly at right angles. Hold them with pincers at g; place the hook of the splicer on the wire f, while the wire e falls into the slot. Twist the pieces around the wire f, when one half of the splice is made. Repeat the operation for the other end. Use about four or five inches of each wire to twist around the other. Another form of splicer, shown in figure 94, is made of cast iron, and is used in the same manner as

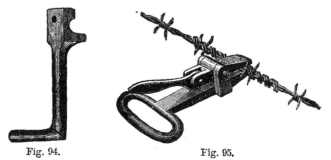

Fig. 94.   Fig. 95.

the first. Figure 95 shows the manner of holding the wire with nippers made for the purpose, and the finished splice.

BUILDING WIRE FENCES ON UNEVEN GROUND.

One of the great perplexities about building wire fences on rolling ground, is how to make the posts in the hollows remain firm, for the pull of the wire in wet

Fig. 96.—FENCE ON UNEVEN GROUND.

weather, or when the frost is coming out, lifts them and causes the wire to sag, and they cease to be an effective barrier. Posts should not be used in the lowest depressions, but in their place at the lowest spots a heavy stone should be partially sunk into the ground, about which a smooth fence wire has been wrapped, as seen in figure 96. When the fence is built, the fence wires are brought down to their place and the wire about the stone is twisted first about the lower wire, then the next, and so on to the top. This prevents the wire from raising, and does away with all trouble of the posts being pulled out by the wires. In fencing across small streams the same plan is successful.

CHAPTER VI.

FENCES OF BARB WIRE AND BOARDS.

COMBINED WIRE AND BOARD FENCE.

A very cheap fence is made of two boards below and three strands of barb wire. To make the fence pig-proof without the boards, five strands of wire, three inches

Fig. 97.—MANNER OF BRACING END-POST.

apart, would be required at the bottom. Two common fencing boards will occupy the same space, when placed three inches apart, and cost less. But for the upper part of the fence, wire is much cheaper than boards. The most considerable item in this greater economy is the saving of posts. The wire requires a post every sixteen feet; hence half the posts are saved. A stout stake, driven midway between the posts, holds the center of the boards in place. These stakes need extend only eighteen inches above ground. Posts that have rotted off in the ground will be long enough for these stakes. Some say that the posts can be set thirty feet apart, but sixteen feet is better. The posts should be at least thirty inches in the ground and well tamped. It is easy to stretch the wire. Its durability depends upon the quality of the wire and posts, and the proper setting of them. Nail on the two boards, three inches apart; the first strand is six inches above the top board, the second strand is twelve inches above the first, and the third sixteen inches above the second. When banked up, as hereafter described, this fence will turn all farm stock. An im-

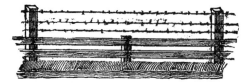

Fig. 98.—SECTION OF FENCE COMPLETED.

portant point is the bracing of the end-posts. If this be neglected or improperly done, the fence will be a failure. Figure 97 shows how the end-post should be braced. It should be a large post and set at least three feet in the ground. The short post which holds the lower end of the brace, should also be well set. Wrap the wire around the end-post several times, and drive staples to hold it on all sides. If the line of fence is more than forty rods long, at least two posts at each end should be braced. After the posts are set, and before attaching the boards or wire, plow a deep furrow along each side, throwing the earth inward. This makes a bank along the line, allowing the fence to be several inches higher; and the furrow drains the water away from the posts, and also restrains an animal that may be tempted to jump the fence. A section of the completed fence is shown in figure 98. Do not hang pieces of tin, etc., upon the top strands of wire, as often recommended, that the animals may see the fence, and be able to avoid it, because it is never necessary.

A modification of this combined fence is shown in figure 99. It is made of one rail along the top, and three wires below. After setting the posts plow a fur-

Fig. 99.—A CHEAP AND GOOD FENCE.

row two feet from the posts on each side, throwing the furrow slice towards the fence, and forming up the ridge neatly with a spade; then stretch the three wires, and nail a two by four scantling edgewise. To prevent an unpleasant sagging of the rails, the posts should be eight feet apart, and the rails sixteen feet long. For common fencing, good straight poles will answer well.

A BRACKETED FENCE.

The features shown in figure 100 are: first, in having two six-inch boards at the bottom. Second, in placing the wires very close together. It being necessary to have barbs only on one side of each space between the wires, plain galvanised wire may be used for every alternate strand, thus greatly lessening the expense. Third, by the use of strips and short stakes, the posts may be placed sixteen feet apart, and the fence remain as perfect as if there were posts every eight feet. Fourth, to make the fence man-proof, make use of a bracket of three-eighth-inch iron, or of one by two-inch wooden strips. The form of the brackets is shown in figures 101, 102 and 103. A barb-wire is attached to the short arm of the brackets, which are fastened to the posts in such a manner as to

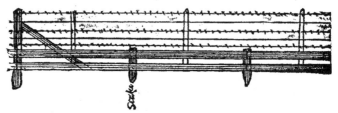

Fig. 100.—ONE PANEL OF IMPROVED WIRE FENCE.

stretch two wires on the same horizontal plane, and fifteen inches apart. The material required for each panel of the fence shown in figure 100, are: Two posts, three barb-wires, two plain wires of No. 12 galvanized iron, two six-inch boards, sixteen feet long, three stakes about three feet long, and sharpened at one end, four strips, four feet long and one and one-half-inch square. To build the fence: Lay off the ground by setting small pegs eight feet apart, then dig the holes, and set the posts at

Fig. 101.—IRON BRACKET.

every fourth peg. Drive the sharpened stakes into the ground at the three pegs between the posts, so that the top of the stakes will be nineteen inches above the ground. Nail the boards on the first stake near the ground, and the second one three inches above the first. Then mark off the place for each wire on the first post, fasten the bottom wire, and put up as far as the first stretching post; then add the other wires, using first a barb-wire, and then a smooth one. The wires should be fastened to the posts with long staples. The strips are to go in the middle of the eight foot spaces; they should not quite touch the ground; fasten them to the boards

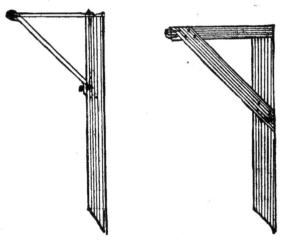

Fig. 102.—ATTACHED BRACKET.　Fig. 103.—WOODEN BRACKET.

with nails and to the wire with short staples. These strips can be made of poles or saplings, and the stakes of short or crooked pieces from the posts. To attach the man-proof part: If the brackets are of wood, nail them to the posts, sawing off the horizontal arm to fifteen inches from the top wire, as in figure 103; stretch the wire and fasten to the end. If the brackets are of iron figure 102, spike the horizontal arm to the top of the post, then put up the barb-wire loose under the oblique arm, and stretch it. Then spike the foot of the oblique arm to the post, and slip the wire into the angle, and close the bracket by closing the arms on the wire. Figure 102 shows the method of attaching the iron bracket to the post.

DOG-PROOF FENCES.

Figure 104 shows a sheep-yard fence, built of wire and boards, as a safeguard against vicious dogs. It consists of

Fig. 104.—A FENCE AGAINST DOGS.

ordinary posts, and three lengths of boards, with an equal number of barb-wires for the upper portion, and a single strand placed near the ground. The sheep are in no danger of injuring themselves with such a fence, and it is an effective barrier to blood-thirsty dogs.

Figure 105 shows a cheaper fence for the same purpose. It has one strand of barb wire below the boards,

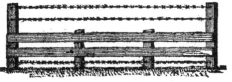

Fig. 105.—A CHEAPER FENCE.

which prevents attempts of dogs to dig under it. For fencing sheep against dogs, the "thick-set" barb wire is the most effective of any.

CHAPTER VII.

HEDGES.

THE BEST HEDGE PLANTS.

The first emigrants from England to the American shores brought with them memories of green hedge-rows, like those which still adorn the motherland. But they found the country whither they had come covered with a dense growth of timber, which furnished abundant material for fences. Hedges were almost unknown in this country until after civilization had reached the treeless prairies. Then, the want of fencing material turned attention to hedges, and they became so popular that many miles of them were planted, not only in the prairie region, but also in the more eastern States where cheaper fencing material was plenty. Now the invention of barbed wire supplies a material so cheap and easily put in place, that hedges have ceased to be regarded as economical for general farm purposes. But they have by no means gone wholly out of use. As a boundary fence, especially upon the roadside, there is much to be said in favor of the hedge. Nothing gives a neighborhood such a finished rural aspect, as to have the roads bordered by hedges. The grounds around the summer cottages on the New Jersey coast, and other popular summer resorts, are largely enclosed with hedges. For interior divisions, as they cannot be removed, they are not to be commended. An orchard, the most permanent of all the plantations upon the farm, may be appropriately enclosed by a live fence. Hedges are either protective barriers, really live fences, or merely ornamental. In properly regulated communities, where cattle are not allowed to run at large, the roadside hedge may be ornamental, while one around an orchard should be able to keep out animals and other intruders. After many experiments and failures, the Osage Orange (*Maclura aurantiaca*), has been found to make the best hedges. Being a native of Arkansas, it has been found to be hardy much farther North, and may be regarded as the most useful hedge plant in all localities where the winter is not severe. Where the Osage Orange is not hardy, Buckthorn, Japan Quince and Honey Locust are the best substitutes. Honey Locust is a most useful hedge-plant, as it is readily raised from seed, grows rapidly, bears cutting well, and in a few years will make a barrier that will turn the most violent animal.

PLANTING AND CARE OF OSAGE HEDGES.

The first requisite for a hedge of any kind is to secure thrifty plants of uniform size. Osage Orange plants are raised from seeds by nurserymen, and when of the right

Fig. 106.—BADLY PLOWED GROUND.

size, should be taken up in autumn and "heeled in." The ground, which it is proposed to occupy by the hedge, should be broken up in autumn and then re-plowed in spring, unless it is a raw prairie sod, which should be broken a year before the hedge is planted. It is a very usual, but very bad practice, to plow a ridge with a back-furrow, as shown in figure 106. This leaves an unplowed strip of hard soil directly under the line upon which the hedge is to stand. When harrowed, it appears very fair on the surface, but it is useless to expect young plants to thrive on such a bed of hard soil, and its result will be as seen in figure 107. The first growth is feeble, irregular, and many vacant spots ap-

Fig. 107.—HEDGE PLANT ON HARD RIDGE.

pear. The land should be plowed as in figure 108. When the sod is rotted, the land should be harrowed lengthwise of the furrows, and the dead furrow left in the first

Fig. 108.—PROPERLY PLOWED GROUND.

plowing closed by twice turning back the ridge. There is then a deep, mellow, well-drained bed for the plants in which the roots have room to grow and gather ample nutrition. Figure 109 shows the effect of this kind of

Fig. 109.—HEDGE PLANT IN MELLOW SOIL.

cultivation. As a barrier against stock, or a windbreak, it is best to plant in double rows, each row being set opposite the spaces in the other, thus : *   *   *   *   *
                                                 *   *   *   *

It is highly desirable that the hedge should be in true, uniform rows, either straight or in regular curves. This can be done only by setting closely to a line. Osage Orange plants may be raised from seed, but as this is a difficult operation, it is usually best to buy young plants from a reliable nurseryman. They are best cut down to about six inches high, and the roots partially trimmed. It is an advantage to "puddle" the roots, which is done by dipping them in a mixture composed of one-half earth and half fresh manure from the cow stable, wet to the consistency of a thin paste. There are various methods of setting the plants. Some use a trowel with a blade about ten inches long; others a dibble, and a larger number than either of the others, a spade. For setting long lines, in situations where appearances are of

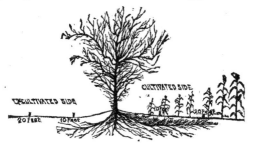

Fig. 110.—EFFECT OF CULTIVATION.

secondary importance, young Osage plants are set very rapidly by running a furrow where the rows are to stand, laying the plants with their roots spread on the mellow soil, one side of the furrow. A furrow is next turned upon the roots, and the plants which may have been disarranged are restored by hand. A tread of the foot will consolidate the earth around each plant. Unless the subsoil is naturally very porous, the ground must be thoroughly underdrained. A line of tiles should be laid six or eight feet from the line of the hedge. The ground for four or five feet on either side of the hedge, should be kept thoroughly cultivated the first three or four years after planting. This cultivation is to be done early each season and cease the first of July, to give the new wood a chance to ripen. The plants should be permitted to grow the first year undisturbed. The following spring, the hedge should be cut off close to the ground with a scythe or mowing machine, and all vacancies where plants have died out or been thrown out by frost, should be filled. The ground on both sides of the ridge is to be kept well cultivated. Figure 110 shows the difference in root growth in cultivated and uncultivated ground.

A thick growth of young shoots will appear, and these are to be cut back to four inches high, the middle of summer and again in September. The object is to obtain a dense growth close to the ground. The third year the pruning is to be repeated, only the shoots must be left four to six inches above the last previous cutting. The lateral shoots which are near the ground, are to be left undisturbed. The trimming should be such as to leave the hedge broad at the base, with a regular slope to the summit like a double-span roof.

Another method is to permit the hedge to grow untrimmed for four or five years. It is then plashed, or

Fig. 111.—HEDGE "PLASHED."

laid over sidewise. This is done by cutting the plants about half through on one side with a sharp axe, and bending them over as shown in figure 111. The hedge is first headed back and trimmed up to reduce the top. In a short time new shoots will spring from the stubs and stems, making a dense growth of interlacing stems and branches. Another method of laying a hedge, is to dig away a few inches of earth on one side of each plant to loosen the roots, then lay the plant over to the desired angle and fasten it there. The earth is then replaced around the roots, and tread down firmly. We believe that a patent is claimed for this process, but its validity is seriously questioned.

It is essential that hedges, whether planted for ornament or utility, shall be kept in shape by trimming every year. It is less labor to trim a hedge three times during the year, when the branches are small and soft, than once when the branches have made a full season's growth. If the hedge is trimmed once in June and again in August, it will be kept in good shape, and the labor will be less than if the trimming was put off until spring. In August the branches can be cut with shears or a sharp corn knife. The foliage on them will aid in their burning, when they have dried a few days in the sun. The thorns are not so hard as in the spring. The brush will be less, and on account of their pliability and greater weight, will pack into the heap much better. If trimmed in August, the hedge will not make any considerable growth during the fall. August trimming does not injure the hedge, rather helps it, as it tends to ripen the wood, preventing a late Autumn growth to be injured by the winter. The loss of sap is less than when the trimming is done in the early spring, as then the wounds are larger, and do not heal before the sap flows. Do not neglect to burn the brush as soon as it has dried sufficiently. If allowed to remain on the ground, it will harbor mice and other vermin. Trim the hedge in August and burn the brush. The trimming should be done in such a manner as to expose the greater amount of foliage to the direct action of the light, air, rain and dew. This is attained by keeping the sides at every trimming in the form of sloping walls from the broad base to the summit

like a double-span roof. They are sometimes trimmed
with vertical sides and broad, flat top, but this is not a
favorable plan for permanency. The lower leaves and
stems die out, leaving an unsightly open bottom of naked
stems, with a broad roof of foliage above. Such trimming and its results have done much to bring hedges
into disrepute.

HEDGES FOR THE SOUTH.

The Osage Orange is a native of the Southwestern
States, and flourishes on good soil anywhere in the South.
Yet there are certain succulent plants which grow so
rapidly in the South, and require so little care, that
they are very successfully employed for hedges in the
Gulf States. One of these if the *Yucca gloriosa*, or

Fig. 112.—CACTUS HEDGE.

Spanish Bayonet. Its natural habit of growth is to produce a dense mass of leaves on a long stem. But by cutting back the growth of the stiff, armed leaves is produced low down, and a hedge of this soon becomes an
impassable barrier. Large panicles of beautiful white
blossoms are produced at the summit, making such a
hedge very ornamental during the flowering season.
Various species of cactus are also employed in the South-
west for hedges. In some of the Middle-Western States
may be seen a hedge like figure 112. At some distance
from the highway, a field had been enclosed with the
tree cactus, which there grows only from four to ten feet

high. The plants that were in the line of the fence were left growing, and those cleared from the field were woven into a formidable barrier to anything larger than a rabbit. While no two rods in this fence are alike, its general appearance is like that shown in the engraving.

ORNAMENTAL HEDGES AND SCREENS.

Hedges and screens for ornamental purposes alone, do not come strictly within the scope of this work, but we will briefly mention a few desirable plants for the pur-

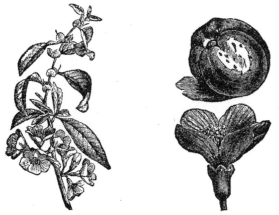

Fig. 113.—BRANCH OF JAPAN QUINCE.   Fig. 114.—FRUIT AND FLOWER.

pose. The Japan Quince, *Cydonia Japonica*, of which figures 113 and 114 show a branch, flower and fruit, is one of the best deciduous plants for an ornamental hedge. It will grow in almost any soil; if left to itself it forms a dense, strong bush, but it may be clipped or trained into any desired form. Its leaves are of dark glossy green, they come early in spring and remain until late in Autumn. This is one of the earliest shrubs to bloom in spring; its flowers are generally intense scarlet, though there are varieties with white, rose-colored, or salmon-colored flowers. A hedge of this plant is not only highly ornamental, but its abundant thorns make a good barrier. Privet, *Ligustrum vulgare*, makes a very neat screen, but will not bear severe cutting back, and is therefore suitable only for grounds of sufficient extent to admit of its being allowed to make unrestrained growth. The common Barberry, *Berberis vulgaris*, also makes an exceedingly pretty screen in time, but it is of slow growth. The Buffalo Berry, *Sheperdia argentea*, has been tried for hedges, but for some reason it has never attained any popularity. In the Southern States, the Cherokee Rose has been found quite successful for the purpose, and nothing in the shape of a hedge can exceed, in striking effect, one of these in full bloom. For evergreen screens nothing is better than the Hemlock, *Tsuga Canadensis*. The Norway Spruce is of rapid growth and bears cutting well. The Arbor Vitæ, *Thuja occidentalis*, is also very successfully employed for the purpose.

CHAPTER VIII.

PORTABLE FENCES AND HURDLES.

PORTABLE BOARD FENCES.

Figure 118 shows a very strong and secure board fence, composed entirely of ordinary fence boards. The triangular frames, which serve as posts, are each of two pieces of inch boards, crossed and braced as shown in figure 115. The panels, figure 117, are sixteen feet long, each composed of four boards, six inches wide. The space between the lower two boards is two and a half inches, second space three and a half inches. A convenient way of making the panels is to use three horses, like that shown in figure 116, the length of each being equal to the total

Fig. 115.—THE POSTS.

width of the panel, and the three short upright strips marking the respective spaces between the boards. The top is covered with iron to clinch the nails used in putting the panel together. The boards are laid on these horses, and the upright cross-pieces nailed on. The second board from the top of each panel is notched at both ends, as shown in figure 117. A good way to make the trian-

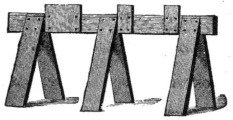

Fig. 116.—"HORSES" FOR MAKING THE FENCE.

gular frames alike, is to cut the pieces by a uniform pattern. Then make one frame of the size and form desired, and at each of the three places where they are nailed together, fasten a plate of iron, thick enough to prevent the penetration of a common wrought nail driven against it. Now lay this pattern frame on the floor with the iron bolts uppermost. Then lay three pieces on this in exactly the right position, drive wrought nails through the two pieces and against the iron plates, which will clinch the nails firmly as fast as they are driven. This will enable the man to nail the frames together quite

Fig. 117.—A SINGLE PANEL.

rapidly. In setting up the fence, each triangular frame supports the ends of two panels. The upper and lower boards of each panel interlock with the frame, as shown in figure 118, making a very strong fence. On open prairie or other wind-swept situations, it may be necessary to stake down some of the frames, to prevent their blowing over. This is quickly done by sharpening pieces

Fig. 118.—THE FENCE IN POSITION.

of inch boards, twelve inches long, and one inch wide, and driving one beside the foot of the triangle, where it rests on the ground, and putting an eight-penny nail through both.

PORTABLE FENCES OF POLES OR WIRE.

Figures 119 and 120 show styles of portable fences, which are used to some extent in the territories. The base of each is the half of a small log, split through the center. For the fence shown in figure 119, two augur holes are bored a few inches apart, and small poles driven to serve as posts. Rails or round poles of the usual length are laid to the desired height, and the top

Fig. 119.—PORTABLE POLE FENCE.

of the posts tied together with wire. In situations where timber is less plentiful, a single stake is set into the base, as in figure 120, braced, and barbed or plain wire attached by staples. Besides the advantage of being

Fig. 120.—PORTABLE WIRE FENCE.

easily moved, these fences can be prepared in winter, when there is little else to do, and rapidly set in place at any time when the ground is clear of snow.

Figure 121 is a fence made of either sawed stuff, or of rails or poles, having their ends flattened and bored. An iron rod, or piece of gas-pipe, any where from half an inch to an inch in diameter, is run through the holes, and through a base block into the ground as far as necessary. A round stick of tough durable wood, an inch or more in diameter, will answer. The size of this rod and its strength will depend upon the amount of zigzag

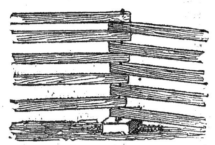

Fig. 121.—PORTABLE FENCE OF POLES OR RAILS.

that is given to the lengths. If the corners are one foot on each side of a central line, the fence firmly held together by the rods, will in effect stand on a two feet wide base. Less than this would perhaps sometimes answer, and there are no sharp corners, or deep recesses for weeds and rubbish.

PORTABLE FENCES FOR WINDBREAKS.

A fence that can be easily moved and quickly set up is shown in figure 122. It consists of panels made of strips

Fig. 122.—PORTABLE FENCE.

eight or ten feet long, nailed to two by four posts, which are beveled to a sharp corner at the lower end. These panels are supported by posts, placed as shown in the engraving, and pinned to the fence posts by wooden pins, driven in by a light mallet. The panels are light and can be loaded upon a wagon from which the sides and ends of the box are removed. A box of pins and the mallet are all the tools required to set up the fence. This fence is not easily overthrown by the wind, which holds it down firmly when blowing on the face of it. For this reason in windy localities, the fence should be set facing the windy quarter.

Another good form of movable fence is seen in figure 123. It is made of common fence-boards, securely

Fig. 123.—RAILROAD WINDBREAK.

nailed on very light posts or on the edge of narrow boards and braced as shown in the engraving. This style of panel is largely employed by railroads as windbreaks in winter to keep the tracks from becoming covered with drifted snow. It is equally convenient on the farm, when a temporary inclosure is needed.

PORTABLE POULTRY FENCES.

It is often very convenient when poultry are inclosed during the growing season, to have a fence for the hen-yard which can be readily moved from place to place. The illustration, Figure 124, shows one of these. Cut the posts the same length as the pickets, and to the inner side of each attach two strong iron hoops bent into a semi-circle, one near the bottom and the other half way up. Through these hoops drive stakes fitted to fill them

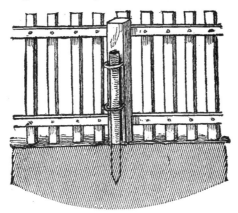

Fig. 124.—PORTABLE POULTRY FENCE.

closely, with sharpened points for easily entering the ground. When removing the fence the posts can be slipped off.

Turkeys, even when they have attained a considerable size, should be shut up until after the dew is off the grass, and other fowls must be confined in limited runs,

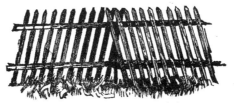

Fig. 125.—MOVABLE FENCE FOR TURKEYS.

while the young are small. It is quite an advantage if these runs can be changed easily, and this can be accomplished only when they are enclosed in a light movable fence. Such a fence is shown in figure 125, on preceding page. It is made in twelve or sixteen feet sections by nailing laths to light pieces of the proper length. The upper end of the laths is sharpened; the end ones are of

Fig. 126.—CROSS-SECTION OF MOVABLE FENCE.

double thickness. The sections are placed with the end-laths intercrossing at the top, and about six inches apart at the bottom, as in cross-section, figure 126. They are held apart by blocks, figure 127, which rest on the upper edges of the cross-pieces and against the laths. They are held together, and to the ground, by stakes driven against the outer side of the end laths. As these stakes have the same angle as the laths, they hold the sections together, and also the fence in its place and down to the ground. The triangular space where the sections join is

Fig. 127.—CROSS-BLOCK FOR FENCE.

closed by a lath driven in the ground or tacked to the block between the cross-pieces. Corners must be formed of two sections inclined inward, and in the same way that sections are joined. The stakes are readily withdrawn, and the sections are so light that they are easily handled.

PORTABLE FOLDING FENCE.

A very convenient form of portable fence or hurdle is illustrated in figures 128, 129 and 130, which was

Fig. 128.—FENCE IN POSITION.

Fig. 129.—FENCE FOLDED.

Fig. 130.—AS A SIDE HILL FENCE.

brought out some five or six years ago. It may be constructed with two or three upright pieces of two-by-four-inch scantling, and four bars, figure 128, held together by carriage bolts in such a manner, that each panel can be closed when desired, as a parallel ruler is folded together. As the bars are on alternate sides, the panel, when closed, takes up the space of two bars only, figure 129. The fence may easily be removed, and fits itself to rolling ground or side-hill, as shown in figure 130. When in position it may be supported by stakes of the same thickness as the upright bars, and driven close beside them.

TEMPORARY WIRE AND IRON FENCES.

Several kinds of wire and iron fences are used in France to make temporary enclosures for exhibition purposes. Two forms are illustrated herewith. Figure 131

Fig. 131.—TEMPORARY WIRE FENCE.

is made of plain iron wire with cast or wrought iron posts. Each post has a plate on its lower end, which is set eighteen inches below the surface of the ground, and the earth filled in compactly about it. The front of the engraving shows the holes in section, with the plates. The top strand is a wire rope made by twisting several strands together. The fence seen at figure 132 is made of narrow strips of sheet iron attached to iron posts driven into the ground. The gate, like that of the other form, is provided with small wheels, which run on a track. The two fences may be modified by using wooden posts sharpened

Fig. 132.—TEMPORARY IRON FENCE.

at the lower end, and driven into the ground, then fastening to them with suitable staples strips of rather broad hoop iron at the top, with plain wire below.

CHAPTER IX.

FENCES FOR STREAMS AND GULLIES.

FLOOD FENCES.

In a situation where a line of fence crosses a stream or a gully liable to be flooded, it is necessary to make special provision for it. A fence extending down near the surface and sufficiently rigid to withstand the current, would arrest the drift wood and other objects floated down on the flood, and soon become a dam. The right kind of a fence must therefore yield to the force of the flood, and renew its position, or be easily replaced after it has subsided. Figure 133 is a very effectual flood-gate for a running stream. The posts, *B, B,* are firmly set on the bank, and a stick of timber, *A,* mor-

Fig. 133.—STRONG FLOOD-GATE.

tised on the top of them. The three uprights, *C, C, C,* are hinged to the cross-timber, and the boards, *F,* fastened in place by tenpenny steel fence nails. The gate easily swings with the current, *D.* Figure 134 shows a form which operates in a similar manner like the other.

Fig. 134.—A CHEAPER FLOOD-GATE.

It consists of two stout posts, five feet high bearing a heavy cross-bar, rounded at each end, and fitted into sockets, in which the bar with gate attached can swing. The construction of the gate is easily seen from the engraving.

The above forms are self-acting, and swing back to their places as the water subsides. For larger streams, it is necessary to construct fences that give way before the flood, and can be brought into position again when it is over. One of these, for a stream which is liable to bring down much drift wood, is shown in figure 135.

Fig. 135.—FENCE FOR A FOREST STREAM.

The logs are the trunks of straight trees, about eighteen inches in diameter, which are hewed on two sides; posts are mortised in each of these logs, and on them planks are firmly nailed. The logs are then linked together with inch iron rods, and the first one connected by **means of** a long link to a tree or post firmly set in the **ground** upon the banks of the stream. The links must all work freely. When high water occurs, the fence is **washed** around and left on the bank; after the water has subsided sufficiently, the logs may be dragged back to **their** places, as shown in the engraving, by means of a **horse** hitched to a staple in the end of the log. Figure 136 shows a lighter fence made of poles or rails, held by interlinking staples to the posts on the side of the stream. As the floods come down, the rails are washed from the

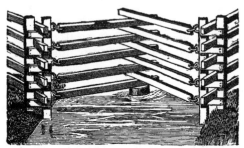

Fig. 136.—FENCE OF MOVABLE RAILS.

center, and float freely at either side of the stream. They can be laid up in place again when the water subsides.

The fence shown in figure 137, though rather rude and primitive, has the advantage of being cheaply constructed and permanent. Two strong posts are driven into the banks on the margin of the stream, to which a log, a foot or more in diameter, is fastened by pins, spikes or withes, about twenty inches above low water mark. Then

Fig. 137.—AN EXTEMPORISED FLOOD-FENCE.

fence rails are sharpened at one end, driven into the stream above the log, upon which the other ends rest, projecting about a foot. They are then securely spiked or pinned to the log, and the work is done. The pointed ends of the rails are up the stream, and in case of flood, the water pours over the obstruction, carrying with it brush, driftwood, etc.

The flood-gate, figure 138, is designed to prevent small stock from passing from one field to another through a water-course under a fence where there is low water, while in time of high water the gate will rise sufficiently

Fig. 138.—AUTOMATIC FLOOD-GATE.

to allow the floating trash to pass through, but not higher, as it is self-fastening. The invention consists of a gate constructed of perpendicular slats hinged above, and moving. This hangs across a stream or ditch. On the down-stream side of the gate a swing paddle is fixed, which hangs in the water. This, marked a in the illustration, is attached to an angular bar, b, which is moved when the flow of water presses with force against the paddle. Two notched pieces, c c, attached to the gate, rest upon the angular bar, b, at low water; when both the paddle and the gate hang at rest, perpendicularly, these notched pieces, c c, hold the gate firmly shut; when, however, the water rises and the paddle is moved sufficiently to disengage the notches, the gate will be moved by the force of the water, and if sticks or rubbish of any kind float down against it they will be swept under it by the water. When the water subsides, the paddle swings back, the pieces, *c c*, catch and keep the gate closed at any height it may fall to. Let the cross-piece, *d*, that is halved into the posts, be about one foot above the banks of the ditch. The pieces, *f f f f*, represent the fence above the ditch, the small posts, *g g*, with the pieces nailed to them, are to prevent the stock from passing when the gate is partly closed, at the same time bracing the posts, *e e;* the holes at *h* are to raise and lower the paddle *a;* if small, a cleat on one of the arms upon which the piece *B* is hung, prevents the paddle from swinging towards the gate.

Figure 139 shows a kind of fence used in Missouri to put across sloughs. It is in effect two panels of

Fig. 139.—A MISSOURI FLOOD-FENCE.

portable fence. The posts are set three to four feet deep, with the tops about one foot above ground; the other posts, to which the planks are nailed, are bolted to the top of the inserted posts. The ends of the panel that connect with the post on the bank are slightly nailed with cross-strips near the top, so as to be easily broken loose when the flood comes. There are also temporary braces bearing upstream, put in to prevent the fence from falling, but are easily washed out, when the fence falls down stream, and logs and other obstructions pass by readily. As soon as the flood goes down, the fence is easily raised, a panel at a time, to a proper place.

Figure 140 shows a cheap and effective form of flood fence. The material used are square-hewn timbers, seven

Fig. 140.—FRESHET FENCE.

or eight inches for sills, stone pillars, split rails about ten feet long. The rails are driven in the ground about two feet deep; the upper ends project above the sill two or three feet, and are spiked down to the sill with large spikes; when the freshet comes, logs and drift-wood are carried over, and the fence will be left in as good order as before the high water.

Figure 141 represents a gulch fence or gate which is in common use in some parts of the Pacific Slope. It

Fig. 141.—CALIFORNIA GULCH FENCE.

is particularly adapted to the gulches of the foot hills and the irrigating ditches of the plains. The whole gate swings freely by the upper pole, the ends of which rest in large holes in posts on either bank, or in the cross of stakes. The upright pieces may be of split pickets or sawed lumber, as may be the most convenient. If the stream is likely to carry floating brush, logs, etc., the slats should be of heavier material than is necessary when this is not the case. When constructed properly the gate will give, allowing rubbish and freshets to pass, and then resume its proper position. The principal advantage claimed for this gate is that it is not apt to gather the passing debris.

A gully is sometimes difficult to fence properly, but by hanging a frame over it, as is seen in figure 142,

Fig. 142.—FENCE FOR A DRY GULLY.

the object may be quickly accomplished. The frame can be spiked together in a short time, or framed together if a more elaborate one is desired. To make it serve its purpose completely, the rails must be closer together near the bottom than at the top of the frame, in order to prevent small animals from going through it.

A modification of this last named device, seen at figure 143, gives greater space for the passage of brush wood or other large objects, which may be swept down on the flood. The width, strength and size of the bases supporting the side posts, and of the braces, will depend upon the width and depth of the channel. The base pieces can be firmly anchored by stakes driven slanting over the ends and outsides, or by stones piled on. For wide, shallow streams, three or even more braced uprights can be anchored eight or ten feet apart in the bed with heavy stones, with two or more swinging sections.

Fig. 143.—A FRESHET FENCE.

If small trees or long timbers are likely to float down, the swinging gate may be twelve or fifteen feet wide. For smaller streams, with strong high banks, five or six feet will suffice.

PORTABLE TIDE FENCE.

Figure 144 represents a fence for tide-creeks. It is made usually of pine, the larger pieces, those which lie

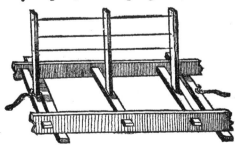

Fig. 144.—SECTION OF A TIDE FENCE.

on the ground and parallel with the run of the fence, are three by four-inch pieces, hemlock or pine, and connected by three cross-bars, of three by four-inch pieces, mortised in three feet apart. Into the middle of these three cross-pieces, the upright or posts are securely mortised, while two common boards are nailed underneath the long pieces, to afford a better rest for the structure, when floating on the water or resting on the ground. Barbed or plain wires are stretched along the posts, which are four feet high.

WATERING PLACE IN A CREEK.

Cattle naturally select a certain place in a water-course to drink at, where the bank is not precipitous. During a good part of the year this bank is muddy, on account

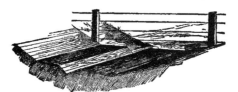

Fig. 145.—A CLEAN WATERING PLACE.

of its moisture and trampling of the animals. As a result, the horses get the scratches, the cows come to the milking pen with muddy udders, and frequently animals are injured by the crowding in the mud. Hogs are often seriously injured, because the mud becomes so deep and tough, that they are well nigh helpless in it. Another objection is that the animals wade to the middle of the creek, and soon make its bottom as muddy as the bank, and the water becomes unfit for drinking. The arrangement shown in our illustration, which may be built of heavy plank, brick, or flat stones, prevents all this. It is constructed by first making an incline to a level platform for the animals to stand on while drinking. This plane terminates in an abrupt descent, forming a trough for the water to flow through. The trough should not be more than two feet wide, that the animals may easily get across it. The level floor permits the animals to drink at their ease, often a matter of importance. Such a drinking place should be made at the upper end of the creek, where it passes through a field to prevent the animals from soiling the water by standing in it above where they drink.

CHAPTER X.

MAKING AND SETTING POSTS.

MAKING FENCE POSTS.

There is quite an art in splitting logs into posts. Every post should have some heart wood, which lasts the longer, for two reasons: That there may be durable wood into which to drive the nails, and without it some of the posts, composed entirely of sap-wood, will rot off long before others, making the most annoying of all repairing necessary. If the log is of a size to make twelve posts, split along the lines of figure 146, which will give each post a share of heart wood. This will make a cross section of the posts triangular, the curved base being somewhat more than half of either side. This is a fairly well shaped post, and much better than a square one having little or no heart wood. Although the log may be large enough to make sixteen or eighteen posts, it is better to split it the same way. It should first be cut into halves, then quarters, then twelfths. If it is attempted to split one post off the side of a half, the wood will "draw out," making the post larger at one end than the other—not a good shape, for there will be little heart wood at the small end. When the log is too large to admit of it being split in that way, each post may nevertheless be given enough heart wood by splitting along the

Fig. 146.

Fig. 147.

lines, shown in figure 147. First cut the logs into halves, then quarters, then eighths. Then split off the edge of each eighth, enough for a post—about one-fourth only of the wood, as it is all heart wood, and then halve the balance. A good post can be taken off the edge, and yet enough heart wood for the remaining two posts remain.

A POST HOLDER.

A simple arrangement for holding a post while it is being bored or mortised, is shown in figure 148. It con-

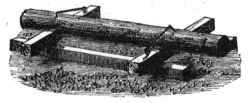
Fig. 148.—A POST HOLDER.

sists of two long pieces of round or square timber, lying parallel upon the ground, and two shorter sticks resting upon them at right angles. The upper pieces have saddles cut out for the posts to fit into. A staple with a large iron hook or "dog," is fastened into one end of each cross-piece, as shown in the engraving. When the post is laid in position, the hooks are driven into it holding it firmly.

DRIVING FENCE POSTS BY HAND.

Where the soil is soft, loose, and free from stone, posts may be driven more easily and firmly than if set in holes

Fig. 149.—DRIVING FENCE POSTS.

dug for the purpose. An easy method of driving is shown in figure 149. A wagon is loaded with posts and furnished with a stage in the rear end of the box, upon which a person can stand to give the posts the first start. Another man holds the posts upright while they are driven. When one post is driven to its place, the wagon is moved to the next place, and this operation repeated,

To drive posts, a wooden maul should be used. This is made of a section of an elm trunk or branch, eight or nine inches in diameter, figure 150. An iron ring is driven on each end, and wedged all around, the wood at the edge being beaten down over the rings with a hammer or the poll of an axe. To prevent the posts from splitting or being battered too much, the ends of the maul should be hollowed a little, and never rounded out, and

Fig. 150.—MAUL FOR DRIVING POSTS.

the ends of the posts should be beveled all around. The hole in the maul for the handle should be made larger on one side, and lengthwise of the maul, and the handle spread by two wedges driven in such a way as not to split the maul.

TO DRIVE POSTS WITHOUT SPLITTING.

Posts are very liable to split in driving, unless some precaution is used. This damage and loss can be avoided in a great measure by proper preparation of the posts before they are driven. The tops of sawed posts should have the sides cut off, as in figure 151, or simply cut off each corner, as in figure 153, while a round post should be shaped as in figure 152. The part of the post removed need not be more than half an inch in thickness, but when the corners only are cut away, the chip should be thicker. In driving, it is very important to strike the post squarely on the top, and not at one corner or side. In most soils at the North, the frosts heave posts more or less each season, and they need to be driven down to the usual depth. To do this with little injury to the post, the device shown in figure 154 may

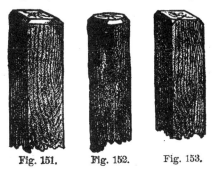

Fig. 151.   Fig. 152.   Fig. 153.

be used. It is a piece of tough hard wood scantling, *e*, eighteen inches in length, with tapering ends. It is provided with a handle, *h*, three feet in length, of quite small size, and if possible, of green timber. In using it, let one person (a boy will do) lay the bit of scantling on top of the post to be re-driven, when, with the beetle or

Fig. 154.—SCANTLING WITH HANDLE IN POSITION.

sledge, the scantling, instead of the post is struck, thus preventing the splitting of the post. When the top of a fence is surmounted by a stringer, as in the engraving, the effect of the blow is distributed over a large space, and both stringer and post escape injury. The attendant should keep hold of the handle, *h*, while the posts are being driven, and move the scantling from post to post as required.

A POWERFUL POST DRIVER.

For a farmer who has a large number of posts to set, a special apparatus for driving them will be found useful.

Fig. 155.—THE POST-DRIVER.

The accompanying illustrations show a machine of this kind. An axle, *a*, figure 155, of hard wood, eight and one-half feet long; a hickory sapling will do. It has spindles shaved to fit the hind wheels of a wagon, which are fastened by linch-pins, leaving about six feet space between the hubs. A coupling-pole, *b*, thirteen feet long, is framed in and strongly braced at right angles with the axle, and connects in front with the forward axle of a common wagon. The main sill, d, figure 156, is one stick of timber, six by eight inches, by fourteen feet long and has a cross-piece, e, framed in the end. Two side-pieces, f, two by four inches by five feet long, are pinned or bolted to the main sill at g, and cross-pieces framed into them, as shown in figure 156, so framed that the lower edges of the side-pieces will be two inches from the axle, when the main sill rests on the axle. The side-pieces, f, should be twenty-two inches apart at the ends. The front end of the main sill rests on the front axle, in place of a bolster, and the "king-bolt" passes through it at h; the upright guides, i, are two by four inches by fourteen feet long, bolted to the side-pieces, f, with a space of fourteen inches between; a cap, j, two by three by twenty-six inches long, is framed on top. Two braces, k, two by four inches by sixteen feet long, are bolted to the upright guides, two feet below the cap, and connect at the bottom with a cross-piece, l, two by eight by twenty-two inches long, between the braces. It has rounded end passing through two-inch holes in the braces, and fastened by a pin outside, to form a loose joint. This cross-piece, l, is held down on the main sill by a strip, m, and steadied by cleats; it is free to slide back or forward, and is held in place by a short pin. By moving this cross-piece, the upright guides, i, are kept perpendicular when going up or down hill. A small windlass, o, figure 155, is placed under the axle, a, between hangers framed into the axle, close to the hubs. Two brace-ropes, or wires, p, are fastened to this windlass at the extreme ends, and wound around it a turn or two in opposite directions, drawn tight and fastened to the main braces near the top. By turning the windlass, o, slightly, by means of a short bar, the machine may lean to either side, to conform to sliding ground, thus being adjustable in all di rections. The maul, *r*, figure 157, of tough oak, fourteen by eighteen inches, by two feet long, weighs about two hundred pounds, is grooved to fit smoothly between the guides; the follower, *s*, is more plainly shown in the engraving, also the simple latch, by which the follower and maul are connected and disconnected. The square clevis, *t*, is of three-quarter inch iron, suspended from the

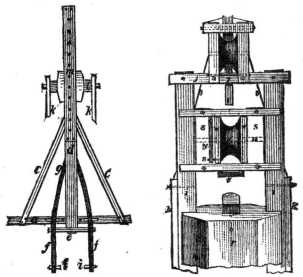

Fig. 156.—BOTTOM OF DRIVER.   Fig. 157.—TOP OF UPRIGHT.

same iron pin, *u*, on which the pulley, *v*, is placed. It is partly imbedded in the wooden casing, *w*, which is eight by eighteen inches; this casing serves to inclose the pulley, *v*, and also to trip the latch when brought together; the clevis, *t*, is caught under the hook fastened in the maul, is pressed into place by a small hickory spring, *y*, acting on a small iron pin, *z*; when it reaches the top, the crotch, 1, suspended from the top, comes in contact with the pin, 2, and the clevis, *t*, is pressed back, and releases the hook, x, when the maul drops. The windlass, 3, figure 155, has two cranks, and a ratchet for convenience. The rope passes from the windlass over the pulley at the top, down and under the pulley, v, then up, and is fastened at 7, on the cap, j, wire braces at 8. By releasing the cranks and ratchet, the follower will run down the guides, and, striking the maul, will "click" the latch into place, ready for another hoist. For two men it is easy work, and can be handled quite rapidly. Drive astride the proposed line of fence; lay a measuring-pole on the ground to mark the spot for the next post; drive forward with the post-driver, having the maul partly raised, set up a post, and proceed to drive it.

SETTING A GATE POST.

No matter how strong or how well braced a gate may be, it will soon begin to sag and catch on the ground, if

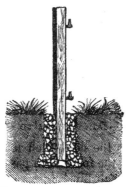

Fig. 158.—A GATE POST SET IN CEMENT.

the gate post is not firmly planted. Sometimes, owing to the soft nature of the ground, it is almost impossible to plant the post firmly, but in such cases the work can generally be done satisfactorily by packing medium-sized stones around the post, in the hole, as shown in figure 158. If it is thought that this will not insure sufficient firmness, add good cement. Place in a layer of stones, then cement enough to imbed the next layer of stones, and so on, until the hole is full and the post planted. Do not cover up the stones with earth or disturb the post for a few days, until the cement has "set." Remember that the post must be set plumb while the work is going on, as it can never be straightened after the cement has "set." Only durable posts should be used, and this method of setting should only be followed with gate posts which are supposed to be permanent, and not with posts liable to be changed.

A still better method is shown in figure 159. Before the post is set into the hole, a flat stone is laid edgewise

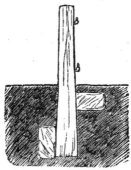

Fig. 159.—GATE POST BRACED WITH STONES.

in the bottom, on the side which is to receive the **greatest pressure** from the foot of the post. When the post is set, and the hole half filled with earth, a second stone is placed against the post on the side to which it will be drawn by the weight of the gate. The stones receive the pressure and hold the post firmly in position.

OLD-FASHIONED LABOR-SAVING DEVICES

Low meadow and other marsh land is subject to heaving by the frost, and much difficulty is experienced in securing firm fences upon such ground, as the posts are drawn up by the freezing of the surface. To avoid this, much may be done in the way of selecting posts that

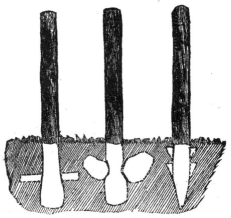

Fig. 160.—DIFFERENT METHODS OF TREATING POSTS.

are larger at one end than the other. It will help very much to put a strong, durable pin through the bottom end of the post, or to notch it at each side, as in figure 160, and to brace the bottom with a flat stone, driven well into the side of the hole with the rammer. When the soil is very soft and mucky, it is best to drive the posts and to make them hold well in the ground, to spike wedge-shaped pieces to them on either side, by which they are held firmly in their places.

LIVE POSTS.

A living tree which stands in the right place, makes a very durable and substantial fence-post. In the great treeless regions of the Mississippi Valley, where it is difficult to obtain timber for posts, it is not an unusual practice to plant trees for the purpose on street boundaries, and other places where the fence is to be permanent. White willow is well adapted for the purpose on suitable soils, as it grows rapidly and bears close pruning. In situations where the soil is even moderately damp, white willow posts, four inches in diameter, cut green and set

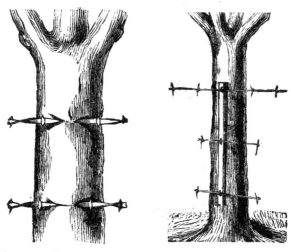

Fig. 161.   Fig. 162.

in spring, will take root and grow. The new branches soon form a bushy head, which may be cut back from time to time. It is not advisable to nail boards or drive staples directly into the tree. With a board fence, the swaying of the tree loosens the nails, and if barbed wire is stapled to the tree, the bark and wood will in time grow over them as in figure 161. To obviate this, a stick is nailed to the tree as in figure 162, and to this the fence is attached. A still better method is to secure the strip of wood to the tree by two or three pairs of interlocking staples.

MENDING A SPLIT POST.

Fence posts split from a variety of causes, and when they are in this condition they make a very insecure

Fig. 163.—MENDING A SPLIT POST.

fence. The usual way is to merely nail an old horseshoe or two across the split part, just below the holes in the posts. This answers fairly well, but does not draw the cleft together, and horseshoes are not always on hand. A better method of doing this is shown in figure 163. A short, stout chain is put around the top of the post, just tight enough to admit of a strong lever. The parts of the posts are then brought together by a heavy downward pressure of the lever and held there, while a strip of good tin, such as can be cut from the bodies of tin cans, is put around and securely nailed. If the post is a heavy one and the cleft large, it is well to take the entire body of a can and double it, to give it additional strength before nailing it on. The dotted lines show where the tin is nailed.

HOOK FOR WIRING POSTS.

Figure 164 shows a modified cant-hook for drawing together the upper extremities of fence stakes that are to be

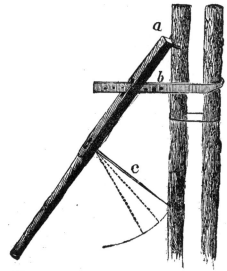

Fig. 164.—A STAKE DRAWER USED IN WIRING FENCES.

wired, as in the engraving. The half-moon shaped iron, a, is riveted fast to the top end of the lever, and is to prevent the end of the lever from slipping off the stake when in use. The second iron from the top, b, is twenty-five inches long, with two hooks at the end, though one will do; this is to catch the stake on the opposite side of the fence. This iron is fastened in the lever by a bolt in a long mortise, in the same way, as the hook in an ordinary cant-hook. The iron rod, *c*, has a hole in one end, and is drawn out to a point at the other—this is fastened to the lever by a bolt in a long mortise, and serves to catch in the stake or rail, and hold the stakes together, while the man adjusts the iron around the stakes. When the stakes are drawn tightly to the fence, this rod is drawn up until it strikes the stake or one of the rails, when the man can let go of the "drawer," and it holds itself. The lever is four feet and three inches long, and two inches square, with the corners taken off part of the way down, the lower end being rounded for a handle, as shown in the engraving.

DRAWING FENCE POSTS.

Figure 165 shows a practicable method of drawing out fence posts by the aid of an ox team. A stout piece

Fig. 165.—DRAWING FENCE POSTS.

of timber with a large flat "foot" is placed under the chain to change the direction of the draft. Two men and a steady yoke of oxen can extract fence posts very quickly and easily by this method. A good steady team of horses will do quite as well as oxen.

LIFTING POSTS BY HAND.

A convenient and sensible implement, for taking up fence posts without the aid of a team, is shown at figure 166. It consists of a stout pole of the size and shape of

Fig. 166.—A CONVENIENT POST LIFTER.

a wagon tongue. The thicker part of this pole, for about fifteen inches from the end, is shaped into a wedge. This is sheathed with a frame made of iron, half an inch thick and two and a half inches wide, and securely fastened with screws or bolts. The end should be pointed and slightly bent upwards. The manner of using this convenient implement is shown in the illustration.

Frequently a farmer has occasion to lift posts, and has not time to wait for the construction of an iron-shod lever. Figure 167 shows a very simple, inexpensive contrivance for such cases. A spadeful of earth is taken from each side of the post, and a short, strong chain loosely fastened around the lower end of the post, as far down as it can be placed. A strong lever—a stout rail will answer the purpose—is passed through the chain, as shown in the engraving, until the end of the rail catches firm soil. By lifting at the other end of the lever the post is raised several inches, when both chain and lever are pushed down again for a second hold, which general-

Fig. 167.—LIFTING A POST.

ly brings the post out. The chain is furnished with a stout hook at one end, made to fit the links, so that it can be quickly adjusted to any ordinary post.

SPLICING FENCE POSTS.

There are places, as crossing over gullies, etc., where unusually long posts are desirable, though not always easy to obtain. In such cases properly spliced posts are almost as durable as entire ones. The engraving of the front and side views, figure 168, shows how the splice may be made to secure strength and durability. The splices should be made with a shoulder at the lower

end, and well nailed together, after which one or two
bands of hoop-iron may be passed around the splice and

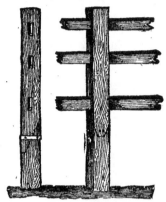

Fig. 168.—SPLICING FENCE POSTS.

securely fastened. The hoop-iron band is one of the
most important points in a splice of this kind.

APPLICATION OF WOOD PRESERVATIVES

To prevent decay at the center, as well as of all that
part of the post placed below ground, by use of wood
preserving solutions, the following system is both novel
and valuable: It is to have a hole in the center of the
post, from the bottom upward, to a point that shall be
above the ground when the post is in position. Then
bore another hole in the side of the post with a slight inclination downward, making an opening in the center
hole, as shown in figure 169. A wooden plug, two
or three inches long, should be driven snugly into the
hole at the bottom of the post, in order to prevent the
escape of any liquid that may be used in the operation.
When the posts are set in an upright position, a preserv-

ative solution may be introduced into the hole in the side and the centre one filled with it, after which a cork plug of some kind should be inserted in the side hole, to prevent evaporation, as well as to keep out dust and insects. The solutions thus introduced will gradually be absorbed by the surrounding wood, until all parts along the entire length of the central cavity must become completely saturated. When the solutions used have been taken up by the surrounding wood, it will only be nec-

Fig. 169.—SECTIONAL VIEW OF BORED POST.

essary to withdraw the cork or plug, and apply more, if it is thought desirable. A common watering pot with a slender spout will be a handy vessel to use in distributing the solutions.

Petroleum, creosote, corrosive sublimate, or any other of the well known wood preservatives may be used in this way. Telegraph posts might be prepared in the same way, and if the central reservoirs were kept filled with petroleum, they would last a hundred years or more. Where a large number of posts or poles are to be prepared, it would be cheaper to have the holes bored by steam or horse power than by hand. With very open and porous wood it is quite probable that a hole bored in the side of the post and above the ground, and deep enough to hold a half pint or more of creosote or some other similar solution, would answer, but a central cavity reaching to the bottom, would perhaps, be best.

IRON FENCE POSTS.

The advent of wire fences was followed by a call for posts in the prairie regions, where timber is scarce. Sev-

Fig. 170.—POST.   Fig. 171.—DISC.

eral forms of iron posts have been devised, of which the leading ones are illustrated herewith. Figure 170 is of iron, one quarter of an inch thick and two and a half inches wide, rolled to a curve and pierced at the proper intervals for the staples, which are to be clinched on the concave side. The disc, figure 171, is swedged out of one fourth inch iron. It is sunken a little below the ground, and the post driven through the curved opening, into which it fits closely. Figure 172 is a flat iron bar, with slots cut diagonally into one side to receive the wire. The post is supported by two tiles with holes to fit the post, which is thrust through them.

Figure 173 is made of angle iron braced at the surface of the ground, with an angular iron plate rolled for the purpose, and driven to its place. Figure 174 shows an

Fig. 172.—POST WITH TILES.   Fig. 173.

iron post, with the ground-piece and driving tube to the left of it. The post is a round iron bar or tube, with notches for the wires, which are held in place with short pieces of binding-wire, wound around the post. The ground piece, which is shown in the middle of the engraving, is of cast iron, eleven inches long, and five inches across the top, with two loops for inserting the iron post. This is driven into the ground, and the iron post driven through it. At the left of the engraving is shown the device for driving the post. It is a piece of common gas-pipe, just large enough to slip easily over the top of the post, and provided on the top with an iron cap to receive the blow of the large hammer or maul used in driving. Figure 175 shows a cast iron ground piece, and at the right is the lower end of a post resting in one of them. The three flanges are cast in one solid piece, with a hole through the centre of any desired form and

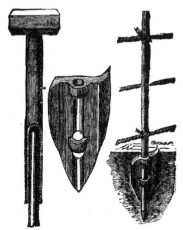

Fig. 174.—POST WITH IRON GROUND PIECE.

size. The wings or flanges are three inch plates, running to sharp edges on the bottom, so that they can easily be driven into the ground. They may be of any desired size, larger sizes being required for a light yielding soil

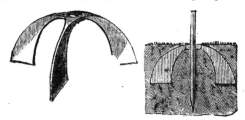

Fig. 175.—CAST-IRON GROUND-PIECE.

than for a stiff one. Figure 176 is an iron post on a wooden base, for situations where the ground is soft and wet. The base is preferably of cedar, three to four feet long, four inches thick, and four to six inches wide. It is to be sunken in the ground cross-wise with the line of fence. The post is of iron, set and stapled into the end-piece, as shown in the engraving. Before being put in place, the whole is saturated with hot coal tar, as a preservative. There is less call for iron posts than was an-

Fig. 176.

ticipated when wire fences first came into general use. It is found that wooden posts can be delivered in any location reached by railway at less cost than iron posts.

CHAPTER XI.

GATES AND FASTENINGS.

WOODEN GATES.

As board and picket fences have gradually replaced rail and other primitive fences, useful but inconvenient "bars" have begun to disappear, and tidy gates are seen. The saving in time required to take down and put up bars, rather than open and close gates, amounts to a good deal. A good wooden gate will last a long time. Gate-ways should be at least fourteen feet wide. All the wood used in the construction of the gate should be well seasoned. It is best to plane all the wood-work, though this is not absolutely necessary. Cover each tenon with thick paint before it is placed in its mortise. Fasten the brace to the cross-piece with small bolts or wrought nails well clinched. Mortise the ends of the boards into the end posts, and secure them in place with wooden pins wedged at both ends, or iron bolts. The best are made of pine fence-boards six inches wide; the ends should be

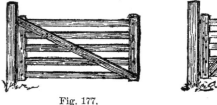
Fig. 177.

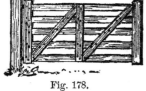
Fig. 178.

four by twenty-four inch scantling, although the one at the latch may be lighter. Five cross-pieces are enough. The lighter the gate in proportion to strength, the better it is. There is but one right way to brace a gate, and many wrong ones. The object of bracing is to strengthen the gate, and also to prevent its sagging. Gates sag in two ways; by the moving to the one side of the posts

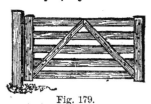
Fig. 179.

Fig. 180.

upon which the gates are hung, and the settling of the gates themselves. Unless braced the only thing to hold the gate square is the perfect rigidity of the tenons in the mortises; but the weight of the gate will loosen these, and allow the end of the gate opposite the hinges to sag. It is plain that a brace placed like that shown in figure 177 will not prevent this settling down. The only opposition it can give is the resistance of the nails, and these will draw loose in the holes as readily as the tenons in the mortises. A brace set as shown at figure 178 is not much better, as the resistance must depend upon the rigidity of the upright piece in the middle, and the bolts or nails holding it will give way enough to allow the gate to sag.

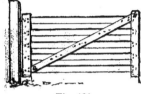 

Fig. 181. Fig. 182.

The method shown in figure 179 is fully as faulty, while the form shown in figure 180 is even worse. It seems strange that any one should brace a gate in these ways, but it is quite frequently seen attempted. The only right way to brace a gate is shown in figure 181. The gate may be further strengthened as shown in figure 182. Before the gate can sag, the brace must be shortened; for

Fig. 183. Fig. 184.

as the gate settles, the points a and b must come closer together, and this the brace effectually prevents.

The posts should be set in such a way that they will not be pulled to one side and allow the gate to sag. The post should be put below the line of frost, or else it will be heaved out of position; three feet in the ground is none too deep. Have a large post and make a big hole for it. Be careful to set the post plumb and stamp the earth firmly in the hole—it cannot be stamped too hard. While stamping, keep walking around the post, so that the earth will be firmed on all sides. Blocks may be arranged as shown in figure 183;

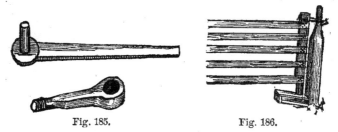

Fig. 185.   Fig. 186.

but this is not really necessary, when the posts have been rightly set, although it may be advisable to take this further precaution.

To remove the pulling weight of the gate when closed, the swinging end may rest upon a block; or a pin in-

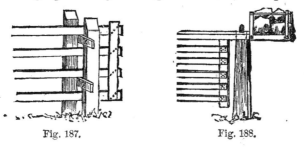

Fig. 187.   Fig. 188.

serted in the end piece of the gate may rest in a slot sawed in the post, or on a shoulder of the post. Figure 184 shows one end of a combination of two plans—the iron rod from near the top of the high post holds the gate while the strain upon the post is lessened by the opposite end of the closed gate being supported on the other post.

For hanging the gate the best hinges are doubtless those shown in figure 185. One part passes through the end-piece of the gate, and is secured by a nut on the end. The other piece is heated and driven into the post, following the path of a small augur-hole. Next to this comes the strap hinge, which should be fastened with bolts or screws. Three easy, cheap ways of supporting the gate are shown in figures 186, 187, and 188. In figure 186, a stout band of wood, or one of iron, may be used in place of the chain. And in place of the stool for the reception of the lower end of the end-piece, a block resting on the ground, or a shoulder on the post, may be substituted. The mode shown in figure 187 is common in the West. Its construction needs no explanation. By sliding the gate back until it almost balances it may be carried around with ease. In figure 188, the fastening, or latch, must be so arranged as to hold the lower part of the gate in position. The box of stone renders it easier to move the gate. A heavy block of wood serves the same purpose.

A VERY SUBSTANTIAL FARM GATE.

Figure 189 shows a gate which combines great durability with much rustic beauty. The cedar posts, $A A$, should be four feet in the ground, and at least ten feet out of the ground. B represents a piece of 2 by 6 hard pine, into which the posts are mortised. C is a 4 by 4 clear pine, turned at both ends and mortised as shown in figure 191. $D E F$ are 1 by 4 pine strips. G is a 1 by 6 pine strip, a sectional view being given in figure 190. It is best to use one piece each of D and E, letting F come between them, as it gives more stiffness to the gate. H is a block of cedar with a hole bored or dug large enough to receive the post, C, and to make it more lasting, a small hole should be bored through the block, so as to let whatever water collects in it pass away; the block should not be less than eighteen inches long—four inches above ground. *I* shows wire fence connected. *J* is a strong wire carried

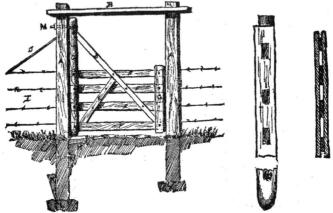

Fig. 189.—A SUBSTANTIAL GATE.   Fig. 190.   Fig. 191.

and secured to the bottom of the first fence post. *K K* are cleats attached to posts to keep them more firmly in the ground. *L* are stones for posts, *A A*, to stand on. *M* shows the hinge, made so as to take up the sag after the gate settles, and as the wood wears out.

A STRONG AND NEAT GATE.

The posts, *a, a,* figure 192, of oak or other durable wood, are eight inches square, and stand five and one half feet above the ground. The posts, *b, b,* three and one third inches thick, four and three quarter feet long, are mortised to receive the slats, *c, c,* which are of inch stuff, three inches wide and ten feet four and three-quarter inches long. They are let into posts, *b, b,* at the distance marked in the engraving. The slats, *d,* are three inches wide, and one inch thick, and are placed opposite each other on front and back of the gate as braces ; *e, e,* are simply battens to make a straight surface for the hinges, *f, f ;* all except the upper and lower ones are very short and carried back to the post. ·The hinges, made by a blacksmith from an old wagon tire, are one and one-half inch wide, three-sixteenth inch thick, and are fastened by light iron bolts through the battens at *e,* and to the rear post.

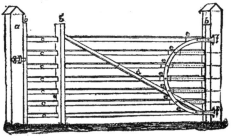

Fig. 192.—A WELL-MADE GATE.

The above describes a cheap, light, durable gate, which in over twenty-three years' use has never sagged, though standing in the thoroughfare of three farms, and also, for years past, used for access to a sawmill. It is made of the best pine. The hinge is an important point. It is not only cheap and easily made, but acts as a brace for the gate at every point, and thus permits the gate to be lightly made. With this hinge sagging is impossible. A gate of this kind will rot down first.

LIGHT IRON GATES.

The gate shown in figure 193 may be made of wrought iron an inch and a half wide and half an inch thick, or preferably of iron gas-pipe of any diameter from half an inch to an inch. In the vicinity of the oil-regions, pipe can be bought very cheaply, which is in condition good

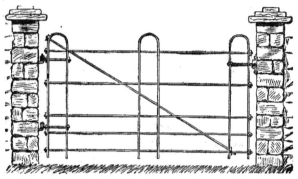

Fig. 193.—A LIGHT IRON GATE.

enough for this purpose. For guarding against hogs, it should be hung near the ground, and have one or two more horizontal pipes near the bottom.

Figure 194 shows the construction of a gate intended for situations much exposed to trespassers. It is made

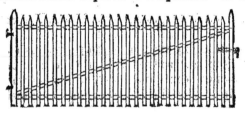

Fig. 194.—A WROUGHT IRON GATE.

of upright strips of flat iron, pointed at the top, and fastened by rivets to a stout frame-work of iron. The "pickets" are placed two to three inches apart, as desired, for the appearance of the gate, or according to the size of the poultry or animals to be kept from passing.

Every self-closing gate should be provided with a drop or spring catch, a suitable bevel for it to strike against and notch to hold it. Gates opening into the garden or out upon the street, should be so hung that they will swing either way. Figure 195 shows a hinge and slide for such a gate. In opening the gate from either side, the arm of the upper hinge slides upon the iron bar, raising the gate a little as it swings around. When loosed, it

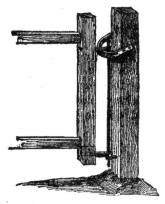

Fig. 195.—HINGE AND SLIDE FOR GATE.　　Fig. 196.

slides down without help, and closes by its own weight. Figure 196 shows another form of the iron slide, suitable for a wide gate post, and more ornamental than the plain slide in figure 195.

Figure 197 shows a very good and common hanging. The upper hinge consists of a hook in the post and a corresponding eye in the hinge-stile of the gate. The lower hinge is made of two semi-circular pieces of iron, each with a shank, one of which is shown above the gate in the engraving. They are made to play one into the other. This style of hanging may be used on any ordi-

Fig. 197.

nary kind of gate, but is specially useful for a small street gate opening into a door-yard.

There is a style of gate for foot-paths, which is not uncommon, that keeps itself always closed and latched, by means of a single upper and double lower hinge, which

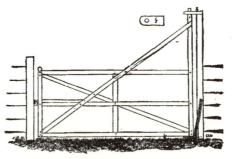

Fig. 198.—SELF-CLOSING FARM GATE.

are to be obtained at most hardware stores. The lower hinge has two "thumbs," which are embraced by two open sockets. When the gate is opened, it swings upon one socket and its thumb, and being thrown off the center, the weight of the gate draws it back, and swinging too, it latches. A farm gate, entirely home-made, may be constructed, of which figures 198 and 199 show the gate and the hinge. The gate is braced and supported by a stay-strip, extending to the top of the upright, which forms the upper hinge, f being attached to the top of the gate-post, by an oak board with a smooth hole in it. The lower hinge is separately shown at figure 199. It consists of an oak board, c, an inch and a half thick, into

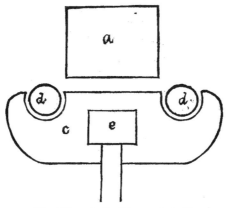

Fig. 199.—LOWER HINGE OF GATE.

which the upright, e, is mortised. In this, two sockets are cut, a foot from center to center. The sockets in this case are three inches in diameter, and when the gate is in place and shut, they fit against two stakes of hardwood (locust), two and a half inches in diameter, d, which being curved, are nailed to the gate-post, a. A smooth stone, laid across in front of these stakes, takes the weight of the gate, and relieves in a measure the pressure on the top of the post. The hinges must be kept well greased, and it is well to black-lead them also, to prevent creaking.

GATE FOR VILLAGE LOT.

Figure 200 shows a light, strong gate made of wood and wire. The top wire is barbed to prevent stock from pressing against it, and beaux and belles from hanging

Fig. 200.—CONVENIENT GATE.

over it. The bottom wires are also barbed to prevent cats, dogs, and fowls from creeping under. This gate is cheap, may be easily constructed, and is suitable for either front or back yard.

A CHINESE DOOR OR GATE SPRING.

Figure 201 shows the manner in which the Chinese use a bow as a spring for closing the light doors and gates. The bow is fastened to the gate by a cord or chain. Another cord or chain is attached to the middle of the bow-string by one end, and the other end is made fast to the gate post, in such a manner that when the gate is opened, the bow will be drawn, and its elasticity will serve to shut the gate when released. Our artist has

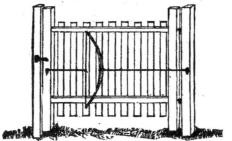

Fig. 201.—CHINESE DOOR OR GATE SPRING.

shown the Chinese invention attached to a gate of Yankee pattern.

LIFTING GATES.

There are various forms of gates not hung on hinges at all, but either suspended from above to lift, and pro-

Fig. 202.—GATE SHUT.

vided with counterweights, or made in the form of movable panels. Figure 202 represents a gate for general use, which is peculiarly well adapted to a region visited by deep snows in winter. The post, firmly set, extends a little higher than the length of the gate. In front of this and firmly fastened to it at bottom and top, is a board at sufficient distance from the post for the gate to move easily between them. An iron bolt through the large post and the lower end of the tall, upright gate bar serves as a balance for the gate to turn on. A rope attached to the bottom of the gate runs over the

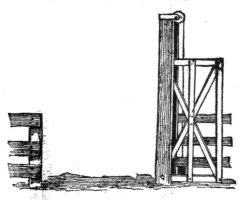

Fig. 203.—GATE OPEN.

pulley and has a weight of iron or stone that nearly balances the gate. The opened gate is shown in figure 203.

Figure 204 shows a gate balanced in a similar manner, and arranged so it can be opened by a person desiring to drive through, without leaving the vehicle. It is suspended by ropes which pass over pulleys near the top of long posts, and counterpoised by weights upon the other ends of the ropes. Small wheels are placed in the ends of the gate to move along the inside of the posts, and thus reduce the friction. The gate is raised by means of ropes attached to the center of the upper side of the gate, from which they pass up to pulleys in the center of the archway, and then out along horizontal arms at right angles to the bars which connect the tops of the posts. By pulling on the rope, the gate, which is but a trifle heavier than the balancing weights, is raised, and after the vehicle has passed, the gate falls of itself. In passing

Fig. 204.—A "SELF-OPENING" GATE.

in the opposite direction, another rope is pulled, when the gate is raised as before.

Figures 206 and 207 show a gate specially designed for snowy regions. The latch-post, figure 205, is fixed in the ground and connected with the fence. It is an ordinary square fence-post, to the side of which a strip of board is nailed, with a space of an inch between the board and the post. At the opposite extremity of the gate a heel-post is set slanting, as shown in figures 206 and 207. The gate is made by laying the five horizontal bars on a barn floor or other level place, with one of the sloping crossbars under them and the other above them. Half inch holes are bored through the three thicknesses, carriage bolts inserted from below, and the nuts screwed on. The gate, thus secured at one end, is carried to the place

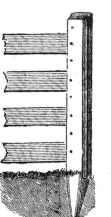
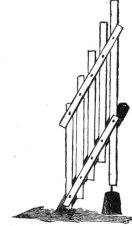

Fig. 205.—LATCH-POST.   Fig. 206.—THE GATE OPEN.

where it is to remain and the other ends of the horizontal bars secured to the heel-post by similar bolts. These should work freely in the holes. The lower bar is **four**

Fig. 207.—THE GATE CLOSED.

feet long and the upper bar seven feet. To the heel of the upper bar is hung a weight nearly heavy enough to balance the gate, so that it may easily be swung up, as shown in figure 206, and the weight will keep it raised.

Figures 208 and 209 illustrate a very cheap way of making a hole through a picket fence in a place where there is not sufficiently frequent occasion for passing, to call for a more elaborate gate. Strips of inch board, as

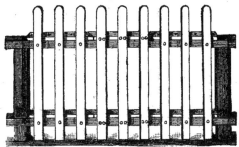

Fig. 208.—THE GATE IN POSITION.

wide as the rails of the fence, and five or six feet long, are nailed to the upper side of the rails and three pickets are nailed to the strips. The pieces are then sawed off, beveling, and the pickets detached from the fence-bars

Fig. 209.—THE GATE OPEN.

by drawing or cutting the nails. The gate can be lifted up and set at one side, but can not be pushed in or pulled out. No rope or other fastening is required, besides it is almost invisible, which is many times an advantage. The gate, as lifted out of the fence and set on one side, is shown in figure 209.

Figure 210 shows an improved form of this gate without posts. In this case the small board strips are cut only as long as the gate is to be made wide, and a diagonal cross-brace running between them, as shown in the

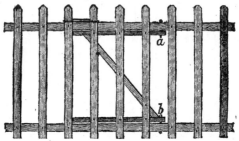

Fig. 210.—A SMALL GATE IN A PICKET FENCE.

engraving. The hinges are fastened to the horizontal bars of the fence by wooden pins shown at a and b. A piece of rope or a short wire passing over the ends of two of the pickets serves to keep the gate securely fastened. These openings are not designed for a regular gate, and

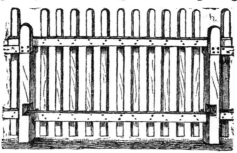

Fig. 211.—MOVABLE PANEL.

could not be used for the passage of any vehicle, as the horizontal bars would be in the way. For a back gate to the garden such an opening would frequently be found convenient and save many steps.

Figure 211 shows a lifting-gate, or rather, a movable

panel, wide enough to permit the passage of a team and vehicle. This might be useful in places where it was not desired to pass frequently.

Figure 212 shows another very convenient form of gate for use in a country where the snow is deep. It is fitted

Fig. 212.—A GATE NOT CLOGGED WITH SNOW.

in a strong frame, and is balanced by weights, so that it can be easily raised. The engraving sufficiently explains how this very useful gate is made and hung in the frame.

RUSTIC GATES.

A picturesque rustic gate is shown in figure 213. The fence and posts are made to correspond. Its manner of construction is clearly shown in the illustration. The vases on the top of the posts may be omitted, unless time can be taken to keep them properly watered.

A very neat, cheap, and strong rustic gate is shown in figure 214. The large post and the two uprights of the gate are of red cedar. The horizontal bars may be of the same or other wood. The longer upright is five and a half feet long, the shorter one four and a half feet.

The ends of the former are cut down to serve as hinges, as shown in the engraving. Five holes are bored through

Fig. 213.—ORNAMENTAL GATE.

each of the upright pieces, two inches in diameter, into which the ends of the horizontal bars are inserted and

Fig. 214.—LIGHT RUSTIC GATE.

wedged securely. For the upper hinge a piece of plank is bored to receive the gate, and the other end reduced and driven into a hole in the post, or nailed securely to its top. A cedar block, into which a two-inch hole has been bored, is partially sunk in the ground to receive the lower end of the upright piece. A wooden latch is in better keeping with the gate than an iron one.

BALANCE GATES.

Figure 215 is a modernized form of a gate which has for generations been popular in New England and the Middle States. In the primitive method of construction, the top bar consisted of the smoothly trimmed trunk of

Fig. 215.—BALANCE GATE.

a straight young tree, with the butt end projecting like a "heel" beyond the post upon which it turned. Upon its extremity a heavy boulder, or box of smaller stones, served as a counterweight. In the gate represented herewith the top stick is of sawn timber, upon the heel of which the large stone is held by an iron dowel. The other end of the top bar rests, when the gate is closed, upon an iron pin, driven diagonally into the post, as shown in the illustration. A smaller iron pin is pushed into the post immediately above the end of the top bar, to secure the gate against being opened by unruly animals, which may attempt to get in.

Figure 216 shows a balance gate which is used in some parts of North Carolina. It is a picket gate framed into

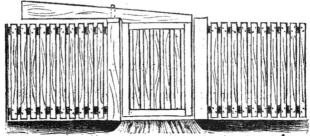

Fig. 216.—CAROLINA BALANCE GATE.

the lower side of a long pole, which is hung near its middle to a pivot driven into the top of the gate-post.

Fig. 217.—A TIDY BALANCE GATE.

Figure 217 shows a more elegant form, the "heel" of the gate remaining on a level with the top line of the fence.

GATE FOR SNOWY WEATHER.

The gate shown in figure 218 is suitable for all weather, but especially useful when there is a deep snow; for it is easily lifted up above the snow, and kept in place by putting a pin through holes in the hinge-bar, which is firmly fastened to the gate post. The hinge-bar should be of good, tough wood, and made round and smooth, so that the gate can swing and slide easily. Boards can be used in place of pickets if preferable. The latch-post to the

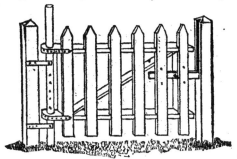

Fig. 218.—GATE FOR SNOWY WEATHER.

right, has a long slot for the latch to work in, instead of a hasp, so that it can be fastened when the gate is at any height.

WEST INDIA FARM GATES.

The illustrations, figures 219 and 220, show two forms of gates used on the island of Jamaica. These gates are

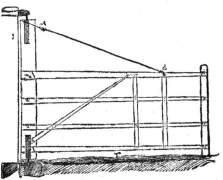

Fig. 219.—WIDE FARM GATE.

twenty-one feet long, each, and cannot possibly sag, even if any number of small boys swing on them. In gate figure 220 the main post is nine by six inches; the bars—marked 2, 3, 5 and 7—are let in the wood three inches on the upper side and one and a half inches on the lower. The tenons, indicated by the dotted lines, go entirely through the posts, and are fastened with pins. Brace 6 is attached to the upper bar eighteen inches beyond the center, F; D is a stout fence wire

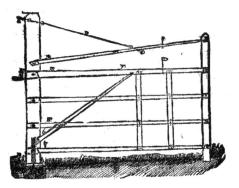

Fig. 220.—ANOTHER WIDE FARM GATE.

fastened by a screw nut at E; the wire, B, is held tightly by the screw hook, A; the iron band, 9, is an inch thick and is bolted to the post. It works on a pivot one and a quarter inches in diameter, and which turns on a flat piece of iron at the bottom of a piece of a one and a half inch iron pipe, which is soldered with molten lead in the stone, 10. Only hard wood is used in the construction. In the gate shown in figure 219, the construction differs from the one just described in that it has a light chain fastened in the shackle, C, and is screwed firmly at A. It is attached to the post, H, by a pivot, as seen in our illustration.

It is often convenient and economical, especially in newly settled regions, where blacksmiths and hardware stores are not at hand, to supply hinges for gates, to make them of wood. The simplest and most primitive form is shown in figure 221. A post is selected having a large limb standing out nearly at right angles. A perpendicular hole in this secures the top of the rear gate standard. The foot rests in a stout short post, set against the main

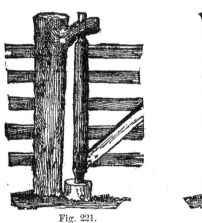
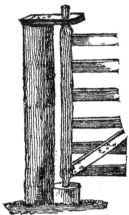

Fig. 221. Fig. 222.

post. A small gimlet hole should extend outward and downward from the lowest side or point in the hole in the short post, to act as a drain, or the water collecting in it would be likely to soon rot both the standard and the short post itself. Another form is to hold the top by a strong wooden withe. A third form is illustrated in figure 222, in which the top of the standard passes through a short piece of sawed or split plank, spiked or pinned upon the top of the post.

The form shown at figure 223 is made of a stout lithe sapling or limb of beech, hickory or other tough hard wood or, if it is attainable, a piece of iron rod.

Fig. 223.—A WITHE HINGE.

A gate can be made without hinges by having the hanging stile somewhat longer than the front stile, and making both ends rounded. The lower one is to work

Fig. 224.—GATE WITHOUT HINGES.

in a hole in the end of a short post raised so that the soil will not readily get in, and the upper one works in a hole made in an oak piece attached to the top of the gate post. Gates of this kind can be made and hung with but little more expense than bars, and will be found far more convenient and saving of time than the latter.

Figure 225 represents a small hand-gate hung upon an iron pin driven into a hole bored in the bottom of the hinge-post, and one of similar size and material bent to a

Fig. 225.—SOCKET HINGES.

sharp angle, and fitted in the top. The lower pin rests in the sill and the upper one extends through the post to which the gate is hung.

DOUBLE GATES.

Figure 226 shows a substantial method of hanging two gates to the same post. The post may be of masonry

Fig. 226.—A DOUBLE GATE.

and the hinge bolts pass through the post, thus preventing any sagging. It is frequently convenient to have gates in the barnyard hung in this manner, then yards

Fig. 227.—DOUBLE BALANCE GATE.

may be shut off one way or the other by simply swinging the gates.

Figure 227 represents a balanced gate for a double driveway. The total length is thirty feet—sixteen feet on one

Fig. 228.—DOUBLE BALANCE GATE WITH STONE POST.

side of the supporting post and fourteen feet on the other. The horizontal top-piece may be of sawn timber, or better still, of a round pole cut from a straight young tree, the larger end being on the short side, its additional thickness serving to counterbalance the longer extremity of the gate. The vertical strips of the original gate, from which the sketch was made, were lag-sticks from an old tread horse-power, and the chain was a part of the remains of a worn-out chain pump. It is held in place by staples driven into the vertical pieces, as shown in the illustration. A pin pushed into the post at either end of the large top bar fastens it securely when closed.

Fig. 229.—THE GATE LATCH.

Figure 228 is a gate which combines some of the features of the preceding two. The stone pillar is round, three feet across and four and a half feet high. A post is placed in the center, upon the end of which the bar rests, bearing the two gates. The fence is arranged in a sweeping curve, so that only one passageway can be open at once.

Figure 230 shows a style of double gate, which has

Fig. 230.—A DOUBLE HINGELESS GATE.

been found very useful on large stock farms, where it is necessary to drive herds of cattle through it. Two high posts are set in the ground about twenty feet apart, and a scantling is put on, which extends from the top of one post to that of the other. A two-inch hole is bored in the center of this scantling, and a similar hole in a block of wood, planted firmly in the ground in the center of the gateway. The middle post of the gate frame is rounded at each end to fit these holes, and this post is the pivot on which the gate turns. With this gate one cow cannot block the passage, besides there is no sagging of gate posts, as the weight of the gate is wholly upon the block in the center. To make the latch, figure 229, a bar of iron one and a half inch wide and eighteen inches long is bolted to one of the end uprights of the gate, and a similar bar to one of the posts of the gateway. For a catch, a rod of three-eighth inch iron passes through a half-inch hole near the end of the bar upon the gateway. This rod is bent in the form shown in the engraving, and welded. It will be seen that the lifting of this bent rod will allow the two bars to come together, and when dropped it will hold them firmly.

DOUBLE-LATCHED GATES.

Figure 231 represents a substantial farm gate with two latches. This is a very useful precaution against the

Fig. 231.—A DOUBLE-LATCHED FARM GATE.

wiles of such cattle as have learned to unfasten **ordinary** gate-latches. The latches work independently of **each** other, the wires, b, b, being fastened to the hand lever a, and then to the latches *e, e.* A roguish animal will sometimes open a gate by raising the latch with its nose, but if one attempt it with this, it can only raise one latch at a time, always the upper one, while the lower one remains fastened. As soon as the animal lets go, the latch springs back and catches again. A hog cannot get through, for the lower latch prevents the gate from opening sufficiently to allow it to pass. A cow will find it difficult to open the gate, because she cannot raise the gate high enough to unlatch it. The latches *e, e,* work up and down in the slides *c, c,* and when the gate is fastened they are about half-way between the top and bottom of the slides.

Figure 232 shows another form of double latches, which are closed by absolute motion, instead of depend-

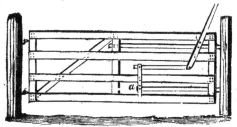

Fig. 232.—A GATE FOR ALL LIVE STOCK.

ing upon their own weight. There are two latches fastened to a jointed lever, so that when the upper end or handle is pushed backward or foward, the latches both move in the same direction. The construction of the gate, and the form and arrangement of the latches and lever, are plainly shown.

IMPROVED SLIDE GATE.

The old style slide gate is an unwieldly contrivance, and the only excuse for its use is its simplicity and cheapness. Numerous devices have been invented and patented to make it slide easier and swing easier, but their cost has prevented them from coming into general use, and the old gate still requires the same amount of tugging and heaving to open and close it.

Figure 233 shows the attachment. The blocks at top and bottom are hard wood, one inch and a quarter thick. The two boards should also be of hard wood. Between the boards are one or two small iron or hard wood wheels, turning upon half inch bolts, which pass through both boards. The bars of the gate run on these wheels. The

Fig. 233.   Fig. 234.—THE GATE COMPLETE.

gate complete, with attachment, is shown in figure 234, the gate being closed. To open the gate, run it back nearly to the middle bar, then swing open. As the attachment turns with the gate, the lower pivot should be greased occasionally. It is well to fasten a barbed wire along the upper edge of the top bar, to prevent stock from reaching over and bearing down on the gate. Where hogs are enclosed, it is advisable to fasten a barbed wire along the lower edge of the bottom bar, as it keeps small pigs from passing under, and prevents large ones from lifting the gate up, or trying to root under.

A COMBINED HINGE AND SLIDING GATE.

The illustrations, figures 235 and 236, show a gate very handy for barnyards. It is fourteen feet wide for ordinary use, and has three short posts. The middle one is movable. A box of two inch boards made to fit the post is planted in the ground; in this the post is set, and can be removed at pleasure. This post is placed three feet from the outside one. The hinge is made of hard wood,

Fig. 235.—THE GATE OPEN.

with a wheel six inches in diameter, as shown in the engraving. It should be so constructed that the gate will move freely, but not too loosely. It is supported at the top by a cap, placed diagonally across, and at the bottom by a block of locust or cedar under it. The middle up-

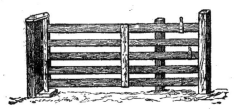

Fig. 236.—THE GATE CLOSED.

rights of the gate should be placed a little to one side of the center, so that the gate can be balanced under the roller. Wooden catches are placed in the middle post, upon which the gate rests. To open the gate, push it back to the middle post, elevate the gate slightly, and it will roll down to the center, where it can be readily opened. Figure 235 shows the gate open, and in figure

236 it is seen closed. This gate has no latch. A barnyard gate is not usually opened wide. A space large enough to admit a man or horse is all that is necessary in most cases. It is more easily opened than the ordinary gate, and it will stay where it is placed. By cutting a notch in the third board, and elevating it to the upper catch on the middle post, a passage is made for hogs and sheep, excluding larger animals.

GATES OF WOOD AND WIRE.

One of the cheapest and most popular styles of farm gate is made of plain or barbed wire, supported by

Fig. 237.—A NEAT GATE OF SCANTLING AND WIRE.

wooden frames. Figure 237 shows a very neat form of combination gate. To make it, obtain three uprights, three inches by one and a half inches, five and a half feet long, and four strips, three inches by one inch, eleven feet long. Cut shoulders in the ends of the strips, and saw out corresponding notches in the uprights;

make these one and a half inch, or half the width of the strips. The bottom notch is two and a half inches from the end of the upright, and the upper one nine and a half inches from the top end. Fit the strips into the notches. There is then a space of one inch between the strips, into which put inch strips, so as to make all solid, and fasten together with carriage bolts. Braces three by one and a half inches are inserted, and held in place by bolts or wrought nails. Bore as many holes in the end-pieces for one-quarter inch eye-bolts, as it is desired to have wires. Twist the wire firmly into the bolts on one upright, and secure the other end to the corresponding bolts on the upright at the opposite end. In stretching the wires, pass them alternately on opposite sides of the center piece, and fasten in place by staples. This will, in a measure, prevent warping. By screwing down the bolts with a wrench, the wires may be drawn as tightly as desired. The hinges are to be put on with bolts, and any sort of fastening may be used that is most convenient. Barbed or smooth wire may be used.

A GOOD AND CHEAP FARM GATE.

Figure 238 shows a gate of common fence boards and wire, which can be made by any farmer. The longer upright piece, seven feet long, may be made of a round stick, flattened a little on one side. The horizontal bars are of common fence boards cut to the desired length, and the shorter, vertical piece may be made of scantling, two by four inches. Three wires, either plain or barbed, are stretched at equal intervals between the upper and lower bar. A double length of wire is extended from the top of the long upright to the opposite lower corner of the gate. A stout stick is inserted between the two strands of this diagonal brace, by which it is twisted until it is

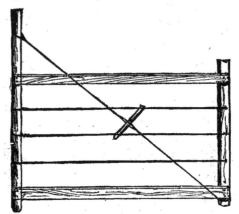

Fig. 238.—GOOD AND CHEAP FARM GATE.

sufficiently taut. If the gate should at any time begin to sag, a few turns brings it back.

AN IMPROVED WIRE GATE.

Figure 239 shows an improved form of wire farm gate, in which the wires can be made tight at pleas-

Fig. 239.—IMPROVED WIRE GATE.

ure. Instead of attaching the wires to both of the end standards of the gate, a sliding standard is put on near the end, to which the wires are fastened. This is secured to the main standard by two long screw bolts, leaving a space between the two of five or six inches. The wires are tightened by turning up the nuts.

A plainer but very effective gate is shown in figure 240 The uprights are three and one quarter by two inches, the horizontals twelve or thirteen feet long, by three and a half by two inches, all of pine. The horizontals are mortised into the uprights, the bolts of the hinges strengthening the joints. The barbed wires prevent ani-

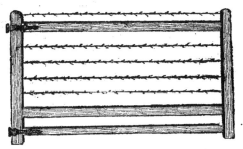

Fig. 240.—GATE OF WOOD AND WIRE.

mals from reaching over and through the gate. To put in and tighten the wires, bore a three-eighth inch hole in the upright, pass the wires through, one or two inches projecting, plug up tightly with a wooden pin, and bend down the ends of the wire. Measure the distance to the other upright, and cut the wire two inches longer. Pass the wire through the whole and tighten with pincers. When the wire is stretched, plug up with a wooden pin, and then bend down the wire. If the wire stretches, it .n be tightened very easily.

Figure 241 represents a light gate, that a child can handle, which does not sag or get out of repair, and is cattle proof. The materials are two boards, twelve or fourteen feet long, three uprights, the end piece three and one-half feet and the center four and one-half feet. two strands of barbed wire, one between the boards, and

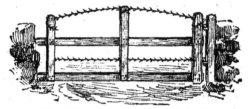

Fig. 241.—BARBED WIRE IN A GATE.

the other at the top of the uprights. It is hung the same as the common form of gate.

TAKING UP THE SAG IN GATES.

Various means have been devised for overcoming the sagging of gates. In figure 242 the hinge-post of the

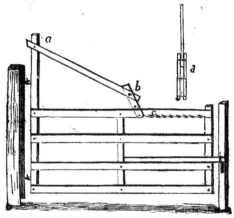

Fig. 242.—REMEDY FOR A SAGGING GATE.

gate-frame extends somewhat above the upper bar of the gate. A board is fastened to the top of this post, a, which runs downward to b, near the middle of the upper cross-bar, and then connects with a short double band— one on each side of the long board—which is provided with a bolt fitting into notches, c, cut in the under side of the upper bar of the gate. The form of the double-latch piece, with its bolts, and its attachment to the board is shown at d.

Figure 243 represents an arrangement which not only provides for taking up the sag, but also for raising the gate above encumbering snow. The gate is made of ordinary inch boards put together with carriage bolts, upon which the joints play freely. The end of the gate, a, is made of two boards, and the post, b, is four by six inches.

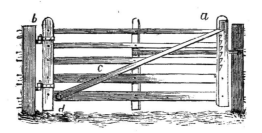

Fig. 243.—A LIFT-BAR FOR A GATE.

One board of the end, a, is notched. The diagonal piece, c, is fastened at d, by means of a bolt through it and the lower board. The end, a, of the diagonal piece, is shaped to fit the notches, by means of which the gate can be raised and lowered. It can also be used as a passage for pigs between fields, by simply raising the gate sufficiently to let them go through. A board, not shown in the engraving, is tacked to the notched board, to prevent the diagonal piece from slipping out of its place.

A much firmer gate is shown in figure 244. The hinge-post is about twice the height of the gate, and has a cap-piece, a, near the top. This cap is of 2 by 6 hard-

wood, strengthened by two bolts, *e. e,* and held in place
by two wooden pins, driven just above it and through

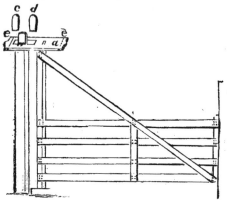

Fig. 244.—A REMEDY FOR A SAGGING GATE.

the tenon end of the post. Wedges *c* and *d* are driven
in the cap on each side of the post. Should the gate
sag, the wedge, *d*, may be loosened, and *c* driven further
down. The lower end of the gate turns in a hole bored
in a hard-wood block placed in the ground near the foot
of the post.

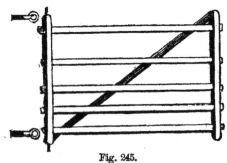

Fig. 245.

Figure 245 shows a gate similarly hung on pivots
driven into the ends of the hinge-bar. These play in eye-

bolts which extend through the post to which the gate is hung, and are fastened by nuts on the other side. As the gate sags, the nut on the upper bolt is turned up, drawing the upper end of the hinge-bar toward the post, and lifting the gate back to a horizontal position.

GOOD GATE LATCHES.

Some cows become so expert, they can lift almost any gate latch. To circumvent this troublesome habit, latches made as shown in figure 246 will fill this bill exactly. It is a piece of iron bar, drawn down at one

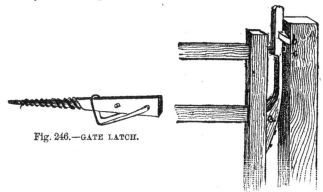

Fig. 246.—GATE LATCH.

Fig. 247.—SPRING GATE CATCH.

end, and cut with a thread to screw into the gate post. A stirrup, or crooked staple, made as shown, is fitted by a screw bolt and nut to the bar. A small bolt must be driven in to keep the stirrup from being thrown over. A projecting slat on the gate, when it is shut, lifts the stirrup and holds the gate. This latch is too much for breechy cows, and they are never able to get "the hang of it."

A simple catch for a gate may easily be made from a

piece of seasoned hickory, or other elastic wood, cut in the shape as shown at *a* in figure 247. This is fastened strongly to the side of the gate, with the pin, *c*, working through the top loosely, so that it will play easily. The catch, *b*, is fastened to the wall or post, as the case may be. The operation will be easily understood from the illustration, and it will be found a serviceable, sure, and durable contrivance. The gate cannot be swung to without catching, and it may swing both ways.

A very simple and convenient style of fastening is illustrated in figures 248 to 251. It can be made of old

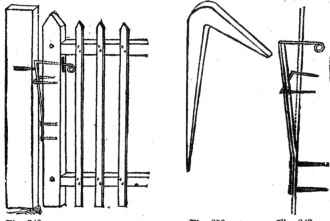

Fig. 248.—LATCH IN POSITION.   Fig. 250.   Fig. 249.

buggy springs, or any flat steel, and should be one inch broad by three six-tenth inch thick, and about eighteen inches long, at the distance of four inches from the lower end. The lever is slightly bent, and has two screw the bolt holes for fastening, figure 249. Eight inches of the top portion is rounded and bent at right angles. The upper part passes through a narrow mortise in the headpost of the gate figure 248. A flat staple, large enough to go over the spring holds it in place. An iron hook, figure 250, driven into the post, holds the latch. A wooden lever, bolted to the top board of the gate, figure

Fig. 251.—LATCH WITH TOP LEVER.

251, enables a person on horseback to open or close the gate. This latch can be applied to any kind of a gate, and is especially desirable in yards or gardens, when, by the addition of a chain and weight, one may always feel that the gate is securely closed. The latch does not cost more than fifty cents, and if properly made and put on will last as long as the gate.

Fig. 252.—GATE LATCH.

In figure 252 is represented a style of gate latch in use in some Southern States. It possesses marked advantages, for certain purposes, over others. It holds to an absolute certainty, under all circumstances, and by allow-

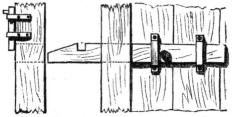

Fig. 253.—LATCH AND PIN.

ing the latch pin to rest on the bottom of the slot in the post, it-relieves the hinges and post from all strain. The latch may be formed by a common strap-hinge, made to work very easily, and the pin should be either a strong oak one or an iron bolt or "lag screw."

Figure 253 shows a latch which cannot be opened by

Fig. 254.—GATE LATCH.

the most ingenious cow or other animal. The latch of wood slides in two iron or wood bands screwed to the gate. It is moved by a knob between the bands, which also prevents it from going too far. The outer end is sloping and furnished with a notch. It slides through a mortise in the gate post, indicated by dotted lines. When the gate is closed, the latch is slid through the mortise, and the drop-pin, which plays vertically in two iron bands, is lifted by the slope on the latch, and drops into the notch. It can be opened only by lifting the drop-pin, and sliding back the latch at the same time.

Figure 254 shows a very ingenious and reliable form of latch. The curved tail must be thin enough and sufficiently soft to admit of bending, either by a pair of large pincers or a hammer, just so as to adapt it to the passage of the pin bolted through the front stile of the gate. As the gate closes, the latch lifts out and the tail-piece advances. The catch-pin cannot possibly move out, unless the whole end of the gate moves up and forward.

TOP HINGE OF FARM GATE.

Continual use, more or less slamming, and the action of the weather, make the gate settle somewhat, but

Fig. 255.—TOP HINGE OF FARM GATE.

the illustration, figure 255, shows a hinge which obviates this trouble. The upper hinge is made of a half-inch rod, about sixteen inches long, with an eye on one end, and a long screw-thread cut upon the other. This thread works in a nut, which nut has a bolt shank and nut, whereby it is firmly attached to the top bar of the gate. If the gate sags at all, it must be simply lifted off the thumbs, and the hinge given a turn or two in the nut; and the same is to be done in case of subsequent sagging. The hinge bolt must, of course, have some opportunity to move in the stile, and must be set long enough at first to allow the slack to be taken up whenever found necessary.

GATEWAYS IN WIRE FENCE.

Regular posts and bars at a passage-way through a wire fence are inconvenient and unsightly. A good sub-

Fig. 256.—GATEWAY IN A WIRE FENCE.

stitute for a gate is illustrated in figure 256. Light galvanized iron chains have a "swivel" near the end, by which they may be loosened or tightened, so as to be of

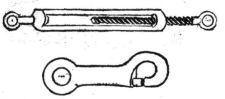

Figs. 257 and 258.—BUCKLE AND SNAP HOOK FOR CHAIN GATE.

just the right length, and a snap-hook at the other. These are both shown of larger size in figures 257 and 258.

The chains are attached by screw-eyes to the posts, and should correspond in number, as well as in position, with the wires. Thus they appear to be a continuation of the same, and as they are larger, they appear to the animals to be stronger, and even more dangerous than barbed

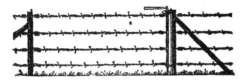

Fig. 259.—THE GATE CLOSED.

wire—hence are avoided. A short rod of iron may be made to connect them at the hook-ends, and so in opening and closing the way, they may all be moved at once. A cheaper and simpler form of wire gate is shown in figures 259 and 260. It consists of the same number of strands as in the adjoining fence, attached to a post in the ordinary way at one end, while the other wire ends are secured to an iron rod. This rod is pointed at the lower end, and when the gate is closed, as seen in figure

Fig. 260.—THE GATE OPEN.

259, this end passes down through a loop, and the upper end is secured to a hook. In opening the gate, the rod is loosened and swings out, when the sharp end is thrust into the earth, or a hole in a wooden block set in the ground at the proper place to receive it.

Figure 261 shows a somewhat similar arrangement. The gate wires are fastened to one post with staples, and attach the loose ends to a five-foot pole. To shut the gate, take this pole or gate-head and put the lower end

Fig. 261.—A WIRE GATE.

back of the lower pin, and spring the upper end behind the one above. If the wires are all of the right length, they will be taut and firm. Two slats fastened to the gate wires will keep them from tangling. A short post set at one side of the gateway may be found convenient to hold the gate when open.

CHAPTER XII.

WICKETS AND STILES.

IRON WICKETS.

Wickets and stiles are convenient passageways through or over fences crossing foot-paths. The bow wicket has the advantage of providing a gate "always open and always shut," and not apt to get out of repair. A wrought iron bow wicket, with short vertical bars, is shown in figure 262. Figure 263 has the bars horizontal, and folds in the middle for a wheel-barrow or small animals to pass. To go through it, a person simply steps

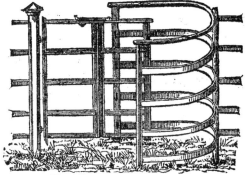

Fig. 262.—WICKET WITH HINGE.

into the bow, swings the gate away from him, and swings it back in passing out. There is no latch to fasten, and

Fig. 263.—WICKET WITH UPRIGHT BARS.

no fear of the entry of live stock. Similar wickets may be constructed of wood for board fences.

WOODEN WICKETS.

Figure 264 shows a wicket gate common in England, where it is much used in foot-paths across fields, etc. It is an ordinary small gate, which swings between two posts, set far enough apart to permit the passage of a person. These two posts are the two ends of a V-shaped

Fig. 264.—A GATE FOR FOOT-PATH.

end in the fence. The engraving shows the construction of the end of the fence, with the two posts, between which the gate swings.

Figure 265 is another form of gate, which consists of a V-shaped panel, filling the opening in the fence—the open

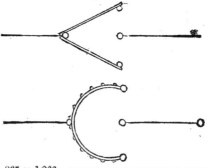

Figs. 265 and 266.—COMMON AND IMPROVED WICKETS.

ends of the V being fixed to posts equally distant from and in a line with one of the posts in the fence, and at right angles to it. This is improved by using bent wheel-rims, figure 266, instead of the straight pieces forming the V-shaped panel. Kept well painted, the hickory rims will bear the exposure to the weather perfectly. The palings should be of oak, an inch wide and half an inch thick, fastened on with screws. The opening in these stiles must be sufficient to allow a corpulent person to pass easily, even if a frisky bull is in uncomfortable prox-

Fig. 267.—A CONVENIENT STILE.

imity, and for this figure 266 is really the most convenient form. The objection to both of these stiles is, that there is no actual closing of the passage. Calves, sheep and pigs, not to mention dogs, work their way through. To prevent this, the gate-stile, figure 267, was invented. It has a small gate swinging on the middle post, but stopped in its movement by the end posts of the V. A

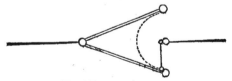

Fig. 268.—A GATE STILE.

person can pass by stepping well into the V and moving the gate by him, where he has free exit. This form is efficient, but inconvenient. A fourth form, the best of all, is the swinging A-stile, figures 268 and 269. In this there are two light gates, made upon the same hinge-post, spreading like the letter A, and braced with a crosspiece between the rails of each side, like the center part of the A. This gate is set to swing on each side of the center-post, as shown. It is so much narrower than the V-stiles, that it is almost impossible for small animals to pass, but it is easily hung so that it will always remain

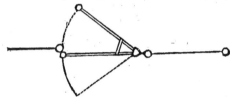

Fig. 269.—SWINGING STILE.

closed, and so offer no temptation to animals on the outside. At night, or when not in use, a wire ring or withe-hoop thrown over the top of the post and the upright part of the gate frame, will securely fasten it. To make

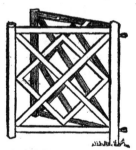

Fig. 270.—A NEAT GATE.

the gate swing shut, all that is necessary is to set the eye of the lower hinge of the gate well out towards the outside. In figure 270 we give a neat A-gate, made of pine or any strong and light wood.

STILES FOR WIRE-FENCES.

The extensive use of wire-fences calls for a farm convenience, heretofore but little known in this country—the stile. The manner of constructing one suitable for barb-wire fence is shown so plainly in the engraving, figure 271, that no description is necessary. The cross piece, upon

Fig. 271.—STILE FOR BARB WIRE FENCE.

which one passes from one flight of steps to the other, may be of any desired width.

Stiles of convenient forms for wire fences are shown in

Fig. 272.—FENCE STILE.

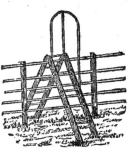

Fig. 273.—ANOTHER STILE.

figures 272 and 273. The one seen in figure 272 takes less space on each side of the fence, but it is not so simple as that shown in figure 273.

Figure 274 shows a passageway in a wire fence, which

requires no climbing, and while it presents an effectual barrier to large animals, is readily passed by any but very

Fig. 274.—WIRE FENCE PASSAGE.

corpulent persons. It originated and was patented in England, but we believe there is no restriction on its construction and use in this country.

CHAPTER XIII.

FENCE LAW.

FENCING OUT OR FENCING IN.

The common law of England, which to a large extent became the law of the original States, bound no one to fence his land at all. Every person is bound under that law to fence his own cattle in, but not bound to fence other cattle out. Every owner of domestic animals is liable for injury committed by them on the lands of others, even though the land was wholly unfenced. But this feature of the English common law was not suited to the conditions which surrounded the early settlers in any part of this country. So long as any region is sparsely settled, the amount of unoccupied land is so much greater than the occupied, that it is cheaper to fence stock out, than to fence it in. Hence the English common law in regard to fencing has been superseded by statute in many of the States. In others it has always remained in force, or has been revived by later statutes. There is such great diversity on this point in the statutes of the several States, that, to quote from Henry A. Haigh's excellent "Manual of Farm Law," "every one having occasion to look up any point of law, should ascertain the statutory provisions concerning it from some official source. Do not depend upon this book or any other book for them, because they are liable to change, and do change from year to year; but go to your town clerk or justice of the peace, and examine the statutes themselves."

DIVISION FENCES.

The legal obligations of adjoining owners to build and maintain division fences, rests entirely upon the statutes of the respective States, save in cases where long usage has created prescriptive rights, or special agreement exists. Such fences are to be built on the boundary line, the expense to be borne equally by the parties, or each one shall make and maintain half the fence. If they cannot agree, or either refuses or neglects to do his share, the statutes provide methods by which the matter may be determined. In some of the States, two or more public officers, called fence-viewers, are elected annually in each township, whose duties, as prescribed by statute, are, when called upon, to hear and decide questions relating to fences in their respective towns. In other States, these duties are performed by overseers of highways or selectmen, *ex-officio*. Whenever any owner or occupant of land refuses to build or maintain half the division fence, or cannot agree with his adjoining neighbor as to which portion they shall respectively maintain, the fence-viewer may be called. Upon being so called, the fence-viewer shall upon reasonable notice, and after viewing the premises, determine and assign the respective portions of the fence to be maintained by each. The assignment when so made and recorded by the proper officer, becomes binding upon the present and all subsequent owners of the land. (2 Wis. 14). When by reason of a brook, watercourse, or natural impediment, it is impracticable or unreasonably expensive to build a fence on the true line between adjacent lands, and the owners thereof disagree respecting its position, the fence viewers may, upon application of either party, determine on which side of the true line, or whether partly on one side and partly on the other, and at what distances, the fence shall be built and maintained, and what portions by either party, and if either party refuses or neglects to build and maintain his part of the fence, the other shall have the same remedy as if the fence were on the true line. When a division fence shall be suddenly destroyed or prostrated by fire, winds or floods, the person who ought to repair or rebuild the same should do so in ten days after being notified for that purpose, and in the meantime he will be liable for damages done by estrays.

There is no legal obligation in any of the States, upon any proprietor of uncultivated, unimproved and unoccupied land, to keep up division fences. When a proprietor improves his land, or encloses land already improved, the land adjoining being unimproved, he must make the whole division fence, and if the adjoining proprietor afterward improves his land, he is required to pay for one half the division fence, according to the value thereof at that time. The laws of the respective States are not uniform touching the obligations to maintain one half a division fence after the owner of the land ceases to improve it. In Rhode Island and some other States, the proprietors are required to maintain these respective proportions, whether they continue to improve their land or not. In Maine, New Hampshire, Vermont and several other States, it is provided that if one party lays his lands common, and determines not to improve them, he may, upon giving due notice, cease to support such fences. But in most of the States, he must not take away any part of the division fence belonging to him and adjoining the next enclosure, provided the other party will allow and pay for his part of such fence. If the parties cannot agree as to its value, it may be decided by two or more fence-viewers. Where adjacent land is owned in severalty and occupied in common, and either party desires to occupy his in severalty, and the parties disagree, either party may have the line divided by the fence-viewers, as in other cases.

Owners of adjoining lands may agree between themselves as to the building and maintenance of division fences, and such agreements are valid, whether they are in accordance with the law or not. In some States such an agreement, if in writing, and filed with the clerk of the township, becomes binding upon all subsequent holders of the land. If not in writing, however, such an agreement may be terminated by either of the parties at pleasure.

HIGHWAY FENCES.

Under the common law, the land owner is under no obligation to fence his land along a public highway. But in Missouri, Iowa, Illinois, Oregon, and some other Western and Southern States, the common law rule has been modified by statutes depriving the land-holder of his action for trespass, unless he maintains sufficient fences around his land. In these States, the owner of land must enclose it with sufficient fences if he would cultivate it. Even where there is no such statutory provisions, it is practically necessary to maintain highway fences, as a protection against cattle which are driven along the highway. The use of barb wire for fencing along the public roads has given rise to questions for which there were no precedents. A case was decided in the United States Circuit Court, at Watertown, New York, December 17, 1885. The action was brought by a horse breeder to recover damages from his neighbor for injuries sustained by the plaintiff's horse from a barbed wire fence, stretched along the roadside in front of the defendant's premises. A non-suit was granted on the ground that the animal received the injuries through the contributory negligence of its owner. Among the rulings of the court was one permitting the plaintiff to be questioned, to show the fact that he had on his own farm a similar fence, but of sharper form of barb. The court further held that it might be a question whether it would not be competent testimony to show the common employment of barb wire fence in that region, and held that for the purpose of this case, a barbed wire fence, if properly constructed upon the highway, must be deemed a legal fence.

It may be said in a general way, that though there is no legal obligation resting on the land holder to maintain fences along the public highway, he neglects to do so at his own risk and peril.

WHAT IS A LEGAL FENCE?

What shall be necessary to constitute a legal and sufficient fence is specifically defined by the statutes of the several States, but there is no uniform rule among all. In Maine, New Hampshire, Massachusetts and many other States, it is provided that all fences four feet high, and in good repair, consisting of rails, timber, boards, or stone wall, and all brooks, rivers, ponds, creeks, ditches, hedges, and other things deemed by the fence viewers to be equivalent thereto, shall be accounted legal and sufficient fences. In Vermont, Connecticut, Michigan, and some other States, a legal fence must be four and a half feet high. In Missouri post fences must be four and one half feet high, hedges four feet high, turf fences four feet high, with ditches on each side three feet deep in the middle and three feet wide; worm fences must be five and one-half feet high to the top of the rider, or if not ridered, five feet to the top of the top rail, and must be rocked with strong rails, poles or stakes; stone or brick fences must be four and one-half feet high. In New York the electors of each town may, by vote, decide for themselves how fences shall be made, and what shall be deemed sufficient. No part of the fence law is so definitely regulated by the statutes of the respective States as the requirements of a legal fence. In all cases where practical questions arise involving this point, it is best to consult the statutes, which will be found in the office of the township clerk.

RAILROAD FENCES.

In nearly every State, railroad companies are required by statute to construct and maintain legal and sufficient fences on both sides of their roads, except at crossings of public highways, in front of mills, depots, and other places where the public convenience requires that they shall be left open. The legal obligations of railroad companies to fence their roads rest wholly upon such statutes. In New Hampshire it is provided that if any railroad company shall neglect to maintain such fences, the owner of adjoining land may build them, and recover double the cost thereof of the company. It is generally held by the courts in all the States that, in the absence of such fences the railroad company is liable for all resulting damage to live stock, and no proof of contributory negligence on the part of the owner of live stock is allowed as a plea in defence, the statute requiring such fences being a police regulation. When the railroad company has built a sufficient fence on both sides of its road, it is not liable for injuries which may occur without negligence on its part. If the fence is overthrown by wind or storms, the company is entitled to reasonable time in which to repair it, and if cattle enter and are injured, without fault on the company's part, it is not liable. If cattle stray upon the track at a crossing of a public road, and are killed, the owners cannot recover damages, unless the railroad company is guilty of gross negligence or intentional wrong. A law in Alabama making railroad companies absolutely liable for all stock killed on the tracks, was held to be unconstitutional.

CHAPTER XIV.

COUNTRY BRIDGES AND CULVERTS.

STRENGTH OF BRIDGES.

Bridge building is a profession of itself, and some of the great bridges of the world are justly regarded as among the highest achievements of mechanical science and skill. But it is proposed to speak in this work only of the cheap and simple structures for spanning small streams. The measure of the strength of a bridge is that of its weakest part. Hence, the strength of a plain wooden bridge resting upon timber stringers or chords, is equivalent to the sustaining power of the timbers in the middle of the span. The longer the span, other things being equal, the less its strength. The following table shows the sustaining power of sound spruce timber, of the dimensions given, at a point midway between the supports:

LENGTH OF SPAN.	WIDTH AND THICKNESS OF TIMBER.			
	6 by 8 inches.	6 by 9 inches.	6 by 10 inches.	6 by 12 inches.
Feet.	Pounds.	Pounds.	Pounds.	Pounds.
10	2,800	2,692	4,500	6,480
12	2,400	3,042	3,750	5,400
14	2,058	2,604	3,216	4,632
16	1,800	2,280	2,808	4,050

A stick of timber twenty feet between supports, will bear a load in its center only one half as great as a timber of the same dimensions, ten feet between supports. Thus four timbers six by twelve inches, in a span of sixteen feet, would bear a load of eight tons; in a twelve foot span, the same timbers would support a weight of nearly twelve tons.

BRACES AND TRUSSES.

The above is the initial strength of the timbers which support the weight of the superstructure, and any load that it may have to sustain. But in bridge building these timbers are reinforced by trusses or braces, which add greatly to the sustaining power of the bridge.

Figure 275 shows the simplest form of a self-supporting bridge, which will answer for spans of from ten to fifteen feet in length. The braces, $c, c,$ reach from near the end of the sill to about four feet above the center. The truss rod, *d*, is one inch in diameter for short bridges

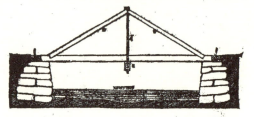

Fig. 275.—A SIMPLE FORM OF BRIDGE SPAN.

up to two inches for longer spans; it is provided with an iron washer at the top. The rod passes through the sill,

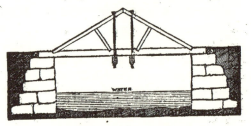

Fig. 276.—A STRONGER SPAN.

and a cross sill, *e*, which passes under the main sills, thus adding firmness to the whole structure. Logs, *f, f,* are

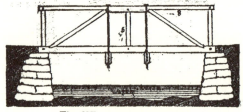

Fig. 277.—A SHORT BRIDGE.

placed against the ends of the sills to keep them in place, and where the wheels will first strike them instead of the floor plank, thus greatly equalizing the pressure. Figure 276 represents a modification of the above. The two truss rods and braces give the structure greater strength and solidity, adapting it for spans eighteen feet in length. For the latter length, sills should be of good

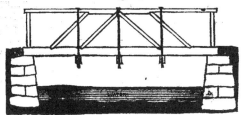

Fig. 278.—A BOLT TRUSS.

material, ten inches wide and fourteen inches deep, with three middle sills of about the same size.

Figure 277 is a more improved style of bridge, the truss serving both to support the structure, and as a parapet. The top railing is of the same width as the sill, about one foot. The lower side may be cut away, giving the bridge a more finished appearance. The railing at the center is six inches thick, and three inches at the ends. The tie, h, is full width and four inches thick. A bridge of this kind will answer for heavy traffic, even if twenty

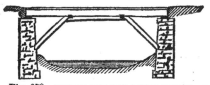

Fig. 279—BRIDGE BRACED FROM BELOW.

feet in length. The bolt truss, in figure 278, is adapted for a span of twenty-five feet. This makes a bridge of great firmness. Each set of truss-rods support a cross sill. The road planks are laid crosswise of the bridge. The middle sills are sometimes half an inch lower than those along the sides, and should be four or five in number. The ends of the planks fit closely against the inside of the truss sills, thereby keeping the planks securely in place.

A common method of bracing is from below as shown in figure 279. This is not usually a good practice, as the braces are liable to be carried away by ice or floods.

ABUTMENTS, PIERS AND RAILINGS.

If the sills of a bridge are laid directly upon the dry walls of an abutment, or upon a heavy plank, the jar of passing teams soon displaces some of the stones, and brings undue strain upon certain portions of the wall.

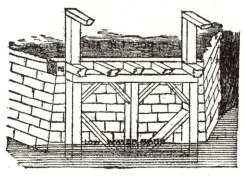

Fig. 280.—END OF A BRIDGE.

To avoid this, abutments are best made of cut stones, and laid in cement. A wooden bent for the support of the ends of the bridge may be made as shown in figure 280. The whole should be constructed of heavy timber, pinned together. A coat of white lead should cover the interior surface of all joints. The number and position of the posts of the wooden abutment are seen in the engraving. A log should be laid upon the wall at *m*, to re-

Old-Fashioned Labor-Saving Devices

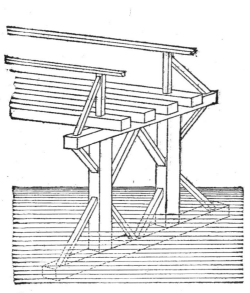

Fig. 281.—FRAMED PIER.

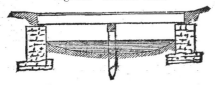

Fig. 282.—BRIDGE SUPPORTED BY PILES.

Fig. 283.   RAILING OF BRIDGE.   Fig. 284.

lieve the bridge from the shock of the passing wagons. A center pier should be avoided as much as possible, as it offers serious obstruction in floods, and ice, drift wood and other floating matter become piled against it, seriously imperiling the entire structure. But in cases where the length of the bridge is so great as to require one or more piers, they may be constructed on the plan

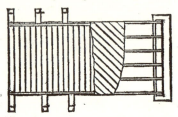

Fig. 285.—PLANK FLOOR OF BRIDGE.

shown in figure 281, or in case the bottom is so soft as to render the mudsill insecure, a line of piles supporting a cross-timber, as in figure 282. A strong, reliable parapet or railing should always be provided. The want of one may be the cause of fatal accidents to persons and horses. Figure 283 gives a side view of a good railing, and figure 284 shows the manner of bracing the posts to the ends of the cross-beams. They should be thus braced at every alternate post of the railing. The floor should be double, as shown in figure 285, the lower planks laid diagonally, and the upper layer crosswise.

BRIDGES FOR GULLIES.

For small gullies which cross roadways or lanes in farms, and are not the beds of constant streams, but are occasionally filled with surface water, a very simple bridge is sufficient. One like that shown in figure 286 is as good as any. The sills, *a*, *a*, are sunk in a trench dug against the bank and at least to the level of the bed of the creek. The cross-sills, *b*, *b*, are not mortised into them, but simply laid between them. The pressure is all from the outside, hence it will force *a*, *a*, tighter against the ends *b*, *b*, which must be sunk a little into the bed of the creek at its lowest point. The posts are mortised into the sills, *a*, *a*, and plates, *c*, *c*, and *d*, *d*, upon

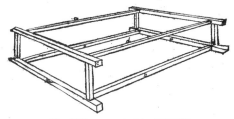

Fig. 286.—FRAME FOR BRIDGE.

which the planks are laid. Props may be put against the lower sides of the posts to hold the bridge against the stream.

A cheap but practicable bridge is shown in figure 287. Two logs are laid across the gully, their ends resting on the banks, and to them puncheons or planks are spiked to form the bridge. Stout posts, well propped and reaching above the highest water mark, are placed against the lower side of the logs. If the creek rises, the bridge,

Fig. 287.—CONVENIENT FARM BRIDGE.

being free, will be raised on the surface of the water, while the posts will prevent its being carried away. Should it not rise with the water, it opposes so little surface to the current that the posts will hold it fast.

ORNAMENTAL BRIDGES.

No feature adds more to the appearance of ornamental grounds than tasteful bridges. A stream or narrow channel connecting two parts of a small sheet of water, affords an opportunity for the introduction of a bridge.

Fig. 288.—RUSTIC BRIDGE.

In the absence of such features a bridge may be thrown across a dry ravine. Whatever style may be adopted, should harmonize with the general character of the surroundings. An elaborate bridge of wood or masonry would be as much out of place on grounds unadorned by other structures, as a rude rustic one would be near highly

Fig. 289.—A BRIDGE OF ROCKS.

finished summer-houses and other architectural features. On most grounds a neat rustic bridge, something like the one shown in figure 288, would be in good keeping with its environments. Such bridges may be made of red cedar logs and branches, resting upon stone abutments. Where boulders are abundant, a stone bridge, something like figure 289, may be built at very little cost, and will last for generations. The pleasing effect of rustic or other ornamental bridges is enhanced by training Virginia creeper or other climbing plants upon them.

ROAD CULVERTS.

A culvert under a road is, in effect, a short bridge. The simplest form of plank culvert, resting upon stone abutments, is shown in figure 290. Such a structure is cheaply built, and serves a good purpose while the woodwork remains sound. But the planks wear out and the timbers decay, requiring frequent renewing. Where stone is abundant it is much cheaper in the end to build wholly of stone, as in figure 291. After the abutments

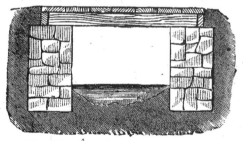

Fig. 290.—CULVERT WITH PLANK FLOOR.

are built, a course of flat stone, along each side, projects inward from six to ten inches, as at a, a, which are covered with a broad stone, b. Where the stream to be crossed is so narrow that a row of single stones is sufficient to cover the opening, a culvert like that seen in figure 292 is cheaply made. Such structures will remain serviceable for a generation, if the foundations are not undermined by the action of the water.

Where flat stones enough cannot be easily procured, culverts may be built of concrete. The abutments are first made, as in other cases; then empty barrels or sugar

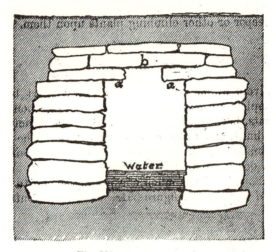

Fig. 291.—STONE CULVERT.

hogsheads, according to the capacity of the opening, are fitted in, or better still, a temporary arch is made of rough, narrow boards. The concrete of cement, sand

Fig. 292.—CHEAPER STONE CULVERT.

and gravel, is then prepared and poured in, temporary supports of lumber having been fixed across each end of the culvert to keep the concrete in place until it hardens.

Small stones may be mixed with the concrete as it is poured into place, and the whole topped off with a row of them. This protection of stones on the top is valuable, in case the covering of earth is worn or wasted away

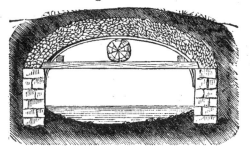

Fig. 293.—ARCHED CONCRETE CULVERT.

at any time while it is in use. For a longer culvert a flattened arch is made of concrete, as shown in figure 293. Light timbers are laid across, the ends resting lightly on the abutments. Across the middle of these a round log is placed to support the crown of the arch. Elastic split poles are sprung over all, and upon these are

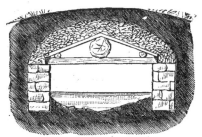

Fig. 294.—ANGULAR CONCRETE CULVERT.

nailed thin narrow boards, extending lengthwise of the culvert. The ends being temporarily protected, the concrete is mixed and poured on, as before. When the concrete has "set," the woodwork is removed.